W9-AXA-578

The
PRO-GROWTH
PROGRESSIVE

An Economic Strategy
for Shared Prosperity

Gene Sperling

SIMON & SCHUSTER
New York   London   Toronto   Sydney

SIMON & SCHUSTER
Rockefeller Center
1230 Avenue of the Americas
New York, NY 10020

Copyright © 2005 by Gene Sperling
All rights reserved, including the right of
reproduction in whole or in part in any form.

SIMON & SCHUSTER and colophon are registered
trademarks of Simon & Schuster, Inc.

For information about special discounts for bulk purchases,
please contact Simon & Schuster Special Sales:
1-800-456-6798 or business@simonandschuster.com

Designed by Dana Sloan

Manufactured in the United States of America

10 9 8 7 6 5 4 3 2 1

Library of Congress Cataloging-in-Publication Data
Sperling, Gene B.

The pro-growth progressive: an economic strategy for shared prosperity /
Gene Sperling.
        p.   cm.
Includes bibliographical references and index.
    1. United States—Economic policy—21st century.   2. Globalization—Economic
aspects—United States.   3. United States—Economic conditions—21st century.
4. Saving and investment—United States.   5. Social planning—United States.
I. Title: Prosperity in a changing economy.   II. Title.

HC103 .S715   2005
330.973—dc22   2005051748

ISBN-13: 978 0-7432-3753-6
ISBN-10:   0-7432-3753-6

*For my wonderful, creative, caring, and
inspiring wife, Allison*

*And in memory of the life, courage, and compassion
of my dear friend, Chris Georges*

Contents

The
PRO-GROWTH
PROGRESSIVE

Introduction

During my eight years in the Clinton White House, I suggested to the president's chief speechwriter, Michael Waldman, that he make the theme of a State of the Union "Will we grow together or grow apart?" It was an update of Benjamin Franklin's warning to fellow revolutionaries that "we will hang together or hang separately," that we must have shared growth if we are to remain a nation with enough economic room for anyone willing to work hard to succeed. Every year I would get the same response: policy wonks should stick to policies, let us take care of the overarching message. Perhaps White House policy aides write their own books to voice the ideas left on the State of the Union cutting-room floors.

The signature description of growing together—cited by Democrats and Republicans alike—is John F. Kennedy's "a rising tide lifts all boats." This line has been misinterpreted by many conservatives to suggest that economic growth alone will always benefit even the most disadvantaged among us—a relationship that history has shown to be far from automatic.[1] The real genius of Kennedy's phrase is that it evokes what our *aspiration* for economic growth should be and suggests a way to judge our economic policies: Do they *both* raise the tide and lift all boats?

This inquiry takes on heightened importance in an economy characterized by the dizzying acceleration of global competition and technological change. The same forces that allow American families to scan the Internet or shelves of a mass superstore for everything from diapers to DVDs are also making a broad segment of the American workforce, from textile workers to X-ray technicians, anxious that their jobs could be eclipsed by technology or performed more cheaply by armies of high-skilled, low-cost workers in countries such as India and China. Americans are wrestling with deep questions about whether the pace of our dynamic economy will be a source of wondrous efficiency, innovation, and high-wage job growth in unimaginable industries, or whether global labor competition and downward pressure on wages will threaten the hallmark of the American economy: a strong and growing middle class that always makes room for those who want to work hard and move up the economic ladder.

Our ability to craft economic policies that allow us to both grow and grow together in a dynamic global economy and create an expanding middle class may be the paramount economic challenge of our era. Yet we will fail to meet it if the debate is dominated by the short-sighted calculus of electoral politics. Conservatives make a serious mistake if they interpret the razor-slim victories in the last two presidential elections as confirmation that their economic policies provide surefire answers to the anxiety more and more Americans are feeling about our economic future. Democrats will err if, in their hunger for an immediate answer to "What now?" after consecutive presidential defeats, they bypass this larger economic inquiry in the search for a magical quick-fix political strategy to tip a few red states blue. Debates between politicians stressing the electoral turnout potential of chest-thumping populism and those pushing the swing-vote potential of centrism based on locating the arithmetical mean between the far right and left trivialize the economic challenges that working America faces.

The fact is that traditional divides in American politics are increasingly ill suited to a serious inquiry about how to ensure we grow together in a dynamic global economy. While I have tried to avoid crude generalizations on the divisions between right and left, conservative and progressive, the fact is that major groups on both sides of the political aisle remain focused on only part of the economic picture. Those on the right who believe that less government will always lead to more robust economic growth may find themselves out of step with the growing imperative for public policies to help workers adjust to the uncertainties of the global market and ensure that growth is fair and consistent with our values. Those on the left whose legitimate concern about protecting hardworking families leads them to call for limiting the pace of change may find themselves trying to hold back the inevitable global competition and innovation that are critical to sparking the next burst of high-paying jobs and wealth in our economy.

America needs a new pro-growth progressive consensus. We need a deeper appreciation of the inevitability of change, the benefits of open markets, and the upward aspirations and entrepreneurial nature of Americans—alongside a greater understanding of how smart, active public policies are vital to ensuring that lightning-quick global competition and technological change are actually being structured to lift all boats.

Instead of dissecting the electoral map, this book will explore three major questions that should frame a pro-growth progressive consensus on economic policy: One, what progressive values should we stand for and demand that a successful economic strategy promote? Two, what hard-nosed economic realities must we accept and embrace in a competitive global economy capable of both tremendous productivity and painful dislocation? Three, in this dynamic economy characterized by accelerating globalization and technological change, what is the role for public policy in ensuring that we enjoy strong economic growth that truly lifts all boats?

PART ONE

■

The Pro-Growth Progressive

1

Growing Together in the
Dynamism Economy

In the 1990s, a new economic era was created when a period of intense globalization collided with an information technology revolution. Yet precisely defining a "new" economy is less important than understanding the nature of the change. I believe a more descriptive label is the "dynamism" economy. Of course, dynamic change in market economies is hardly new. The mid-twentieth-century economist Joseph Schumpeter identified the process of "creative destruction," positing that a healthy market economy is continually moving forward, replacing old capital, old industries—and existing jobs—with more productive alternatives.[1] Yet, what feels most "new" for average citizens is the breakneck speed at which the increased globalization, rapid technological advance, and the explosion of the Internet are putting fierce competitive pressures on the economy and accelerating change not only in products and services, but also in entire job categories and industries.

Markets are moving to what would have been considered an ideal of global efficiency in which producers can look anywhere for the place, people, and technology to produce a good or service as cheaply and efficiently as possible. Thanks to the Internet, consumers can instantaneously compare the price and quality of almost every good and service produced in the world and choose the one that best meets their needs.

In 2000, about half the companies that had comprised the 100 largest industrial firms in 1974 had either gone bankrupt or been taken over.[2] Between 1970 and 1990, the rate at which companies fell out of the Fortune 500 quadrupled.[3] It is as if the search for the best product, service, or input went from a regional athletic competition to a never-ending global economic Olympics in one generation. Yesterday's champion is less secure, and as new products and services redefine the market, profit margins drop.

Dell Computers, the last major PC maker to manufacture in the United States, typifies this Olympic-level competition. Dell's factories attract awe and intense scrutiny for streamlined production. According to the *New York Times,* "Designers give one another high-fives for eliminating even a single screw from a product, because doing so represents a saving of roughly four seconds per machine built—the time they've calculated it takes an employee, on average, to use the pneumatic screwdriver dangling above his or her head."[4] Dell rates each of its suppliers each week in a cut-throat search for better, cheaper parts.[5] The result is that today it takes a single worker only five minutes to build a PC; a task that took two workers fourteen minutes only five years ago.

Nokia, the world's largest cell phone maker, is acclaimed for its efficient supply chain—managing 60 billion parts a year from more than 29 countries—but has found that in the new global marketplace, efficiency is not enough. In 2004, it saw its market share drop from 35 percent, where it had been for five years, to 29 percent when it fell behind in the fashion-driven market for flip-phones, color screens, and camera phones. Nokia responded by slashing prices and retooling its supply chain to be more responsive to operator networks. It sped development, moving more quickly from concept to commercial application, introducing 35 new models in 2004 and 40 new models in 2005. Nokia is now leading the next wave of "cool" phone technology using third-generation networks that were first introduced in the United States in 2004—releasing one phone that can hold up to 3,000 songs and another that can capture as much as an hour of video.[6]

THE UPSIDES AND DOWNSIDES OF THE DYNAMISM ECONOMY

This fierce competition drives a never-ending focus on improving quality and efficiency and lowering prices for consumers. Many experts on competitiveness argue that one reason the U.S. economy outperformed Europe and Japan in the 1990s was that our open competitive economy put more pressure on businesses to modernize and innovate. Research by economist Martin Baily and the McKinsey Global Institute confirms that the intensity of competitive pressure in the U.S. economy drove a widespread adoption of technology across broad sectors of our economy, as even traditional bricks-and-mortar firms were forced to incorporate cutting-edge innovations to stay ahead.[7] Competition kept average prices for consumer goods in the U.S. to only 21 percent above the lowest world prices, while prices exceeded global lows by 38 percent in Germany, 61 percent in the United Kingdom, and 102 percent in Japan.[8] Productivity, which had averaged an anemic 1.5 percent over a twenty-three-year period from 1972 to 1995, has now averaged 3.1 percent from 1995 to 2004.[9]

Yet the same competitive pressures generate wider economic anxiety. Previously, the threat that global competition would lead to downward pressure on a worker's wages, force her out of a job, or even decimate her entire industry was limited to a clearly identifiable portion of our workforce—mainly factory workers in globally traded manufacturing industries. As globalization and technology now allow consumers and producers to scan the globe to maximize efficiency in everything from accounting to machine-tool production, the very forces that bring efficiency and lower prices raise new concerns about whether armies of new workers from China or India will eliminate jobs and force wages in the United States down for decades to come. Many fear that these trends will hollow out middle-class jobs and that the only workers who will not be vulnerable to this dramatic increase in global labor arbitrage will be either the super-educated and very hard to replace, or those in jobs that require a physical presence in the United States and are not subject to automation—construction, cutting hair, and restaurant service.

These new concerns cloud today's economic debate. Often in politics it is easy to identify opposing interests: environmentalists versus loggers; union leaders versus corporate management; uninsured working parents versus small businesses struggling to keep health care costs low. Today's conflicts are far more nuanced and complex. Individuals can hold conflicting opinions in their many roles as consumers, workers, parents, and community members. As a consumer and parent, a low-income mom wants to make her money go as far as possible at Wal-Mart, but as a neighbor and worker she fears that Wal-Mart is driving down wages and forcing other firms to cut back health care benefits. The member of Congress may want to pursue greater economic ties with the country his parents emigrated from and yet fears that a new trade agreement could hurt workers in his district.

Clearly, consumers benefit from the low-cost products and services that global competition provides. But if that competition also reduces wages it could leave consumers with less buying power. From a worker's perspective, it may seem obvious that a dynamic economy poses a threat in the form of greater dislocation, but the same competitive pressure can also be the source of the next wave of good high-paying jobs for American workers in the industries of the future. For a concerned global citizen, the market openings and foreign investment that can shake up old, illegitimate, and corrupt power structures in developing countries can also be used—at least temporarily—to exacerbate income inequality and enrich an illegitimate status quo.

These tensions require deep, honest exploration that does not easily fit within any right-left, pro-globalization–anti-globalization perspective. Too many on the right side of the political spectrum approach these challenges of the dynamism economy with an unhelpful ideological presumption that less government always leads to higher economic growth. And too many on the left start with the presumption that restricting competition to protect jobs or ensure wages and benefits can be counted on to help working families in the long term. We are left with a deficit of serious discussion on policies that *both* respect and even embrace the power of markets while ensuring that growth does not come at the expense of our progressive values.

Consider the debate over outsourcing in 2003 and 2004. In speeches I used to say we had a two-party system on outsourcing: the "Sky Is Falling Party" and the "Don't Worry, Be Happy Party." Neither really examined the realities of the dynamism economy and the legitimate needs and anxieties of workers. The Sky Is Falling Party disproportionately blamed outsourcing for job loss while giving the impression that policy could easily restrict market behavior and companies could protect U.S. jobs. The Don't Worry, Be Happy Party trivialized the concerns of workers at risk and failed to see that the lack of government policies to spur job growth, increase competitiveness, and cushion devastating dislocation was partly responsible for the economic pain and legitimate worry of an increasing number of workers and communities.

My solution was a third-party movement on outsourcing—the Humility Party. The platform would recognize that because outsourcing is primarily a function of unstoppable forces such as the spread of global information networks rather than trade, there was no way to completely eliminate it without hurting long-term U.S. job growth. With hundreds of millions of new middle-class consumers coming into the world economy, we should be confident that in the long run America will win more than it loses from an open global economy. Yet the Humility Party would admit that we do not know for certain that global labor competition will not present a serious problem for American workers in terms of lower wages or dislocation in the future.[10]

The Humility Party would ask hard questions: What practical options do we have between simply assuming greater globalization will lift all boats, and resorting to self-defeating protectionism? How can we lower the cost of job creation in the United States, in light of global labor market competition? Can we use tax incentives to encourage job creation or make investment more attractive in low-cost areas of our country? Can we, as Intel founder and chairman Andy Grove suggests, spark greater job creation in the United States by investing in basic research, a modernized technology infrastructure, and math and science education?[11] Are we willing to accept slightly higher prices to ensure that global competition does not lead to a race to the bottom with firms squeezing every last penny—not through innovation but by clamping down on employees' health and pension benefits? With the outsourcing debate dominated by one side condemning it and the other simply yawning at it, these questions received too little serious policy consideration.

MEMO TO PROGRESSIVES: EMBRACE GROWTH AND ECONOMIC DYNAMISM

Too often in progressive policymaking circles, if an analyst raises concerns about whether a proposed progressive policy is inefficient, hurts growth, or might have the unintended consequence of creating negative incentives for work or job creation, many assume the motivation for such objections is to push for a centrist position or the moderation of progressive goals. The purpose of this book is not to moderate progressive goals, but to look for the most pro-growth means to achieve those goals. The "most-pro-growth alternative" test requires examining how progressive policies can be achieved at every step while maximizing economic growth and minimizing negative unintended consequences for the very workers, employers, and investors our policies are designed to empower. Of course, there are goals—banning child labor in our factories; preventing racial, religious, and gender discrimination in the workforce—that require direct intervention in the market regardless of their efficiency or economic impact. Yet on a host of policy goals, decision makers have many avenues to find policies that are both pro-growth and progressive. It will be easier to find those avenues if policymakers follow the six pro-growth progressive guideposts.

1. Dealing with the Inevitability of Economic Dynamism

Imagine you are a member of Congress and are approached by a patriotic CEO of a small electronics firm in your district. She desperately wants to keep buying from U.S. suppliers, but a direct competitor has cut prices by making insulated wiring more cheaply abroad. The CEO tells you that if she continues using her U.S. wiring supplier, she will not be price competitive, will risk losing business, and may have to cut jobs. She is committed to doing everything she can to keep buying American, but asks you to sponsor legislation restricting her competitor from buying from overseas suppliers.

What are your options? Congress could forbid all U.S. electronics firms from outsourcing overseas, but the CEO's competitor may then move his whole operation abroad and future start-ups may relocate in nations that allow them to search the globe for suppliers. You could enact quotas or higher tariffs on imported wiring to reduce the incentive to locate overseas or import from foreign producers. Even if this means higher consumer prices for electronic goods in the United States, you may decide it is worth it to protect the high-paying jobs in your district. But other companies in your district rely on low-cost electrical inputs from other nations to stay competitive, and local exporters could be hurt if other nations retaliate with quotas and higher tariffs to protect their own producers.

Furthermore, you have a sinking feeling that shutting off global competition in the long run might dampen the pressure for U.S. companies to innovate and seek higher value-added services or production, leaving your community more dependent on a product or service where they no longer have a competitive edge.

This all-too-real hypothetical illustrates that however admirable it is to want to take every imaginable step to save existing U.S. jobs, when we impede the economic logic of producers seeking to meet consumer demands by finding the lowest-cost inputs, we are engaging in a losing game. It is, as Robert Reich once explained, like building sand barricades on the beach to try to keep the tide from coming in.

What drives much of the economic upheaval in the dynamism economy is not simply globalization, but technological advance as well. The introduction of ATMs and self-service gas pumps would have shaken up jobs in the United States, even if we had a completely closed economy. Fifteen years ago, the Bureau of Labor Statistics predicted that travel agents would be among the fastest-growing U.S. job categories; instead those jobs contracted by 6 percent and are projected to shrink further over the next decade as more Americans book their travel online—an option that did not exist fifteen years ago.[12] Today, 25 percent of supermarkets now offer self-checkout services, and the IHL Consulting group predicts by 2010, 95 percent of checkout lanes will be self-serve.[13]

Even countries that are often accused of robbing American jobs face constant price pressure from new technologies and even lower-cost nations. Advances in natural language speech recognition software are already responsible for automating many Indian call center jobs.[14] A host of African countries are luring outsourcing with new strategies and even tax cuts. Indeed, when I mentioned outsourcing to a group of students at the Indian Institute of Management in Bangalore in 2003, they thought I meant outsourcing jobs *from* Bangalore to poorer parts of India and Africa. In China, low-cost manufacturers are already being squeezed by growing wages. Loh Sai Kit, manager of Yuh Fai Toys company in Dongguan, saw several local companies close in 2004 and move production to Vietnam.[15] The Indian outsourcing company MsourcE has recently opened up a call center in Mexico—where per capita income is about ten times higher than India's—but has a workforce of native Spanish speakers to serve the U.S. market.[16] Neeraj Bhargava, CEO of WNS, India's largest third-party offshore company, says, "I see ourselves eventually operating out of three or four clusters—one for European languages, one for Asian languages, and then for risk reduction we may want to be in places like Mexico, Canada, or Latin America, which incidentally offers Spanish language capability too."[17] At the 2005 World Economic Forum in Davos, the buzz was that as a new wave of outsourcing expanded to business processes like accounting and data entry, language would play a less significant role, sparking an even more intense global competition for providing these services.

Understanding the inevitability of change does not mean we should sacrifice progressive policy aspirations at the altar of economic efficiency or resign ourselves to an unrestricted, unforgiving global market where the tide may rise but many boats sink. It does mean that progressives must be pragmatic about the realities of the dynamism economy and choose the most pro-growth alternative to achieve any progressive goal.

2. Unintended Consequences:
Thinking Seven Steps Down the Road

Shaping a pro-growth progressive agenda requires acknowledging the difficulty of anticipating how any action or inaction can create negative unintended consequences. Mitigating these unintended consequences was a key goal when, during the presidential transition in December 1992, we sought to implement President Clinton's vision for a National Economic Council—a corollary to the National Security Council that I would direct from 1997 to 2001. Bob Rubin, who was the first head of the National Economic Council, stressed to Bo Cutter, Sylvia Mathews, and me that while the immediate impact of many decisions might be predictable, the challenge was to try to "look seven steps down the road." To me this was the policy maker's Hippocratic Oath—first do no harm by avoiding cures that are worse than the disease. Process is crucial here. In the face of an immediate or lingering economic problem, the pressure to "do something" can overwhelm careful consideration of unforeseen or unconsidered consequences.

For example, when gas prices spike, there are calls for the U.S. government to release oil from the Strategic Petroleum Reserve (SPR), a government-controlled reserve of 590 million barrels established after the energy crises of the 1970s. The first-order effect of a release is straightforward: increasing the supply of oil in the market should lower prices. Yet having felt this pressure on several occasions as NEC director—and yielded to it on one occasion[18]—I found that calculating the second-, third-, and fourth-order effects is far more complicated. If releasing reserves is seen as an aggressive or even hostile tactic, and OPEC officials signal they will pull back supply in retaliation beyond the amount of the SPR released, the action could lower supply expectations in the market and raise prices. If using the SPR raises expectations that it will be tapped whenever there are shortages or price hikes, oil companies might hold fewer reserves in the future, increasing the likelihood of oil shocks. If investors viewed it as a politicization of economic policy, it could raise the costs of borrowing and discourage foreign investment in the United States. The one time that the Clinton administration did a "swap"—a short-term release that had to be replaced—the National Economic Council and Energy Secretary Bill Richardson foresaw some of these second- and third-order effects and managed the release and diplomacy well enough to avoid these pitfalls. But it is a far more complicated calculation than those who often call for SPR releases recognize.

Avoiding unintended consequences requires carefully considered policies, not minimalist government. Inaction or maintaining the status quo can have unintended consequences as well. Consider the corporate reforms that were not instituted in the mid-1990s, particularly SEC Chairman Arthur Levitt's recommendation to separate auditing and consulting practices to prevent conflicts of interest. Few policy makers anticipated that *not* acting would help lead to the stunning corporate scandals in the summer of 2002.

Whether or not one agrees with President Clinton's economic policies, his decision to create a National Economic Council as a coordinating body helped promote a process that subjected new ideas to rigorous scrutiny. It was not uncommon for our economic team to seize on a seemingly good idea, only to have it crumble under our own hard questioning. The process of collective deliberation and scrutiny can at times be harder in Congress, where offices tend to work more independently, often without the benefit of an honest broker.

3. Taking Silent Trade-offs Seriously

Progressives should be particularly concerned with an unintended consequence I refer to as a "silent trade-off," when well-intentioned policies to protect certain workers or communities impose burdens on similarly situated or worse-off workers who were not included in the immediate cost-benefit calculations. These trade-offs are silent because often the potential downsides to other workers are never openly considered and weighed in making the decision.

European "hire-and-fire" policies are meant to provide greater security for workers by mandating generous severance pay, notice periods, and firing restrictions. In Germany, employers must inform workers weeks or months in advance of firings; in Norway the permissible reasons for employers to dismiss workers are so narrowly defined that it is extremely difficult for anyone ever to fire an employee. But as economists like to say, high barriers to exit (i.e., lots of hurdles to firing workers) means higher barriers to entry (i.e., employers might be less likely to hire new workers). Such policies result in greater protections for workers with jobs, but can have a chilling effect on hiring, resulting in slower job growth and higher unemployment—often referred to as Eurosclerosis. Some European policies have dramatically increased the average length of unemployment, putting the jobless at a higher risk of being permanently marginalized from the workforce. They have also made employers less likely to hire "risky" workers, increasing employment among working-age men at the expense of women and youth.[19] More and more progressives in Europe now seem to grasp this; a main goal of New Labour in Britain and many Social Democratic parties across the continent has been implementation of labor market reforms designed to reduce these painful trade-offs while maintaining crucial support for workers.

4. Empowering People Directly

When pro-growth progressives take seriously the law of unintended consequences and the potential for silent trade-offs, a common theme often emerges: *empowering people directly rather than trying to protect them by restricting or impeding markets.* When hardworking families are forced to raise their children in poverty; when parents struggle to take time off to care for a sick kid or parent; when workers are devastated by a plant closing in their community, the well-intentioned progressive instinct is often to restrict market behavior to prevent such outcomes. Sometimes such intervention is the best or only option. Yet too often progressive policy makers rush to restrict market behavior without considering whether the same goal could be achieved by giving workers the resources they need and avoid new burdens on employers that risk negative consequences.

Consider the fact that too few part-time working parents have 401(k) retirement accounts. If politically feasible, some progressives would support requiring all businesses to offer part-time workers a generous pension with matching employer contributions. Such a regulation might cause some employers—especially small businesses—to hire fewer part-time workers and therefore reduce job opportunities for some working parents. The question for the pro-growth progressive is not whether to give up on the goal of better pension protection for working parents, but whether there is a better way to achieve that goal. In chapter 13, I describe new Universal 401(k) accounts with generous matching contributions that the government could offer directly to all workers, which could achieve the goal of increased pension and retirement security for part-time working parents while imposing no new restrictions on employers and avoiding any potential harm to part-time job prospects.

5. Recognizing the Potential Link Between
Dynamism and Progressive Goals

When a company draws raves from Wall Street analysts and is rewarded with a higher stock price for a corporate restructuring that involved moving jobs overseas, it is easy for some to conclude that the benefits of the dynamism economy reflected in the Gross National Product (GNP) are reaped only by multinational corporations while the costs are carried by typical hardworking families and their communities. Yet the pro-growth progressive must be careful not to place inordinate blame on dynamic global competition for job losses or downplay the potential for such dynamism to play a key role in furthering progressive economic goals.

There is little question that our labor market performance in recent years has been exceptionally weak and that poor economic policy choices contributed to the worst jobs recovery since the 1930s. Three and one-half years after the end of the 2001 recession, we were still more than 8 million private sector jobs behind where we should be in a normal economic recovery. Yet it is far less clear that too much dynamism, technological change, or globalization were the primary drivers of our labor market troubles. The main difference between the historic job creation of the late 1990s and the historically weak job market of Bush's first term was not the number of jobs destroyed by economic change, but the economy's failure to create new jobs to replace them.

Consider that in 1999, fierce competition destroyed an astounding 32.9 million private-sector jobs, the equivalent of more than 20 percent of our workforce, according to the Business Employment Dynamics Survey published by the Bureau of Labor Statistics (BLS). Yet that same competition also helped create 35.5 million. The result: a net creation of 2.6 million jobs. At the same time, unemployment fell to its lowest level in thirty years and poverty to its lowest level since 1979.[20]

Compare that to 2003, the second year of our anemic "job-loss" recovery. We might have expected many more jobs destroyed in such a weak year. Yet only 30.2 million jobs were eliminated, nearly 3 million *fewer* than in 1999. The force behind our net job loss was that only 30.1 million new jobs were created in 2003, nearly 6 million fewer than in 1999. In the end, rather than the solid 2.6 million net jobs created in 1999, we saw a loss of 120,000 jobs in 2003, according to this BLS survey.[21]

This shift offers a crucial caveat for progressives. The increased pace of change and competition in our economy can be both a cause of great upheaval at the expense of workers and a powerful engine of job creation and economic opportunity.

Intense global competition and dynamism partly stimulated growth in the 1990s and delivered progressive results. The pace of technological change, together with open markets, sound fiscal policies, and investments in workers and technology did not prevent dislocation to millions, but it did foster the longest sustained economic expansion in our nation's history where the fruits of growth were broadly shared. From 1992 to 2000, every quintile of the income distribution, from the highest 20 percent to the lowest 20 percent, saw incomes increase. Indeed, those in the bottom fifth saw the largest increase in income growth of 22.5 percent. This presented a sharp reversal from 1979 to 1993, when the top 20 percent gained 28.4 percent while those at the bottom saw their incomes decline by 13 percent. The typical family saw its income rise $7,200 in inflation-adjusted dollars, an increase of 15.3 percent. African American families saw even higher income growth of $8,900, a striking 33 percent increase.[22]

During the late 1990s, the poverty rate in America fell to its lowest level since 1978, and a lower proportion of blacks and Hispanics lived in poverty than at any time in history.[23] For the first time more than two-thirds of Americans owned their homes.[24] The fact that these outcomes occurred amidst such a burst of dynamism may not validate any isolated policy, but it should make progressives think twice about whether slowing the pace of change is a surefire way to achieve progressive goals.

6. Passion for Economic Growth

The Democratic Party should disband if it ever stops being the party that stands by the little guy, leads the fight against racial and economic disadvantage, sticks by working families when times are tough, and takes on those with privilege who don't play by the rules.

Yet when the public *only* hears Democrats taking on powerful interests or fighting for those who have fallen on hard times, they may believe that progressives' and the Democratic Party's passion is limited only to helping those in distress, and not to spurring economic growth and helping families create wealth. Democrats cannot just be the party for you when something bad happens. They also need to be the party of your optimistic aspirations. Friends are most important during hard times, but most of us want friends who support our dreams and hopes as well. While any pro-growth progressive strategy must include a cost-sharing compact to help

Americans manage risk and dislocation, progressives will make a serious mistake if they believe that Americans only aspire to a "safety net nation." The distinctive feature of the American character is the desire both for a safety net to ensure economic dignity in hard times and the chance to create wealth and move up the economic ladder. Even ultimate populist Huey Long deeply understood this. While he often resorted to shameless populist demagoguery, the first line of the theme song he played at virtually every public appearance was "Every man a king, every man a king, you can be a millionaire."

Indeed, this optimistic belief in upward mobility lies deep within the American psyche. Geographical expansion allowed early Americans who wanted wealth and opportunity to move to a new territory and try their hand; they did not have to wrestle it from those who had it. When the historian Frederick Jackson Turner declared the closing of the Western frontier in 1893, he predicted that "the American energy will continually demand a wider field for its exercise."[25] And, as historian David Noble has chronicled, the movement from the farms back to the cities and urban areas had become the next great American expansion.[26] While geographic expansion may be limited, growth and innovation remain the perpetual American frontier.

Continuing to push for a growing economic pie should be critical for those who believe in an America that always makes room for more people from diverse economic, cultural, and ethnic backgrounds who want to work hard to move up into the broad middle class. Simply put: it is easier to have a melting pot if it is a growing pot. When the economy stagnates, competition for a set number of jobs and resources becomes a war for scarce resources that can break down along racial and ethnic lines.

That is why the failure to "grow together" increases the risk that we will "grow apart" and become divided as a people competing for a shrinking pie of resources and opportunity.

Even when Democrats have taken correct and important stances on issues such as Social Security privatization and corporate misconduct they have often failed to appeal to the optimistic pro-growth aspirations of Americans because their strongest messages are seen only as critiques.

On Social Security privatization, Democrats have been right to criticize conservative plans to introduce unnecessary market risk into Social Security's guaranteed progressive benefit, and to level a broader critique of President Bush's misnamed "ownership society," which does virtually nothing to help 95 percent of Americans save and build wealth. In the summer of

2002, Democrats led by Senator Paul Sarbanes rightfully pushed for tough new legislation to address the conflicts of interest and corporate malfeasance that decimated wages and pension savings of millions of employees. Democrats also had good reason to question the practices of energy companies during the California energy crisis and whether pharmaceutical companies were subject to adequate pressures to keep prices low.

Yet if the only time most Americans hear leading Democrats speak with passion about investing in the stock market or large corporations is in a negative context, some may question whether the party is sufficiently passionate about helping individuals who want to invest more in the market or find a job with a large, growing company. Senator John Kerry recognized this in May 2004 when he acknowledged to the Business Roundtable that he had gone too far in broadly using the term "Benedict Arnold CEOs." "You can't love jobs but hate the people who create them," he explained.[27]

The key for Democrats is not to pull our punches, but to match our critiques with passionate words and bold policies to spread wealth creation, and encourage entrepreneurship, risk-taking, and small business creation. A recent Pew poll found that the nearly 40 percent of crucial undecided voters respond overwhelmingly to the optimistic empowerment and growth messages that Democrats too often fail to deliver.[28]

Imagine a very troubled company whose workers must choose between two finalists for a new CEO. One candidate lists a number of specific populist actions to improve the company, including selling off a private jet for top executives and closing down the executive dining room with its high-priced chef. Each change reflects good values and is overwhelmingly popular with the workers. The other CEO candidate brushes aside these symbolic changes and outlines his long-term plan to restore profitability. In an ideal world, the company's workers might want a CEO with both a long-term vision for profitability and a commitment to slashing lavish executive perks. But given the choice, they are likely to go with the CEO who has a plan to save their jobs, even if he doesn't share their values on corporate fairness.

President Clinton had an intuitive feel for defining his economic agenda within an optimistic and pro-growth vision. He never shied away from populist positions like addressing skyrocketing CEO pay, taking on the tobacco industry, critiquing foreign corporate tax avoidance, and pocket vetoing bankruptcy reform that he believed was a sop to the credit card industry. Yet he paired these positions with a future-oriented "economy, stupid" focus that highlighted the positives of technological advance, open markets, and "building a bridge to the future." On the issue of fiscal discipline, for example, he defined deficit reduction as critical to both creating a pro-confidence and pro-investment climate and achieving the progressive goals of saving Social Security and restoring trust in government. He also realized the importance of always providing a positive progressive alternative. When the Republicans won congressional majorities and pushed for a balanced budget in 1995, most of their specific measures were so unpopular with the public that most of Clinton's staff believed he could simply criticize individual spending cuts in the Republican budgets. Yet Clinton and Gore understood that without a progressive balanced budget plan of their own, they would cede the field to Republicans and drive voters concerned about fiscal discipline to the Republican plan by default, even with all its unpopular details.

Being a pro-growth progressive does not mean compromising progressive values or moving to soulless centrism or Republican-lite positions. It means having plans to realize progressive values and economic growth, understanding that those two goals can be consistent and even complementary.

MEMO TO CONSERVATIVES: A HANDS-OFF APPROACH WILL ALSO FAIL TO HELP US GROW, OR GROW TOGETHER

If the dynamism economy means accepting some degree of economic upheaval and dislocation as inevitable, it also requires rethinking the traditional conservative bias that smaller government is inherently pro-efficiency and pro-growth. Indeed, what may matter most today is the design, not the size, of government policy. Far from restricting markets or burdening employer choice, ambitious policies to improve the knowledge base of our workforce and help American families adjust to fast-paced change may be increasingly vital to both growing the economy and ensuring more Americans believe they are benefiting from its dynamism.

This should provoke a rethinking of fiscal policy among supply-siders: deficit-exploding tax cuts that are designed to starve the beast of government, rather than produce unrestrained free enterprise may cripple the government's ability to institute the policies necessary to avoid a backlash that could lessen support for open trade, vibrant markets, and fast-paced competition.

1. Conservative Humility

Much of the comfort that the "don't worry, be happy" crowd takes in a less-government-is-more approach is based on a faith that "sooner or later" markets will sort things out. Of course, this is sometimes the case in the long run. For example, fears of a "hollowing out" of middle-class jobs have characterized numerous periods in our history ever since the post–Civil War period when Northerners worried that their industrial jobs would all shift to the low-wage South. At each juncture, we have eventually created new jobs and new industries that might have seemed unimaginable years before. In addition, demographic trends suggest that our main challenge in years to come may be too few workers, not too few jobs. Americans also have reason for long-term optimism if, in the coming decades, the explosion of workers entering the global economy in countries like India and China come to constitute a new army of middle-class consumers that can purchase U.S. goods and services.

Yet even if history and long-term trends suggest that disruptive change sorts itself out, free-market conservatives should not assume that the recent trends in the dynamism economy are inflicting only mild or temporary pain for workers and their communities. In the early 1990s, fears over the temporary impact of competition from South Korea and Japan turned out to be overstated, but there is no precedent for the explosion of globalization and information technology combined with the integration of the economies of China and India, which together make up 40 percent of the world's population and have a seemingly limitless supply of cheap labor. While economic theory and experience may say that when poor nations grow, workers demand more wages, thus reducing the gap in labor costs, none of us knows how long it will take before we see significant wage increases in those countries. Even Paul Samuelson, the Nobel Prize–winning economist and ardent free trade supporter, has questioned whether the U.S. will always enjoy "surplus of winnings over losings" if trading partners like China and India simultaneously increase their numbers of highly skilled workers and maintain lower labor costs.[29] What if new domestic industries are slower to materialize than the industries and jobs leaving? The absence of any targeted government responses to spark jobs, supplement wages, or help with economic adjustments could lead to far more protectionist, anti-growth backlashes.

Those who base their arguments for more open markets only on long-term macroeconomic forecasts must also recognize there is something disturbingly cold and utilitarian about people at comfortable jobs at comfortable think tanks and law offices opining that for the good of the economy, we must tolerate other people's pain. In the Clinton campaign war room in the fall of 1992, James Carville told George Stephanopoulos and me that he was willing to be for NAFTA, but he could hardly stand the way elite trade supporters discounted the cost of others' dislocation. "I am all for NAFTA and open trade," he said, "but I just wonder how the argument would go if all the facts showed that NAFTA would be good for the economy as a whole, but it would cost 50 percent of Washington elites the ability to get their children into a good private school. I wonder how much we would hear about the overall good of free trade then?"

Of course, many pro–free trade economists would rightly argue that while dislocation driven by globalization and technology can be extremely painful, sooner or later economic openness will raise all boats. When I hear that argument, I am reminded of President Clinton's "iron law" of politics that when someone said a problem was not about money, he was always talking about someone else's problem. My own iron law is that whenever someone says that dynamic economic change will benefit everyone sooner or later, he is always talking about someone else's job. When it is your livelihood, there is a profound difference between sooner and later.

The problem with our current discourse is that while those who call for increased trade barriers often have no strategy for how their company or industry will compete and prosper over the long term, those who argue against protectionism often have nothing to say to those facing pain and devastation today but "tough luck." This leads to an impoverished impasse: *when it comes to workers and communities threatened by global competition, protectionists have no vision for the future and free traders have no vision for the present.*

Conservatives and free traders have to recognize that we cannot break out of this deadlock if the only option we offer communities suffering economic devastation because of global competition is protectionism. Even where I have differed on proposals to raise trade barriers, I never accepted the callous claim that calls for such protection were the result of selfish special interests. When United Steelworkers of America President George Becker explained to me that despite the flurry of antidumping cases brought by the Commerce Department in 1999 and 2000, he still thought the administration needed to do more, I did not see a man fighting for an extra tax break or a special privilege. He was fighting for the jobs, the livelihoods of his workers. If the only choice is between economic devastation and protectionist policies, what union leader or elected official is not going to choose trade barriers?

For Erskine Bowles, President Clinton's former chief of staff, the lack of meaningful policies for communities threatened by global trade tore at him as he traveled to hard-hit areas during his first run for the United States Senate in 2002. Like many in the administration, he had supported trade expansions. But on the campaign trail in North Carolina he reversed those positions after talking with families in devastated mill towns. I asked him whether his new stance represented a change of heart or just the political realities of running for office in a state where politicians have to look out for globally vulnerable industries like textiles. He paused a while, and then said that after seeing the devastation of entire mill communities, he could not maintain the presumptions about free trade that he had in the White House if we could not come up with better alternatives. "The values my mom and dad brought me up on just tell me that it is wrong," he explained. In those communities, "there were no new jobs to even train people for. Whole communities were spiraling downward toward death." He still believed in the benefits of open markets, but now he felt that we could not go any farther until we found effective means to alleviate or prevent such economic suffering. If free traders continue to ignore the need to engage in serious discussion on solving the problems of dislocation and providing vulnerable communities with viable choices, they risk a further depletion of their ranks.

2. The Economic and Political Danger of Encouraging a Winner-Take-All, Loser-Lose-All Society

Conservative free marketers must also acknowledge that without more thoughtful government policies, the dynamism economy could become a winner-take-all, loser-lose-all environment with dangerous consequences.

In his thought-provoking book *The New Financial Order,* Yale economist Robert J. Shiller explains that the difference between who wins and who loses is increasingly a function of chance and unforeseen choices. "Individual careers," Shiller explains, "can be as dramatically harmed by being just marginally less productive as by discovering a key scientific result a week later than others."[30] The savviest investors in the world have been unable to predict which industries will be the wealth and job creators of the future and which will fall by the wayside or become victims of global competition. Workers or high school and college students making choices about their careers should hardly be expected to do better.

Unfortunately, this unpredictability can wound our national psyche and our economy's potential if people believe that the difference between a sudden nest egg and a devastating fall is the result of luck and timing and not the traditional American virtues of hard work and education. In a flourishing free market, differential outcomes based on chance are inevitable. But the real question is whether our public policies mediate the role of chance—and recycle opportunity for those with high aspirations and strong work ethics—or exacerbate the inequities of market outcomes. The less-government, supply-side policies of the Bush administration are moving us toward a dangerous situation where not only market forces, but also our government policies, strongly promote a winner-take-all and loser-lose-all economy.

Most middle-class workers have traditionally believed that there was an unspoken economic compact in America: if they did all the right things— got an education, found a job, and worked hard—they would be guaranteed a basic level of comfort for their families. It is similar to the contract-law definition of "reliance"—what a prudent, reasonable person would believe based on statements and promises, even without an explicit contract.

In the 1990s, when dynamism brought both record job growth and considerable dislocation, many Americans accepted President Clinton's view that this unspoken economic compact simply needed to be updated. People could still rely on a degree of economic security in a dynamic global economy if they added a commitment to pursue higher education, computer literacy, and lifelong learning to improve skills on the job. Even if it was too late for some older or less-skilled workers, they could take comfort in the fact that their children could rely on this updated social compact to succeed.

When economists downplay concerns of outsourcing by pointing out that the number of jobs being sent overseas is small compared to the size of our workforce, they miss the fact that even anecdotal stories of radiologists and investment bankers losing their jobs to overseas competition creates a sense of economic anxiety far beyond the immediate numbers affected. It causes millions of working Americans to question whether or not there is any economic reliance left. If only the super-educated are assured of being able to surf the waves of the global economy, what can the average hard-working American—even with a solid college education—rely on? One of the most frequently heard comments from people who have lost their jobs is: "This wasn't supposed to happen to me—I did everything I was told to do: went to school, got a college degree, worked hard." Mike McGeehan, a member of Pennsylvania's state legislature, recently noted, "When the steel work went overseas, when the auto work went overseas, the textile work went overseas, everyone said it won't happen to my industry. Well, guess what, people? No one's safe in America anymore."[31] As forty-nine-year-old Michael Tucker, a laid-off software developer, lamented, "Computer programmers are the textile workers of the future."[32]

The Economic Danger: Less Risk Taking and Investment

If the government is seen to sanction an uncertain environment where workers have no economic reliance, an increasing number of people could decide that taking risks and investing in training and education will still leave them vulnerable—stifling innovation and productivity in our economy. Over dinner recently, Clyde Prestowitz, president of the Economic Strategy Institute, mentioned that his son had been laid off as a computer programmer in Silicon Valley and had decided to start a snow removal business in Aspen. As his son explained, "At least I'll know they'll never be able to shovel our snow from India."

Robert Shiller envisions a scenario where millions of workers shun high-skilled career paths out of fear that they will be subject to an unforgiving global economy combined with minimal government assistance. "Brilliant careers go untried because of the fear of economic setback. The educations people undertake, the occupational specialties they choose, the ventures they set out on, are all limited by the knowledge that economically we are on our own and must bear all of the losses we incur."[33]

We in the United States recognize that if a single bankruptcy resulted in a lifetime of oppressive debt or even debtors' prison, the cost would be not just in disappointed lives, but in less risk taking and entrepreneurship. The "fresh start" rationale of bankruptcy always had economic growth content: we did not want to discourage risk taking or leave viable entrepreneurial talent shackled due to bad luck or even a single bad business calculation. A one-strike-and-you're-out economy could undermine the willingness of Americans to do what we know is in our national interest—take risks, innovate, and invest in higher education and skills.

The Political Danger: Rejection of Pro-Growth Policies

With an increasing share of the public concerned that their jobs are, as economists say, "globally contestable" there is a greater risk of a broader political backlash against open markets and globalization. If accepting other people's pain is the only way to support dynamism, an increasing portion of the American public will translate their anxieties into a political voice. The *Wall Street Journal* reported that the number of high-skilled and technology workers' groups like Mad in the U.S.A. and the Organization for the Rights of American Workers support the anti-trade anti-openness position.[34] Conservative free-market advocates could find that their laissez-faire view sparks a backlash that results in anti-growth outcomes.

3. Recycling Opportunity:
The Increased Importance of Progressive Taxation

Much of the push for tax reform in conservative circles, like the consumption tax or flat tax, would make our system less progressive and less flexible in moderating the ups and downs of the dynamism economy. Most Americans support our progressive tax system because they agree with the basic fairness of asking those who benefit most from our economy to bear a somewhat higher burden of taxation. The increasing role of chance in the dynamism economy is another compelling reason to maintain a progressive tax structure.

No one makes the case for progressive taxation more passionately than Bill Gates Sr., whose son is, of course, the richest man in the world. Gates Sr. explains that the "great man" theory in the United States—that great wealth is amassed by the individual efforts of individual men—"borders on mythology."[35] Those who create great wealth do so on the backs and shoulders of previous generations of taxpayers whose money has helped construct the most reliable intellectual property system in the world, a strong judiciary, universal public education, stable capital markets, and government research investments. The "great man" in America is the beneficiary of the investments of millions of average people. As Gates Sr. told Bill Moyers, "The notion that 'You earned it' is more correctly 'you earned it with the indispensable help of the government.' If you'd been born in West Africa, you would not have earned it. It would not have occurred." Gates believes that progressive taxation is a means for those fortunate individuals "to pay a return" on the investments of millions of average workers who, over many generations, helped lay the foundations for that individual's success.[36]

Gates's notion of "paying a return" takes on new significance in an economic environment increasingly characterized by chance for those whose jobs are tied to the accelerating pace of technological change and global competition. Consider the following scenario: three friends graduate from average colleges with a computer science degree. None of them finished at the top of their class or has the education to begin executive-track jobs, but each is hardworking and received the latest training. One friend chooses the next Intel and through stock options makes a small fortune. Meanwhile, one of his equally talented friends ends up at a company that was on top but is now struggling to survive, and the third finds himself at a company that is completely eclipsed by a new wave of technology. As Shiller stresses, it is hard to argue that skill has defined who is well off and who is unemployed. We accept such variance in financial well-being—even due to pure luck—as an inevitable outcome of a free-market economy. A progressive tax code ensures that those who have prospered the most provide resources to cushion the blows and provide new opportunities to those who end up with the short straw. If all workers are taxed at a flat 15 percent rate rather than through a progressive rate structure, the government has fewer revenues to support bold education and retraining policies, and the two losing friends will have less chance of gaining the new skills they need to take another shot. A tax code that is regressive and allows tax-free accumulation of large amounts of wealth can exacerbate winner-take-all outcomes in the dynamism economy instead of moderating them.

To the extent that progressive taxation can mediate such chance-driven outcomes, foster vital investments in workers, and lead more people to embrace our dynamism economy, it will make our entire workforce and our economy more productive. The 1990s is a perfect example. While income taxes were raised on the highest earners as part of the 1993 deficit reduction plan, by 2000 the top 1 percent of earners on average were making $423,000 more a year *after* taxes due to a stronger economy.[37] The dramatic transformation of our fiscal situation after 2000 from projected surpluses to projected deficits as high as $4.8 trillion over the next decade could not have come at a worse time. Beyond the harm these growing deficits pose to our financial stability, investment climate, and ability to address the baby boom retirement crisis, starving-the-beast with high-income tax cuts saps the government of the vital resources it needs to recycle opportunities and to help workers survive—and hopefully thrive—in a fast-paced dynamism.

4. A New Cost-Sharing Compact
That Goes Beyond the Business Cycle

We need to recognize that the anxiety of workers at risk in the dynamism economy represents not only their fear of losing their paycheck, but losing health insurance for their kids, losing their home because they can't make mortgage payments, or suffering other dramatic setbacks. We need adjustment policies that are comprehensive and protect families against devastating economic falls. In chapter 4, I describe a set of bold new adjustment policies in areas such as retraining, health care, and wage and mortgage insurance.

We also need to break free from the outmoded view that seeks to determine why a worker lost her job before determining the level of adjustment assistance she should receive. Our current policy of offering increased income and health insurance support if you can show your job was lost due to trade is inequitable and out of touch with the complex nature of the dynamism economy. Indeed, even in manufacturing there is nothing to suggest that losing your job due to trade leads to a harsher adjustment process. Data from the Displaced Workers Survey in 2002 shows that while manufacturing workers who lost their jobs to import competition experienced an average 13 percent wage loss, manufacturing workers who lost their jobs for reasons unrelated to import competition experienced an average wage loss of 12 percent.[38]

Imagine three brothers living next door to each other, each earning $50,000 and supporting three children. Brother One loses his machine tool factory job due to new low-cost competition from a new trade agreement. Brother Two loses his position at a bank because new online banking makes his job obsolete. Brother Three loses his job because a new Korean product has shrunk his company's market share. In our current system, Brother One has lost his job due to trade and therefore is eligible for generous training assistance and substantial assistance to buy health care for his family. Since Brother Two lost his job due to new technology, he will receive no health care benefits and a far less generous training assistance. Whether Brother Three gets the more generous or less generous assistance will come down to a complex and nuanced judgment from the government as to whether his job was lost due to trade or simply the creation of a new product line.

Treating the families of these three brothers so differently based on a causal analysis of how they lost their jobs is not just unfair but increasingly hard to determine. In the dynamism economy more and more job loss will resemble that of Brother Three: a mix of technological change, global competition, shifting consumer tastes, and product lines that will not be easy to sort out.

Beyond the Business Cycle

We should shed the antiquated practice of conditioning expansions of our adjustment efforts on downturns in the business cycle. The traditional justification for providing extra relief in times of overall economic distress contends that it may be harder for a worker to be rehired when jobs are scarce. This is why we provide extended unemployment insurance—which is paid out for just thirteen weeks and to just 35 percent of job losers—only when we are in or near a recession.[39] Indeed, one reason lawmakers did not include temporary health insurance assistance for unemployed workers in the economic stimulus package in 2002 was their concern that, once enacted, the measure might become permanent.

This kind of business-cycle thinking is out of date in an economy where job loss is increasingly a permanent, not cyclical phenomenon. A study by New York Federal Reserve economists Erica Groshen and Simon Potter identified the job loss in the previous five recessions in industries that were experiencing cyclical change (jobs came back at the end of the recession) versus those that were undergoing structural change (job losses or gains continued independent of the rebound). Compared to the recessions of the 1970s and 1980s, where job loss was roughly split between permanent and temporary, 79 percent of jobs lost in the 2001 recession occurred in industries experiencing permanent structural change.[40] Yet even this study misses a fundamental component of the dynamism economy: permanent job loss happens constantly, under both good and bad economic conditions. Our adjustment policies must catch up to this new reality.

5. Increasing the Pool

A presumption in favor of minimalist government will also prevent us from addressing two of the paramount challenges to America's competitiveness: how to ensure that we have an increasing number of highly skilled workers and how to stay at the cutting edge of the technological change that creates whole new industries and drives job growth in the dynamism economy. Conservatives will need to look beyond the simple assumption that all government investment slows growth and embrace bold investment to educate workers and spur technological innovation.

Harvard economist and current Dean of the Kennedy School of Government David Ellwood, through work with the Aspen Institute, has highlighted the stark reality that the robust 44 percent growth in our native-born workforce over the past two decades is coming to a halt. Over the next twenty years we will see *zero* growth. And as minorities and traditionally disadvantaged groups with lower education levels make up a larger share of our workforce, if these patterns are not changed the growth in average education among the workforce will slow dramatically. Over the past two decades, the share of workers with at least a college degree grew by 50 percent; over the next two decades it will grow by only 4 percent.[41] Even in manufacturing, retiring baby boomers will create a need for ten million new skilled workers over the next twenty years, according to a study by the National Association of Manufacturers.[42]

We can no longer rely on natural labor force growth to fill the high-skilled jobs of the future—we must increase the share of our workforce that is highly skilled and educated.

China and India have made aggressive investments in their workers and in scientific research. While graduate enrollment in the U.S. in math and science has declined by 20 percent since 1993 and the President's 2006 budget cuts funding for R&D in real terms, the number of Ph.D.s awarded in China grew fivefold in the 1990s and China has doubled the percentage of its GDP invested in R&D between 1995 and 2002.[43]

Every year billions of dollars flow through Washington lobbying shops as businesses and corporate leaders seek even the slightest regulatory advantage, yet national priorities like increasing investments in education are treated like hobbies. When it comes to equipping every child in America with a strong foundation of education from birth and opportunities throughout their childhood and adult life to increase their education and skills, most corporations substitute lobbying muscle for an occasional speech or small grant from their corporate foundation.

While no doubt many corporate leaders are concerned about these workforce issues, to become the "Statesman CEOs" that Peter Peterson has called for,[44] challenges that are critical to our nation's long-term bottom line like universal quality preschool and opportunities for Hispanics, blacks, and women in the fields of math and science, must be given at least the same priority as the narrow and short-term issues that often dominate current corporate lobbying and advocacy.

Every child in America should obtain the kind of experiences and brain stimulation in their first years of life that builds a foundation for strong cognitive and analytical skills. We need a bold commitment to universal preschool. We should expand Head Start, provide universal after-school care and make it easier for kids from disadvantaged backgrounds to get a college education. In part III, I will explore key strategies to "increase the pool" of high-skilled workers that must be an integral part of a progressive pro-growth economic strategy.

The fight to attract high-wage jobs will grow increasingly competitive in this new environment. To remain a magnet for innovative companies and high-value added industries, we have an imperative to maintain economic stability, the strongest research capacity, and the best high-tech infrastructure. America should be pushing our investment in innovation and science into overdrive, not dragging our feet because some will label such critical investment "big spending." Particularly in basic research, government funding is critical to a continual stream of scientific and technological innovation. First, we cannot rely on the private sector with its product-driven research to expand the borders of knowledge. As MIT physicist and Nobel Laureate Jerome Friedman explains, "If you know what you are looking for, you are limited by what you know." [45] Second, proactive government research investment increases the speed at which new ideas, discoveries, and technologies are disseminated. Private companies need monopoly prices to pay for their investment, so they receive patent exclusivity for seventeen years. However, many products and services would not have been possible without the foundation of basic research that doesn't require an immediate commercial application. For instance, the work on quantum mechanics by Albert Einstein, Niels Bohr, and Max Planck that led to the creation of the transistor and the laser also made the Internet and DVD possible. [46]

Before diving into the specific areas of pro-growth progressive policy, I want to define the foundations of the approach. What does it mean to be progressive? What values do progressives want to support through economic policy?

2

Three Progressive Values

Readers looking for a rigid definition of what it means to be progressive based on the historical roots of the Progressive era or the teachings of particular modern philosophers will be disappointed with the pages that follow. My definition is based on my own observations. I believe that as a community we have a collective responsibility to support three basic values: economic dignity for those who take responsibility for their lives, opportunity for upward mobility, and fair starts so that the accident of birth does not overly determine one's life outcomes. Conservatives may also share these aspirations, but often argue that government is not as responsible for ensuring these aims or that such public policy intervention will do more harm than simply letting markets take their course. Being a progrowth progressive means respecting the power of the markets and being humble about the unintended consequences that conservatives and libertarians fear while still firmly believing that we have a collective responsibility to design public policies that lift all boats.

1. Economic Dignity for Those Who Take Responsibility for Their Lives

There is an implicit social compact in the United States that those who accept the responsibility of working hard to support themselves and their families should be able to maintain the basic necessities of life without humiliation, exploitation, poverty, or devastating falls in their standards of living.

New Deal social assistance programs were designed to help people who were not capable of helping themselves, such as orphans, the severely disabled, and the elderly. But as government assistance has expanded to include those who find themselves in oppressive economic circumstances—such as unemployment and poverty—Americans want to know that those recipients of assistance are doing everything in their power to help themselves. "Within the U.S.," Michigan Public Policy Dean Becky Blank writes, "the distinction between the 'deserving' and the 'undeserving' poor is often based on whether poor individuals are viewed as behaving in ways that contribute to their poverty."[1]

While many see this ethic as a heartless rationale for denying assistance to those deemed "undeserving," understanding the power of this social compact is critical to unlocking public support for more compassionate and progressive policy. President Clinton recognized that the public would be far more willing to support generous assistance to lower-income families and individuals if it was tied to a willingness to work. Indeed, Clinton often noted that even in the suburbs one of the most popular statements was "no parent who works full-time should ever have to raise a child in poverty," even though policies he was calling for—the Earned Income Tax Credit, the minimum wage, and child care—fundamentally focused on the working poor.

Indeed, this call for individual responsibility is heard from a wide spectrum of progressive thinkers. Marian Wright Edelman's first lesson in her essay "25 Lessons for Life" is "Don't feel entitled to anything you didn't sweat and struggle for."[2] It is inherent in the "Opportunity and Responsibility" theme that Bill Clinton and the leaders of the Democratic Leadership Council—Al From, Will Marshall, and Bruce Reed—successfully pushed in the 1992 campaign and that became a central tenet of the Clinton presidency. It taps into an intrinsic component of the American social contract: a willingness to help those who help themselves.

I was struck by how deeply the public values this compact when Democrats were fighting to extend unemployment insurance in the wake of September 11, 2001. Even with 8 million Americans out of work and 860,000 exhausting their unemployment benefits in the last quarter of 2001,[3] Democratic pollster and strategist Stan Greenberg told me it was crucial to describe those needing benefits not as "the unemployed" but as "hardworking Americans who are desperately looking for work."

Government efforts to help ensure economic dignity can take many forms. One of the most basic is to provide a "floor" or minimum standard of living for the working poor or those with disabilities who cannot work on their own. As Barbara Ehrenreich powerfully captured in her book

Nickel and Dimed, securing economic dignity requires an income well above the official government poverty line—$18,000 for a family of four. When Ehrenreich spent a month working as a server in a hotel restaurant in Key West, Florida, she found that none of her colleagues earning at or near the minimum wage could even save enough for the security deposit on rented apartments and were forced to live in a semipermanent flux of week-to-week rooms, friends' houses, and their cars.[4]

In the dynamism economy, a new and growing threat to economic dignity is the anxiety that job loss will result not in temporary hardship, but in a permanent decline in economic well-being. Progressives may have legitimate philosophical concerns about whether it is appropriate to focus limited resources on preventing falls in the standard of living of workers who may still be better off than those who don't have any economic security to lose. I was forced to confront this philosophical dilemma when I pressed Congressman Charlie Rangel for his support on a trade agreement and told him about the administration's plans to increase job search and training assistance for displaced workers.

Rangel, a veteran and former civil rights leader who has represented his Harlem district for twenty-five years, posed a compelling question: "Why do we do so much for the people who are losing good jobs and so little for those who never had a chance to have a good job in the first place?"

Pro-growth progressives must be committed to securing economic dignity on both fronts. A working family that is forced to sell its home, lose health insurance, or abandon retirement plans suffers a special assault on economic dignity. Anthropologist Katherine Newman, in her book *Falling from Grace: Downward Mobility in an Age of Affluence,* describes this condition as "eviction from the American dream." "Downward mobility is not just a matter of accepting a menial job, enduring the loss of stability, or witnessing with dismay the evaporation of one's material comfort. It is also a broken covenant. It is so profound . . . that it calls into question the assumptions upon which their lives have been predicated."[5] Progressives must make policies that protect economic dignity both for those who are working their way up and those in danger of a devastating economic fall.

Another hard balance is between ensuring basic economic necessities and reducing income inequality. Large-scale inequality tears at our social fabric, weakens our sense of national community, and raises fears that the well-off can cheat, lobby, or use accounting gimmicks or inside networks to further protect and increase their wealth at the expense of average Americans. The desire to balance inequality against economic gain has surprising resonance with the American public. When an NBC/Wall Street Journal poll asked Americans in May 2003 whether they would rather see income gains that led the wealthiest to do significantly better than the poor or see lower gains for *both* groups with greater income equality, they chose the latter 60 percent to 27 percent.[6]

While I believe that progressives should work to minimize income inequality, I also believe that our primary goal should be raising all middle-class and poor boats substantially, even if the well-off boats rise at a similar or faster pace. Certainly the trend of family income we saw between 1993 and 2000 is the ideal. All five economic quintiles experienced substantial income growth and the bottom quintile's income grew 23.6 percent— faster than the most well-off fifth of families.[7] Yet I would have rather seen the bottom quintile's income grow 30 percent and the top quintile's income grow 31 percent, because even though income inequality would have slightly increased, the poorest families would have seen a substantial increase in their standard of living.

2. Opportunities for Upward Mobility

When writing his seminal work on American democracy, Alexis de Tocqueville noted that, "The privileges and disqualifications of caste being abolished, and men having shattered the bonds which held them fixed, the notion of advancement suggests itself to every mind, the desire to rise swells in every heart, and *all men want to mount above their station: ambition is the universal feeling.*"[8] [Emphasis added.]

This vision of America as a place where everyone who works hard can move upward has always been our aspiration, even when it was notoriously denied to African Americans, Hispanics, Native Americans, and women at points in our history. A poll from the Pew 2004 Political Landscape Project found that Americans by a margin of two-to-one reject the statement that "success in life is pretty much determined by outside factors," and more than two-thirds of Americans disagree with the notion that "hard work offers little guarantee for success."[9]

Yet America is moving quickly away from this ideal. Noted European sociologist Gosta Esping-Anderson has found that the correlation of incomes between parents and children is twice as strong in the United States as it is in Scandinavia.[10] A recent study by Gary Solon, an economist at the University of Michigan, has shown that the degree to which children find themselves in different income brackets than their parents—what is known as "intergenerational" mobility—is actually lower in the United States today than in a number of industrialized countries including Germany, Canada, and Scandinavia.[11] Data compiled by Katharine Bradbury and Jane Katz at the Federal Reserve in Boston suggest that income mobility has slowed in the United States since 1970.[12] Earl Wysong, a sociologist at Indiana University, tracked upward mobility using father-son pairs from 1979 to 1998: he found that 70 percent of sons in 1998 were doing the same or worse than their fathers had done in 1979.[13] Such research consistently finds that it is becoming increasingly unlikely that the lowest 20 percent of earners will escape poverty. Upward mobility is particularly limited for African Americans. Economist Tom Hertz at American University has shown that 63 percent of blacks born in the lowest quartile will stay there in adulthood and only 4 percent will move to the top quartile.[14]

Designing public policies that address this worrying trend should be a priority for progressives. Traditionally, they have highlighted educational inequities as a barrier to upward mobility and made the strong case for increasing investments in education. The example of Bill Clinton, who grew up without a father in a family of humble means but became president through hard work and access to education, is the prototypical example of the foundational role that education can play in promoting upward mobility for all.

Yet outside of education, progressives have missed an opportunity to promote policies on savings, wealth creation, small business creation, and entrepreneurial opportunities that respond to Americans' aspiration for upward mobility.

3. Fair Starts: Life Outcomes Should Not Be Determined by the Accident of Birth

Intrinsic to the American belief that individual economic well-being should be determined by talent and effort—not by government fiat—is ensuring that entire groups in our society are not denied a reasonable opportunity to move upward by virtue of the accident of their birth.

In his *Thoughts on Government* in 1776, John Adams was emphatic that the government should literally spare no expense to provide equal educational opportunities for all children. He explained that "laws for the liberal education of youth, especially for the lower classes of people, are so extremely wise and useful that to a humane and generous mind, no expense for this purpose would be thought extravagant."[15] It was of no small consequence that in 1779 Adams wrote into the Massachusetts Constitution, "it shall be the duty of legislatures and magistrates, in all future periods of this commonwealth, to cherish . . . public schools and grammar schools in the towns."[16] Thomas Jefferson also made an outspoken commitment to fair starts through equal education, calling for a constitutional amendment guaranteeing free public education in 1806.[17]

Yet as we look at the real-life circumstances of millions of children in the United States, we have to ask ourselves whether we are not moving backward from our Founders' vision of reasonable opportunity for all children. Conservatives avoid the cognitive dissonance between the hard facts of child poverty and their belief in the ideal of America as a land where all can rise without more proactive public policies by noting that no specific laws prevent any child from rising up and escaping their economic circumstances. They celebrate the few who can be portrayed as having pulled themselves up by their bootstraps. Yet how much comfort should we take in the equality of our laws when we knowingly tolerate millions of children being born into a low and increasingly unbreakable economic class? Americans would not tolerate a law saying that only 7 percent of American children born to single mothers in housing projects are permitted to go to college. Yet this is in fact the situation today,[18] and we take little action to rectify it.

It undercuts our values in fair starts and upward mobility when the lives of an entire class of children have been fundamentally predetermined by age five. Poor mothers are three times as likely to get insufficient care during their pregnancies—leading to infant mortality rates 60 percent higher than the rest of the population.[19] Children in families with income below $15,000 are more than fourteen times as likely to be abused and more than forty times as likely to be neglected;[20] poor children are four times as likely to experience hunger.[21] Poor children are significantly less likely to be read to or get the kind of intellectual stimulation in the first years of life[22] that we know is a major factor in their ability to do well in school or even perform well in a job interview. Poor children who do attend preschools spend their days in decrepit classrooms with disengaged, undertrained teachers, while only miles apart in most American cities the most well-off parents spend thousands of dollars grooming and training their children to pass entrance exams into elite preschools. By the time these two different groups are ready to enter elementary school, the gap has widened. It should surprise no one that poor children are twice as likely to repeat a grade and more than twice as likely to drop out of high school.[23]

If Americans truly believe that everyone must take personal responsibility for his or her success or failure, we have a compelling moral responsibility to make sure that every child gets to the starting line with at least a chance to compete. We should, as Adams said, spare no expense to ensure that every child has the same opportunities to succeed and to promote a society that embodies the notion of distinction based on merit not the accident of birth.

Public policy is nudging us toward an America that turns this value on its head. There have been no significant new efforts to ensure that the poorest children in America have a fair shot early in life, but we are promoting tax policies designed to lock in a perpetual economic elite who can accumulate and pass on wealth to their heirs tax-free.

Nowhere is this contradiction more evident than in recent policies on quality preschool and the estate tax. Proposals to spend $20 billion a year to ensure quality preschool for all children age 0–5 are considered too expensive to be politically viable. At the same time, the Bush administration and conservatives are in a frenzy to permanently repeal the tax on our nation's wealthiest estates at an eventual cost of $75 billion–$100 billion a year. Indeed, eliminating the tax for the wealthiest one-half of 1 percent of estates—or about 10,000 total estates—would eventually cost over $40 billion per year. This aggressive effort is exactly what Thomas Jefferson feared when he called for reformed inheritance laws to "prevent the accumulation and perpetuation of wealth in select families."[24] As FDR echoed over a century later, "inherited economic power is as inconsistent with the ideals of this generation as inherited political power was inconsistent with the ideals of the generation which established our government."[25] More recently, Warren Buffett has compared repealing the estate tax to picking the 2020 Olympic team from the first-born children of the 2000 team.[26]

If we are truly committed to a nation where accidents of birth do not determine life outcomes, we need to refocus our priorities from repealing the estate taxes paid by a few thousand of our wealthiest families to helping the millions of poor children who through no fault of their own are born into poverty and whose opportunities will say much about our nation's potential to grow and live up to our progressive values.

PART TWO

■

*A New
Compact on
Globalization*

3

Toward a New
Consensus on Trade

On the morning of November 18, 1999, I was holed up in a hotel room with Secretary of State Madeleine Albright, U.S. Trade Representative Charlene Barshefsky, Commerce Secretary William Daley, Agriculture Secretary Dan Glickman, and Senior Advisor Karen Tramontano, staring out at throngs of angry protesters. After several hours we were escorted to special armored cars and driven to the back entrance of the nearby conference center. We weren't in a foreign nation in the midst of a coup. We were in Seattle for the opening session of a World Trade Organization meeting to launch a new round of global trade negotiations. Left-of-center activists were protesting the policies of a left-of-center president during one of the greatest economic booms of the twentieth century.

While the protesters dressed as turtles may have made the evening news, I knew our biggest challenge was the silent but growing number of voters who saw expanding trade as a source of anxiety, not an engine of growth in our dynamic economy—even while job growth and income were soaring and unemployment was at historic lows.

President Clinton's record on trade reflected both the tension and ambivalence of the 1990s. While we failed to launch a new round of WTO talks in Seattle and Congress blocked the extension of presidential "fast-track" trade negotiating authority in 1997, there was nonetheless substantial progress on open markets. In addition to the creation of the WTO in 1995, the Clinton years saw the passage of the North American Free Trade Agreement (NAFTA), a historic trade pact with China, the first African Growth and Opportunity Act, a Caribbean Basin Initiative, and the inclusion of labor and environmental provisions in the core trade agreements (as seen in the historic bilateral agreement with Jordan). We negotiated a model agreement on textiles and labor standards with Cambodia, started normalizing trade relations with Vietnam and Laos, largely resisted trade barriers that could have deepened the damage of the Asian financial crisis in 1997–1998, and secured a crucial international agreement to keep the Internet duty-free and to set standards for international payments.

As he completed his second term, President Clinton was painfully aware that these accomplishments usually faced substantial opposition from his own party. In the House of Representatives, NAFTA passed with 40 percent Democratic votes; China with 35 percent; Africa with 60 percent. When we pulled the bill to give the president trade promotion authority in 1997, we barely had 25 percent of Democratic votes. (Six years earlier Bush I received nearly half of Democratic votes in the successful passage of fast track.) This sharp drop in support reflected deep opposition to trade policy among the traditional liberal base, a feeling of betrayal among some House Democrats that the business community had not done more to support pro-NAFTA Democrats in the 1994 election, and a growing anxiety at the pace of change and dislocation in the economy.

While the Republican Party—particularly in the House of Representatives—tends to be more supportive of new trade-opening agreements, the demarcations are not entirely predictable. The majority of Democratic senators have traditionally voted for market openings and trade votes often break down less by party lines than by the region or constituency likely to be hurt by the trade issue at stake. Even President Bush has faced significant opposition from his own party on several aspects of his trade agenda and has had to make special-interest concessions to move trade deals through. During the 2004 presidential campaign when Chairman Greenspan chided me because he felt one of Senator Kerry's positions was too protectionist, I told him that he "had no idea how hard it was to be a pro-trade Democrat." He whispered back, "You have no idea how hard it is getting to be to be a pro-trade Republican."

A POLARIZED, IMPOVERISHED DEBATE

While not all votes are predictable, the debate on trade and globalization remains bitterly polarized, and the outcome of virtually all analysis is predetermined by the views of the sponsoring organization or individual. As a result, there is a serious deficit of open-minded exploration of how to harness and expand the benefits of globalization and trade to ensure that trade is supporting progressive outcomes at home and abroad. While many on the left claim to be for open markets as long as the right conditions and standards are met, often those conditions are designed virtually to ensure no further trade liberalization. On the right, while some agree to minimal labor and environmental standards or a sprinkling of retraining assistance, the concessions tend to be minor and grudging. When a brave soul like Democratic Congressman Sander Levin pushed human rights and labor conditions as a sincere effort to get to yes on a major trade agreement with China—though he is from a heavily union district in Detroit, Michigan—he was treated as an oddity worthy of major newspaper features.[1] While President Clinton will be seen for years as the most consequential pro-trade progressive, and while he broadened the constituency for open markets, stronger labor and environmental standards, and funding for dislocated workers, he left office deeply frustrated that his efforts to forge a new consensus on trade and globalization remained very much a work-in-progress.

I continue to believe that the Clinton administration's orientation toward open markets and our overall support for the major trade agreements were the right positions and that expanding trade will remain a vital mechanism to both spur competition and productivity growth in our own economy and reduce global poverty. Yet I am also painfully aware and not afraid to admit where our critics have proved right and most importantly, where there is room for new solutions that combine the best points from all sides. We will never build a new consensus on open markets unless all parties are willing to take a humble, practical look at where their arguments are not supported by the evidence and to learn from those hard realities going forward.

Take NAFTA. One can search in vain for a balanced, objective analysis of the agreement's impact on Mexico and the United States. Instead, both sides marshal every piece of evidence possible to support their position, fearful that even the slightest concession to the other's position can and will be used against them in the court of public opinion.

Opponents routinely make three major points: real wages have dropped and poverty has increased in Mexico in the ten years since NAFTA; the agreement has forced factory closings and job losses in the United States (the Economic Policy Institute estimates that NAFTA cost 900,000 U.S. jobs between 1994 and 2002); and our trade deficit with Canada and Mexico has widened from $13 billion in 1994 to more than $110 billion in 2004.[2] My nineteen-year-old nephew, and frequent anti-trade protester, Erik constantly argues that the labor violations, human rights abuses, and environmental damage in the export-oriented maquiladora factories that line the Mexican border are evidence of the degradation and exploitation that NAFTA has wrought.

NAFTA supporters respond with their own compelling arguments: it has helped boost trade in Mexico by 232 percent since 1993, a rate of growth twice the rest of the world, and has created half of the 3.5 million new jobs in Mexico from 1995 to 2000. U.S. exports to NAFTA countries also grew at twice the rate of those to the rest of the world, and instead of a "giant sucking sound" of job loss after NAFTA, our nation experienced the longest economic expansion in our history—with more than 22 million jobs created between 1993 and 2000.[3]

Yet an objective analysis of NAFTA should provoke humility and reflection—not certainty—from all sides. Advocates and opponents conveniently leave out complicated factors that muddy their clearly stated positions.

Critics who point to the fact that in Mexico real wages are lower today than when NAFTA was signed often fail to mention that the primary reason for this deep decline and the increase in poverty was the 1995 peso crisis, which can hardly be blamed on NAFTA. If anything, NAFTA helped Mexico make a strong economic recovery in the second half of the 1990s because it prevented the government from pulling back on its important economic reforms and resorting to protectionism as it did after the 1982 peso crisis. NAFTA helped Mexico gain the confidence of global investors within only seven months of the crisis; it took them seven years to return to international capital markets after the 1982 crisis.[4] While about a third of Mexicans remain in poverty today, overall poverty levels have declined since their peak in the wake of the 1995 peso crisis.[5] And while critics are right to highlight the wage suppression and violence that has plagued the export-oriented maquiladoras, they often fail to mention that the deepest poverty in Mexico remains in the southern provinces that are least touched by globalization.

At the same time, proponents of NAFTA need to be more clear-eyed about its unfulfilled promises. In Mexico, some vulnerable constituencies—most notably small farmers—have been hit extremely hard by rapid market opening. Despite an agreement to phase out Mexican corn tariffs, the Mexican government quickly allowed for the importation of large quantities of subsidized American corn. Oxfam International has argued that these policies have devastated the lives of 15 million people who depend on small farming.[6] While the Clinton administration created side agreements that mandated labor and environmental standards and while we have not seen the dramatic race to the bottom in Mexico that many feared, these agreements have not lived up to their promise, particularly in the maquiladoras, due to a lack of planning and inadequate enforcement. NAFTA supporters should be candid about the need to strengthen these provisions, and address deficiencies going forward.

In the United States, the unprecedented job growth in the 1990s coincided with NAFTA, but it cannot be primarily attributed to the agreement. While the majority of economists dispute the contention that NAFTA caused a net job loss in the U.S., most also conclude that it has had a negligible or only mildly positive impact on net job creation. And, while jobs in industries exporting to Canada and Mexico have wages 13 percent to 18 percent higher than the national average,[7] the Economic Policy Institute points out that some employer surveys have found that they are willing to use NAFTA as a bargaining tool in wage negotiations.[8]

For the pro-growth progressive, wrestling with these hard realities on trade is an unavoidable part of the larger challenge: how do we marshal the long-term pro-growth benefits of global competition and technological change while promoting a stronger governmental role in ensuring dynamism promotes equity, prevents devastating economic falls, and creates new opportunities not only in the United States, but also for our trading partners.

HONEST DISCUSSION OF TRADE'S IMPACT

Reducing Mutual Exaggeration: "Trade Over-blame" and "Discounting Pain"

The first step in moving beyond our polarized national debate on trade is to reduce the exaggeration on both sides about the costs and benefits of open markets. The typical heated political battle over a trade agreement goes as follows: those opposing the trade agreement put out stark facts about likely job losses and ignore jobs that might be gained through exports or competitive advantages gained from lower-cost imports. Advocates publicize the number of jobs likely to be created from new exports in the industries most likely to benefit, giving short shrift to job losses caused by a rush of new imports and the possibility that a new trade agreement might make it easier to move jobs to a trading partner and export products back to the United States.

Trade supporters discount the degree of pain that trade can precipitate in particular industries and communities, while trade critics play on the public's tendency to see trade opening as a larger cause of job loss than it is. Critics are able to play an "over-blame game" on job loss for two reasons. One, in a dynamic global economy dislocation increasingly takes place without leaving a clear causal villain. When a company goes bust or lays off hundreds of workers, it can be caused by new technology, new product development, changes in consumer tastes, ineffective management, global competition, or any combination of those factors. Yet because trade agreements are identifiable and concrete events, they are easy targets when the actual cause is considerably more complex. During one of our many Oval Office meetings to sway lawmakers leaning against fast-track trade authority in 1997, a Southern Congressional Democrat told President Clinton that he could not give him his vote because his constituents blamed the closing of a major plant in his district on NAFTA. Thinking I was scoring a big point, I said that the product made by the factory was not even covered by NAFTA. He calmly replied, "You think I don't know that? The fact is that over 80 percent of people in my district think that NAFTA caused that factory to close, and that public perception is my political reality!"

The other reason for the over-blame game is that the benefits of free trade are relatively invisible and diffuse while its harm is often concentrated and highly visible. When I lobbied for passage of trade agreements, I often explained that when a trade opening helped one hundred companies each create or save ten jobs, no one noticed the cumulative thousand jobs. Yet when a single company laid off one thousand employees, it was often a heartbreaking news story that shook confidence and caused anxiety far beyond the laid-off workers and their families.

In retrospect, I must note that this example fails to describe the reality many communities face. Consider two scenarios. In the Macroeconomy Scenario, one thousand jobs are lost in a highly publicized layoff, but one hundred companies in the same geographical area create ten jobs each, and these jobs are in higher-paying fields where the United States has a competitive edge. Most economic analysis shows that open markets shift the jobs to those with higher wages in more competitive industries. Economists J. David Richardson and Howard Lewis found that in the late 1990s exporting firms not only paid higher wages, but also experienced 2 percent to 4 percent faster annual employment growth and were "simply better performers in apples-to-apples comparisons."[9]

While open-trade advocates might like to end the discussion there, consider the Textile Community Scenario. A new trade agreement creates one thousand decent jobs in several states, yet one thousand jobs are lost from a single town that has been dependent on textile manufacturing for generations. The number of jobs lost and gained nationally may be a wash, but the losing community suffers declining revenues and declining hopes for an economic recovery. While trade may shift the national composition to higher-wage jobs, the families in Textile Communities experience just the opposite—a downward shift in probable future wages, especially for older workers. The theory of trade and comparative advantage is of little relevance for these communities. As anthropologist Katherine Newman explains:

> When steel mills close their gates, oil fields fall silent, and farm areas experience epidemics of foreclosure, downward mobility engulfs entire communities. The blight spreads from the shuttered factory to the town beyond its gates, undermining the firms that supplied the factory; the restaurants, supermarkets, and clothing stores where workers used to spend their money; and the public sector, which must struggle to support schools, police, and fire departments on a reduced tax base.[10]

These scenarios suggest that the damage wrought by dislocation depends critically on the skills and ages of workers who lose their jobs, the concentration of job loss within communities, and the degree to which new jobs can replace the lost wages. While the overall number of workers dislocated from jobs is smaller than many might think—between January 2001 and December 2003 only 4 percent of our labor force was displaced from jobs they had held for at least three years[11]—labor economist Lori Kletzer estimates that displaced workers consistently earn less in their new jobs and for one-quarter of them salaries decrease by more than 30 percent. Wage loss is the worst for older workers with minimal education who have worked a single job for a significant period of time. Such older displaced workers often find no new job opportunities that fit their narrow skill set and are forced into low-paying service jobs.[12]

For the pro-growth progressive, there are no easy long-term solutions. Trade barriers can shelter such communities for a period of time but are rarely a permanent solution. It is worth noting that many European countries that opted for higher trade barriers over the past two decades were no more successful in stemming the loss of manufacturing jobs, and have paid a price in persistently high unemployment. In West Germany, for example, one quarter of the manufacturing workforce was lost between 1970 and 1990, and since reunification, manufacturing employment has shrunk by another 25 percent, while unemployment remained above 10 percent for much of the 1990s.[13] Japan lost 16 percent of its manufacturing jobs between 1995 and 2002, and even developing economies lost jobs due to higher productivity: Alliance Capital Management estimates that Brazil lost 20 percent of its manufacturing jobs and China lost 15 percent during that period.[14]

Where lower cost imports are cutting into the market share and employment of U.S. competitors, U.S. trade barriers are usually at best a short-term strategy to allow vulnerable communities the breathing space to innovate. At worst they can make a community even more dependent on a threatened product or service and lead to silent trade-offs for other workers in other communities who are hurt by trade retaliation or higher prices. I first struggled with this tension when I was a midlevel economic staffer for the Dukakis presidential campaign. Steel tariffs had become a major campaign issue because whoever won the election was going to have to decide whether to renew so-called surge control protections that had been in place since 1984. Pennsylvania was shaping up as a critical battleground state, and I talked to labor leaders, local politicians, and the families of steelworkers there to prepare background memos for Governor Dukakis's visits. For many of these communities, trade barriers had provided too little protection to save their jobs in the long run, but enough to delay the process of economic diversification. While those communities with steel plants wanted new surge protection, when I asked families in communities where the factories had already closed what Dukakis could do to help, the response was: "Tell him not to talk about bringing steel back. We are tired of being lied to. No more false promises. We want to hear how he is going to bring new jobs, new industries."

A BALANCED ASSESSMENT OF IMPORTS AND PROGRESSIVE VALUES

The costs and benefits of cheaper imports rarely get a full and fair discussion in trade debates. Many conservatives and free-trade purists assume that when push comes to shove American consumers will always choose the more convenient, lowest-price option, regardless of circumstances. They point to the overwhelming popularity of discount superstores like Wal-Mart and Target and to the Web-based lender and broker E-Loan, which found that when consumers were offered a choice of having their loans processed faster in India or slower in the United States they chose the more efficient option about 85 percent of the time.[15]

Yet the fact that consumers may downplay the importance of national origin or choose lower prices does not mean that, given the chance, they would not act collectively against their narrow consumer interests to achieve a larger social or community goal. No doubt mass superstores are wildly popular, yet even lovers of lower prices may support public policies that halt the most egregious labor practices of some of these chains. While Americans may deeply appreciate the benefits of fierce competition between Microsoft, Google, and Yahoo to create the best search engine technology, there are increasing concerns that the competition between Wal-Mart and its competitors is forcing down wages and creating a race to the bottom on cutting health care benefits. A recent survey by a North Carolina hospital found that 47 percent of Wal-Mart employees who sought treatment were either on Medicaid or had no insurance; Georgia officials estimate that more than ten thousand children of Wal-Mart employees were on the state's health program at a cost of $10 million to taxpayers.[16]

Indeed, several communities have voted against the opening of new Wal-Marts—subverting their personal interests as consumers to their collective concerns about protecting jobs and benefits in their communities. In the mid-1990s allegations that Kathie Lee Gifford's clothing line was being manufactured in sweatshops using child labor sparked a wave of successful anti-sweatshop consumer campaigns. After Nike came under scrutiny for the conditions in its sneaker factories, the company found the negative reputation affected not only consumer behavior but also the morale of its workforce. "[Workers] were going to barbecues and people would say: 'How can you work for Nike?' " explained Nike Vice President

Maria Eitel. "I don't know if we were losing employees, but it sure as hell didn't help in attracting them." [17]

While these examples serve as an important reminder that the benefits of low-cost imports do not always trump all other considerations, progressives too often discount or dismiss the progressive impact of low-cost imports. How can cheap imports be progressive? Think about a more familiar argument—why a sales tax is considered regressive. In a state with a 5 percent sales tax, a CEO making $1 million a year pays the same $5 tax on a $100 clothing purchase as her housekeeper who makes $15,000. When you impose protectionist measures that increase prices for all consumers, they act as a de facto sales tax that hits the poor hardest. When you remove restrictions and allow imports to lower the price of basic goods, you achieve a progressive goal of keeping more money in the pockets of the poorest Americans.

Take Christmas toys. In the early 1990s, imported toys carried tariffs of about 5 percent to 10 percent. These tariffs had long ceased protecting jobs, because nearly all toy manufacturing had moved abroad and jobs in the U.S. toy industry were in design and research. The tariff had essentially mutated into a wholesale tax of 5 percent to 10 percent on every Cabbage Patch Kid, Pokémon, or Nintendo sold in the States.

In 1994, through the Uruguay round of the World Trade Organization (WTO) the Clinton administration decided to eliminate the tariffs, making toys one of the relatively few consumer sectors in which the United States has fully liberalized its trade policy. The result? Since 1997 toy prices have fallen 22 percent, while prices for all goods in the economy have risen 15 percent. [18] Eliminating tariffs has made it significantly easier for low- and moderate-income American families to fill their kids' Christmas stockings.

In a paper entitled "Toughest on the Poor: Taxes, Tariffs, and Single Moms," Edward Gresser of the Progressive Policy Institute calculated the net impact of our remaining import tariffs on the prices of a representative basket of consumer goods for an average American family. Gresser found that protectionism imposes a silent tax on American consumers that is more regressive than the sales tax, payroll tax, or excise tax. The effective tax rate of protectionism for a low-wage working mother is about 2 percent of income, four times the average 0.5 percent rate for a high-income family. [19]

This situation is hardly limited to the United States. In Japan, agricultural protectionism costs consumers an estimated $60 billion per year in higher food prices. [20] In India, because of the tariff structure on women's creased economic engagement push the country in the right direction, or is it a case where we must hold firm until basic rights are reached?

In my tenure at the White House, these issues were most contentious during the debate on whether China should be allowed to enter the WTO. Large segments of the American public held strong arguments both for and against China's entry into the WTO. Those against ranged from labor unions to conservative Christians upset that the United States would trade with a nation that engaged in repressive tactics against dissidents, union organizers, and ethnic minorities, and was accused of using slave labor and promoting forced abortions. Many opposition groups wanted the United States to demand major commitments and verification from the Chinese government that these practices had stopped as condition for open markets. It was hard for the Clinton administration to dismiss such requests, for Clinton himself had drawn a strong link between human rights and trade with China during his 1992 presidential campaign and the first year of his presidency.

Yet President Clinton questioned whether an unbendable linkage—while best in an ideal world—was actually the best course, both from a human rights and foreign policy point of view. The question we faced was whether spurring economic engagement with China would be more likely to foster economic and political freedom than taking a hard stand and not achieving open markets at all.

During the fight over China's WTO membership, National Security Advisor Sandy Berger and I carried to all of our meetings a series of *Washington Post* articles by John Pomfret reporting that Chinese reformers supported engagement and trade while the opposition was formed from the military, the entrenched state-owned manufacturing sector, and Communist officials clinging desperately to state control over how people work and live. As Pomfret explained, the hardliners feared "that joining the WTO will mark another step toward privatizing China's economy and importing even more Western ideas about management and civil society—a headache for those whose job it is to ensure the longevity of the one-party Communist state."[28]

There was also reason to believe that as China began working more closely with the United States and moved into the realm of rules-based international trade, economic reforms would become inevitable and would undercut Communist control and promote economic freedoms. The transparency requirements we fought for sought to codify this imperative of greater fairness and openness. Demanding that prices, quotas, tariffs,

cotton skirts, wealthy women face a 30 percent mark-up on high fashions from Milan while poor families in rural districts often face a 100 percent mark-up in the price of cheap cotton prints from Bangladesh or Nepal.[21]

Pointing out the regressive impact of protectionism does not mean that we should turn our backs on potentially hard-hit communities or never accept any cost or inconvenience to prevent socially unacceptable conditions. Yet it does reinforce a major premise of this book: that empowering people and communities directly is often preferable to trying to impede economic change. Even for those who believe the government should take action to protect jobs or health care benefits threatened by lower-cost global competition, progressives would normally want to fund such efforts through our progressive income tax, not a regressive tax that hits a single working mom four times harder than it does the CEO of the company she works for.

After the Seattle WTO meetings in the fall of 1999, President Clinton asked me for ways he could lay out a robust vision of his "Globalization with a Human Face" theme. I presented him with a brief outline for a tell-it-like-it-is speech that critiqued all sides—including ours—for not doing enough to reach a consensus on globalization. We agreed that one area where we deserved some criticism was our sole focus on exports when defending new trade openings.

In January 2000, during his speech to the World Economic Forum in Davos, Switzerland, President Clinton went off-text to emphasize this point:

> We can also, I must say, do better in the developed countries if we are able to make a more forceful case for the value of imports. None of us do this enough, and I must say, I haven't done this enough . . . Every time we talk about trade agreements in our countries, we always talk about how many jobs will be created at home because we're opening markets abroad.
>
> I wish everyone here would look at yourselves and ask yourselves if you are wearing anything made in a country other than the country where you live.
>
> There are benefits to imports. We don't just do a favor to developing countries, or to our trading partners in developed countries, when we import products and services from them. We benefit from those products. Imports stretch family budgets; they promote the well-being of working families, by making their dollars go further; they bring new technology and ideas; they, by opening markets, dampen inflation and spur innovation.[22]

Unfortunately, most progressives are hesitant to offer a balanced view of the costs and benefits of American imports. The modern consumer movement, for example, tends to oppose almost all trade opening with virtually no mention of the regressive costs to lower-income consumers. In the 1940s, 1950s, and even 1960s, consumer groups often fought vehemently for more open trade because it would benefit all consumers, especially the poorest Americans.[23] Few would dispute the lasting influence of Ralph Nader's Public Citizen organization on establishing food and auto safety regulations, but in the area of trade, it and most other consumer groups—with the notable exception of the Consumers Union—have ignored the regressive impact of protectionism on consumers.

OPEN MARKETS AND BROADER POLITICAL AND ECONOMIC REFORM

Progressives must not lose sight of their long-standing commitment to market opening as means of promoting open societies and greater understanding between nations.

In 1936, President Franklin D. Roosevelt took the stage at the Peace Conference in Buenos Aires and addressed the issues of trade: "Every nation of the world has felt the evil effects of recent efforts to erect trade barriers of every known kind. Every individual citizen has suffered from them. It is no accident that the nations that have carried this process farthest are those, which proclaim most loudly that they require war as an instrument of their policy. It is no accident that attempts to be self-sufficient have led to falling standards for their people and to ever-increasing loss of the democratic ideals."[24]

After witnessing the negative effects that economic isolation had on Germany and Japan in the 1930s, FDR and Harry S. Truman considered trade liberalization as well as the establishment of the GATT (General Agreement on Tariffs and Trade), World Bank, and IMF crucial to making the world more secure. Trade was an important foreign policy tool throughout the Cold War. In 1962, President John F. Kennedy justified his Trade Expansion Act by explaining, "a vital expanding economy in the free world is a strong counter to the threat of the world Communist movement."[25] Most recently, President Clinton saw the membership of Russia and China in the major

global economic institutions as vital to building a post–Cold Wa structure for greater global cooperation.

The recent tension in French-U.S. relations illustrates how im economic engagement is. In response to the French government's tion to the invasion of Iraq, some members of the U.S. government and public directed their disdain not just at the French governm inexcusably, at French people and businesses. Following the lead congressional dining room some U.S. restaurants changed "Frenc to "freedom fries" on their menus. But in a number of instances, o economic ties helped cooler heads to prevail. In March 2003, th Carolina legislature abandoned a measure to boycott all French p after realizing that the French company Michelin employed six th South Carolinians and had invested more than $2 billion in the stat

With a constant threat of terrorism there can be little questi closer economic ties between the United States and the Middle E Africa are in our interest. The Middle East is least touched by trade ization and among the most ridden by conflict. Its share of world t dropped by 75 percent since 1980, increasing its isolation and the of young people who are frustrated and unemployed.[27] At a U.S Forum in Doha, Qatar, in January 2004, I witnessed enormous su and misunderstanding of the United States, but one of the few everyone agreed on was that further economic cooperation cou move things in the right direction.

LEVERAGE OR EXCHANGE?

In considering the foreign policy benefits of trade, the toughest c over whether to use trade as leverage—by conditioning access to o kets on whether countries abide by our values and make progress nomic, democratic, and human rights reform. Many argue th conditionality is a counterproductive imposition on sovereignty a freedom will come through exposure to our values, not by denyin to our markets until a nation gets in line. Our values will always inf trade decisions, so policy makers must be willing to ask practical qu considering the history, culture, and sensitivities of a potential partner, is leverage likely to encourage reform or backfire? Will and rules be publicly listed was a precondition for establishing a functioning and efficient business environment by curtailing Communist officials' power to set prices, stymie competition, or demand bribes from investors and businessmen.

Further, the Clinton administration felt that given China's immense population and pivotal role in ensuring world security, gambling on increased economic cooperation was the only choice. Thirty years from now, was there a greater chance of China being a peaceful, constructive partner with the United States if we denied them open trade or if we brought them into the international community and made our two nations more economically interdependent? The latter meant potentially weakening a tool for coercing greater respect for human rights. Yet our hope was that over time, openness would create new avenues for encouraging progress on human and labor rights, and that we could create other means—including a U.S.-China Economic Commission—to pressure China to reform.

In fact, the precarious U.S.-China WTO negotiating process shows how even the prospect of greater economic engagement can stave off dangerous foreign policy divisions and prevent escalating misunderstandings and miscalculations. In April of 1999, USTR Charlene Barshefsky reported that Chinese Premier Zhu Rongji, in the days leading up to his state visit to Washington, suddenly made significant concessions that she felt signaled a desire to return from the United States with a deal. While our foreign policy and economic teams were unanimously for a deal, this news set off a tactical debate. Barshefsky and the foreign policy team, including Secretary of State Madeleine Albright, Secretary of Defense William Cohen, and Berger, feared that failure to finalize a deal in April, even if it was not perfect, would undercut Zhu—whom we all regarded as an unusually enlightened and pro-market reformer. The rest of the economic team including Bob Rubin, Larry Summers, Bill Daley, Lael Brainard, and me, as well as Legislative Director Larry Stein and chief of staff John Podesta feared that if we did not gain key concessions on antidumping and import surges, we would lose key Democratic votes and risk being unable to get congressional passage of the agreement. In a meeting in the Yellow Oval on the third floor of the White House, Sandy Berger and I watched as President Clinton candidly explained to Zhu that the administration was unanimously for an agreement but that there was a divide among his advisors on the best timing for finalizing an agreement. After explaining the pros and cons, President Clinton told Zhu he was willing to wrap up negotiations in the coming weeks or instruct Barshefsky to work through the night with him to try to close the deal. Zhu said he was happy to finish the negotiations later. The two teams decided to document the progress in a public memo. But then everything seemed to go wrong. False leaks suggested that a deal had been reached, and the White House had scuttled it for crass political reasons. The Chinese negotiating team did not realize that the concessions they had put into the document would find their way onto the Internet before they had a chance to explain their decisions to the government officials in China. Suddenly, Zhu was on the defensive and attacked President Clinton, who was furious about the false press reports that he had balked at the deal for political reasons.

In retrospect, we made a major mistake in not announcing exactly when and where negotiations would continue so that everyone would understand that both sides were completely committed to reaching an agreement that year. Many in the American press and business community incorrectly believed that some in the administration were opposed to a deal; they didn't realize that our only internal differences involved the timing and strategy for successful completion. Nevertheless, the misunderstanding was seen as a temporary setback that would be put to rest when a deal was struck within two months, probably by June or July. But on May 8, I woke up to a CNN report that the U.S. military had accidentally bombed the Chinese embassy in Belgrade the night before. To President Clinton's great dismay, the overwhelming majority of Chinese thought it was on purpose.[29] Now we had a problem.

It took months of careful communications—including secret calls from Clinton to Chinese President Jiang Zemin—before Jiang gave us a nuanced yes to Clinton's request to restart negotiations. Despite the bitter sentiment generated by the Belgrade bombing, we convinced the Chinese that our shared economic interests deserved continued attention at the negotiating table.

As we prepared to restart the process, Barshefsky decided to have me co-negotiate the final agreement with her in Beijing to show the Chinese that the administration was united. Barshefsky, a highly skilled and relentless negotiator, also felt that since I would be viewed as a personal representative of the president, I could be used to make the political case for the strong antisurge, antidumping, and auto provisions we would need to secure congressional passage. After several days of roller-coaster talks, negotiations seemed to break down when the Chinese walked out during a break and never returned—though they were to later claim that it was Barshefsky and I who had abandoned the negotiations by leaving too early.

That evening Barshefsky and I called Clinton from the basement of the U.S. embassy in Beijing to say that negotiations had failed and that we were coming home unless there was significant movement by the morning. Only an hour before we left for the airport, Madame Wu Yi, one of China's highest-ranking officials, approached me in the hall during a break to inform us that Premier Zhu, accompanied by the Chinese foreign minister, had made what we were told was his first trip to the Ministry of Trade. He pulled Barshefsky and me into a side room for one last try to save a deal. When the Premier and I first exchanged differing views over which side had "walked out" the previous day, an impatient Barshefsky scribbled on my notepad that this was starting to resemble a *Seinfeld* episode. Once we made clear that it was just a misunderstanding, Zhu gave us not only his final demands but also the concessions we needed to take home a deal we thought would pass. Barshefsky—who had pursued this agreement for years—and I commandeered a women's bathroom just long enough to place a call to President Clinton—who had to be pulled out of the shower—and tell him that the deal was closed. *New York Times* reporter David Sanger later described the incident to colleagues as an act of bathroom-to-bathroom diplomacy.

A misunderstanding over something as simple as who walked out of a negotiating session was a stark warning that without engagement our misunderstandings could spread to the national security realm. There was no question that only Jiang Zemin's desire to reach an agreement kept him from exploiting anti-American sentiment after the accidental Belgrade bombing.

During the first months of the Bush administration, the United States and China found themselves embroiled in another diplomatic standoff. In April 2001 a U.S. spy plane collided with a Chinese fighter jet and was forced to make an emergency landing on the island of Hainan, leaving twenty-four crew members and an $80 million high-tech surveillance plane in the hands of the Chinese. The Bush administration refused to admit responsibility for the collision. President Bush demanded that China return the crew and not examine the plane. Tensions escalated as China insisted on an apology before releasing the crew. A few days later Bush and Jiang backed off their hard lines and agreed on a letter of regret that allowed both sides to save face. The crew was released eleven days after the collision, and the plane was eventually returned.[30]

Two major foreign policy misunderstandings; two problems solved. I cannot help but think that had we walked away from the 1999 trade talks, the resolutions to both crises could have been far worse. As the *Los Angeles*

Times explained in 2001, "With China's membership in the WTO still pending, Chinese officials have also avoided threats of economic retaliation and gone out of their way not to inflame nationalistic sentiments that could threaten U.S. interests in China."[31]

As with NAFTA, both supporters and critics of increasing economic engagement with China can find a multitude of evidence for their positions. Critics point out that a half decade after the WTO agreement, China remains disturbingly repressive. The State Department's 2005 human rights report details a litany of human rights deficiencies, including the harassment and detainment of dissidents, wanton disregard for due process, widespread religious suppression, and the continued use of "reeducation-through-labor" camps.[32] There has been an uptick in the intimidation of journalists and scholars—twelve writers were arrested in the spring of 2005 and a lawyer who tried to defend them was disbarred[33]—and an AFL-CIO brief filed with the U.S. trade representative last year documented unconscionable labor abuses, including the violent suppression of peaceful strikes, the excessive use of forced overtime, and the coercion of workers who depend on their employers for housing and legal status.[34] Even the Bush administration's USTR has found that piracy of intellectual property remains epidemic and that many of the important trade rules and regulations issued in accordance with their WTO obligations still exist on paper only. Finally, despite making a minor adjustment to their currency on July 21, 2005, a wide array of economists still believe that China is unfairly distorting trade flows by manipulating its currency.[35]

Yet while these substantial problems cannot be taken lightly, supporters marshal their own evidence that more trade with China has been, on the whole, a positive force. In 2004, China accepted a WTO-dispute-resolution case ruling in favor of the United States over China's unfair support for domestic semiconductor producers. China has also dramatically increased its involvement with regional organizations such as ASEAN (Association of South East Asian Nations) and APEC (Asia-Pacific Economic Cooperation) and played an ongoing role in U.S.-led multilateral talks over North Korea's nuclear arsenal.[36] In addition to listing troubling labor rights abuses the most recent State Department Report on Human Rights in China notes that recent economic reforms have sparked "rising urban living standards," "a burgeoning middle class," and "greater independence for entrepreneurs," while increasing employment options and reining in state involvement in workers' daily lives.[37] While many correctly argue that the gains of China's record growth have not been evenly distributed—and that the rural poor cotton skirts, wealthy women face a 30 percent mark-up on high fashions from Milan while poor families in rural districts often face a 100 percent mark-up in the price of cheap cotton prints from Bangladesh or Nepal.[21]

Pointing out the regressive impact of protectionism does not mean that we should turn our backs on potentially hard-hit communities or never accept any cost or inconvenience to prevent socially unacceptable conditions. Yet it does reinforce a major premise of this book: that empowering people and communities directly is often preferable to trying to impede economic change. Even for those who believe the government should take action to protect jobs or health care benefits threatened by lower-cost global competition, progressives would normally want to fund such efforts through our progressive income tax, not a regressive tax that hits a single working mom four times harder than it does the CEO of the company she works for.

After the Seattle WTO meetings in the fall of 1999, President Clinton asked me for ways he could lay out a robust vision of his "Globalization with a Human Face" theme. I presented him with a brief outline for a tell-it-like-it-is speech that critiqued all sides—including ours—for not doing enough to reach a consensus on globalization. We agreed that one area where we deserved some criticism was our sole focus on exports when defending new trade openings.

In January 2000, during his speech to the World Economic Forum in Davos, Switzerland, President Clinton went off-text to emphasize this point:

> We can also, I must say, do better in the developed countries if we are able to make a more forceful case for the value of imports. None of us do this enough, and I must say, I haven't done this enough . . . Every time we talk about trade agreements in our countries, we always talk about how many jobs will be created at home because we're opening markets abroad.
>
> I wish everyone here would look at yourselves and ask yourselves if you are wearing anything made in a country other than the country where you live.
>
> There are benefits to imports. We don't just do a favor to developing countries, or to our trading partners in developed countries, when we import products and services from them. We benefit from those products. Imports stretch family budgets; they promote the well-being of working families, by making their dollars go further; they bring new technology and ideas; they, by opening markets, dampen inflation and spur innovation.[22]

Unfortunately, most progressives are hesitant to offer a balanced view of the costs and benefits of American imports. The modern consumer movement, for example, tends to oppose almost all trade opening with virtually no mention of the regressive costs to lower-income consumers. In the 1940s, 1950s, and even 1960s, consumer groups often fought vehemently for more open trade because it would benefit all consumers, especially the poorest Americans.[23] Few would dispute the lasting influence of Ralph Nader's Public Citizen organization on establishing food and auto safety regulations, but in the area of trade, it and most other consumer groups—with the notable exception of the Consumers Union—have ignored the regressive impact of protectionism on consumers.

OPEN MARKETS AND BROADER POLITICAL AND ECONOMIC REFORM

Progressives must not lose sight of their long-standing commitment to market opening as means of promoting open societies and greater understanding between nations.

In 1936, President Franklin D. Roosevelt took the stage at the Peace Conference in Buenos Aires and addressed the issues of trade: "Every nation of the world has felt the evil effects of recent efforts to erect trade barriers of every known kind. Every individual citizen has suffered from them. It is no accident that the nations that have carried this process farthest are those, which proclaim most loudly that they require war as an instrument of their policy. It is no accident that attempts to be self-sufficient have led to falling standards for their people and to ever-increasing loss of the democratic ideals."[24]

After witnessing the negative effects that economic isolation had on Germany and Japan in the 1930s, FDR and Harry S. Truman considered trade liberalization as well as the establishment of the GATT (General Agreement on Tariffs and Trade), World Bank, and IMF crucial to making the world more secure. Trade was an important foreign policy tool throughout the Cold War. In 1962, President John F. Kennedy justified his Trade Expansion Act by explaining, "a vital expanding economy in the free world is a strong counter to the threat of the world Communist movement."[25] Most recently, President Clinton saw the membership of Russia and China in the major global economic institutions as vital to building a post–Cold War infra-structure for greater global cooperation.

The recent tension in French-U.S. relations illustrates how important economic engagement is. In response to the French government's opposition to the invasion of Iraq, some members of the U.S. government, media, and public directed their disdain not just at the French government, but inexcusably, at French people and businesses. Following the lead of the congressional dining room some U.S. restaurants changed "French fries" to "freedom fries" on their menus. But in a number of instances, our close economic ties helped cooler heads to prevail. In March 2003, the South Carolina legislature abandoned a measure to boycott all French products after realizing that the French company Michelin employed six thousand South Carolinians and had invested more than $2 billion in the state.[26]

With a constant threat of terrorism there can be little question that closer economic ties between the United States and the Middle East and Africa are in our interest. The Middle East is least touched by trade liberalization and among the most ridden by conflict. Its share of world trade has dropped by 75 percent since 1980, increasing its isolation and the number of young people who are frustrated and unemployed.[27] At a U.S.-Islam Forum in Doha, Qatar, in January 2004, I witnessed enormous suspicion and misunderstanding of the United States, but one of the few things everyone agreed on was that further economic cooperation could only move things in the right direction.

LEVERAGE OR EXCHANGE?

In considering the foreign policy benefits of trade, the toughest debate is over whether to use trade as leverage—by conditioning access to our markets on whether countries abide by our values and make progress on economic, democratic, and human rights reform. Many argue that such conditionality is a counterproductive imposition on sovereignty and that freedom will come through exposure to our values, not by denying access to our markets until a nation gets in line. Our values will always inform our trade decisions, so policy makers must be willing to ask practical questions: considering the history, culture, and sensitivities of a potential trading partner, is leverage likely to encourage reform or backfire? Will the increased economic engagement push the country in the right direction, or is it a case where we must hold firm until basic rights are reached?

In my tenure at the White House, these issues were most contentious during the debate on whether China should be allowed to enter the WTO. Large segments of the American public held strong arguments both for and against China's entry into the WTO. Those against ranged from labor unions to conservative Christians upset that the United States would trade with a nation that engaged in repressive tactics against dissidents, union organizers, and ethnic minorities, and was accused of using slave labor and promoting forced abortions. Many opposition groups wanted the United States to demand major commitments and verification from the Chinese government that these practices had stopped as condition for open markets. It was hard for the Clinton administration to dismiss such requests, for Clinton himself had drawn a strong link between human rights and trade with China during his 1992 presidential campaign and the first year of his presidency.

Yet President Clinton questioned whether an unbendable linkage—while best in an ideal world—was actually the best course, both from a human rights and foreign policy point of view. The question we faced was whether spurring economic engagement with China would be more likely to foster economic and political freedom than taking a hard stand and not achieving open markets at all.

During the fight over China's WTO membership, National Security Advisor Sandy Berger and I carried to all of our meetings a series of *Washington Post* articles by John Pomfret reporting that Chinese reformers supported engagement and trade while the opposition was formed from the military, the entrenched state-owned manufacturing sector, and Communist officials clinging desperately to state control over how people work and live. As Pomfret explained, the hardliners feared "that joining the WTO will mark another step toward privatizing China's economy and importing even more Western ideas about management and civil society—a headache for those whose job it is to ensure the longevity of the one-party Communist state."[28]

There was also reason to believe that as China began working more closely with the United States and moved into the realm of rules-based international trade, economic reforms would become inevitable and would undercut Communist control and promote economic freedoms. The transparency requirements we fought for sought to codify this imperative of greater fairness and openness. Demanding that prices, quotas, tariffs, and rules be publicly listed was a precondition for establishing a functioning and efficient business environment by curtailing Communist officials' power to set prices, stymie competition, or demand bribes from investors and businessmen.

Further, the Clinton administration felt that given China's immense population and pivotal role in ensuring world security, gambling on increased economic cooperation was the only choice. Thirty years from now, was there a greater chance of China being a peaceful, constructive partner with the United States if we denied them open trade or if we brought them into the international community and made our two nations more economically interdependent? The latter meant potentially weakening a tool for coercing greater respect for human rights. Yet our hope was that over time, openness would create new avenues for encouraging progress on human and labor rights, and that we could create other means—including a U.S.-China Economic Commission—to pressure China to reform.

In fact, the precarious U.S.-China WTO negotiating process shows how even the prospect of greater economic engagement can stave off dangerous foreign policy divisions and prevent escalating misunderstandings and miscalculations. In April of 1999, USTR Charlene Barshefsky reported that Chinese Premier Zhu Rongji, in the days leading up to his state visit to Washington, suddenly made significant concessions that she felt signaled a desire to return from the United States with a deal. While our foreign policy and economic teams were unanimously for a deal, this news set off a tactical debate. Barshefsky and the foreign policy team, including Secretary of State Madeleine Albright, Secretary of Defense William Cohen, and Berger, feared that failure to finalize a deal in April, even if it was not perfect, would undercut Zhu—whom we all regarded as an unusually enlightened and pro-market reformer. The rest of the economic team including Bob Rubin, Larry Summers, Bill Daley, Lael Brainard, and me, as well as Legislative Director Larry Stein and chief of staff John Podesta feared that if we did not gain key concessions on antidumping and import surges, we would lose key Democratic votes and risk being unable to get congressional passage of the agreement. In a meeting in the Yellow Oval on the third floor of the White House, Sandy Berger and I watched as President Clinton candidly explained to Zhu that the administration was unanimously for an agreement but that there was a divide among his advisors on the best timing for finalizing an agreement. After explaining the pros and cons, President Clinton told Zhu he was willing to wrap up negotiations in the coming weeks or instruct Barshefsky to work through the night with him to try to close the deal. Zhu said he was happy to finish the negotiations later. The two teams decided to document the progress in a public memo. But then everything seemed to go wrong. False leaks suggested that a deal had been reached, and the White House had scuttled it for crass political reasons. The Chinese negotiating team did not realize that the concessions they had put into the document would find their way onto the Internet before they had a chance to explain their decisions to the government officials in China. Suddenly, Zhu was on the defensive and attacked President Clinton, who was furious about the false press reports that he had balked at the deal for political reasons.

In retrospect, we made a major mistake in not announcing exactly when and where negotiations would continue so that everyone would understand that both sides were completely committed to reaching an agreement that year. Many in the American press and business community incorrectly believed that some in the administration were opposed to a deal; they didn't realize that our only internal differences involved the timing and strategy for successful completion. Nevertheless, the misunderstanding was seen as a temporary setback that would be put to rest when a deal was struck within two months, probably by June or July. But on May 8, I woke up to a CNN report that the U.S. military had accidentally bombed the Chinese embassy in Belgrade the night before. To President Clinton's great dismay, the overwhelming majority of Chinese thought it was on purpose.[29] Now we had a problem.

It took months of careful communications—including secret calls from Clinton to Chinese President Jiang Zemin—before Jiang gave us a nuanced yes to Clinton's request to restart negotiations. Despite the bitter sentiment generated by the Belgrade bombing, we convinced the Chinese that our shared economic interests deserved continued attention at the negotiating table.

As we prepared to restart the process, Barshefsky decided to have me co-negotiate the final agreement with her in Beijing to show the Chinese that the administration was united. Barshefsky, a highly skilled and relentless negotiator, also felt that since I would be viewed as a personal representative of the president, I could be used to make the political case for the strong antisurge, antidumping, and auto provisions we would need to secure congressional passage. After several days of roller-coaster talks, negotiations seemed to break down when the Chinese walked out during a break and never returned—though they were to later claim that it was Barshefsky and I who had abandoned the negotiations by leaving too early.

That evening Barshefsky and I called Clinton from the basement of the U.S. embassy in Beijing to say that negotiations had failed and that we were coming home unless there was significant movement by the morning. Only an hour before we left for the airport, Madame Wu Yi, one of China's highest-ranking officials, approached me in the hall during a break to inform us that Premier Zhu, accompanied by the Chinese foreign minister, had made what we were told was his first trip to the Ministry of Trade. He pulled Barshefsky and me into a side room for one last try to save a deal. When the Premier and I first exchanged differing views over which side had "walked out" the previous day, an impatient Barshefsky scribbled on my notepad that this was starting to resemble a *Seinfeld* episode. Once we made clear that it was just a misunderstanding, Zhu gave us not only his final demands but also the concessions we needed to take home a deal we thought would pass. Barshefsky—who had pursued this agreement for years—and I commandeered a women's bathroom just long enough to place a call to President Clinton—who had to be pulled out of the shower—and tell him that the deal was closed. *New York Times* reporter David Sanger later described the incident to colleagues as an act of bathroom-to-bathroom diplomacy.

A misunderstanding over something as simple as who walked out of a negotiating session was a stark warning that without engagement our misunderstandings could spread to the national security realm. There was no question that only Jiang Zemin's desire to reach an agreement kept him from exploiting anti-American sentiment after the accidental Belgrade bombing.

During the first months of the Bush administration, the United States and China found themselves embroiled in another diplomatic standoff. In April 2001 a U.S. spy plane collided with a Chinese fighter jet and was forced to make an emergency landing on the island of Hainan, leaving twenty-four crew members and an $80 million high-tech surveillance plane in the hands of the Chinese. The Bush administration refused to admit responsibility for the collision. President Bush demanded that China return the crew and not examine the plane. Tensions escalated as China insisted on an apology before releasing the crew. A few days later Bush and Jiang backed off their hard lines and agreed on a letter of regret that allowed both sides to save face. The crew was released eleven days after the collision, and the plane was eventually returned.[30]

Two major foreign policy misunderstandings; two problems solved. I cannot help but think that had we walked away from the 1999 trade talks, the resolutions to both crises could have been far worse. As the *Los Angeles*

Times explained in 2001, "With China's membership in the WTO still pending, Chinese officials have also avoided threats of economic retaliation and gone out of their way not to inflame nationalistic sentiments that could threaten U.S. interests in China."[31]

As with NAFTA, both supporters and critics of increasing economic engagement with China can find a multitude of evidence for their positions. Critics point out that a half decade after the WTO agreement, China remains disturbingly repressive. The State Department's 2005 human rights report details a litany of human rights deficiencies, including the harassment and detainment of dissidents, wanton disregard for due process, widespread religious suppression, and the continued use of "reeducation-through-labor" camps.[32] There has been an uptick in the intimidation of journalists and scholars—twelve writers were arrested in the spring of 2005 and a lawyer who tried to defend them was disbarred[33]—and an AFL-CIO brief filed with the U.S. trade representative last year documented unconscionable labor abuses, including the violent suppression of peaceful strikes, the excessive use of forced overtime, and the coercion of workers who depend on their employers for housing and legal status.[34] Even the Bush administration's USTR has found that piracy of intellectual property remains epidemic and that many of the important trade rules and regulations issued in accordance with their WTO obligations still exist on paper only. Finally, despite making a minor adjustment to their currency on July 21, 2005, a wide array of economists still believe that China is unfairly distorting trade flows by manipulating its currency.[35]

Yet while these substantial problems cannot be taken lightly, supporters marshal their own evidence that more trade with China has been, on the whole, a positive force. In 2004, China accepted a WTO-dispute-resolution case ruling in favor of the United States over China's unfair support for domestic semiconductor producers. China has also dramatically increased its involvement with regional organizations such as ASEAN (Association of South East Asian Nations) and APEC (Asia-Pacific Economic Cooperation) and played an ongoing role in U.S.-led multilateral talks over North Korea's nuclear arsenal.[36] In addition to listing troubling labor rights abuses the most recent State Department Report on Human Rights in China notes that recent economic reforms have sparked "rising urban living standards," "a burgeoning middle class," and "greater independence for entrepreneurs," while increasing employment options and reining in state involvement in workers' daily lives.[37] While many correctly argue that the gains of China's record growth have not been evenly distributed—and that the rural poor are falling further behind—many regional governments have recently an-nounced minimum wage increases, and the government has recently announced plans to improve free universal education and tackle the gross inequities between rural and urban populations.[38]

As with most difficult trade issues, the spread of information technology in China demonstrates how not everything is black and white. Supporters of the WTO agreement like me often pointed to the fact that the agreement would offer tens of millions of Chinese access to the Internet and other information technologies, increasing the flow of information and helping reduce the government's stranglehold on free speech and political dissent. Has this been realized? The rapid spread of information technology—with new Internet users coming online at a rate of 800,000 per week[39]—has not stopped the Chinese government from controlling the commanding heights of the Internet, tracking usage, and cracking down on online dissidents. Yet, there are signs that the rise in information technology combined with the need for workers to fuel China's export-led growth are giving some of the most mistreated, unskilled Chinese workers the ability to use cell phones, text messaging, and the Internet to compare their wages and working conditions with other worksites and make greater demands on their employers. Factory workers like twenty-two-year-old Sheng Kehua are gaining the confidence to walk away from abusive employers. "I checked the Internet and learned that the pay level in Shanghai is better than here," she explained after she and more than twenty female co-workers recently left their rural factory.[40] Indeed, some employers are already responding to the increasingly empowered workforce; Li Xinghiao, the owner of the Chigo Air Conditioning plant, has raised salaries and started giving bonuses to workers who stay for three years or more, built new housing, a swimming pool, and a reading room, and gives his workers access to the company's pomegranate orchards. Another plant plans to invest $2 million in air conditioning in order to attract workers.[41]

Beyond the choice statistics from both sides, however, the hard reality is that the final verdict on what impact greater market opening will have on our long-term security and economic relations with China—as well as China's progress on political and human rights—will not be delivered within a few years. For those of us who bet that increasing economic relations with China will over time promote a more peaceful world, it is imperative we not just sit by passively and watch events in China unfold, but act affirmatively to push in that direction.

U.S. companies who argued alongside us that China's WTO entry would bring American values and labor standards to China must help ensure that increased economic engagement moves China in that direction by adopting voluntary codes of conduct, monitoring factories, and standing up to worker suppression. Those who supported the WTO agreement even in light of China's human rights record must now encourage human rights monitors both in the U.S. government and in NGOs to shine light on China's shortcomings and push for strong, sustained progress on human rights. The U.S. government should actively seek partnerships to improve labor standards and safety—especially for products that are being exported or supplied to American companies.

And while we must not allow either side to incite a trade war through exaggerated claims, when we are hard-nosed in pressing China to live up to the letter of its WTO agreements we not only help ensure a more level playing field for U.S. workers but show Chinese citizens an example of their government being bound by the rule of law. The Bush administration, by waiting until the beginning of the presidential election in 2004 to take a harder line with China on currency manipulation, intellectual property disputes, and other aspects of our trade agreement, may have given the Chinese the impression that these positions were driven by political necessity, not a serious commitment to enforcement. Economist C. Fred Bergsten referred to the U.S.'s tepid response to China's "blatant market distortions" as "disturbing."[42] And, regardless of how the USTR would have ruled on the AFL-CIO's petition into China's labor rights violations in 2004, the fact that the Bush administration did not even formally launch an investigation in light of China's serious repression of Chinese union leaders reinforced the damaging impression that the U.S. government is not committed to pushing China to live up to core labor standards.

OPEN TRADE AND GLOBAL POVERTY REDUCTION

In June 1999, at the annual G8 Summit in Cologne, Germany, I went jogging amidst the crowds of protesters. What struck me most was the position of some debt relief protesters that the United States and Europe should reduce unfair trade barriers to poor African countries. Later that year in Seattle, while most protesters seemed either concerned about American jobs or opposed to the entire notion of a global trading system, I again saw groups pushing for more open access to rich markets as a vehicle to reduce global poverty.

When I returned to the White House I told a number of colleagues and journalists that many of the protesters seemed to disagree more with each other than with our administration's position. Those calling for more market access for poor countries were saying that the world's poor were helped by more open trade, not less. They simply wanted to see a global trading system where the rules weren't rigged against the poor. Implicit in their argument was the need for a coordinated global body to set the rules for the international trading system—essentially the WTO.

In 1998, President Clinton met with the presidents of five Central American countries after Hurricane Mitch devastated the region. An estimated 2.7 million people were left homeless,[43] and the total estimated damage was $6 billion—12 percent of the region's total economic output and 42 percent of its exports.[44] Seventy percent of the infrastructure in Honduras had been destroyed, Nicaragua estimated its losses at $1 billion and had lost forty bridges. Yet to my amazement, the five presidents stressed that the most important thing the United States could do for them was to extend and expand the Caribbean Basin Trade Initiative; they wanted the opportunity to compete in U.S. markets.[45]

When Ugandan President Yoweri Museveni toured the United States in late 2003 his main message was, "Africans will live or die depending on whether the world's wealthiest economies—and some of the more advanced developing ones, too—lower import barriers and scale back the agricultural subsidies and overproduction which depress world prices and close rich country markets to Africa's rural majority."[46]

As NEC director, I cannot recall a meeting with one progressive American organization that wanted me to promote more open markets for global poverty reduction, with the exception of the "African Summit"—a grassroots coalition that supported the passage of the African Growth and Opportunity Act in 2000. As Norwegian Minister of Development and leading antipoverty activist Hilde Johnson has put it, "there is a disturbing silence from the NGOs in the United States about the importance of trade to reducing poverty in the world's poorest nations."[47]

The discussion became more balanced in the last few years. In April 2002, Oxfam International, the U.K.-based antipoverty organization with a large and influential grassroots network in the States, put out a report entitled "Rigged Rules and Double Standards: Trade, Globalization, and the

Fight Against Poverty." In the preface to the report, the Nobel Laureate economist Amartya Sen stated in simple, elegant terms, "Global integration rather than insulated isolation has been the basis of economic progress in the world."[48] The report continued:

> *International trade is often viewed as a threat to the poor. The opportunities that it creates for human development and poverty reduction are often overlooked. These opportunities are not an automatic corollary of increased trade; but, when good policies enable poor people and poor countries to participate in markets on equitable terms, trade can act as a powerful force for change.*[49]

The most visible progressive organization in the United States that specifically argues for greater trade as a tool for poverty reduction is DATA, which stands for *D*ebt *A*IDS *T*rade *A*frica.[50] DATA was founded in 2002 by Bono, the lead singer for the legendary rock band U2. In 1999 Bobby Shriver introduced Bono to Treasury Secretary Larry Summers and me, and we formed a strategic partnership that played an important role in the larger grassroots effort that culminated in the Debt Relief Act in 2000. When I asked Bono whether he really understood how pathbreaking—and controversial—it was to make the "T" in DATA stand for trade, he said people "are not used to a progressive organization in the U.S. lobbying for more open trade with Africa. But that's why it's so important. We have to let the citizens of the most powerful and generous nation on earth know just how important trade can be to the lives of hundreds of millions of the world's poor."

We have made some significant progress opening our markets to African products. In 2000, President Clinton signed the historic African Growth and Opportunity Act (AGOA), which provided qualifying African countries with significantly more open access to export to the U.S. market. The AGOA tariff reductions, along with the reductions from the Generalized System of Preferences, mean that 75 percent of imports from AGOA countries now enter the U.S. duty-free. AGOA is only a first step. But for the first time it has given African countries the chance to strengthen their domestic industries and attract new investment, create jobs, and raise living standards.[51]

African countries can make enormous strides by increasing their own domestic commitment to opening markets. By removing import taxes in the early 1990s on agricultural imports such as fertilizer, Uganda helped its coffee farmers increase income and diversify despite falling coffee prices. As one Ugandan farmer explained, "Life is always hard . . . but no farmer here will tell you that life is harder today than it was before. We were given an opportunity to get something out of our coffee—and we took it." [52]

Yet for many developing countries, the rich world continues to play a pernicious game of "do as I say and not as I do" on the opening of markets. Agricultural subsidies in the richer nations cost poor countries $50 billion a year, which happens to be about the same amount that the OECD countries offer poor countries in foreign aid. [53] In Japan, the average cow is paid $7 a day by the government, while the average African citizen makes little more than $1. [54] These policies undercut developing countries in precisely those industries where they have the best chance of competing and building a base from which to expand. More than 60 percent of Africans are currently employed in agriculture, and the International Food Policy Research Institute has found that every $1 increase in agricultural exports translates into $1.42 in increased income in African countries. [55] This is why perhaps the most important aspiration of the Doha Round of WTO trade negotiations is to reach an agreement on reducing agricultural subsidies that is both palatable to developed countries and increases opportunities for millions of farmers in the world's poorest countries.

4

A New Cost-Sharing Compact

During a visit to New York City in 2000, President Clinton showed me a newspaper editorial that called the U.S. textile lobby's opposition to the African Growth and Opportunity Act (AGOA) a classic example of special interests disregarding the needs of poor African workers. Clinton didn't think the criticism was entirely fair. He thought that a lot of the American textile workers might support economic development in Africa as much as anyone else in the country but might not believe that it was right to ask them to pay for the entire cost with their jobs.

This is an important point. It may be economically advantageous and morally compelling to promote open markets with impoverished African nations, but we too often fail to ask how the costs of such decisions are distributed at home. Lowering trade barriers that lower consumer prices and reduce global poverty is a win for most of us. Yet while these benefits may be broadly spread, the costs are often concentrated. If a community needs to take an individual's property for a larger community benefit, the Fifth Amendment requires "just compensation." While it would be foolhardy in the dynamism economy to provide everyone who suffers dislocation a legal right to compensation through courts, fair cost sharing should inform the laws we pass and the economic arrangements we promote.

In his first-year tort class at Yale Law School, Professor Guido Calabresi—now Federal Judge Calabresi—used to ask his students to imagine an Evil God offering a new invention that would dramatically improve the quality of life, allow people to travel to work, see family and friends, and even get emergency health care—all easily, quickly, and for a price most families could afford. There was just one catch: the nation had to sacrifice twenty thousand people to violent deaths each year. His point was that the proliferation of the automobile makes exactly this trade-off, though few of us see it that way. In trade policy, we are essentially asking whether a system that will let one choose from all products around the world, find the best prices, save thousands of dollars a year for families, reduce poverty in Africa, and spur productivity in our nation—is worth sacrificing the sudden dislocation of scores of U.S. workers a year.

Traditionally, one could draw a fundamental distinction between the challenge posed by auto accidents and open markets. In the case of car accidents, individuals sit behind philosopher John Rawls's famous "veil of ignorance," where no matter how smart or wealthy they are—or how good their driving skills—they have no way of knowing whether they will fall victim to a deadly accident. As Rawls suggests, being behind the veil makes all parties more willing to support collective efforts to insure against risk.[1] Not only do individual drivers carry car insurance, but our state laws give us the comfort of knowing that everyone else on the road is obligated to do so as well.

One reason why our social safety net to cushion dislocation and help workers make the transition into new jobs—policies often referred to as "adjustment assistance"—has traditionally been so fragmented, complex, and inadequate is that severe displacement was traditionally a fate limited to a clearly identifiable "them": workers in steel towns, textile communities, and other globally threatened manufacturing industries. Heartbreaking newspaper accounts of entire communities spiraling downward, due to major job loss, told stories that transpired far from the lives of most middle-class Americans.

As the pace of globalization and technological change threaten an increasing number of job categories with dislocation or downward wage pressure, Rawls's veil has enveloped more and more Americans. Anxiety about global competition suddenly feels more like the automobile example, as fewer Americans can confidently separate themselves from those at risk. In Greater Santa Clara County, California—otherwise known as Silicon Valley—more than three years after the dot-com bubble burst, more jobs were still being lost than were being created. In a region only recently hailed as the hub of American innovation and job creation, *Investors' Business Daily* reports that between 2001 and 2008 the largest number of job openings in the county will be in food preparation and services, followed closely by low-wage retail and cashier positions. In an online support group for laid-off tech workers, one resident lamented, "The feeling grows that one isn't contributing anything to the world, and that one's possible contribution is no longer even valued."[2]

As more white-collar and technical workers feel vulnerable to global economic competition, we may see the rise of a broader political constituency to support a bolder, universal system for cost sharing, cushioning dislocation, and helping Americans move into new jobs.

As *New York Times* columnist Thomas Friedman outlined in his brilliant book *The Lexus and the Olive Tree,* the Clinton administration sought to push a series of what he calls "strategic mobilization" efforts—increasing health and pensions assistance for dislocated workers, supporting Community Development Banks, and most notably the Workforce Investment Act of 1998, which strengthened and consolidated worker training programs, created one-stop career centers, and substantially increased funding for youth training programs. Friedman described the 1998 Workforce Investment Act as "one of the best, but most underreported, bipartisan achievements of the Clinton era."[3]

Yet having been closely involved in developing each of those ideas, I know all too well how far we still have to go to offer a comprehensive, universal adjustment system that provides real assurances to all families that dislocation will not lead to devastating falls in economic dignity.

FOUR STEPS TOWARD A NEW COST-SHARING COMPACT

To achieve shared growth in the dynamism economy we must move toward a four-part strategy for cost sharing and adjustment assistance.[4] First, we need a new "preemptive" policy framework that offers broader choices to help workers and communities *before* their only options are to seek protection or accept economic devastation. Second, we need a wider net of social insurance that moves beyond the outdated view that training and unemployment assistance alone are enough to help workers and their families after a job dislocation. Third, we need an adjustment assistance system that is both simpler and more universal. This means not only providing one-stop settings to access all forms of assistance but ending the practice of tying such assistance to how and when a worker loses his job. Fourth, we need a compact between policy makers, employers, and workers to take all reasonable steps to ensure that employers eliminate jobs only when no other economic alternative exists.

The importance of the fourth pillar—a compact on making job loss a last resort—is vital for building workers' trust and support for adjustment assistance. Policy wonks like me know that when most workers hear about a new retraining proposal, their reaction is anything but enthusiastic. After all, retraining and adjustment assistance are the "pre-nups" of public policy: they are options for what to do after a series of unfortunate events you would like to prevent in the first place. A politician promoting dislocation policies often feels like he or she is telling a newlywed husband how much counseling he could receive if his wife leaves him for his best friend. Most happily married people would rather focus on maintaining their marriage, and most workers happy with their paychecks would prefer to focus on keeping their jobs.

Shortly after General Wesley Clark decided to run for president, he talked very optimistically during a conference call about strengthening our national worker retraining system. After the call, I told his economic advisor, Jason Furman, that it was refreshing to hear an outsider like Clark excited about retraining policies because most elected officials grow tired of hearing constituents deride such proposals as "burial insurance." On the next conference call with Clark that I participated in, he asked me to guess the reaction he got when he talked to workers about his adjustment ideas. Before I could answer, he replied, "burial insurance. They called it burial insurance."

Whether or not adjustment assistance is a winner on the campaign trail, the realities of the dynamism economy will sooner or later create a national imperative to mitigate dislocation.

1. Preemption: Moving Beyond the Choice of Protection or Devastation

Imagine you are a senator or union leader watching a new trade opening or global trend threaten the economic base of one of your constituents. Perhaps you know in your heart that they do not qualify for protection under our trade laws, or that protection would lead to retaliation or higher prices that would hurt other workers in other industries. Do you sit back and let your workers or constituents lose their jobs without a fight? Of course not. You would fight for any protectionist measures you could, because you know that is your only option. Although those who call for protectionism often lack a viable long-term vision for how to protect jobs in the years to come, policy makers who say no to trade barriers within our current framework usually have nothing to offer the workers and their families who suffer in the present except for weak, fragmented, and uncertain adjustment assistance. If we want to advance a pro-growth progressive economic strategy, we need to develop preemptive policies that offer workers and communities an option other than asking for protection or waiting for economic devastation.

Can We Employ Reverse Industrial Policy?

Industrial policy—the notion that the government can identify and target investment to the industries most likely to drive our economy in the future—has been appropriately discredited. Without true market failure that prevents private investors from capturing the benefits of important economic and social investment, there is no reason to believe that a set of government employees will be more likely to predict the innovations and industries of the future better than the collective judgment of millions of investors, entrepreneurs, and private sector experts. Indeed, one of the hallmarks of our economy is its unpredictability. About a quarter of all American employees work in jobs today that didn't exist thirty-five years ago. In the 1967 movie *The Graduate,* the young hero Benjamin, played by Dustin Hoffman, received cocktail party counsel to pursue a career in plastics, an industry which Princeton economist Alan Krueger noted "has lost 40 percent of its jobs since the movie was released, contracting even more than the rest of manufacturing."[5] Beyond the challenge of picking winners among existing industries, it's instructive to remember that a little over fifteen years ago all but a few of the wisest or luckiest investors in the country paid little attention to the emerging technology behind the Internet.

We do far better at predicting losers in our economy—those industries and job categories most vulnerable to new technologies or global trends. We know that communities that are highly dependent on a single industry or company confronting significant global price competition are often at risk. At times, watching threatened communities struggle year after year as their core industry declines is like watching a slow-motion car crash. We know that when the major employers that a community relies on close their doors, the community's economic base can spiral down, leading to lower tax revenues, fewer services, and diminishing new job opportunities for laid-off workers. Given this reality, why are the overwhelming number of government policies available to communities and workers only *after* they suffer pain and dislocation?

Narrow industrial policies are usually misguided because they too often hurt market efficiency by either aiding noncompetitive industries or blocking economic change. By contrast, reverse industrial policies could ease and speed the transition for communities and workers so they can devote their capital and resources to more competitive and productive uses.

Designing the precise mechanisms to trigger assistance to communities and workers before the layoffs and factory closings will not be easy, precise, or foolproof. But there is every reason to believe that we could establish rational procedures to decide which communities and workers should be given preemptive options. Petitions to the International Trade Commission for trade relief, for example, or to the Justice Department or Federal Trade Commission for antitrust relief require judgment and discretion, but most believe we are better off with such processes than without them. African governments have used a series of statistical indicators to develop an early-warning system to predict and preempt famine. The Commerce Department could develop a model that includes statistical guideposts as well as an independent commission—including forecasters, retired CEOs, community development experts—to recommend who should be eligible for preemptive assistance based on petitions from workers and communities.

Preempting the Spiral: Community Adjustment Compacts

A preemptive adjustment policy must give communities highly dependent on a globally contested industry wider options for economic diversification and revitalization *before* a downward economic cycle hits.

The Clinton administration used tax incentives for investment and job creation to encourage poor communities to devise strategies for their economic future—this included Empowerment Zones, Community Development Banks, and New Market Tax Credits. Because these pro-growth progressive policies relied on incentives to bring new capital and business financing into low-income neighborhoods, they drew support not only from Representative Charles Rangel and Reverend Jesse Jackson but at times from Jack Kemp and Republican Speaker of the House Dennis Hastert.

Building on the model of the Empowerment Zones, we could create

"Community Adjustment Compacts" offering new business investment incentives and wage credits to communities committed to economic revitalization strategies when faced with the danger of suffering due to massive layoffs or relocation of their major factories or service providers. While it would be an innovation simply to extend such zones to communities hard hit by the dynamism economy, to be most effective we must go another step: such incentives should be available not only after the dislocation, but when it first appears on the horizon.

Both of our secretaries of Housing and Urban Development in the Clinton administration, Henry Cisneros and Andrew Cuomo, often noted that the application process for Empowerment Zones alone provided significant benefit—before a single dollar went out—simply because it forged an unprecedented effort to convene a community's diverse stakeholders to map out an economic strategy for the future. Vice President Al Gore named this the "Dumbo magic feather" approach, because just as Dumbo always had the power to fly without the magic feather, such stakeholders already had this capacity to come together but just needed the lure of a package of tax incentives, wage credits, and grants to make it happen. With a preemptive approach, a Community Adjustment Compacts process might inspire different stakeholders from a vulnerable community—business leaders, union representatives, elected officials, local investors, and nonprofits—to start work on an economic diversification strategy two years before economic devastation hit, instead of two months after.

Beyond diversification, a preemptive approach can instigate the modernization that will help companies adapt to global competition. The Strategic Early Warning Network (SEWN) in Western Pennsylvania involves community, business, and union leaders to identify and assist at-risk manufacturers; SEWN estimates that preemptive efforts have saved more than 8,000 jobs.[6] The Wisconsin Manufacturers Development Consortium has used the threat of global competition to get its member companies to join forces so they can lower the costs and the risks of upgrading technology needed to meet overseas competition,[7] rather than wait until layoffs hit.

Rapid Preresponse Units

When communities implement preemptive diversification strategies, we should make it easier for them to access the full range of potential government economic development programs without forcing a hapless economic development administrator from the community in question to travel to Washington and trek from agency to agency.[8] During the Clinton administration our Office of Economic Adjustment at the Defense Department would bring a one-stop shop to communities hurt by a major base closing. Those responsible for pursuing an economic revitalization strategy could access in one place—or through one coordinator—the range of agencies and adjustment programs that together could help speed an economic revitalization. At the recommendation of White House economic aide Dorothy Robyn, we pushed Congress—unsuccessfully—to draw up a similar one-stop approach for communities impacted by major job loss and economic decline. This coordinated response was never passed. Going forward, however, we should not only look to make such units a reality, but also gear them toward "preresponse" to assist those communities designated at risk before the downsides of the dynamism economy take hold.

Preemptive Retraining Assistance

The common thread in virtually every job retraining initiative is that eligibility is triggered only after you have lost your job. No wonder workers call it burial insurance. Certainly, an unemployed worker has more time to seek the serious, community college training for specific technical or health care jobs that has proved most effective. But why should we not give some workers the choice of getting trained for a new job or career when they first see the writing on the wall?

Imagine if unions, workers, or communities could apply for preemptive training. While some workers in a threatened industry would still choose to ride things out and hope for the best, others, if given the option, might choose to engage in some job search, training, or community college education in advance as an insurance policy.

Moving toward preemptive reemployment policies would mean taking into account the time and financial constraints workers have in their current jobs. Telling working parents that they need to find the time and resources to take courses after work could push already pressed parents over the edge. One important preemptive move would be to expand effective community college training courses over the Internet, allowing more currently employed workers to start training for new job categories from home or their job without having to travel or find additional child care. We need to modernize financial aid regulations to benefit workers who choose online training. While we must protect adult learners from fly-by-night courses, our current laws prohibit colleges from offering student aid if they offer 50 percent or more of their courses online. We also need to join with community colleges and to upgrade online courses for adult education beyond textbooks and lecture notes posted on the Web, particularly in high-growth technical areas. Indeed, as job search services have proven to be one of the most effective reemployment policies—with saved unemployment insurance often exceeding the costs of the services—engaging workers in the question "of what comes next" may itself prove beneficial.

One approach is "entrepreneurial training"—learning how to start your own business. In evaluations of two small programs in Washington and Massachusetts, participation roughly doubled the likelihood that participants started a business in the eighteen months after the training, increased earnings in the period by $7,500, and increased the total time spent employed.[9] A promising program in North Carolina targets entrepreneurial training both at those who have lost jobs and at workers who want to start a business "on the side." The New Opportunities for Workers program operates within twenty-eight community colleges in North Carolina and is integrated with a micro-enterprise program for graduates of the training.[10] For those with an entrepreneurial spirit, getting this training before losing a job could give them a jump-start. Some might want to start a new business with a spouse while still on their job, and if laid off, expand the business.

Flexible Education Accounts

To encourage learning and education before and after dislocation we need to target financial help to the time and circumstances workers need it most. One innovation would be to offer all Americans a $15,000 Flexible Education Account. The account would allow workers to receive a 50 percent credit on all qualified education or training up to $15,000 per decade, and would replace the Clinton administration's Lifetime Learning credit, which offers workers a 20 percent credit on up to $10,000 a year in lifelong learning and retraining expenses. The Lifetime Learning credit was a positive step forward, but it is both more and less than the typical worker needs. It is more in the sense that no worker is going to need an education tax credit each and every year. It is too little in that a 20 percent tax credit may not be enough of an incentive when a worker seeks intensive training or education. The Flexible Education Account, on the other hand, recognizes that what many workers most need is a great deal of new education or training in a concentrated period—a few times in any given decade or more in many cases. The Flexible Education Account gives workers a larger credit when they need training, but gives them the power to concentrate or spread out their resources over a decade as they see fit—not only if they are laid off, but also when they sense their jobs are at risk or simply want a promotion or job change. It would give workers the flexibility to access considerably more financial support for a year or two of intensive training when they actually need it. Although a 50 percent credit is far more generous than what is offered today, requiring workers to pay half ensures that they use the resources wisely and pressure education institutions not to use the accounts to inflate tuition prices.

In addition to such Flexible Education Accounts, proposals like the one Senator Kerry put forward in the 2004 campaign to make college more affordable with a 60 percent credit on the first $4,000 of tuition for four years would yield a double benefit in the dynamism economy. First, it would provide generous credit for students who planned to complete their degrees. Second, it would provide crucial comfort to parents at risk of losing their jobs who are worried about paying for their children's college education. Harvard professor Lawrence Katz has stressed that this is one of the most significant fears of workers who lose jobs.

Preemptive Compensation?

Finally, we should consider if there are circumstances when it would make sense to offer compensation for an economic policy with wide benefits but very concentrated costs on certain workers and communities. Such policies are fraught with potential problems. First, they need to be designed to help innocent workers and their families, as opposed to bailing out investors for the downsides of risks they willingly assumed. Even if they are properly designed, they can still undermine the principle of making assistance universal, lead to generous windfalls for some, and create resentment among those who are left out or who never had a chance in the first place.

Why should we even consider the idea? There are times when the overall economic benefit of a market opening is clear and overwhelming and when the only impediment is the political opposition of a small minority who could suffer dearly from the action and have the power to block it. Imagine an ambitious free trade deal with Africa that would dramatically reduce poverty and significantly reduce the cost of basic goods for poor and working-class families in the United States, but would erode land values for a small set of American farmers. Should we forgo the important benefits of the agreement or should we engage farmers in discussions to find some agreeable mix of compensation and incentives to help transition farmland to more productive uses like production of new bio-fuels that would be critical to America's energy future?[11] If new climate-change legislation benefited us all but threatened coal producers and miners, could some mix of incentives and compensation help us move forward? These hypothetical examples raise serious red flags but also serious questions about how our society shares the costs of change. In the dynamism economy, they will need to be addressed.

2. Broadening Adjustment Insurance: Health, Mortgage, and Wage Insurance

Health Care Between Jobs

Because most Americans receive health care coverage through their employers, the fear of job loss is compounded by the fear of losing one's health insurance. A single illness could result in financial ruin. Harvard Professor Elizabeth Warren reports that more than half of all personal bankruptcies are due not to irresponsible spending, but to excessive, uninsured medical costs.[12] Since 1985, workers have been able to purchase their former employer's health care coverage through a program called COBRA at the average price, plus a 2 percent markup (to help offset the costs of disproportionate numbers of sicker former workers taking this option).[13] Yet, for many, it is like being offered a chance to buy running shoes after they've broken their legs. For a family of four at the median income of $45,000 a year, the annual cost of this coverage averages $10,000—22 percent of their income,[14] which has just fallen to near zero. No wonder only 7 percent of unemployed workers enroll in COBRA.[15] In Clinton's 1997 budget, his top health care aide, Chris Jennings, and I successfully inserted a provision to provide health insurance between jobs. With unemployment falling to historic lows, the proposal never caught on, and we dropped it during budget negotiations in 1997, and instead focused on expanding the children's health insurance initiative that the First Lady had been advocating within the White House. Five years later, with President Bush pushing for normal trade promotion authority amidst significant job loss, Senate Democrats, led by Max Baucus, Jeff Bingaman, and Tom Daschle, made a minor breakthrough. The Trade Adjustment Assistance Reform Act of 2002 included a tax credit for 65 percent of health insurance premiums for the unemployed—but only for those 148,000 workers a year designated as having lost their jobs due to trade.[16]

In the absence of universal health care legislation, our goal should be a system of temporary health coverage that workers can count on if they are laid off—regardless of whether the layoffs occur during a downturn or are the result of trade, outsourcing, or changing consumer tastes. Such a program need not be expensive; expanding the health care tax credit that is currently part of TAA to the 575,000 workers who are displaced each year would cost only $1.4 billion a year.[17] To ensure that such policies do not have the unintended effect of discouraging people from looking for work—if a potential employer does not provide health care—provisions should be made to allow workers to maintain their old coverage for a reasonable time.

Mortgage Insurance

William Schweke, vice president of the Corporation for Economic Development, has examined assistance to dislocated workers and found that all too frequently job loss leads workers to miss mortgage payments and eventually to foreclosure on their most important assets—their homes. Foreclosure ruins credit, uproots families, and destroys a middle-class family's best chance of accumulating wealth. Mortgage foreclosures can also accelerate the downward spiral of whole communities.[18] A number of states and even some private companies are now offering foreclosure protection and mortgage insurance plans to protect families from losing everything when the breadwinner loses his or her job.

Bolder adjustment assistance should at least provide incentives for states to experiment and expand mortgage insurance or protections for dislocated workers. Pennsylvania established a foreclosure protection fund in 1983 during a period of economic downturn and massive job loss. The program intervenes in foreclosure proceedings faced by families because of job loss, and it can supplement mortgage payments for up to two years. In twenty-two years, the Pennsylvania program has assisted more than thirty-two thousand homeowners. In 2003, North Carolina started a small pilot program on a similar model, after foreclosures in the state nearly tripled in five years.[19] We should consider public policies to expand the mortgage insurance option that helps workers preempt the foreclosure process. Both Genworth Financial in West Virginia and MassHousing in Massachusetts now include mortgage insurance against job loss, disability, or death, which provides up to $2,000 a month for six months on all their high-risk mortgages. Although both these programs are less generous than the Pennsylvania and North Carolina programs in the duration of assistance, they offer the significant benefit of not requiring separate approval for help.[20] Yet, without thoughtful incentives or public policies, private insurers are inclined to restrict their packages to those with the best credit.

What About the Fifty-Two-Year-Old Worker?: The Case for Wage Insurance

For workers of any age, losing a job due to a more open, dynamic, and insecure economy is demoralizing and debilitating. Yet with a bold set of adjustment and transition policies, many younger workers should have time to regroup, take advantage of generous retraining assistance, learn new skills, and work on a new career.

The toughest cases are older workers, usually in manufacturing industries, whose wages far exceed the market value of their education or transferable skills and whose potential for wage loss is huge.

Carlton Anderson had worked in manufacturing since he was sixteen, including thirty years at the Philadelphia Glass Bending Company. After he was laid off in 2001 at the age of fifty-eight, he was lucky enough to find a job with a Philadelphia distributor, but his take-home pay dropped by a third.[21] Sandra Larson, a St. Paul, Minnesota, native, had worked at Toro Inc. for nineteen years as an inventory manager before she was laid off in 2001. She considers herself lucky—she found a new job later that year. Yet at $10 an hour, the new job pays only 40 percent of the $24 an hour she was making at Toro. "I made good money there and I'm never going to see that again."[22] If we are serious about a new compact on cost sharing, we must find ways to provide a modicum of economic dignity for people like Ms. Larson and Mr. Anderson.

One well-designed option is for the government to provide wage insurance for older workers moving into new but lower-paying jobs. A 50 percent wage insurance plan means an older worker would get 50 percent of the difference between his new and his old wages. In Ms. Larson's case, if she was making $24 an hour and is now making $10, the gap is $14. Under wage insurance she would get an extra $7—50 percent of the gap—bringing her total hourly wage to $17. That's still 25 percent less than her previous job, but it could be enough to prevent a devastating fall in her standard of living.

Wage insurance is a model for pro-growth progressive policies, because it empowers workers directly and encourages work. Wage insurance that replaced 100 percent of a worker's lost wages or was given to a dislocated worker prior to finding a new job could provide an incentive against looking for new work. But as long as wage insurance covers between 50 and 75 percent of past wages and is triggered only when a worker finds a new job, the policy ensures that workers always have a strong incentive to find both new work and the highest wage possible. A worker who previously made $20 an hour and is reemployed at $10 an hour would end up with a $15 an hour wage; if he is reemployed at $15 an hour he would end up with $17.50.

Economists Robert Litan and Lori Kletzer have spearheaded the call for wage insurance,[23] and Congress created a small pilot program in 2002, but only for the relatively few workers who qualify for trade adjustment assistance. For eligible workers, the program replaces 50 percent of an eligible worker's wages for up to two years, if the worker held her old job for at least three years and she finds a new, full-time job within twenty-six weeks of losing her old one. But the program is not only limited to workers over fifty who can prove that they lost their jobs due to trade; at least 5 percent of all workers at the old firm also have to be older than fifty and the Labor Department has to determine whether the industry is in decline and the worker is unlikely to find another job in that industry.[24]

A bolder adjustment policy for the dynamism economy will require a major expansion of wage insurance: a comprehensive program should offer benefits to all workers over fifty—and possibly somewhat younger—regardless of how they lost their job or whether their company petitions for relief, and should allow eligibility for those who can only find part-time work based on their hourly wage.[25]

A major question is whether privately offered wage insurance options will grow in the dynamism economy, and whether incentives should be offered to employers, unions, or private providers to develop private sector options. For the broader workforce, including younger workers, it is worth exploring other options, including providing incentives for employers and unions to offer such insurance. Offering future wage insurance would strengthen the trust between employers and employees and prove a valuable fringe benefit when worker anxiety about job loss is running high. The McKinsey Global Institute found that for less than 5 percent of the savings companies realized from outsourcing, they could offer a generous wage and health care insurance package to all their full-time employees.[26]

3. A Universal One-Stop System for Adjustment and Reemployment

The fundamental failing of our system of adjustment assistance for dislocated workers is that it is neither bold enough, universal enough, nor simple enough to aid Americans suffering the trauma of losing a cherished job. Nearly everyone knows where to go to get a new driver's license, rent a movie, or see a football game, but virtually no one knows where to go or what their options are when they lose their job. If few policy makers or members of Congress even understand the differences in programs and eligibility, how can we expect a shell-shocked working parent—often with only a high school education—who has just lost her paycheck to expertly navigate a host of government programs?

The United States needs a new, comprehensive adjustment policy with one-stop shopping for those who have lost their jobs. Workers who lose jobs should be able to call a single number, 1–800–NEW–JOBS, where they can get information on all things related to dislocation, including unemployment insurance, job search assistance, training programs, and options for health, mortgage, and wage insurance. In an era where more and more superstores provide one-stop shopping, government must provide the same one-stop, one-call service. The key challenge will be to do so as efficiently as these private sector superstores and provide what Vice President Gore described as a truly customer-oriented government.

Adjustment assistance will never fit the realities of the dynamism economy if it is turned off and on depending on how you lost your job or what phase in the business cycle your job loss occurred. Currently, the most generous assistance—Trade Adjustment Assistance and some health care subsidy—is available to a mere 148,000 workers who can establish their jobs were lost due to trade.[27] Another 365,000 workers are helped by the less generous retraining and job search assistance under the Dislocated Worker program, though these workers get no health benefits.[28] Even eligible workers often find there are not enough slots in either program.[29] By comparison, over 30 million Americans lost jobs in 2003 alone, and the most recent data shows that in July of 2005 there were 1.4 million Americans who had been unemployed for twenty-seven weeks or longer.[30]

Extended unemployment benefits today are tied to the depth of recession or economic weakness in the national economy, even though we know that in the dynamism economy, permanent job loss, and even the loss of whole job categories can have a harsh impact on specific communities even when the larger national economy is not in recession.

In 1994, under the leadership of Labor Secretary Robert Reich, a team of White House and Labor Department officials including Paul Dimond, Barry White, Larry Katz, Doug Ross, and I worked on a broad reemployment and training proposal for President Clinton. Reich was adamant that it give workers income support for in-depth training, and we also allowed for significant personal choice by giving workers individual training grants. While this ambitious proposal died with the Republican sweep of Congress in 1994, the Clinton administration did make some progress in the area of worker training through the bipartisan 1998 Workforce Investment Act. This reform consolidated the delivery of job training programs and created statewide One-Stop Career Centers where any worker, regardless of why he lost his job (or even if he still had a job), could receive core services including job search assistance and basic career counseling. The act also gave workers more flexibility through new Individual Training Accounts, which could be spent on job counseling and career services. In 1994, giving training grants directly to workers was controversial among those who feared that there was not enough accessible information to prevent workers from being taken advantage of by weak or even shady training programs. Yet today, in the world where 147 million people have used eBay,[31] we can be far more confident that workers will be able to navigate an online clearing house of information about eligible programs and provide feedback to create a robust, competitive, and transparent marketplace for training and reemployment programs.

Moving to a unified reemployment system would require major systemic reform to America's social safety net, which will not be achieved overnight. Rob Atkinson at the Progressive Policy Institute has argued that we first need to modernize the state-run unemployment insurance.[32] But we need to go further by integrating unemployment insurance and training programs so that they provide workers with a clear path back to employment. What we now call Trade Adjustment Assistance should be made available to all dislocated workers, regardless of how they lost their jobs.[33] Most dislocated workers want to find new jobs as quickly as possible. Research has shown that what most people really need is basic help in assessing their skills, polishing up their credentials, and focusing their job search—inexpensive services that yield high returns. Indeed, studies show that the return on these programs in lower unemployment payments and increased taxes is about two dollars for every one dollar invested.[34] And of course, we need a continued effort to reform training efforts based on what we know works best. The available studies show that on-the-job training programs create some of the highest returns on wages,[35] while training programs that combine job search with specific vocational training show significant employment and income gains.[36] Longer-term training in community colleges has proven to increase earnings not just for eighteen-year-olds but also for older workers who are in the labor market.[37] Results are especially strong for training in technical and scientific fields, such as health care, that have shown wage gains of 10 percent to 15 percent per year of training.[38]

4. A Compact for Fighting for American Jobs

To answer the argument that these new ambitious adjustment strategies are simply high-class "burial insurance," we must combine these efforts with a commitment to take all reasonable action on behalf of workers' jobs before they are lost and take the bold steps needed to make our nation a magnet for job creation and investment within the global marketplace.

A Competitive Environment for Job Creation

One positive outgrowth of the outsourcing debate may be an increased focus on the policies that maintain a competitive environment for quality job creation: research, fiscal, technology, regulatory, and education policies to improve innovation and build a highly skilled workforce. The United States must always compete for the cutting-edge industries likely to drive higher-wage job creation in the United States. Continually advancing to the cutting edge ensures that as technology and automation increase the ease of outsourcing, we are developing new products and services that create new job opportunities at home.

Still we can do far more to compete even for the jobs that are not on the cutting edge or require advanced technology degrees. When people hear that American jobs are being replaced by foreign workers at 10 percent of the wage costs, they may feel there is no hope of competing for any job that is not highly skilled or requires a physical presence in the United States. Some fear that our economy will see a hollowing-out of middle-class jobs. Yet, to the degree that wages become a smaller portion of the cost of overall production, even automation can increase the ability of the United States to compete for those jobs based on factors we can control: health care costs, modernized technology infrastructure, tax policy, and the skills of our workers. When America loses a job because a poorer nation can provide that service dramatically cheaper, there may be nothing we can do. But why should we ever lose even a single American job because there is better broadband in Bangalore than in Buffalo?

The labor cost of producing a typical Dell computer is about $10, only 2 percent of its total cost. Dell has kept its three major production facilities in the United States and is planning to open its next factory stateside because quality and proximity are more valuable than the savings from lower labor costs abroad.[39] Sidney Harman, president of Harman International Systems, a manufacturer of high-end audio equipment, explains: "A handful of years ago, 15 percent of our total cost was represented by direct labor. Today, it is less than 5 percent, and it is headed lower. I ask you: Does it take a genius to conclude that if it gets down to 1 percent or less, it doesn't matter very much whether we build the product in Indonesia or Indiana?"[40] There is even some evidence that the gap in labor costs between the United States and places such as India may be shrinking. Hewitt Associates, a global HR consulting and outsourcing firm, reports that wages for information technology (IT) professionals in India have grown by 14 percent in the past year and other sources estimate that India may face a labor shortage of highly qualified IT professionals as early as 2007.[41] An economist for Citigroup in China estimates that payroll costs could rise by 40 percent to 50 percent over the next few years as companies compete to attract workers.[42]

These trends alone will not protect every existing U.S. job, but they do demonstrate that when U.S. jobs face lower-wage competition overseas, we have more choices than just giving up or resorting to protectionism. Wages in rural areas, for example, are often low enough to be price-competitive with many outsourcing options, yet America is falling behind in rural broadband infrastructure. While productivity gains in manufacturing are narrowing the importance of wage differentials, the exploding health care costs here add labor costs that foreign competitors simply do not have.

Even in labor-intensive services like call centers, the focus on wage differentials may obscure the importance of technology investment in our ability to keep those jobs here. Average wages in rural America are 30 percent to 40 percent lower than in our urban areas.[43] Moreover, Deloitte and Touche has found that 38 percent of companies find hidden costs when they outsource including quality control, training, and travel.[44] Yet many of these rural areas lack high-speed Internet access. The most recent survey by the International Telecommunication Union reports that after beginning the Internet revolution, the United States has fallen to sixteenth in the world for broadband access.[45] While 67 percent of suburban households have Internet access, only 52 percent of rural households are online—and only one in five rural Internet users has broadband access.[46] Intel founder and chairman Andy Grove points out that Korean and Japanese broadband networks are twenty to fifty times faster than in the United States, yet support from the public policy community for technological infrastructure remains, in his words, "Ho hum."[47] As long as we lag in deploying an advanced IT infrastructure, we risk having more and more jobs migrate to economies that have invested in the twenty-first-century equivalent of roads, trains, and ports.

Where states, cities, and entrepreneurs have taken the lead, these investments are starting to show results. Minnesota and West Virginia have invested in tech corridors,[48] Georgia has partnered with BellSouth to bring broadband to one hundred rural towns since 2000;[49] and Philadelphia is making the whole city a wireless Internet "hot spot."[50] Entrepreneur Kathy White of Jonesboro, Arkansas, has started Rural Sourcing, which is cost competitive with Indian firms, especially when you factor in communication costs, travel expenses, and inconvenience. The company is building on state investments and by 2008, it plans to open fifty IT centers in rural America employing twenty-five hundred people.[51]

Another serious threat to creating our competitive environment for job creation is the cost of health care. American companies have seen health care premiums rise 59 percent over the past four years, while our competitors in Europe and Japan are supported by universal health care.[52] A survey by the National Federation of Independent Businesses (NFIB), a small-business advocacy group, found that health care costs were a "critical" issue for 66 percent of its member companies.[53] General Motors spends more per car on health care than it does on steel—adding $1,500 to every car it makes. As GM Chairman Richard Wagoner points out, our foreign competitors operate in environments where health care costs are broadly shared. Our inaction on health care "places our children and our grandchildren at risk and threatens the health and global competitiveness of our nation's economy."[54] Standard and Poor's specifically mentioned health care costs in their decision to downgrade the bond ratings of GM and Ford to junk levels.

One idea Senator Kerry proposed in the 2004 campaign was to create a federal reinsurance pool to ease the costs of catastrophic health cases for employers. Such a system would reduce catastrophic care costs for employers if they committed to use the type of preventive health and wellness programs and chronic care coordination that have been shown to decrease the use of unnecessary institutional care and make insurance more affordable and predictable for all purchasers. Several Republican CEOs who opposed Kerry privately told campaign policy director Sarah Bianchi and me that they supported Kerry's basic strategy to reduce employers' catastrophic health costs because it was critical to their competitiveness.

We should also increase efficiency and reduce costs by expanding the use of health information technology. Senators Hillary Clinton and Bill Frist have recently introduced legislation to accelerate the transition to computerized record keeping by establishing national standards for sharing electronic health information and providing grants to help local health systems develop the infrastructure they would need to join an eventual nationwide network. They estimate the efficiency improvements from moving to such a system could reduce costs by up to $200 billion a year—about ten percent of what we currently spend on health care annually.[55]

Pro-Jobs Incentives in Our Tax Code

An area of tax reform that needs to be considered is the impact of the tax code on job creation. This inquiry must follow several paths. While both parties have suggested programs that provide incentives to long-term capital investment and risk taking, the United States has to determine to what degree its tax incentives for productive investment and lower taxes for capital gains and dividends are creating distortions that encourage employers to choose technology over new jobs. New technology will always make it more efficient to replace workers with machines or computers but such decisions should be based on relative economic costs, not a tax code that tips the balance against workers.

Americans need to know that their tax dollars are not being used to encourage moving jobs and production overseas. In the 2004 campaign, Senator Kerry suggested removing tax incentives for U.S. firms to shift jobs abroad and creating new incentives to create jobs here at home. The tax code is not the only factor influencing complex strategic decisions made by companies and changing tax incentives alone would not stop outsourcing driven by legitimate economic rationale. But the tax code should not use taxpayer dollars to give American companies an incentive to move jobs to overseas tax havens and then export their product from there.[56] The Congressional Research Service concludes, "Economic theory is relatively clear on the basic incentive impact of the system: it encourages U.S. firms to invest more capital than they otherwise would in overseas locations where local taxes are low. . . . Accordingly, deferral poses an incentive for U.S. firms to invest abroad in countries with low tax rates over investments in the United States." [57] Put another way: if you have two companies, each looking to expand either in Hamtramck, Michigan, or Hong Kong, our tax code puts the company who chooses to create jobs in the United States at a competitive disadvantage with the company who moves jobs overseas. While we don't want to discourage American companies from trying to penetrate new and promising markets or generating profits that could lead to more job creation in the United States, how can we build the public's trust that we are putting American workers first when our own tax code does the opposite?

Increasing the Pool of Entrepreneurs

Beyond preemptive support for communities threatened by global competition, progressives should be far more aggressive in supporting entrepreneurship and small business creation. The economic case is clear. Studies have shown that nations that are most successful in fostering entrepreneurship have consistently sustained growth and maintained low unemployment. [58] Small businesses remain the key driver of American job growth, creating about 75 percent of all new jobs. [59] Small business creation has been an avenue for economic advancement for women and minorities and the means for economic diversity within communities. And clearly, small firms are less likely to find it efficient to move jobs overseas.

Fostering small business development has long been a top public policy priority. Since 1958, the Small Business Investment Company (SBIC) program has provided venture capital that would not otherwise be available through banks or other private sources. Under the program, the government partners with privately operated investment companies, known as SBICs, that provide equity capital, long-term loans, and technical assistance to growing businesses. Early on, Apple, Intel, America Online, Staples, Federal Express, and Costco all received SBIC funding. [60] In addition to investment and technical assistance, progressive and conservative small business advocates should support lowering health care costs, simplifying tax compliance for small businesses, fostering entrepreneurial incubators, and increasing tax incentives for the self-employed.

We also need to increase the pool of entrepreneurs, and as Jesse Jackson has said, "make the dream of entrepreneurship a dream within the reach of all Americans in every neighborhood of this country."[61] Traditionally, the high risk associated with lending in low-income communities has scared away the venture capital that promising entrepreneurs need to get their dreams off the ground.[62] Moreover, as University of Michigan Law Professor Michael Barr argues, the lack of access to even basic personal banking services and low savings in these communities eliminates the most common source of start-up capital.[63] The Clinton administration made this a priority through several successful initiatives, including the New Markets Tax Credit, Empowerment Zones, a community development bank initiative, and reform of the Community Reinvestment Act.

The promising New Markets Venture Capital (NMVC) program needs to be expanded. It uses public funds to back venture financing for entrepreneurs in low-income communities. Adena Ventures, the first venture fund the NMVC program launched, provided financing to four new high-tech companies in the Appalachian region of Ohio, West Virginia, and Maryland in 2001 and 2002.[64] Unfortunately, in 2003, just as the first NMVC funds were getting off the ground, the Bush administration eliminated all funding. Another program that has met the same fate from the Bush administration is BusinessLINC, which seeks to finance local organizations that build mentoring relationships between larger businesses and small business owners and entrepreneurs in economically disadvantaged areas.

Still, many innovative small business mentoring programs have taken root at the local level. One, the Entrepreneurial League System being piloted in West Virginia, Kentucky, and Ohio, creates a tiered system to help individuals start businesses, develop their skills, and build connections with other participants.[65] First-time business owners form a rookie league, seasoned businessmen join the Major League, and others take assignments to A, AA, and AAA divisions—each receiving appropriate training and assistance from "coaches" and mentors in upper divisions. As the participants' businesses grow, they can move up in the ranks to get more advanced training and help those just joining.

Corporate Responsibility and Jobs: The Discretionary Principle

The debate over whether protecting jobs should be a core aspect of corporate responsibility is often misguided. When a company with ten thousand employees needs to lay off one thousand workers as part of a well-designed strategy to reduce costs and stay competitive, it not only can maximize shareholder interests, but also help save the other nine thousand jobs as well. Calls for corporate responsibility through no-layoff or no-outsourcing policies may seem naïve and counterproductive to those business leaders who fight for their market share and even existence every day. Yet it is also often the case that there is often more than one way to peel an apple.

We should expect our CEOs to follow an ethic of corporate responsibility, including what I would call the "discretionary principle," meaning that when CEOs choose among a range of options for achieving efficiency and competitiveness, they should exercise every reasonable option that minimizes job loss and community devastation. Exercising the discretionary principle is not about whether a company chooses its workers over its shareholders, or social responsibility over profit. It is about expecting business management faced with "gray" choices and discretion among economically viable options to strive for the path that minimizes harm to workers and their communities.

This "last resort" ethic is neither unprecedented nor economically naïve. After September 11, Southwest Airlines faced hard choices to cut costs and ride out the industry downturn. Company management used a variety of cost-saving techniques including executive pay cuts to bring costs down without laying off a single worker. As Southwest CFO Gary Kelly explained, "In thirty years we have not had a layoff. That would be the last thing we would do to save Southwest Airlines." [66] The decision was not just symbolic; it paid economic dividends. Southwest was the only U.S. airline to turn a profit in 2002.

A *BusinessWeek* article entitled "Where Layoffs Are a Last Resort" profiled a small group of companies that prioritize jobs as a matter of company policy. The group of companies includes public and private firms across a range of industries from FedEx to SC Johnson, and from Pella windows to AFLAC insurance. The executives insist that they are not making these decisions out of altruism. These plans foster higher productivity, risk taking and innovation, and invaluable loyalty. Keeping workers on board even in tough times can save costs, too, by lowering severance payments and rehiring costs, and sustaining institutional memory and trust, thus preparing the company to return to full capacity as soon as the economy recovers. [67]

Even in those cases where cutting jobs or outsourcing production abroad seems unavoidable, it may make sense to create some breathing room to ensure that a company considers all its options. For example, requiring companies to give ninety days' notice before outsourcing jobs could give workers in vulnerable industries a chance to discuss with management the options that would maintain the company's competitiveness and minimize harm to its workforce. This would not necessarily stop companies from outsourcing, but it could give employees and communities more confidence that if a firm decided to relocate abroad, it was truly the last viable option, not the result of an irrational herd mentality or, as one person who serves on several corporate boards told me, because "everyone else is doing it."

A management that is facing painful competitive solutions can promote this discretionary principle when it engages in constructive dialogue and information sharing with the union, which in turn helps build trust that all parties are committed to finding a solution with the least dislocation possible. During the 2004 presidential campaign, president of the United Steelworkers of America Leo Gerard told me and three other Kerry advisors, Roger Altman, Sarah Bianchi, and Marco Trbovich, about one such collaborative process with Goodyear because workers were brought to the table. In 2003 Goodyear was operating at a two-year loss of more than $1 billion and wanted to shut down a number of American plants. The union could see that the company's position was unsustainable and that compromise was necessary. After heated negotiations and strikes that spring, an agreement was reached. The USWA accepted a combination of pay and benefit cuts, and Goodyear agreed to retain thirteen of fourteen American production facilities. Neither party could prevent some job loss, but the parties developed mutual trust, and the USWA now has a seat on Goodyear's board of directors, the highest union representation in the company's history. As Gerard later said, the agreement made his union a "true partner in the future success of the company."[68]

Rule–Based Trade

Finally, all actors in our economy—from workers and consumers to CEOs—need to believe that our government will enforce the basic set of trade rules it has created to establish a fair playing field.

Our trade laws are structured to prohibit what is known as "dumping" —when foreign countries flood the market with below-cost goods produced through illegal and uncompetitive practices. They also provide an occasional and temporary escape clause (Section 201 relief) for industries to modernize or adjust from potentially devastating trade shocks not necessarily caused by illegal activity.

Some of our nation's most ardent free traders would argue—at least among themselves—that even protections against illegal dumping are politically attractive nuisances that impede efficiency and growth. Some contend, for example, that if Russia wants to give us huge amounts of steel cheaper than it costs them to make, we should view it as a gift and simply say "thank you." Yet our antidumping laws are predicated on a sound tradition of preventing unfair competition from destroying an asset that has, and can continue to have, long-term economic value and viability.

Consider how our antitrust laws guard against what is known as "predatory pricing." If an airline sees a discount upstart flying out of its hub in Dallas and decides to cut airfares to $10 a flight, it will drive the new company out of business before it has a chance to get off the ground. In the short term, predatory pricing looks like a "gift" to consumers—$10 flights would be quite a boon. Driving a viable asset out of business, however, could result in less fare competition in Dallas and undermine long-term growth.

When used correctly, the same economic rationale applies to the Section 201 escape clause provision. If a domestic industry has the capacity to remain competitive, but faces a surge of cheap imports due, for example, to an unforeseen currency collapse in a trading partner, it could strike such a hard blow that the industry would simply be forced out of business.

The challenge, of course, is judgment. At its worst, the Section 201 escape clause can reflect the last-ditch effort of failing business management to get the government to help them escape from their unwise choices. At its best, it reflects cases like that of Harley-Davidson, which on the brink of bankruptcy in 1984, received temporary relief in the form of 50 percent tariffs on finished motorcycle imports for five years. Harley-Davidson used the period wisely, increasing efficiency and strengthening its brand image, and by the end of the decade it was once again an industry leader.

While making these decisions is difficult, giving workers the confidence that they have been treated fairly through a rule-based process is vital to maintaining political support for open market policies.

5

Raising Global Boats

In the past year, I have read several articles about women in the Bangladeshi textile industry who feared that with the scheduled end of the global textile quota system in 2005, China would take away their U.S. market share, forcing hundreds of thousands of them out of work, into poverty and even prostitution.[1] These articles are striking precisely because the women's experiences do not fit neatly into a particular ideological camp on the relationship between trade, globalization, and poverty.

These textile workers force globalization critics to recognize that, however repulsive it may seem that these women work for twenty cents an hour on products for export to the United States, they desperately want these jobs and fear what will happen to them if the jobs go away. Weeks before the January 1, 2005, deadline twenty-year-old Ruma explained: "Our living standards have improved thanks to the textile industry . . . with the salary, I support a whole family . . . we are still poor. If we lose our jobs, we will not belong to any class."[2] Indeed, according to Bangladeshi Foreign Minister Morshed Khan, employment has empowered women in one of the world's few Muslim democracies: "For the first time in a Muslim country, hundreds of thousands of women in their late teens and early twenties are wearing cosmetics, carrying handbags, and walking to work every day. There is no way . . . that this government or any other government can send them back to the kitchen."[3] More fundamentally, progressives tend to ignore the fact that, as Harvard labor economist Richard Freeman and Kim Elliott of the Institute for International Economics point out, the worst conditions and human rights abuses often occur in areas most untouched by globalization, where they "cannot be directly manipulated by trade flows."[4] The ILO recently found that most of the child labor in the world happens in domestic subsistence agriculture, where few if any multinational companies are making investments.[5]

The devastating dislocation that these poor Bangladeshi women could face due to the elimination of textile quotas should also provoke humility from free trade purists who hold the simplistic view that all market openings are unambiguously good for the world's poor. The evidence of how trade affects income inequality, particularly in the short term, is mixed. Without serious, structured efforts to ensure shared growth, there is no guarantee that trade will automatically bring significant benefits to the world's poor. The testimony of these Bangladeshi women reinforces the point that when it comes to trade and poverty, we need hardheaded, humble analysis from all sides about how to ensure that trade benefits the poor in developing countries.

When Bono recently told me he would be speaking at college campuses in the United States, I asked how he handled the trade debate with activist students who, while sympathetic to his calls for more resources to fight AIDS and global poverty, often dismiss free trade as an agenda driven by corporate American greed. "What I say is that the depth of Africa's crisis is such that we cannot afford to posture," he explained. "I tell them, I'm a rock star. It's my job to posture. But there are just too many people dying in Africa for us not to open our minds to whatever strategies will help solve this crisis."

IN SEARCH OF A NEW CONSENSUS

During the 1990s, President Clinton made significant progress toward including labor and environmental standards in trade agreements, which is important both to lift living standards in lower-income trading partners and to ensure that American workers have confidence that competition is not based on a global race to the bottom on core labor rights. While President Clinton was only able to forge side agreements for the already negotiated NAFTA agreement, and while we failed in Seattle in 1999 to establish even a WTO labor standards working group, near the end of the administration, we negotiated a model free trade agreement with Jordan that included enforceable labor standards in the core of the agreement.

Legitimacy and Limits of Enforceable Labor Standards

While in recent years an uneasy consensus has formed over including at least some form of labor standards in trade agreements, the issue—along with environmental safeguards—remains one of the most divisive in trade-related negotiations. In the Clinton administration, dealing with labor standards as a vote-counting exercise was agonizing. When we moved to the left to pick up twelve votes, we lost twenty-five votes on the right. If we agreed to less stringent labor requirements to secure reliable free trade votes—usually from Republicans—we were criticized for abandoning President Clinton's "globalization with a human face." Republican members of Congress have told me that they regard labor standards as a ruse: however far they go, they believe Democrat opponents of trade will always move the goal post ten yards farther down the field. Likewise, some Democrats believe that many who oppose labor standards do not in their heart of hearts even support basic labor protections like collective bargaining, minimum wages, and work safety standards here at home.

Reaching common ground requires that we recognize both the legitimacy and limitations of such standards. Those who argue that labor standards have no place in commercial trade are not on firm ground. We often take moral issues into account when establishing our trading relationships; we did not trade with the Taliban in Afghanistan, for example, or with the government of Burma because of its long record of human rights abuses. In addition, while we may accept the reality of comparative advantage when a factory is able to pay a lower wage in a developing country because of its per capita income and level of development, it is an entirely different issue if a country is gaining comparative advantage by promoting abusive child labor, jailing union leaders, or flaunting its own minimum wage, hours, and safety laws.

Clear and enforceable labor standards cannot be relegated to side agreements and should not be considered secondary provisions. But supporters of labor and environmental standards, like myself, have to recognize that there are limits to how far they will take us—especially given the risk that our trading partners in poor countries see such measures as punitive impositions on their sovereignty designed to unfairly close our market to them. Progressives who understand why the United States is seen as heavy-handed in its dealings with allies in areas such as the invasion of Iraq or the war on terrorism, have to recognize that the same potential exists in a progressive area like labor standards.

At the Seattle negotiations in 1999, central opposition to our calls for incorporating labor standards within the WTO structure did not come from Republican business leaders but from poor nations who interpreted our position as an effort to impose twenty-first-century labor and environmental standards on their economies, which more closely resembled the U.S. economy in the nineteenth century. Even some unions and NGOs in poor countries shared their governments' concerns because "they fear[ed] that such provisions could be abused for protectionist purposes," as WTO Director-General Mike Moore explained.[6]

When I traveled with President Clinton to Auckland, New Zealand, in 2000 for an APEC summit, I was hoping to get participants to reconfirm the ILO's Convention against abusive child labor, which Labor Secretary Alexis Herman and I had long been promoting and which 132 countries including the United States had already ratified. ILO Convention 182 is just about the most noncontroversial component of the labor standards debate: a commitment to work against the worst forms of child labor. Since it had already been ratified by eighteen Asian countries, I figured my request was little more than checking a box. I have to admit that when my National Economic Council associates told me it wasn't going to be possible even to mention Section 182 in the summit document, I couldn't believe it. How could anyone be opposed to such a basic commitment?

The next day, as I watched the off-the-record discussion between President Clinton and the fifteen other heads of state, various presidents and prime ministers from developing nations expressed their contempt for labor standards as a rich nation's way of imposing protectionism that would cost their countries jobs. They were unwilling to endorse the link between labor standards and trade even when they supported the specific provisions. The attitude was almost always the same: now that the United States has succeeded, it wants to impose standards that the United States did not uphold when it was at a similar stage of economic development.

Opposition from the governments of developing countries alone is not a reason to pull back on labor standards, particularly because these governments often represent an elite population and not typical workers. Some of the biggest players in multilateral trade negotiations—such as China and Egypt—are not democracies with leaders who represent the workforce. Yet if developing countries see our positions on labor standards as punitive impositions on their sovereignty—hypocritical positions, designed to punish them for not living up to U.S. standards—it will undermine the larger goal of increased living standards and worker rights in these countries.

We should use our strong commitment to core labor standards as an incentive for nations who want to expand trade with the United States to undertake reforms on their own initiative. The Clinton administration made it clear to the Jordanian government that a precondition of any bilateral agreement would be Jordan's willingness to enforce its core labor standards, and the Jordanians saw it in their interest to do so. The Bush administration, however, sought to soften the Jordan model in the negotiations of the Central American Free Trade Agreement (CAFTA). It sent a signal to such governments as El Salvador—who historically have had a poor record on labor rights—that they did not have to show significant improvement to negotiate an agreement with the United States. In doing so, the Bush administration missed a critical opportunity to inspire greater reform in Central American countries and lessen the intense divisiveness of the fight for congressional approval.

MORE TOOLS IN THE TOOL KIT

Once we use our clear commitment to core labor standards as a way of spurring reform and bringing our trading partners to the table, pro-growth progressives need to increase the number of tools in our tool kit—in addition to labor standards—to show that we can move forward with a model of partnership, not punishment and protection.

1. Taking Enforcement Seriously

While progressives should continue to push trading partners to raise the protections in their labor laws when necessary to meet international core labor standards, it is crucial that we not underestimate the progress that can be made in some countries by ensuring they enforce the laws on their books. A focus on enforcement of existing laws could have a major impact on improving labor conditions, while by definition representing a lesser imposition on sovereignty.

Consider child labor in India. The Indian government has laws on the books forbidding child labor, yet there are millions of children in India engaged in dangerous and difficult work, and in many areas Indian children still suffer under forms of bonded labor. Children work to pay off parents' debt in harrowing and exhausting work, harvesting sugarcane, carrying and breaking slabs of stone in quarries, welding jewelry, and even tanning leather with noxious chemicals.[7] These practices are against the law, but government officials and community leaders are not enforcing these laws because of corruption, poverty, and even cultural reasons. Requiring the Indian government to pass new laws to strengthen their labor standards will do little to address this problem. Instead, our priority should be strengthening enforcement at the national level and empowering NGOs and civil society groups to be more forceful watchdogs. Another example is China, where the labor laws mandate safe and decent working conditions, but where corruption and neglect make labor issues a major concern. In Latin America, research shows that the ratification of ILO labor conventions is near universal; the overwhelming challenge for labor standards in the region is enforcement.[8]

A more substantial commitment to enforcement would have a number of progressive benefits. First, it could empower committed reformers within poor government ministries to increase the resources for enforcement. Second, it puts the United States in a position of working constructively with developing country NGOs and watchdog groups to strengthen oversight and regulation of labor practices with increased financial support and technical assistance, and to empower a sustainable movement to make the enforcement and eventual improvement of labor standards in these countries a national priority.

2. Partnerships and Positive Incentives

While we have no choice but to provide less trade or cut off ties through sanctions in cases of brutal labor violations in developing countries like Burma, these are not always the most effective ways to achieve positive results for workers, and indeed have the potential to backfire. In 1995, when a bill was introduced in Congress to impose trade sanctions on Bangladesh for its systematic violation of its own domestic child labor laws, clothing producers in the country immediately fired fifty thousand underage workers. These children—about 85 percent of whom were young girls—were probably unable to find any other job, and reports confirm that many were forced into prostitution.[9] We need to consider what approaches might be more effective to help workers and communities in these countries. Let me offer three examples.

Between 1997 and 2000, Secretary of Labor Alexis Herman, Senator Tom Harkin of Iowa, and I formed a sort of troika to push for greater support of the ILO's efforts to fight abusive child labor, including a new ILO convention to ban its most abusive forms. Over the period, we increased aid to the ILO from $3 million to $45 million and added an additional $37 million for school-based programs. Senator Harkin pushed for an executive order to draw up a public list of products that might be made with illegal child labor. There was a major dispute over whether products from India should be included, and my deputy, Sarah Rosen Wartell—who had been engaged in long negotiations on the issue—told me the Indian government was appalled that we would humiliate them by putting them on this list only weeks before an Indian state visit to the United States. The world's largest democracy was already annoyed that our attention was focused on China joining the WTO rather than strengthening U.S.-Indian bilateral relations.

NSC director Sandy Berger asked me to head up a U.S.-India Economic Dialogue and travel to New Delhi to resolve the economic disputes, including the issue of child labor, prior to the state visit. It became clear that if we put India's products on the list—or if we forced an agreement on child labor that looked like we were dictating the outcome—they would feel we were trying to embarrass them and negotiations would end in stalemate, worse relations between the two countries, and no real progress in helping Indian children. We decided our best strategy was to seek the equivalent to a consent agreement that would allow India to announce it was making progress without appearing that it was caving to U.S. demands. We initially offered to refrain from citing Indian products while launching a U.S.-funded effort to reduce child labor, but this offer was rejected out of concern that it would look like we were dictating terms to the government. Even when I thought we had reached an agreement to have a $40 million ILO anti–child labor fund that each nation would contribute half to, the chief of staff to the prime minister explained to me in his New Delhi office that we would have to agree that only the ILO and the Indian government could be involved in setting the terms for distribution of the funds. This arrangement led to a true cooperative partnership between the United States, the Indian government, and the ILO, with tangible benefits to tens of thousands of poor children. It was also a stark lesson in the sensitivity those of us who want greater labor standards must have when seeking a benign social outcome that can be interpreted as a heavy-handed imposition on sovereignty.

Examples in Chile and Cambodia reinforce this vision. On several occasions I spoke to Ricardo Lagos Jr., son of Chilean President Ricardo Lagos and a critical actor in the recent U.S.-Chile trade agreement. He admitted that their knowledge of the U.S.'s commitment to core labor standards did indeed act as a "kick in the pants" to improve some of their labor provisions. But he became furious at the idea that the U.S. would threaten sanctions and force Chile to pay the U.S. government if Chile failed to meet the U.S.'s interpretation of Chilean labor laws, a tactic he believed would only lead to an acrimonious standstill. If Chile did fail to live up to its agreements, Lagos thought a far better option would be to force the government to set aside funds to invest in protecting workers and enhancing standards within Chile—with the U.S. playing a monitoring role.

With Cambodia, we were able to use the power of positive incentives rather than brinksmanship in a poor country that was years away from meeting high standards on labor rights and working conditions. Seventy-five to eighty percent of Cambodians work in subsistence agriculture. Their lives are unbelievably hard—people are mostly illiterate and vulnerable to starvation. With little access to medicines for curable diseases, they face infant mortality rates of nearly 100 per 1,000 live births.[10] As in Thailand thirty years ago, people are flocking to cities to get whatever jobs are available.

When the United States normalized trade relations with Cambodia in 1996, it catalyzed the development of a previously nonexistent industrial sector. Many in the "standards or nothing" camp argued that the Cambodian government would be more likely to reform if we set out standards for them, but, in practice, they would not be able to meet those standards for years to come. The new jobs being created were poor by American standards and liable to workplace abuses, yet the alternatives were worse.

While the Clinton administration wanted to help the country industrialize, it did not want to accept subpar labor outcomes as a given. Having won the trust of the Cambodian government, the Clinton administration pursued a positive incentives strategy to push it to improve their labor standards. In 1999, Clinton signed a three-year trade pact that granted the Cambodian government up to 14 percent in additional annual increases in the U.S. quota of garment imports. In exchange, the Cambodians had to allow the ILO to help revise the labor standards code of conduct in the garment industry to include paid overtime, a ban on child labor, and work-break requirements, and to oversee the enforcement of the new provisions. The ILO, for the first time, agreed to monitor all Cambodian labor practices—"everything from toilets to hours to wages."[11]

The prospect of additional access to the U.S. market was a powerful incentive. The Cambodian government agreed to make inspections mandatory for any garment factory that wanted to export to the United States and it even began inspecting factories that were not exporting here. The ILO inspectors found that the factories were actually in pretty good shape for such a poor nation. The AFL-CIO and the ILO sent in workers to train the Cambodians to unionize. Within the first two years of the accord, Cambodia won a 9 percent increase over its original garment quota. The garment industry has become the country's biggest exporter. More than seventy-five garment factories have unionized, and in 2000, the government agreed to its first ever minimum wage law.[12]

Today, Cambodia's 200,000 industrial jobs are virtually all the result of access to the U.S. market.[13] By engaging with the government in a positive way, we were able to achieve both pro-growth and progressive goals: increased trade and higher labor standards.

As in Bangladesh, many in Cambodia are anxious about what will happen with the removal of global textile quotas and the end of preferential access to the U.S. market. Cambodia's commitment to labor standards may actually provide an advantage that could mitigate the loss of global market share to China. Karen Tramontano, president of the Global Fairness Initiative, explains that many retailers today are looking for "brand security" and want to do business in countries not considered socially irresponsible.[14] Locating in such countries reduces the likelihood of embarrassing and costly public relations incidents involving labor rights abuses at local factories. A major report on the Cambodian garment sector by the Carnegie Endowment for International Peace said, "Cambodia plans to position itself as a safe haven for buyers who care about their reputation. This decision represents a consensus between the government and the private sector that improving labor standards has had practical, tangible value in the marketplace."[15] Indeed, this decision may be paying off: a survey of fifteen Western buyers accounting for nearly half the market in the Cambodian garment industry found that that 60 percent planned to *increase* business with the country in 2005.[16]

While Cambodia is far from a model global citizen—as its notorious sex trafficking and poor scores on the World Bank's government corruption indicators remind us—this approach has helped the country make important, sustained progress on both labor standards and economic development. The United States should consider how to use the same positive incentives and monitoring programs in the context of new trade agreements, perhaps by requiring the ILO to establish programs in key export sectors as a condition of new bilateral or regional deals. The United States can also provide stepped-up assistance for the independent monitoring of such programs.

3. Labeling, Codes of Conduct, and the Market for Standards

Transparency about the conditions in factories around the world provides another avenue to create incentives for higher labor standards and a potential weapon against egregious labor abuses. If consumers in a global marketplace insisted on purchasing goods and services that were made under fair working conditions, poor countries could, in theory, profit from implementing such standards. When economists Richard Freeman and Kim Elliott surveyed the literature on consumer behavior, they discovered what you might expect—many more consumers say they are willing to pay a premium than actually do when given a chance. Nonetheless, they identified a significant minority of consumers that both talk the talk and walk the walk, enough for a sustainable and profitable niche market for labor standards.[17] Anne Gust, General Counsel and Compliance Officer for the GAP, stated in a Fortune Brainstorm Panel that their customers are adamant that their clothes not be made with sweatshop labor, and that it is easier to meet that consumer request in countries where the government—either on its own initiative or through a trade agreement—is committed to wide enforcement of core labor standards.

In the wake of a number of highly publicized sweatshop scandals in the mid-1990s, there were calls to legislate a solution and outlaw U.S. companies from setting up production centers in places where sweatshops operated. In 1996, Clinton and Labor Secretary Reich discussed the issue with many of the major players in the U.S. apparel industry to try to find a voluntary, and more politically sustainable, solution.

These discussions began a three-year process that led to the creation of the Fair Labor Association (FLA). When Alexis Herman succeeded Reich as Labor Secretary in 1997, and she and I took over negotiations, we tried to get unions, major companies, labor rights activist groups, and antipoverty NGOs to agree on a code of fair labor standards and a process for monitoring and enforcement. Getting such diverse groups to voluntarily agree on a common framework for standards and monitoring was painful. Some companies were worried that making the code of conduct too stringent would discourage others from joining. Others were concerned that having an FLA "seal of approval" could make them more vulnerable to even a lone incident of worker exploitation or abuse. Labor rights activists pushed hard to make sure the code had teeth, that there would be independent monitoring and that all results would be made public. Unions expressed grave concerns about giving a seal of approval to any company that had any production facilities in China.

Michael Posner of Human Rights First played a brilliant conciliatory role in the negotiations. He gave me a heads-up on when meltdowns were imminent or which back-channel conversations were important, and when my presence at a meeting or a particular commitment from the president was needed. In the end, despite having developed a strong working relationship with UNITE—the largest textile union in the United States—they could not support the initiative. But many stayed in, including the RFK Foundation, Lawyers Committee for Human Rights, and Pharis Harvey, founder and then-director of the International Labor Rights Fund. In early 1999 the FLA began monitoring twelve major U.S. apparel companies, including Nike, Reebok, Ralph Lauren, and Nordstrom.[18]

While the FLA is far from perfect, it has provided a constructive framework to build upon, a virtue that Michael Posner passionately stressed in our negotiations. On the eve of the release of the first FLA monitoring report in 1999, Reebok CEO Paul Fireman said, "we want to show that a detailed, critical report about factory conditions can be disclosed without the sky falling. And we'd like to start changing the attitude that has prevailed among many companies for many years—that they do not have any real responsibility for conditions in factories they do not own, or for the treatment of workers who are not their employees."[19]

The FLA has already established a worldwide network of independent monitors—most small, local NGOs—that conduct random inspections of member-country factories, and it posts the results on its Web site. Recently, the FLA became the repository and arbiter of third-party complaints of factory abuses. In 2003 a textile union in a free-trade zone in Sri Lanka filed a complaint with the FLA because one of the local contracting companies in the region would not recognize them. Nike and Activewear also requested that the FLA intervene. FLA President Auret van Heerden called for mediation, and the union was recognized. A similar case in Guatemala led to the first collective bargaining agreement in the nation's history.[20]

The question going forward is whether the monitoring of corporate practices in poor nations can empower concerned consumers to vote with their purchases to create a true market for products made in adherence to core labor standards. Simply requiring higher wages in one nation could backfire if the higher wages take away the country's cost competitiveness and force production elsewhere. The challenge is to translate the results of reliable monitoring to the consumer and convince many of them to choose goods made under humane conditions—even if at times it means slightly higher prices.

Certainly, an easy and relatively inexpensive first step would be for the United States to increase funding for independent monitoring. Building the capacity of local monitors is crucial for ensuring a steady stream of ac-curate information and will be increasingly important as local employers become more adept at outsmarting the burgeoning inspection processes.

Second, more concerned consumer groups should explore whether or not labeling schemes would empower more consumers to choose prod-ucts that they know were made in accordance with basic labor standards. The consumer movement and activist groups have demonstrated that their power can work in the negative—boycotts and bans do influence consumer behavior. The challenge is to turn that leverage toward the positive—supporting mechanisms that highlight good practice and give others a tangible incentive to emulate them.

The most established example of labeling schemes is the Fair Trade coffee certification provided by the international nonprofit organization TransFair. All coffee that receives the Fair Trade label has been purchased through cooperatives that guaranteed farmers a minimum above-market price. In 2000, responding to intense pressure from activist groups, Star-bucks agreed to begin selling Fair Trade coffee beans alongside their regular brands, although they stopped short of offering a brewed Fair Trade op-tion. Starbucks increased its purchase of Fair Trade coffee by 70 percent in fiscal year 2002—from 653,000 pounds to 1.1 million pounds.[21] Perhaps more important, the Starbucks decision helped prompt others to offer Fair Trade coffee, including two of the four major global coffee distributors—Procter & Gamble and Sara Lee, and such major retailers as Safeway and Dunkin' Donuts.[22]

Another successful labeling scheme is the UN-backed Kimberley Process for "clean diamonds," negotiated in Kimberley, South Africa, in 2002. Responding to intense pressure from advocacy groups like Amnesty International and OXFAM, the diamond industry teamed with the UN and governments of diamond-producing nations to curb the sale of "blood di-amonds" mined during brutal civil wars in Sierra Leone, Angola, and the Democratic Republic of Congo. In 2003, the certification process got fur-ther support when the U.S. Congress passed the Clean Diamond Act, which requires a Kimberley process certification for all diamonds imported to the U.S. Industry leaders like Tiffany now have strict policies against buying conflict diamonds—one Tiffany salesman told me, "you cannot believe how many customers ask for assurance that their diamonds are clean." Though the certification process has been hampered by difficulty monitoring production in some producing nations and by weak compliance in the United States, member countries account for 99.8 percent of worldwide diamond production, and in 2003, 47,600 certificates were issued covering $20 billion of diamonds.[23]

Third, progress could be made if U.S. corporations found it in their interest to initiate and implement ambitious globalization codes of conduct. Currently, a number of voluntary corporate codes of conduct, including the Global Sullivan Principles, the UN Global Compact, and the Global Reporting Initiative offer a broad set of socially responsible principles and ask participating companies to report on their progress. To date, none has moved beyond the self-reporting stage to include external monitoring or enforcement.

If a group of major U.S. corporations, perhaps through a highly respected organization like the Business Roundtable, went beyond these initial codes, it could help spark a new ethic of corporate global citizenship. This would require companies to support a system of truly independent monitoring and transparent reporting. In return, labor advocates would need to be sensitive to business concerns about proprietary information and not fall into the cynical game of raising the bar higher and higher on companies willing to commit to codes of conduct—an approach that leaves people with the impression that no good deed will go unpunished. Starbucks has become a magnet for criticism from activist groups in large part because it was the first major player in the coffee industry to sell Fair Trade coffee and the only company to pioneer a preliminary industry code of conduct. "It's better to start with them. Kraft is never going to do anything," explained one activist candidly. "[W]hen you're the grassroots with limited resources, you have to pick your targets carefully."[24]

4. Foreign Adjustment Strategies

While studies show that, over time, open trade can help raise living standards for even a nation's poorest citizens, in the short term, openness can bring painful dislocation and widen inequity in nations where safety nets are weak but where elites are well-positioned to seize the early economic

opportunities. Even in the absence of new trade agreements, modernization can temporarily exacerbate existing inequities in developing nations.
The harsh dislocation of small farmers after the opening of the Mexican
agriculture market, as well as the horrific accounts of hundreds of young
women workers in the maquiladoras in Ciudad Juárez being raped and
murdered, demonstrate powerfully why pro-growth progressives must be
concerned with the degree to which our trading partners have the capacity
to provide the additional services and protections needed to limit the extreme downsides of accelerated economic change from rapid opening of
markets. Harvard professor Dani Rodrik notes one encouraging finding:
nations with increased trade tend to have larger government programs to
help limit the risks that come with change and openness.[25]

To meet the promise of freer trade, pro-growth progressives must ask
two important questions: How can we ensure that countries have structures in place to protect citizens and cushion workers dislocated by trade?
What can we do to make sure that the initial benefits of trade are invested in
education, health care, and infrastructure to benefit the broad population,
not just the fortunate few?

New Jersey Congressman Robert Menendez proposed creating a new
Social Investment and Economic Development Fund in the context of the
Free Trade Area of the Americas negotiations. The fund would provide $2.5
billion over five years to address Latin America's high structural inequality
and persistent poverty. It would support antipoverty initiatives and training programs to help countries build the institutional capacity to provide a
more robust social safety net on their own.[26] The United States could also
offer developing nations substantial technical assistance to design new social safety net structures as well as mechanisms to ensure and enforce labor
standards and worker safety.

5. Bold Partnerships Beyond Labor Standards: The Case for Universal Education

I cannot recall any discussion in my years as national economic advisor
when a lawmaker declared that his vote on a trade agreement would be
contingent on, for example, more direct aid to the workers and children
of the trading country at stake, or increased investment to improve a
country's health infrastructure. This always struck me as a phenomenal
missed opportunity.

Imagine if progressives said that part of the price for their trade votes was bold new funding to catalyze a global effort to educate the 104 million primary school–age children currently out of school. A half century of evidence shows that even in developing countries, an additional year of education can raise future wages by at least 10 percent,[27] that quality education spurs economic growth and productivity, and that educated citizens tend to build more democratic institutions with greater participation and less corruption.

Educating girls delivers the highest return on investment.[28] Increasing the share of women with a secondary education by 1 percentage point boosts annual per capita income growth by 0.3 percentage points.[29] An extra year of a woman's education has been shown to reduce the risk that her children will die in infancy by 5 percent to 10 percent.[30] And more educated women tend to choose to have smaller, more sustainable families. In Brazil, illiterate mothers have an average of six children while literate mothers have fewer than three children and are better able to care for and invest in their children's well-being.[31]

Finally, simply keeping children in school has been shown to delay sexual activity, increase knowledge about the spread of disease, and reduce the risk of contracting HIV/AIDS. This is critical because half of all new HIV infections occur among fifteen- to twenty-four-year-olds. Prevalence rates are lowest in the five-to-fourteen age group, and reaching this younger generation provides what the World Bank has called "A Window of Hope" for halting the spread of AIDS.[32] For instance, young rural Ugandans with some secondary education are three times less likely than those with no education to be HIV-positive.[33] And school-based AIDS education can reduce risky behavior by as much as 75 percent.[34]

While education, particularly for girls, provides incredible benefits for individuals, communities, and countries, the decision whether to send children to school often falls to parents living in extreme poverty, for whom the costs of schooling may appear to outweigh the benefits. In many developing nations, such impoverished parents still bear the costs of tuition, books, and transportation, even for elementary school, which can take a sizable chunk of their income—especially if they have several school-age children.

Long distances to school impose further disincentives and opportunity costs. Parents fear that their girls will be sexually assaulted or harassed en route, and that long hours traveling back and forth will deny them their children's help with the grueling daily collecting of firewood and water. Some feel they cannot get by without the additional income their children earn by working—which often averages as much as 25 percent or more of total family income. Such cost-benefit calculations too often mean that parents are less likely to invest in education where the return is the highest—for their daughters. Not only do they rely upon girls to care for younger siblings, but in many poor nations parents believe that a daughter's education will benefit only her husband's family once she is married—essentially that sending their girls to school is "like watering someone else's garden."

The good news is that this situation is far from hopeless. When governments align the interests of parents with the best interests of their children and the nation, by reducing their direct costs and opportunity costs, all over the world parents choose to send their children, particularly their girls, to school. When governments eliminate school fees, build schools near villages, and employ quality teachers, school enrollments skyrocket.[35]

The most effective strategy is to tackle the financial disincentives for parents head-on by offering quid pro quo assistance for poor parents to send their children to school—including funds to make up for their children's lost labor. The Bolsa Escola program in Brazil gives mothers a stipend in a government-created bank account, which is used to purchase groceries and other necessities if their children maintain 90 percent attendance at school. The result? It has virtually eliminated dropouts among girls and may have attracted one-third of children who were previously out of school—many of whom were working.[36] In Diadema, a former shantytown an hour outside Brasilia, I met with several mothers who said that without Bolsa Escola they would never have been able to send their children to school and still care for them. The results have been just as powerful in Mexico's Oportunidades program.[37] Bangladesh's national stipend program, which helps poor, rural girls complete secondary school, is considered a model for other countries.[38] The power of the stipend compels parents to keep their kids in school, maintain their grades, and delay marriage. School feeding programs have also been shown to encourage impoverished parents to send their children to school. Although President Clinton's $300 million Global Food for Education initiative was cut back after 2001—despite strong bipartisan support from former Senators Bob Dole and George McGovern—it provided meals to 7.7 million children in 38 countries and was found to increase enrollment by over 10 percent.[39] Hillary Rodham Clinton describes how as First Lady she spoke with village elders in Bangladesh who were amazed at the number of families who were willing to send their girls to school when they could get a stipend or even a bag of rice. These families were compensated for their daughters' lost labor and could "actually make a sensible trade to have their girl remain in school."[40]

While simply banning child labor in certain industries can often have the unfortunate unintended consequence of having children shift to even more dangerous or abusive child labor, aggressive approaches to fund free universal basic education afford poor families better options for their children. When I was in Mumbai, an hour outside of Bombay, in July 2003, I visited the Vidhyaka Sansad boarding school for children who had worked in the backbreaking quarry industry. One seventh grader, Anil Dhane, told me with pride that only a couple of years ago, "I was carrying around six bricks weighing twelve kilograms each." "Now," he beamed, "I have the chance to get a full education." While it may not be possible or practical to prevent nonabusive child labor in the poorest families in the poorest nations, with basic education these children can recapture a portion of their childhood, and educate themselves for a better future.

A bold commitment to universal basic education is something both trade skeptics and trade enthusiasts could agree on, to ensure that more open markets truly raise all economic fortunes around the world. Sadly, the United States provides only about $400 million a year to educate the world's poorest children in South Asia, Africa, the Middle East, and South America. That is about what we spend to build twenty new high schools in the United States. To go beyond the UN Millennium Development Goal for primary education and to achieve universal basic education by 2015, the world needs a new global compact.[41] Developing nations would do their part by finalizing a comprehensive strategy for free universal education that includes adequate domestic commitment and strong transparency, accountability and antifraud protections, while the richer nations would commit an additional $7 billion to $10 billion annually to support poor countries that have already begun serious national reforms and provide strong incentives for those that have not yet begun to design a credible national plan.

In April 2004, Senator Hillary Clinton announced the first Education for All legislation that would commit $2.5 billion from the United States for universal education by 2009,[42] while working through the global Fast Track Initiative. Congresswoman Nita Lowey, who together with Republican Congressman Jim Kolbe has increased funding for education since September 11, has introduced similar legislation in the House.

If we do not commit these funds, we are effectively punishing countries that are doing the right thing. When Uganda, Kenya, and Tanzania eliminated fees for primary education, each country saw between 1 million and 3 million new children enroll in the first year of the reform. Yet without increased support from developed nations, such admirable efforts result in a temporary decline in quality because classroom sizes explode. I saw 140 fourth graders in a single class in Tanzania a year after they had ended school fees. When I visited the Tula Kebale primary school in Ethiopia in April 2002, an amazing female principal had so dramatically improved the quality and community participation of her school that enrollment had skyrocketed. The second-grade class I visited had 170 children. The principal had done everything to increase enrollment but had no resources to appropriately manage the expansion.[43]

We are also failing to realize the potential for universal basic education to be a preemptive strategy for winning hearts and minds in the global battle of ideas and the war on terrorism. America's strategy for supporting education is not only inadequate, it is fundamentally reactive.[44] Our boldest efforts on education in recent years have come after we invade or bomb countries (such as the effort to get girls in Kabul into school for the first time), or when we fear that a lack of quality public education prompts radicals to fund fundamentalist schools that teach extremism. When we fund reactively, we provide the wrong incentives for developing nations and instill skepticism about our motives. On two recent trips to the Middle East, I heard the same refrain: Americans do not care if children around the world starve or go without basic education, as long as they do not grow up to attack the United States.

Rather than waiting until schools have been subverted by extremists or flattened by bombs, the U.S. would do better to support poor countries' efforts to educate their children before conflicts or imminent threats arise. No country better exemplifies the need for such a preemptive strategy than Kenya. After Daniel arap Moi's twenty-four-year dictatorship ended in 2002, President Kibaki announced universal education as a national priority in his inauguration speech, and has eliminated school fees and decentralized school management. Yet as fee elimination has sparked a massive influx of new students, Kenya now faces major financial challenges. While Kenya made significant strides to have their education plan approved by the Fast Track Initiative in July 2005, they still face a financing gap of at least $106 million a year.

Currently the U.S. commits only a paltry $3 million a year for education in Kenya. A substantial U.S. commitment to Kenya's education system at this critical moment would not only signal our support for developing countries that promote democracy and reform, but also would improve U.S. national security. Al-Qaeda terrorists have struck twice and are thought to have operatives in the country. In the North Eastern Province, with a Muslim majority, fewer than 20 percent of primary school–age children are enrolled. Without efforts to expand public education in this region, George Saitoti, Kenya's education minister, fears that schools funded by radical religious groups could emerge.[45] If the U.S. allows Kenya's experiment with universal education to fail solely because Kenya poses no imminent threat today, we may end up paying a high price tomorrow.

Since leaving the White House, I have dedicated much of my time to running the Center for Universal Education at the Council on Foreign Relations, and chairing the U.S. chapter of the Global Campaign for Education. I have marshaled academic evidence and tried to convince policy makers of the importance of education in poor countries. The evidence is overwhelming, but I'm consistently struck by the deep intrinsic support for education among the American public. When tens of millions of Americans learned that the Taliban barred Afghan girls from school, they did not need statistics or studies to know it was wrong and to want our country to respond. If the United States were to lead a preemptive strategy on universal education, it would send a signal to the world of how strongly Americans value the education of every child.

PART THREE

■

A Workforce for the Dynamism Economy

6

A Pro-Growth Model for Rewarding Work

After signing his 1993 Deficit Reduction Plan, President Clinton was more than a little frustrated at how much attention was paid to the 2.5 million upper-income Americans whose taxes were increased and how little notice was given to the substantial tax cut offered to 15 million working poor Americans through a historic expansion of the Earned Income Tax Credit (EITC). In January 1996, George Stephanopoulos, Communications Director Don Baer, and I suggested that President Clinton use the State of the Union to tell the inspiring story of an EITC recipient named Faith Bowman. She had used her EITC tax cut to pay for graphic design courses that qualified her for a good job and allowed her to get her daughter out of foster care.[1] The president mocked his own frustration by explaining that he would have to ask Ms. Bowman to stand in the First Lady's box and introduce her as the only one of 15 million EITC recipients who actually knew she had received a tax cut in 1993.[2]

Fortunately for President Clinton—and more important for America's working poor—lawmakers on both the right and left have grown to appreciate how much the expansion of the EITC (which we should have renamed the Rewarding Work Tax Credit) has helped tens of millions of American workers move toward economic independence. All told, the expansion has provided nearly $100 billion in additional wage supplements to hardworking low-income workers in the decade since its passage. Every year the EITC lifts more than 5 million families above the poverty line.[3] Beyond its benefit to millions of hard-pressed working families, the EITC is also a model policy for pro-growth progressives because by flowing directly to individuals, it does not burden employers or discourage job growth.

The EITC also taps a powerful component of economic dignity: the notion that Americans who work full-time should not have to raise their children in poverty. Indeed, for President Clinton it was the power of this value that made cutting back on the EITC nonnegotiable. Within the administration there was significant pressure to cut back on our EITC campaign proposal when we put together our first budget in January 1993. Because of increases in projected deficits the National Economic Council had to confront a growing tension between Clinton's progressive campaign commitments "Putting People First" and his promise to reduce the deficit. I was often the man in the middle on these debates.

Because I supported increasing our deficit reduction efforts in light of the worsening forecasts, many of our political advisors criticized me for not standing by the "Putting People First" agenda. Within our nearly daily Roosevelt Room budget meetings with President Clinton, some members of the economic team saw me as pushing him too hard to fund his progressive initiatives.

Fulfilling the president's campaign promise on EITC funding would cost over $7 billion a year, and Treasury Secretary Lloyd Bentsen, himself a longtime EITC supporter, reminded me that even cutting our commitment in half still amounted to an impressive multibillion-dollar expansion.

I would love to say that our full EITC expansion prevailed because of my persistence, but it was saved because President Clinton considered sacred his pledge that no parent working full-time should raise their children in poverty. Once it was clear to him that we needed every penny of his EITC increase, together with our proposed minimum wage hike, to meet his pledge, there was no question that he would stand by this campaign commitment.[4]

THE MOST PRO-GROWTH ALTERNATIVE

To see how the EITC achieves this core progressive value in the most pro-growth manner possible, let's look at the traditional conservative and progressive responses to public policies that reward working lower-income families.

The Free Market Position Goes Too Far

For decades, some conservatives have argued that just as we don't impose price controls or a minimum price floor on cars or candy bars, the government should not dictate a "minimum" when it comes to wages.

Economists including Alan Greenspan don't make this argument because they want to return to Dickens-era sweatshops. They believe a minimum wage is the type of direct government intervention that exacts a silent trade-off where some workers are helped but more vulnerable workers pay the price.

In simplified terms, their argument is that if a hypothetical McDonald's has a total of $1,000 a week to pay all of its employees, and the government requires all employers pay $200 a week per worker, McDonald's can hire only five full-time employees. In the absence of a $200-a-week minimum wage, however, McDonald's could hire ten full-time employees at $100 apiece. Minimum wage opponents question why the government should intervene. Not only do they claim that the higher wages for the five employees come at the expense of five others who could be making $100 a week, but they also argue that the other five could be among the economy's most vulnerable workers in desperate need of jobs. With the unemployment rate for black teenagers more than seven times that of the overall population, Greenspan argues that the minimum wage "does destroy jobs and does increase teenage unemployment."[5] Before the passage of the first minimum wage law in 1938, one Arkansas representative asked, "What profiteth the laborer of the South if he gain the enactment of a wage and hour law—40 cents per hour and 40 hours per week—if he then loses the opportunity to work."[6]

This argument has two fatal flaws. First, it ignores lopsided bargaining power in the workplace. Low-wage, low-skill workers usually do not have enough leverage with employers to successfully fight for their own economic dignity. Our courts do not honor contracts made at gunpoint, yet the poor and economically desperate have the economic equivalent of a gun to their heads. An employer cannot legally demand sex from a single mom with three kids, even if she might be willing to take the deal to keep food on the table. But neither should an employer be allowed to take advantage of her desperation by paying her $2 an hour. There is simply no way to ensure basic economic dignity and protection from abuse other than by directly intervening in the market to set a floor on wages.

Second, the conservative argument ignores real-world evidence that a moderate minimum wage does not seem to hurt job creation and may actually help increase productivity and growth. In 1992, when New Jersey raised its minimum wage from $4.25 to $5.05, while Pennsylvania maintained a $4.25 floor, two Princeton economists, Alan Krueger and David Card, saw it as a unique opportunity to test the traditional theory that the minimum wage trades higher earnings for fewer overall jobs in a real-world-controlled experiment. They examined low-wage fast-food chains along the border between the two states before and after New Jersey's minimum wage hike. Market purists would have predicted that New Jersey restaurants, now forced to pay higher wages, would hire fewer workers than those allowed to pay lower minimum wages in Pennsylvania. Yet Krueger and Card found that the New Jersey restaurants increased employment 13 percent, more than in comparable stores in Pennsylvania. Why? Higher wages led to a more stable, better-motivated workforce—delivering enough benefits and reduced recruitment costs to justify increasing employment.

The Card-Krueger studies provide solid evidence to counter the argument that minimum wage increases will, ipso facto, cost jobs. Their conclusion suggests that moderate minimum wage increases are an effective way to achieve the progressive goal of dignity at work without limiting flexibility or costing jobs.[7] Unfortunately, some progressives have misinterpreted these findings to conclude that unlimited increases in the minimum wage never have a negative effect on employment. Card and Krueger would be the first to argue that if one pushes the minimum wage too high, at some point it will lead to the negative outcome Greenspan warns of: employers hiring fewer low-wage workers.

What is that magic level for a moderate minimum wage? My informal poll of progressive labor economists suggests between $7.00 and $7.25 by the year 2006. Such an increase is particularly justified because the entire value of President Clinton's 1997 minimum wage increase to $5.15 an hour has been eroded by inflation. The real value of the minimum wage today is at its lowest point since 1955.[8]

If direct market intervention like increasing the minimum wage was our only tool to reward work, progressives seeking to offer workers a living wage in the range of $10.00–$12.00 an hour would face a dilemma. By forcing employers to pay such a high minimum wage, their admirable goal of a living wage could be achieved by silently trading away a number of lower-wage jobs. This is where the EITC provides a pro-growth alternative. For a working mother with two kids, the maximum $4,300 annual EITC benefit is equal to a $2.00 to $3.00 an hour raise. Combined with a moderate minimum wage increase, the EITC could help get families close to a $10 an hour wage without burdening employers and risking the negative labor market effects that mandating such a level might precipitate.

Indeed, because the EITC adds an extra reward to work, it encourages people on the sidelines to join the labor market. Economists Nada Eissa and Jeffrey Liebman found that mothers who received the expanded benefits increased their labor force participation by up to 2.8 percentage points relative to childless women.[9] Using a different technique, Bruce Meyer and Dan Rosenbaum found that over a twelve-year period, changes in the EITC were responsible for about 60 percent of the increase in employment rates of single mothers.[10] During the late 1990s programs like the EITC helped fuel a virtuous cycle of growth by encouraging a steady stream of new workers into the market to feed our expanding economy.

EXPANDING THE REWARDING WORK MODEL

As we go further to meet our progressive commitment to economic dignity for those who work, the rewarding work model of tying assistance to work and delivering it directly to individuals offers a blueprint for how to make ambitious progress in ways that are truly pro-growth.

Expand the Federal EITC

One way to make the EITC more effective would be to expand the credit for larger families. Despite increases in the EITC, it addresses the needs of larger families less effectively because it provides the same credit to all families with more than one child. But larger families have more mouths to feed, higher child care costs, and more frequent medical needs. While some worry that increasing the level of the EITC for each child provides an incentive to have more children, there is no evidence to suggest that a poor working mother would have another child simply because she would get another $500 through the EITC. Currently wages and the EITC don't increase when families grow beyond two children, but welfare benefits do. Adding the EITC to the current structure would strengthen the incentives to work.

If we do not want to expand the EITC for each additional child, we could certainly lift more working families out of poverty by instituting a moderately higher EITC for families with three or more children. From a pro-growth progressive standpoint, that would be an extremely well targeted policy. Compared to an increase in the minimum wage—which affects a single person and a single mother of four equally—increasing the EITC for larger families would give assistance to working families who need the most help.

Creating Local Rewarding Work Tax Credits

Many states and local communities have become frustrated by the lack of progress in increasing the federal minimum wage. Currently fifteen states and the District of Columbia have minimum wages above the federal level ($5.15)—most around $6 or $7 an hour. Even in traditionally conservative states, there has been substantial political support for such measures. In November 2004, for instance, 68 percent of Nevada voters supported a ballot initiative to amend the state constitution to ensure a minimum wage of $6.15 an hour and adjust it to inflation.[11]

There is little evidence that these moderate increases are impeding businesses or decreasing low-wage employment, and many grassroot advocates have lobbied to go beyond these state campaigns. Beginning in Baltimore in 1994, more than one hundred communities, including Boston, Chicago, Detroit, and Minneapolis have passed living wage ordinances.[12] The so-called living wage campaign shifts the minimum wage debate by asking: what is the wage necessary to provide a family economic dignity in a certain community? Such advocates usually answer between $10 and $12 an hour. "It's fundamental," explained Jen Kern, a living-wage advocate for the antipoverty group ACORN. "If you work, you shouldn't be poor. People in America believe that." [13]

I certainly agree. Yet, until recently living wages were largely limited to employees of local governments or local government contractors where higher wages may hurt local budgets but not job creation. Where there is an effort to guarantee such living wages for private-sector employees, a pro-growth progressive strategy should consider at what point we run the risk of negative impacts on job creation and whether the EITC model would reach this goal more effectively.

A number of communities including San Francisco, California; Denver, Colorado; and Montgomery County, Maryland, have begun experimenting with local EITC programs. Although these communities also have partial living wage laws for public employees, these EITC programs achieve the same goal in the private sector with lower risks to low-wage job growth. Studies by David Neumark of Michigan State University have found that state and local EITC programs fight poverty more effectively than living wage laws.[14] Moreover, the local EITC is a more targeted benefit: while the wage increase from a living wage is partly consumed by federal payroll taxes, state income taxes, and a decline in federal EITC benefits, local EITCs are administered through the tax code and therefore are not subject to any tax.[15]

In Montgomery County the program has expanded every year. In San Francisco, the local EITC will be paid for through a public-private partnership with government foundations, and local businesses.[16] The EITC is an antipoverty program both ACORN and local chambers of commerce should love—an economically efficient and politically sustainable model for rewarding work.

Reducing the Regressive Burdens on Work

All working families must pay for transportation and child care, but these costs impose a heavy burden on poor families and function as a regressive tax on work. For any parent who wants to work, finding or paying for child care is an unavoidable hurdle. A recent Children's Defense Fund study found that child care for a four-year-old runs about $5,000 a year. That may represent only a small fraction of an upper-income family's budget—only 5 percent of pretax income for a family making $100,000—yet for a low-income family making $20,000, child care can eat up a distressing 25 percent of their income.[17] Isabel Sawhill at the Brookings Institution estimates that if working parents were relieved of the burden of paying for child care, it alone would lift 1.9 million people out of poverty.[18]

The working poor also operate under the following paradox: car ownership is essential for finding and traveling to good jobs and has significant positive effects on the employment rates of poor and minority individuals, but without a good job it is difficult to earn enough money to own a car in the first place.[19] According to a recent nationwide survey, while 66 percent of entry-level jobs are created in suburban areas, 75 percent of likely candidates are concentrated in urban center and rural areas.[20] When economists Harry Holzer, John Quigley, and Stephen Raphael studied the effect of new public transportation infrastructure on minority hiring in suburban communities in the San Francisco Bay Area, they found significant increases in minority workers being hired for unskilled jobs, especially Hispanic workers.[21] If people can get to jobs they are most suited for, the result is the most effective allocation of our labor force and an economy working at its maximum productivity.

In 1998, President Clinton increased federal funds to expand public transportation services that connect low-income workers to their jobs, but more funding is needed. Expanding the rewarding work model would mean looking for new policies—or an expansion of refundable tax credits—that provide assistance directly to low-income workers to reduce these financial burdens of child care and transportation without putting new mandates or costs on employers.

ANSWERING CRITICS

The EITC model is not without criticism. Conservative critics argue against the program on the grounds that when benefits get too generous they constitute welfare. To understand this charge, one has to understand why the EITC is called a "refundable" tax credit. Often when Congress decides to provide a tax cut, it does so by giving a credit that can be deducted from taxes owed. If a middle-class family makes $60,000 and owes $10,000 in income taxes, a $1,500 tax credit reduces their bill to $8,500. But if a working single mother with two kids making $20,000 a year owes $1,000 in income taxes, she isn't entitled to the full $1,500 tax credit. And for the over 50 million Americans who do not earn enough money to owe income tax, these nonrefundable tax cuts offer them no benefit at all.

The EITC, on the other hand, is refundable. If Congress wants to give you a $1,500 tax cut, and you only owe $1,000 in taxes, you get a refund check for $500. The crucial value of the EITC's refundability is that even those families who pay little or no income tax get the full benefit and the full incentive to work that it is designed to provide.

Conservative commentators and Republican leaders have often tried to label the refundable portion of these tax cuts as welfare. Indeed, controversy over this issue nearly upended the bipartisan 1997 Balanced Budget Agreement.

As we closed in on a deal, one final sticking point was whether families receiving a refundable EITC could also take advantage of our proposed $500 child tax credit.[22] House Speaker Newt Gingrich seized on "refundability" and argued that "when you take out billions of dollars in tax cuts for working people and put in billions of dollars for people who pay no taxes, that's increasing welfare spending." [23] He was essentially saying that people receiving the EITC who were working full time and making between $10,000 and $25,000 were welfare recipients. The argument backfired when we brought young police officers who received the EITC, including Daniel Mercado of the Savannah, Georgia, Police Department to the White House. "Forgive me for not knowing all the details of this debate," Mercado said at a press conference, "but all I know is I work hard, I pay taxes, I have kids, and a tax cut for each of my children seems to me to make a lot of sense. I would think that if there was going to be a child tax credit given that it would apply to someone like me who is working very hard every day to support my family." [24]

Beyond politics, Gingrich's argument ignored the fact that the EITC was meant to offset not just the federal income taxes, but payroll taxes as well. In other words, if you make $20,000, 15.3 percent of your wages—$3,060— is taken out of your paycheck for Social Security and Medicare taxes. While only half of that—7.65 percent—is taken directly out of a worker's paycheck, labor market economists universally agree that over time the payroll taxes paid by employers eventually work their way out of wages. In other words, for someone making $20,000, even a refundable tax as high as $3,060 would simply refund the impact of payroll taxes. Finally, the EITC helps offset the state and local income tax and other tax burdens such as sales, property taxes, and excise taxes that poor workers often pay.

On the final weekend of the balanced budget negotiations Erskine Bowles and Bob Rubin asked me to be ready to respond to Gingrich's promised compromise. In a Saturday meeting with Senate Majority Leader Trent Lott, Rubin, and Bowles, Gingrich acknowledged that there should be refundable tax credits—but only to the point where they covered the worker's income tax and the employee side of the payroll tax. It was a tense moment. Gingrich's concession was a major breakthrough—he supported the concept of refundability, and I believe was making a sincere effort to find common ground, but because his proposal still left out millions of working poor women making between $12,000 and $18,000, I knew President Clinton would not want to agree to it. When I told Gingrich this, he abruptly ended the meeting, bringing the balanced budget negotiations to a temporary standstill. Fortunately, Gingrich had sent Bowles a book that day as a gift, and Bowles used it as an excuse to call him back. Gingrich grudgingly acquiesced after Rubin agreed to increase an enforcement provision in the EITC program.

This victory to protect refundable tax credits was consequential and lasting. In the 2001 Bush tax cut, a bipartisan effort by Senators Olympia Snowe of Maine and Mary Landrieu of Louisiana overcame administration opposition to expand the refundability of the Child Tax Credit, and even President Bush has endorsed refundable tax credits for health care. However, the issue of whether refundable tax credits should be seen as welfare or a pro-work or pro-family tax cut remains controversial. In 2003, the Congressional Republicans removed a provision that would have accelerated the expansion of the refundable portion of the child tax credit—denying increased assistance to 12 million children in low-income families, including 200,000 low-income military personnel, some of whom were stationed in Iraq. "To me, it's a little difficult to give tax relief to people that don't pay income tax," Republican Majority Leader Tom DeLay explained.[25] The *Wall Street Journal*'s editorial page went so far as to repeatedly call the poorest Americans "lucky duckies" because they don't pay income tax.[26]

Yet refundable tax credits that offset both taxes and the costs of going to work are pro-work, pro-growth, and consistent with the values of upward mobility and economic dignity. We give start-up help to new business and for oil exploration. Why not help reduce the costs for poor families who are working hard to get ahead?

7

The Work-Family Balancing Act

Thirty years ago, people like my mother, who balanced careers with their responsibilities at home and in the community, would have been labeled "super moms." This title is now the norm. As work-family expert Karen Kornbluh explains, "The traditional family—one breadwinner and one homemaker—has been replaced by the juggler family."[1] While some religious conservatives might believe that women should focus solely on raising families and while some economists worried about labor shortages might be relieved if more women chose to work, most parents simply want the greatest flexibility to find a juggling strategy that meets their family's economic and emotional needs without facing excessive punishment from the workplace.

For the pro-growth progressive, providing increased flexibility for working parents presents a significant policy challenge. Most of the balancing decisions—whether Mom can leave work early to pick the kids up from school, whether Dad will still be eligible for benefits if he goes part-time for a couple of years, whether either will be guaranteed their old job if they take off six months to care for a newborn—lie in the hands of private employers. Some with highly valued skills have chosen to become "free agents" so they can set their own work schedules and make their own choices about balancing work and family.[2] But those with less bargaining power—and particularly in periods of market weakness—do not have this flexibility.

Government policies to help extend flexibility to parents will often directly restrict employers' freedom to make decisions about their own businesses—precisely the kind of direct interventions that can have unintended anti-growth consequences. For some in the business community, policies dealing with work and family can be summed up by the reaction of the New Jersey chapter of the National Federation of Independent Businesses (NFIB) to an early version of the Family Medical Leave Act, which guaranteed workers the right to take unpaid leave for the birth of a child or for specific medical emergencies: "in the area of employer-employee relations," the New Jersey NFIB argued, "government has no role."[3]

But this opinion ignores not only values and social policy questions but the degree to which participation and contribution of women in the workforce is critical to our ability to stay ahead in a dynamic, competitive global economy. Policies that make it easier for workers to both be better parents and make more and better contributions to the workforce can be pro-growth progressive "win-wins."

MAINTAINING OUR COMPETITIVE EDGE

Many overlook the extent to which the strength of the U.S. labor market over the past half-century, and particularly in the past decade, has been the result of women's participation. Consider that from 1955 to 2002, the percentage of women in the labor force nearly doubled from 36 percent to 60 percent, enough to keep the overall participation rate increasing modestly even as the rate for men fell from 85 percent to about 73 percent. Among mothers of children under eighteen the rate nearly tripled, from 27 percent in 1955 to 72 percent in 2001.[4] Harvard economist Richard Freeman found that in 1998 alone, women moving into the workforce—and primarily into full-time jobs—not only increased the U.S. employment rate by 9 percent but also explained two-thirds of the difference between U.S. and OECD employment rates.[5] In Japan only 50 percent of the female population participates in the labor force and women account for only 30 percent of full-time workers.[6] Our ability to maximize women's potential in the labor market could be a key factor in maintaining a competitive edge in the future.

ALLOWING THE BEST TO RISE TO THE TOP

Imagine you're the coach of a high school basketball team and are told that every year 50 percent of the most talented freshman would never be allowed to try out for the varsity squad. This is how much of the American workplace is structured; mothers are often prevented from moving up to the varsity level after taking time off or reducing their hours to raise children. A survey by the National Parenting Association shows that 42 percent of female corporate executives age forty-one to fifty-five and 49 percent of women who earn more than $100,000 a year are childless, compared to 19 percent of the female population as a whole.[7] The *Wall Street Journal* recently highlighted the story of Catherine King who has an MBA from Stanford and impressive job history at Credit Suisse First Boston and Chase Manhattan Bank. After taking a number of years off to raise her kids, she was told by corporate recruiters that she had only a 15 percent chance of getting a job in her own field of finance and virtually no chance of moving into an executive position.[8]

The "mommy track" problem extends beyond those who aim at the executive suite. In middle-class families, women who never aspired to be a CEO still often find that when they return to work full-time, they are handicapped by ongoing barriers in the workforce. In fact, researchers have found that the wage gap between men and women is actually becoming more of a "mommy gap." While childless women with comparable educational and work experience make 90 percent of what their male counterparts do, mothers as a group earn only 73 percent of what men with the same education, experience, and occupation do. A first child lowers a mother's earnings by 7.5 percent, a second child lowers them by another 8 percent.[9]

Of course, for some working mothers—and working dads—such mommy-track jobs may provide a much-desired opportunity to do meaningful work without an all-consuming "fast track" schedule, what *New York Times* writer Lisa Belkin calls the "opt-out revolution."[10] Yet why should so many career paths—from law firm partnerships to the tenure track at academic universities—be structured so that the only way to get to the top is to commit to an all-consuming work schedule during one's late twenties and thirties that makes parenthood so difficult? If such career tracks offered greater flexibility for working parents to return to the workforce or choose a faster track at later ages, they would not only allow for more equal opportunity but also increase the talent pool competing for the varsity squad. As George Harvey, former CEO of Pitney Bowes, has said, "If I'm going to get the best talent, I've got to look at the entire population."[11]

FAMILY-UNFRIENDLY WORKFORCES AND
FEWER WORKERS FOR TOMORROW

At a recent conference for current and former high-level progressive policy makers in London, I was struck by the serious discussion concerning the low birthrate in Europe and the new innovations to encourage childbirth that pop up at the local level. In the Spanish town of Calzadilla, the mayor awards an Iberian pig—worth about $300—to every family upon the birth of a child. "I'd rather have free day care than a free pig, but every little bit helps," remarked one new mother as she accepted her swine.[12]

For most industrialized countries, maintaining a growing labor force with an aging population by making it easier for people to be both workers and parents is no joking matter. A survey of twenty-two industrialized countries has found that a 25 percent increase in direct support for parents can increase the birthrate by as much as 4 percent.[13] A Duke University survey suggests that public policies to support women's flexibility to earn income and maintain autonomy while working could actually increase fertility rates.[14] In Sweden, researchers found that both birthrates and women's labor force participation increased in the 1980s after the government increased parental benefits and child care assistance, "allowing working women to have an [additional] child."[15] When a recession in the early 1990s forced the government to cut back on these reforms, the birthrate declined markedly. In Japan, women cite cultural expectations and rigid workplace rules as reasons why they are delaying or avoiding marriage and children, leading to fears of *shoshika*—a land without children.[16] German researchers believe that a main reason for their country's low birthrate is the poor state of preschool and child care facilities. The head of German Chancellor Gerhard Schroeder's panel of economic advisors, Bert Rurup, notes that many young women there believe that it simply will not be possible to have both families and careers.[17]

This is not to say that encouraging childbirth should be an explicit aim of government policy. But it may be doubly foolish—neither pro-family nor pro-growth—to allow unnecessary workforce barriers to prevent families from having the number of children they want.

LOOKING FOR THE MOST PRO-GROWTH ALTERNATIVES

Many progressives have rightly looked to public policy to help ensure that all working parents can balance their work and family obligations. This is an area where it is particularly important for pro-growth progressives to design such policies to avoid negative unintended consequences.

Consider the issue of the "contingent" workforce. Many of the jobs most conducive to work-family balancing are part-time, but these are much less likely to include the health and pension benefits that come with less flexible, full-time jobs. Indeed, 31 percent of working women are employed in a "nonstandard arrangement," working part-time, as independent contractors, or from home,[18] and employers have no obligation to provide them with health care benefits. A similar dynamic occurs with pensions: although pension laws are gender-neutral, most benefit plans require five years of full-time work to earn full benefits, which puts women at a disadvantage because their median stay at a job is only 3.8 years, compared to 5.1 for men.[19] Women are also dominant in service-oriented jobs such as child care and secretarial work that are less likely to provide benefits.

Americans would never tolerate a law that gave women with children fewer benefits than other workers. So when progressives see the labor market moving in this direction, they rightly want to narrow these divides. One way to close these inequalities would be to federally mandate full benefits to workers in temporary or part-time jobs. But many businesses would find the costs so high that they would either shift to full-time workers, which would mean fewer part-time and temporary jobs for precisely the parents we are trying to help, or reduce the benefits for all workers, which would also move us in the wrong direction.

Certainly there are some cases where offering benefits to all employees can lead to a positive outcome. Starbucks offers full health benefits, pension, and paid family leave to every employee working twenty or more hours per week. Starbucks CEO Howard Schultz explained to me that these generous benefits have been a positive factor in the quality and retention of part-time employees that make up two-thirds of their workforce and have contributed to the company's astounding growth.[20] Yet if we required companies to offer part-time workers the health and pension benefits given to full-time workers, we have to accept that employers might offer fewer part-time jobs. A better pro-growth alternative would be to offer a Universal 401(k) with matching tax credits directly to all workers—

including part-timers—as a means of offering pension benefits without any negative consequences to part-time workers.

FINDING WORK–FAMILY WIN–WINS

1. Moving Forward on Family Leave

When President Clinton signed the Family and Medical Leave Act in 1993 (FMLA), he understood that the only way to achieve the progressive goal of allowing parents to take time off to be with a newborn or a sick relative was to restrict employers' flexibility and guarantee the right to unpaid family leave for all workers in firms with more than fifty employees. His belief that this limited intervention would not have the doomsday impact its business opponents predicted turned out to be correct.

In Department of Labor surveys in 1995 and 2000, 90 percent of companies reported that the FMLA had a positive or neutral effect on growth; 90 percent reported a positive or neutral effect on profitability; and 83 percent reported a positive or neutral effect on employee productivity.[21]

While the act does protect workers' ability to take time off for serious illness or to bond with newborns or adopted children, it does not ensure that parents can afford to take that leave. For a family struggling from paycheck to paycheck, the abstract right to take unpaid leave may not mean much. A 2001 survey of people who wanted to take family leave but had not done so found the reason was economic 77 percent of the time.[22] Many workers lack even the most basic protections like sick leave or the flexibility to attend a parent-teacher conference—76 percent of low-wage workers have no paid sick leave, and 41 percent have no paid leave of any kind, no sick days, and no vacation days.[23]

The key policy question now is how we can go further than the basic protections afforded by the FMLA in the most pro-growth way possible. The debate is often stalemated between work-family groups and business organizations, such as the Chamber of Commerce. Yet, there is a growing need to find policies that make it more financially tenable for working parents to care for newborns or very sick family members, while also recognizing the legitimate concerns of small businesses and entrepreneurs.

Business organizations should at least be willing to recognize that a significant body of evidence suggests that some form of financial assistance allowing working parents to care for newborn children is effective in promoting the pro-growth and progressive goal of fair starts.[24] Professor Chris Ruhm of the University of North Carolina looked at nine European countries that have increased paid leave over the past three decades. Ruhm found that a ten-week increase in paid leave is associated with a 5 percent to 7 percent decline in post-neonatal mortality and a 3 percent decrease in child mortality.[25] These findings should weigh particularly heavily on the United States, where the post-neonatal mortality rate is one of the highest of any industrial country and where the four leading causes of death among young children are SIDS, accidents, pneumonia/influenza, and homicide.

Second, paid maternity leave is hardly cutting edge: Otto von Bismarck implemented paid family leave in Germany in the 1880s, and the International Labor Organization (ILO) called for paid maternity leave at two-thirds of regular wages in the months following World War I. The average industrialized country offers fourteen to sixteen weeks of paid maternity leave, and even low-income countries such as Vietnam, India, and Indonesia offer comparable paid maternity leave—twelve to sixteen weeks.[26]

Third, a number of U.S. companies are already offering paid leave to their employees without adverse consequences. Deloitte & Touche, Amoco, and Aetna Life have actually documented considerable savings from offering more generous leave both in terms of increased retention and worker productivity. Furthermore, evidence shows that paid maternity leave may be good for overall growth by encouraging more women to work. In one study of the evolution of paid leave policies in Europe, paid leave for a mother with a newborn increased female employment by almost 10 percent.[27]

The power of these arguments suggests that we should look for ways to go beyond the guarantee of unpaid leave. Yet those of us who support greater work-family protections must be willing to recognize the importance of designing policies that take legitimate small business concerns seriously and avoid unintended consequences for the women and working parents these measures are designed to assist. While it is illegal for employers to directly discriminate by gender or pregnancy, MIT economist Jon Gruber has shown how a direct mandate on employers on behalf of working women can have the unintended consequence of financially burdening women. Gruber examined a number of states that passed laws in the 1970s requiring any employer offering health insurance to cover pregnancy as a form of illness (such laws have since been repealed). He found that rather than raising the cost of employees' health care or hiring fewer female employees, businesses covered the cost of the mandate by providing less generous wage increases to women of childbearing age, eventually resulting in a pay gap between them and the rest of the workforce.[28] In short, the cost of this new benefit was being financed by a de facto wage tax on women of childbearing age.

The intense divisions between business and work-family groups over sweeping expansion of family leave should not prevent us from taking commonsense steps now. First, we should be able to give workers at least twenty-four hours a year to attend doctor's appointments or school emergencies, like the proposal President Clinton made in 1996. Employers may fear misuse, but a twenty-four-hour limit per year would be a very small burden, and it is hard to argue that employers should have the right to fire someone for having a doctor's appointment or having to pick up a sick child at school. Second, we should flatly reject any efforts to backtrack on current protections for seriously ill workers who need regular treatments such as chemotherapy or dialysis. Further, business groups and work-family advocates should support the basic value that no one should be fired because they or their child has the flu or any other routine illness. Third, though business groups have vigorously opposed any extension of FMLA protections to smaller businesses, we should at least expand the number of firms covered by FMLA protections for childbirth or adoption. The lack of a gray area when dealing with pregnancy and adoption allows zero room for fraud or overuse, and pregnancy, by definition, gives employers plenty of time to prepare for a key worker's absence. As a nation we will need to do more to make it easier for Americans to be both workers and parents, but these three commonsense provisions would at least begin to bring work-family policies in line with our values.

A Newborn Leave Tax Credit

One pro-growth progressive proposal that could achieve the benefits of paid maternity leave while minimizing unintended negative consequences on growth or women's wages would be a Newborn Tax Credit. This proposal, which I first published in *Blueprint* magazine in February 2003 at the request of DLC President Bruce Reed, would offer families making less than $100,000 a $3,000 refundable tax credit every time a child is born. First, it would add no new mandate to employers, thereby minimizing any new costs or burdens on their flexibility; second, unlike the scenario above where women of childbearing age would end up shouldering the burden through lower wages, the cost of the Newborn Leave Credit would be shared equally by the population as determined by our system of progressive taxation; third, by providing resources directly to parents, it would give them maximum flexibility. New parents would receive $3,000 in untaxed income during their child's first year to use as they saw fit. If a parent chose to take ten weeks of leave, the credit would offset $300 a week in lost after-tax income; likewise a parent could choose to take off a month at $500 a week and go part-time at $200 a week for an additional five weeks. Some families might choose to have a grandparent stay for the first few months and use the credit to cover associated costs.

Going Farther on Paid Leave?

One potential criticism of the Newborn Leave Credit is that it covers only one component of the unpaid leave options protected by the FMLA. Shouldn't there be paid options for parents to take time off to care for a sick child or parent as well?

The answer may very well be yes, but we have to get the policy right. We need policies that are both bighearted enough to support parents who must cross the country in search of the best cancer treatments for their child, and hardheaded enough to recognize that policies that pay people not to work are always subject to abuse.

Perhaps the most important test will come from our largest laboratory of democracy. In July 2004, California started the first paid family leave program in the country. It expands the state's disability insurance system to allow 12 million of the state's 15 million workers to draw up to 55 percent of their average wage (though no more than $728 a week) for up to six weeks for family and medical leave, not just for newborn leave. The California legislature is funding this plan by charging all 12 million workers subject to the state's disability program an extra 50 cents a week—or $26 a year—in the employee's disability tax.[29]

California businesses argue the new program will be a "job killer" because it will encourage overuse and abuse—they contend the 55 percent wage supplement alongside savings on child care and transportation could make it economically attractive for parents to simply take time off to spend with their kids. Advocates rightly point out that—like the Newborn Tax Credit—the cost of the new law is spread across all employees, imposing no new financial burden on employers. They also point to a study conducted by economists Arin Dube of the University of Chicago and Ethan Kaplan of the University of California at Berkeley, which showed that California businesses could save $89 million due to increased retention while the state could save $25 million as fewer ex-employees go on food stamps or welfare.[30] While it is too early to draw definitive conclusions, the fact that, of the first 158,000 workers to receive assistance in the first eight months of the program, more than 89 percent took a leave in order to bond with a new child indicates that fears of overuse and abuse have so far not been realized.[31] The success or failure of the California program will be followed closely by both sides and may say a lot about the momentum and design for expansions of family and medical leave.

2. Universal After-School: Increasing Parents' Productivity

While after-school care is often promoted as an important education policy for keeping young people from delinquent behavior and improving academic standards, its pro-growth contribution to improving the productivity of working parents is far less acknowledged. After-school programs can give parents, especially in two-income families, peace of mind, help reduce absenteeism, and increase productivity, providing a true win-win for employers and families.

Consider the challenge that families face in the absence of after-school options. According to the National Institute on Out of School Time, kids spend only about 20 percent of their time in the classroom.[32] This means that the gap between parents' work schedules and children's school schedules can amount to at least twenty to twenty-five hours a week,[33] and the struggle to navigate weekly gaps, along with vacations and summers, often ends up outweighing the benefit of a second wage.[34] In a survey of 143 New York City public schools with comprehensive after-school programs, 94 percent of parents said the programs were convenient; 60 percent said they missed less work than before because of them; 59 percent said the programs supported them in keeping their job; and 54 percent said they allowed them to work longer hours.[35]

The Los Angeles Public School District's BEST (Better Educated Students for Tomorrow) provides homework assistance, library services, and other activities until 6:00 P.M. More than three-fourths of the parents surveyed claimed the program significantly lessened their fear about their children's after-school activities and gave them more energy in the evenings. More than half of the parents said that the program resulted in a "sizable savings" of their time.[36]

By virtue of the structure of our school day, U.S. schools already provide more support to parents than our European counterparts. Extending the school day through community-based after-school programs could help increase our competitive edge over other major industrialized countries. In many European countries, a combination of short school days and years, inconvenient vacation schedules, and limited after-school programs makes it difficult for women with school-age kids to work at all. In Germany and Luxembourg, kids are sent home for lunch every day. French schools are often closed on Wednesdays, while in Italy, Denmark, and the Netherlands, schools do not always supervise children during the lunch hour. This explains why, when economists measure the overall "cost" of having children across countries, parents in Germany and Italy have higher burdens than those in the United States.[37]

Moving Toward Universal After-School

Despite the strong pro-growth arguments, universal after-school is seen predominantly as a pet liberal cause. As recently as 1997, we had no organized federal effort to help fund after-school programs. In 1998, the Clinton administration established the 21st Century Community Learning Centers Program (CCLC) to award grants for schools to work with local organizations in their communities to establish centers where children could receive educational assistance, cultural enrichment, and other after-school activities. By 2001, we had increased the CCLC program and expanded federal spending to $1 billion a year. While the program successfully targets low-income communities and schools where the need is greatest, it covers only 7 percent of the nation's public schools.[38] In 2003, a committed constituency in Congress beat back the Bush administration's proposal to cut $400 million from the CCLC program.

To get serious, we need an affordable after-school option for every parent at every child's school or in their neighborhood. Every effort should be made to coordinate after-school programs with the existing public school system, but funding should also be available for nonprofits such as Big Brothers Big Sisters of America and the Urban League that have implemented innovative and successful after-school initiatives. The cost of a universal after-school program is estimated to be between $5 billion and $10 billion a year, but could be kept manageable by having parent contributions—on a sliding scale based on income—supplement federal funding. In one study, 74 percent of elementary and middle school parents were willing to pay for an after-school program, while fewer than half had kids in schools with such programs.[39]

3. Overcoming the Double Standard for Mothers: Universal Preschool

Another extremely emotional and complex challenge is minimizing the double standard in work expectations for middle-class and poor women. Conservatives seem to suggest that public policy should encourage middle-class women to stay at home and compel poor mothers to work. Rich Lowry, a conservative commentator and editor of the *National Review*, argued that 70 percent of parents would prefer to have one parent stay home: "It should be a goal of public policy to make it easier for these parents to act on their natural instincts." Yet at the same time he argued for the need to "reestablish tough work requirements" for welfare recipients, with no mention of the burden this would put on poor single mothers.[40] President Bush has advocated the same pernicious double standard: pushing an increase in the work participation requirement for welfare mothers from thirty to forty hours a week while speaking to the importance of allowing more women to be stay-at-home moms.

The challenging reality that progressives must face is that while we want to minimize this double standard, we have to recognize that work, especially when combined with the EITC, can help families raise themselves out of poverty more effectively than cash assistance.[41] And, as research shows, poverty, especially in early childhood, is linked to lower educational development and a higher likelihood of being poor as an adult.[42]

If we accept that poor women need to work to best care for their children while many middle-class women have the luxury of balancing how much they work and how much they stay at home, it should compel us not to exacerbate this double standard by raising work requirements without offering poor women additional support in caring for and educating young children.

Universal 0–5 year education is an example of a policy that could help support low-income families in a difficult work-family balance. Providing a safe, nurturing environment for children enables parents—particularly poor single mothers—to hold a job without having to worry that their absence is harming their children. An evaluation of Early Head Start, for example, found that parents with children enrolled in the program were significantly more likely to be employed or enrolled in education or job training programs than parents in a control group. In North Carolina's Smart Start Child Care Subsidy Program, parents' participation in the labor force added nearly $590 million to the state's economy.[43]

Other studies have shown that child care and early childhood education can minimize parents' absenteeism and improve concentration. For example, a 1990 study found that nearly one out of every six mothers employed outside the home had lost work time due to a failure in their regular child care arrangements.[44] In a 1999 survey of mothers on the waiting list for state child care assistance in Houston, 40 percent said they had missed work or worked fewer hours because of problems with child care.[45] In New York City's garment industry, which is made up of predominantly low-income workers, about one in four mothers reported missing a month or more of work a year because of child care problems. In some alarming cases, children have died because their mothers, pressured to work without child care, have resorted to leaving their kids in their cars.[46]

4. Creative Win-Wins in the Private Sector

Companies are finding that creative approaches to increasing family flexibility can be good for their bottom lines. The number of major employers providing programs to help employees balance work and family quadrupled during the 1990s; these programs reduce stress and improve motivation, making workers more productive. Employees who participated in DuPont's work-life programs, for example, were 45 percent more likely than their coworkers to say they were willing to "go the extra mile" to ensure the company's success. And by reducing employee turnover companies who help working parents also reduce their costs. A 2001 study of one hundred U.S. companies found that offering paid parental leave was associated with a 2.5 percent increase in profits.[47]

Moving beyond the traditional five-day, 9-to-5 workweek allows employees to work when they can be most productive. Johnson and Johnson reports that absenteeism is 50 percent lower among employees who use the company's flextime and family leave program.[48] Aetna has reported annual savings of over $1 million in recruiting costs after permitting formerly full-time employees to work part-time after taking family leave—cutting employee attrition in half. Today, more than half of major employers offer formal flextime programs.[49]

Many other companies offer on-site care or assist parents in making child care arrangements. SAS Institute, a North Carolina-based software company well known for its employee benefits program, runs a child care center staffed with one person for every three children. As a result SAS has a turnover rate of around 5 percent, compared to 25 percent for the rest of the industry, saving the company an estimated $75 million a year.[50]

8

Increasing the Labor Pool: A New Role for Colleges

The same demographic forces that are challenging Social Security and Medicare are producing what Harvard economist David Ellwood calls a "creeping crisis" in our labor market that could undermine our future productivity and growth. For decades, our economy has relied on a healthy increase in the working-age population. In the past two decades alone, the pool of workers age twenty-five to sixty-four grew 44 percent. But in the next two decades, we will see *zero* net increase in our pool of native-born workers; minorities and traditionally disadvantaged groups who usually have less education will make up a larger share of our workforce. Over the past two decades, the share of workers with at least a high school degree grew by 19 percent; over the next two decades it will grow by only 4 percent.[1] At the same time high-skilled technical jobs have grown five times faster than the population since 1980. Unless we expect massive new immigration or increased fertility rates, *we will need to increase the pool of highly skilled workers* or face a growing labor shortage.

The challenge is great because this period of declining labor market growth coincides with a dramatic increase in global competition in skilled labor and technological development. China and India together now graduate more than five times as many engineers as the United States,[2] and China alone awards twice the number of bachelor degrees each year.[3] Nine nations have a higher percentage of twenty-four-year-olds with some form of science degree,[4] and U.S. twelfth graders finished eighteenth out of twenty-one nations participating in the leading international assessment of math and science skills.[5] The United States, once so dominant in technological innovation, now trails five other countries in the percentage of GDP devoted to scientific research.[6]

Higher skills will be more essential even for what have previously been considered low-skilled jobs. As a recent *Wall Street Journal* series on the changing nature of blue-collar work explained, "Gone are the traditional assembly jobs that required little skill and less education, those tasks being automated or sent overseas to less-industrialized countries. Remaining in the U.S., as well as in most industrialized countries, are blue-collar jobs involved in making products with proprietary technology, or items that require frequent tweaks and updates. . . . Today's blue-collar workers are more involved in customized manufacturing, coming up with solutions to a particular customer's needs, rather than churning out standardized parts and commodities."[7] This trend, known as "upskilling," is responsible for 72 percent of the growth in jobs requiring postsecondary education.[8]

Today business organizations put out well-meaning statements about the need for school reform and accountability, but there is so much head nodding that we seem to have lost our ability to think boldly. In the Millennium Development Goals established by the United Nations in 2000, the world set ambitious goals for putting all children in school and cutting poverty in half. Yet here at home, we do not address priorities like getting all children a decent preschool experience, dramatically increasing the number of U.S. citizens with four years of college education, or expanding public investment in basic research. We need an Apollo equivalent on education and research: a rethinking of the entire pipeline from birth through college and beyond to ensure that more of our nation's workers are trained, motivated, and equipped to maintain a strong middle class in the dynamism economy.

REACHING OUT, REACHING DOWN: A NEW ROLE FOR COLLEGES

The current discussion on how to increase the number of minority and disadvantaged college students is dominated by a debate over whether affirmative action should guide admissions decisions *among the existing pool* of college-eligible twelfth graders. While reasonable race-based affirmative action on college admission is no doubt still necessary to ensure diversity and spread opportunity, we spend far too little time on the larger question: what can we do to increase the pool of college-ready students from minority or disadvantaged backgrounds? How can we reach disadvantaged kids at younger and younger ages to give them the motivation, hope, and tools to realize higher dreams and have access to higher education? While the recent policy focus on reforming and reducing the size of high schools is an important step, millions of children will not make it unless we reach them earlier. As Laura Rendon of California State University explains, "By the time students get to 12th grade, it is too late to improve college-eligibility . . . It could be said that students begin to drop out of college in grade school."[9]

If we want to increase the pool of disadvantaged students capable of completing a quality higher education, we have to reach them early in life. Personal experience and observation first motivated my own inquiry into how to reach economically disadvantaged children at an earlier age. In 1984, while I was at Yale Law School, I participated in a Street Law program and taught tenth graders at local New Haven public schools. My class may have been 90 percent poor and black, but I was struck by the quality of our discussions—first-rate debates on constitutional law issues; displays of critical thinking equal to classrooms in wealthy suburbs. Yet when it came to their writing assignments, incredibly bright tenth graders performed at a fifth- or sixth-grade level. I asked how many in my class had a family member or a close friend who had gone to college. Not one hand went up. After an awkward silence, a couple of boys proudly offered that their older brothers had gone into the military. No one in the entire class had a personal relationship with a college graduate.

From Yale, I moved on to Wharton Business School. In one of my weekly columns for *The Daily Pennsylvanian,* I wrote a piece on a *60 Minutes* story about a CEO named Eugene M. Lang, who in June 1981 delivered the graduation speech at P.S. 121, the East Harlem elementary school he had attended as a child. When Lang saw that the school was now filled with poor minority students who were unlikely to go to college, he made a spontaneous promise that he would give college scholarships for any of the sixty-one sixth graders who graduated from high school. He later offered them tutoring, weekend trips to colleges, and education about financial aid options.

When *60 Minutes* checked on the story years later, they found that where P.S. 121's projected high school graduation rate had been 25 percent, 62 percent of the kids from that sixth-grade class Lang spoke to had enrolled in college.[10] Though Lang's promise did not instantly lift all students out of their impoverished circumstances, it gave them something many of us take for granted: the expectation that they were supposed to go to college. When I grew up in a middle-class neighborhood in Ann Arbor, Michigan, my friends and neighbors were threatened by the same teenage behaviors that tempt most poor kids: reckless drug use, irresponsible sex, lawbreaking, skipping school. Yet in Ann Arbor and suburban communities all over America, we had a gift we were not aware of: the ingrained expectation that whatever trouble we got in, we were supposed to stay on track and not screw up our shot at going to college. That expectation often serves as a virtual magnet to pull kids back from the edge over and over again.

While I admired Lang's effort, I couldn't help thinking that colleges themselves could play precisely the same role, using their resources to provide young kids with the magnet of higher expectations. This notion crystallized for me when I read exchanges in the Wharton School's newspaper over whether Penn's recruitment of Hispanic students was too focused on a few select private schools in Puerto Rico. A school official replied that they were trying, but the pool of qualified Hispanic twelfth graders in the Philadelphia school system was so small they had to look elsewhere. More recently, two former college presidents, William Bowen of Princeton and Derek Bok of Harvard, in their book *The Shape of the River* have made a compelling case for the benefits of affirmative action for both colleges and society at large, yet come to similar conclusions: that the academic rigor of Ivy League and other top schools simply "makes it unrealistic to expect them to serve large numbers of students who come from truly impoverished backgrounds."[11] This sentiment summarizes everything that is wrong with how colleges approach diversity. Instead of accepting the lack of qualified twelfth graders from minority and disadvantaged backgrounds in their cities as a given, why don't the Penns, Harvards, Yales, and Columbias of the world take responsibility for reaching down to elementary and middle schools to help increase the pool of qualified, but disadvantaged, twelfth graders in their own backyards?

Investigating this question led me to my first ever policy proposal. In 1987, I outlined an Urban Excellence Corps, where colleges would adopt poor students in sixth grade and work study students would provide long-term mentoring, with the assurance that kids would receive college aid if they made it all the way through high school. I failed repeatedly to get anyone to take this proposal seriously, striking out in the 1988 Dukakis campaign, Governor Cuomo's office, the 1992 Clinton campaign, and even in Clinton's first term. But in 1997, when I became NEC director, the stars were aligned and everything broke my way. Domestic Policy Advisor Bruce Reed, his deputy Elena Kagan (now Dean of Harvard Law School), and Education Secretary Richard Riley were looking for ideas to increase minority college enrollment and encouraged me to push for this idea internally. When I first pitched it at a State of the Union meeting, President Clinton told me that he and Mrs. Clinton were longtime fans and friends of Eugene Lang and enthusiastic about the I Have a Dream Model. Bruce Reed and I had already recruited college presidents for the America Reads program, and I was able to get three hundred presidents along with sixty-six public- and private-sector organizations to support the concept. The Hispanic Congressional Caucus and its tireless education advocate, Representative Ruben Hinojosa, were particularly enthusiastic about working with us on this proposal.

Perhaps most important, Leslie Thornton, Secretary Riley's deputy chief of staff, introduced me to the inspired Philadelphia Congressman Chaka Fattah, who was sponsoring a proposal to give poor students certificates that told them how much education aid they would receive if they stayed in school and wanted to go to college. Fattah's legislation did not include the significant mentoring programs or structured college involvement of our broader proposal, but his philosophy seemed the same: change the expectations of poor children. Since Fattah already had one hundred cosponsors for his modest bill, I feared he might feel that putting aside his proposal to join our far more expansive legislation would cost the cosponsors he had worked so hard to line up. He was stunned that I would have doubted his response. "I'm a second-term congressman whose party is in the minority," he said. "The president wants to partner with me on a bigger proposal that he will put in the State of the Union, and you are worried I won't go along? Are you out of your mind?" Fattah became the chief congressional champion of the final bill.

On February 4, 1998, President Clinton announced this new initiative as the High Hopes for College program (later renamed Gaining Early Awareness and Readiness for Undergraduate Programs, or GEAR UP). In our initial effort to get the High Hopes/GEAR UP legislation through the Republican-controlled House Education Committee in 1998, our innovative White House higher education advisor Bob Shireman was not hopeful that a new Clinton initiative would attract Republican support despite Fattah's inspired effort. But after the committee's majority shot down amendment after amendment in the higher education bill, Representative Mark Souder, a conservative Republican from Indiana, said that Republicans had to support such a proposal if they were serious about reaching out to all Americans. It did not use race as a factor in determining eligibility, he argued, nor was it big government; it looked to local schools, colleges, and community groups to do the implementation. Souder voted for it, another Republican followed, then another, and the amendment passed out of committee by a vote of 24–18. Once it got through the House, my first call was to Senator Jim Jeffords—then a Republican and a longtime mentoring supporter—who struck a deal with us that led to the ultimate legislation. The program passed into law as part of the Higher Education Amendments of 1998. By our last year in the White House GEAR UP had grown to a $295-million initiative, providing mentoring, college visits, tutoring, and financial aid education to 1.3 million children.[12]

A MODEL PROGRAM

The GEAR UP model addresses the challenges that disadvantaged students face in staying on track for college. When we first floated the GEAR UP legislation to outside experts, Steven Zwerling of the Ford Foundation agreed that the evidence showed that reaching out to disadvantaged children at young ages and staying engaged with them through high school was the single most promising way to increase the pool of college-ready young people from disadvantaged backgrounds.[13]

GEAR UP starts early and stays with students all the way through school. This component is modeled on the successful I Have a Dream programs in sixty-three cities that grew out of Lang's initial commitment and on a nationwide program called Project GRAD, founded by Houston businessman and former Teneco CEO James Ketelsen. Ketelsen had become frustrated that a college scholarship he had funded was not having a substantial effect and designed his new program for K through 12 to support students at every stage of the process. In one school in Davis, Texas, a 25-point gap in math scores between the school's students and the rest of the state was closed within two years; the reading gap was narrowed by 30 percentage points.

To ensure that GEAR UP would not simply "skim off" the highest-performing kids—or those with the most motivated parents—Bob Shireman added the requirement that the program work with entire classes and grades, rather than individual students. This feature, often referred to as a "cohort" approach, has helped spur broader reform in many GEAR UP schools. When an entire class—or even an entire middle school—takes part in the program, parents and teachers tend to be more motivated to push for across-the-board improvements.

Indeed, polls have shown than more than two-thirds of parents have little information about what their children should be doing to prepare for college, but most want to know more. GEAR UP provides a catalyst and a means for them to get engaged. The director of a West Virginia GEAR UP program told me of an eighth-grade math teacher in Appalachia who bitterly complained that before the GEAR UP program, not a single parent had ever challenged her curriculum. But now, the teacher lamented, she had to put up with parents calling to ask her what she was teaching and how it would help prepare their kids for college.

In its first six years, GEAR UP has grown to almost three hundred partnerships between colleges and local schools, and thirty state grant programs. While it is too soon to present a comprehensive evaluation of the program's impact (the first students are just now graduating from high school) GEAR UP is substantially increasing student expectations and achievement and improving school environments. In the East Texas GEAR UP Project, the number of students taking algebra in eighth or ninth grade has jumped 20 percent. Performance on statewide math and reading exams has markedly improved in a number of participating schools, with one evaluation noting that GEAR UP was "seen as a force for academic improvement." A California GEAR UP Partnership between Palomar College and the San Marcos School System doubled the number of kids taking the PSAT test by tenth grade.[14]

While Congress has continued to fund GEAR UP, the Bush administration has repeatedly proposed to eliminate it even though both Florida under Governor Jeb Bush and Texas when George Bush was governor were top users of GEAR UP funding for successful programs. The last thing we should do is cut back early intervention initiatives for children from disadvantaged families. Currently, students from poor backgrounds are twenty-five times less likely to attend one of America's top colleges or universities than students from the richest quarter of American families. At the most selective private universities in 2003, more freshmen had fathers who were doctors than all those whose fathers were hourly workers, teachers, clergy, or members of the military.[15]

CALLING ON COLLEGES

Over the next twenty years, we should work for a new ethic of college involvement, including the expectation that our institutions of higher learning—particularly the strongest among them—should reach down into their communities to increase the pool of qualified students from disadvantaged backgrounds. One of the strongest innovations of the GEAR UP model is that it requires that each partnership include a college to commit to work with local schools and provide mentoring and guidance. Precedents for this approach included the University of Washington "Early Scholars Outreach Program," and Indiana's Twenty-First Century Scholars program, which linked top students from the University of Washington and University of Indiana with area middle schoolers and offered study skills workshops for both students and parents through the high school years. Participants had GPAs 30 percent higher than non-participants, and 97 percent of participants graduated from high school with 77 percent going on to college.[16] The Indiana program, started by Indiana Governor (now Senator) Evan Bayh, also promised full tuition to low- and moderate-income seventh and eighth graders who stayed crime- and drug-free, maintained at least a 2.0 grade point average, and applied to a state college during their senior year—helping the state climb from fortieth to seventeenth in the percentage of students attending college.[17]

We need to expand on this model. GEAR UP partnerships should be seen as a foundation for wider state initiatives and private initiatives by colleges themselves. While some might argue that this is not an appropriate role for colleges, we need to remember that colleges are fundamentally social institutions and there is no single answer for the role they are supposed to play. As a society we have decided over time that universities are where basic research should be conducted and where the best amateur athletic competition should take place. These are not laws of nature, but roles we believe colleges are uniquely positioned for. There is no reason why twenty years from now the definition of college in the United States could not include a commitment to help disadvantaged young kids in local communities aspire to go to college.

Some of the best schools in the country are located within or nearby some of the most acute urban poverty in America, but there are precious few connections between college and community. As the kids in my Street Law class reminded me, living down the street from Yale didn't guarantee that they would have any exposure to the college's benefits. On-site visits have been a fundamental element of GEAR UP's success, because they open a new sense of perspective and opportunity. Giving kids from disadvantaged backgrounds the chance to visit the campus and even stay over in the dorm, and see, touch, and feel the environment can be transforming. As one student put it, "For the first time, I could see the goal."[18] Even colleges in rural areas or separated by distance from disadvantaged communities find new opportunities are available in online tutoring and mentoring alongside occasional college visits and summer programs for kids and communities that need support.

Colleges can tap into the idealism of youth to give college students, many of whom are on work-study to afford college in the first place, a chance to act as tutors and mentors for disadvantaged kids—something they will likely benefit from as well. Currently, we spend more than $1 billion on the federal work-study program, and we require that schools spend 7 percent of this money on community service. As long as we ensure college students are adequately trained, it seems crazy to not spend far more on supporting mentoring and tutoring programs to help increase the pool.

For colleges to scale these efforts and play this new role, we will need a major expansion of GEAR UP and similar initiatives like Project GRAD and components of the TRIO program. With additional public support, we should not shy away from asking colleges themselves to lead this effort. One idea would be for a group of top universities, particularly in the Ivy League, to start a High Hopes Coalition that any state or private college could join. Each school would agree to institute new long-term early intervention programs in their communities and to give free tuition to participating students who are admitted to any participating college.

Finally, the GEAR UP model and expanded efforts at early intervention and outreach offer colleges common ground with supporters and opponents of race-based affirmative action. GEAR UP is a race-blind policy, but because it is geographically targeted toward poor areas, it inevitably helps a disproportionate share of African American and Hispanic students. While strong early intervention from colleges would not end the need for reasonable affirmative action, as Rep. Souder's support for GEAR UP demonstrated, it could offer a vehicle for those from differing political perspectives to join together and promote college opportunity and upward mobility for disadvantaged youth.

Addressing a Hidden Crisis: The College Completion Gap

Colleges and policy makers also need to face an enduring dirty secret of college opportunity in the United States: while we can be rightfully proud that the growth in college enrollment for blacks and Hispanics outpaced the national average in the 1990s,[19] *the number who actually graduate has continued to lag.*[20] Only about half—52 percent—of minority students entering college in 1995–1996 finished their bachelor's degree within six years. Of this group, only 38 percent of black students and 40 percent of Hispanics had received their BA over that period, and those who were the first in their family to attend college were only graduating at a 43 percent rate.[21] The graduation rate for high-income students is 60 percent higher than the rate for low-income students. America may have the highest college enrollment rate in the world, but its graduation rate is near the bottom of OECD countries.[22]

One important step in tackling this problem is to make higher education more affordable. In the 2004 Democratic primary campaign, Senator Kerry and others put forward several good ideas for consolidating and expanding the Hope Scholarship and establishing education tax cuts to ensure that low-income and middle-class students receive adequate financial support for all four years of college. Another strategy worth considering is a system of "income contingent" loans, where students are required to pay back only a certain share of their income—say 8 percent. Especially for low-income students—who have to borrow the most and whose family work histories give them the least confidence in future financial success—such loans would assure them that no matter what happened, their college expenses would not sink them financially. Income contingent loans might also encourage more students to choose careers in public service because they would be under less pressure to pay down their debt immediately. Although we created an "income-contingent" option on many student loans during the Clinton years, we were not able to make it as broad or as generous as we would have liked.

The problem of low college completion rates involves more than just money. A crucial factor is preparedness: many American high school students are not equipped with even the basic skills. As Bill Gates points out, two-thirds of American high school students, "most of them low-income and minority students, are tracked into courses that won't ever get them ready for college or prepare them for a family-wage job . . . This isn't an accident or a flaw in the system; it is the system."[23] The Bill and Melinda Gates

Foundation has invested more than $1 billion in Redefining the American High School to focus on college preparation through smaller, more rigorous and more technical high school education. Although the initiative is only in its second year, an evaluation of it conducted by the American Institutes for Research and SRI International showed that the program has had success improving students' attitudes towards school.[24]

Once students get to college, they face a social and emotional struggle to adapt to an unfamiliar culture.[25] Minority graduation rates are particularly low in institutions without strong histories of minority enrollment or in communities with few minorities. Colleges need to take more responsibility for lowering these barriers. One promising approach is intensive precollege "boot camp." In Georgia Tech's Challenge program, participants spend five weeks before freshman year living together, taking classes in science and math, and building leadership skills. The results have been outstanding. Retention rates and GPAs are above average for the university, and in the 2002–2003 school year Georgia Tech awarded more undergraduate and graduate engineering degrees to blacks than any other institution.[26] Another creative strategy to address the social dimensions of college is using residential situations to help foster peer support and smaller, less threatening learning communities within large universities. For example, Florida State University has created Living Learning communities in freshman residence halls. The smaller communities facilitate student interaction with some faculty members. Students can take classes in their residence hall and attend weekly meetings to help them utilize available services.[27]

Attrition is a particular problem at community colleges, where many students have children and 42 percent of first-year students do not stay on for a second year, compared to only 16 percent who leave after the first year at four-year institutions. Data presented by Cecilia Rouse and Tom Kane show that among community college students who say they are working toward at least a bachelor's degree, only a third had done so after ten years, compared to 72 percent of four-year students.[28] Strategies that could help include expanded tuition assistance, curriculum reforms to create bridges between remedial courses and credit courses (too many noncredit remedial courses can burn up both students' resources and their determination), nontraditional scheduling and classroom options such as distance learning, and greater access to support services, like on-campus child care, help accessing public assistance programs, and mentoring.[29]

College Completion Bonus Fund

We should design education assistance incentives based on college completion, not just college entry. The Clinton administration launched a College Completion Challenge Grants program, which offered assistance and targeted scholarships to schools that demonstrated success in helping retain students. We should extend this model into a College Completion Bonus Fund that would reward universities for increasing the number of low-income students that they graduate. The College Completion Bonus Fund would have two key elements. First, it would require colleges to report and share with parents and students annual data on the number of low-income, middle-income, and minority students both enrolling and graduating. Second, the financial incentives would focus on increasing the *number* of low income or Pell Grant students who graduate, rather than the *percentage*. If the fund focused on the percentage of students who graduate, it could give colleges an incentive to take fewer chances on low-income students. By rewarding increases in the number of students who graduate, it would encourage all colleges to invest in early intervention, educational assistance, and other programs to recruit low-income students and ensure they reach graduation.

9

Take Universal Preschool Seriously, Please

The progressive case for investing in education in the first five years of every child's life has always been compelling, but the pro-growth imperative of this investment gets stronger every day. For all the evidence, studies, and rhetorical support, if we measure our nation's commitment to fair starts by the resources we devote to it we're forced to say, to quote John McEnroe, "You *cannot* be serious."

We lament the poor performance of youngsters from economically disadvantaged backgrounds and know that children from upper-middle-class families have multiple advantages even in the first year, yet we allow hundreds of thousands of children to enter kindergarten without positive preschool opportunities. As Ron Haskins at Brookings and Cecilia Rouse at Princeton explain, "Although the achievement gap is normally seen as a problem affecting school-age children, in fact the gap first opens during the preschool years."[1] While recognition of the growing importance of preschool has sparked increased enrollment across the demographic spectrum, many poor kids who manage to see the inside of a classroom or care center before age five endure subpar facilities, untrained teachers, and large class sizes. We begin to see disparities as early as age three—children from well-off families have average vocabularies of 1,100 words, compared to 750 words for middle-income children, and 530 for low-income kids.[2] When they enter kindergarten, children from high-income families score 60 percent better on basic cognitive tests[3] and perform consistently better on evaluations of social and emotional development.[4]

THE TRADITIONAL ECONOMIC CASE FOR PRESCHOOL: HIGH RETURNS

The classic argument for investing in preschool is that investments made early in a child's life can pay educational and economic dividends down the road.[5]

The foundational study on the benefits of investing in preschool began forty-two years ago in Ypsilanti, Michigan. There, a group of researchers and educators began a remarkable experiment at the Perry Preschool. They split 123 poor African American kids into two groups. One was enrolled in a quality preschool program and the other was not. The study followed the two groups up through high school and recently published the findings through age forty. The results are striking. At age forty, 65 percent of the preschoolers had graduated from high school or received an equivalent degree, while only 45 percent of the non-preschoolers had progressed that far. The preschoolers had an average income of $20,800—just enough to keep a family of four above the poverty line of $18,000; non-preschoolers' average incomes were $5,000 less. Perhaps most dramatically, men in the preschool group were nearly twice as likely to be involved in raising their own children.[6] A similar experiment begun in 1972 at the Abecedarian Preschool in Chapel Hill, North Carolina, found that an intensive preschool program from infancy to age five was linked to higher IQ, higher math and reading scores, and a higher likelihood of college attendance. Even though Abecedarian is one of the more expensive early childhood programs, at $13,000 per child, researchers Leonard Masse and Steven Barnett found that the returns far outweighed the expense. The program boosted lifetime earnings of the enrolled children by $143,000 and boosted the lifetime earnings of their mothers by $133,000.[7]

In 2003 Rob Grunewald and Art Rolnick, two economists at the Federal Reserve Bank of Minneapolis, analyzed programs like Perry and Abecedarian and found that quality preschool has a social return as high as 16 percent a year. "Early childhood development programs are rarely portrayed as economic development initiatives, and we think that is a mistake. Such programs, if they appear at all, are at the bottom of the economic development list . . . They should be at the top."[8] The Business Roundtable has called for a dramatically larger government role in providing preschool, particularly for less-well-off families, because the return "ranges from $4 to $7 for every dollar spent."[9] The Committee for Economic Development, which has an Invest in Kids Working Group chaired by economist Rob Dugger, calculates that a $13,800 investment in Head Start returns $182,000 over a child's life, and aims to make early investment in children our nation's highest economic priority by 2015.[10] In 1996, the nation's law enforcement community started a group called Fight Crime: Invest in Kids to publicize how important they believed preschool was to reducing crime and delinquency. In a recent study in Chicago, kids who did not attend preschool programs were 70 percent more likely to be arrested for violent crime by age eighteen.[11] Indeed, Indiana once used the number of second graders reading below grade level as a factor in planning future prison construction.[12]

When states have examined the impact of quality preschool both on reducing crime and improving the workforce, they have found considerable budgetary savings. Massachusetts, for example, saved $2,705 per child on early intervention *after* factoring in the cost of the care, and Montana saved $2 for every dollar spent.[13]

But despite the evidence, when it comes to appropriations, early childhood education is no match for tax cuts and corporate subsidies. From 1993 to 2001, President Clinton more than doubled Head Start funding from $2.8 billion in 1993 to $6.2 billion in 2001 to make overdue quality improvements and expand enrollment. Yet funding has gone up less than 10 percent during Bush's entire first term. For fiscal year 2005, Congress increased the appropriated funds for Head Start by less than $70 million.[14] That same year, they passed a single $231-million tax break to support bonds for building four shopping malls.[15] President Bush's first budget of his second term calls for a spending freeze that will lower the number of kids in Head Start by twenty-five thousand. While the total costs of legislated increases in tax cuts and prescription drugs will, when fully implemented, cost over $500 billion each and every year, the typical Head Start increase in the last few years has been just one-tenth of one-tenth of a single percent of that increase.[16]

WHY THE CASE IS EVEN STRONGER IN THE DYNAMISM ECONOMY

Despite the lack of progress, the pro-growth case for universal preschool has only grown stronger in recent years as we have come to better understand that the cognitive skills needed to succeed in the dynamism economy are developed at the earliest ages. As the notion of a worker learning a single trade or specific set of skills and using them for an entire career has become an anachronism, the most basic cognitive, language, and social abilities that affect people's ability to write, speak clearly, work together, and make decisions have already become the currency of our twenty-first-century workforce. "A person's ability to understand, interpret, and productively utilize information is sine qua non in knowledge economies where technologies and skill requirements are apt to change rapidly," explains sociologist Gosta Esping-Anderson. "These [cognitive skills] are developed very early in a child's life—in large part *prior* to school age."[17]

Yale psychologist Edward Zigler, a preeminent expert on children's neuroscience, emphasizes how a child's ability to develop critical cognitive and noncognitive skills depends on stimulation from both parents and teachers and has permanent effects on a person's ability to reach his full potential as a worker. In 1997 Hillary Clinton sought to highlight dramatic new research on the importance of early brain development in a White House Conference on Early Childhood Development and Learning. The critical finding was that much of the basic hardwiring occurs soon after we are born, when our brains are extremely malleable. A baby is born with about 100 billion neurons, and in the first few years, a quadrillion neural connections are formed. The density of these connections reaches its peak at about two years old and levels off. After about age ten or eleven, the process becomes one of refinement, clearing away the clutter of neural connections that are needed the least.[18]

The neurological research is backed up by social science studies that showed that at-risk children who receive early education during the 0–3 period have better social, emotional, cognitive, and language outcomes at age three; they have higher IQ scores and better school performance than children who receive similar services programs in later years.[19] Other studies have shown that chronic exposure to stress- or fear-inducing situations can interfere with the development of the parts of the brain involved in complex thought.[20]

TAKING THIS SERIOUSLY

Currently, our most expansive effort to provide quality preschool to under-privileged kids is the federal Head Start program. Launched as a pilot in 1964 and standardized as an official program of the Department of Health, Education and Welfare in 1969, it provides grants to local school systems and nonprofit organizations to provide preschool services. Almost 80 percent of Head Start families have annual incomes of less than $15,000, and the average Head Start kid comes into the program with literacy skills that are a full standard deviation below the national average.[21]

In the past two decades, Head Start has battled constant misguided criticism about its efficacy. Critics highlight faulty research to suggest a "fade-out" effect where the IQ gains made in preschool years seem to disappear in later years of schooling.

Steven Barnett of the National Institute for Early Education Research is one of the academics who have found that many of these fade-out studies overemphasize IQ scores, ignore the consistent benefits like reducing grade repetition and improving high school graduation rates, and contain serious methodological errors that when corrected, show persistent improvements in test scores.[22] Nevertheless, the debate highlights a sad aspect of our national dialogue on preschool. Critics seem eager to use any evidence of less than complete success as a rationale for scrapping the entire program. As Cato researcher John Hood, who wrote one of the key studies on the fade-out problem in 1992, asserted, "instead of expanding Head Start, we should end it."[23]

We cannot afford this kind of defeatist bias. As Heather Weiss, director of the Harvard Family Research Project, explains: "We need to shift from a system of 'gotcha accountability' on Head Start to a system that embraces constant experimentation and learning for continuous improvement *and* accountability."[24] Three goals are paramount: extending access so that all children can benefit from a preschool education; improving quality beyond mediocre and overcrowded child care so that kids develop the cognitive capacities we now know are so critical; and expanding the effort to support children from infancy until they enter kindergarten.

FROM HEAD START TO A COMPREHENSIVE 0–5 INITIATIVE

As part of the Head Start expansion during the Clinton administration, we used the 1994 reauthorization to broaden the program with the creation of the Early Head Start program for children age 0 to 3. By 2003, Early Head Start was funding more than six hundred fifty programs providing sixty-two thousand families of infants and toddlers with a package of employment services for out-of-work moms, child care options for those who work, parental training classes, and home visits.[25] Now we need to transform Head Start and Early Head Start into a truly comprehensive 0–5 education and child care initiative that offers all children from modest and low-income families access to quality infant, toddler, and preschool programs.[26] Launching such an effort might cost between $20 billion and $30 billion annually, but that is only 25 percent of what recent tax cuts for the most affluent 1 percent of Americans will cost each year.

Ensuring quality care and services for children 0–3 will be the bulk of the expense. The most promising strategies involve giving states the leeway to experiment and scale successful programs. North Carolina's Smart Start partnership was launched in 1993 under the leadership of Governor Jim Hunt. By subsidizing education for child care providers and investing in better centers, this public-private partnership increased the number of children receiving high quality child care from 20 percent to 70 percent, and increased the proportion of teachers with college degrees or some college training from 41 percent to 83 percent.[27] A ten-year review of the program found that participating children were more likely to be immunized on time, had better math and language skills, and exhibited fewer behavioral problems when they began kindergarten.[28] Karen Ponder, president of the North Carolina Partnership for Children, which administers the Smart Start partnership, told me, "A four-year-old at risk was an infant at risk . . . We can't keep moving back our approach to early education by a year, and think that a pre-K program serving four-year-olds will address problems that have existed since the child was a toddler." Top early education expert Joan Lombardi points to Educare, which started in Chicago and has now expanded to four other cities, as another promising model for future expansion of comprehensive 0–5 education.

The controversy surrounding the possible fade-out effect should motivate us to develop students' cognitive skills throughout the education system. Schools that are under increasing pressure from politicians, parents, and advocacy groups to get results on high-stakes tests under the No Child Left Behind Act too often pursue rote learning and mind-numbing homework designed to teach to the test, not train critical, creative thinking. While we need standards and accountability, school reform must continue the benefits of Head Start by stressing problem solving and cognitive skills, and training teachers to assess how well children are learning within the classroom.

Finally, the public needs to pressure politicians to sponsor universal 0–5 programs. For a governor or a president the economic benefits of investment in preschool education are experienced only in the future—during the terms of their successor's successors. The contribution to a more competitive workforce may come two decades after early childhood investments, but the benefits of realizing the core American value of fair starts —where one's opportunities are not predetermined by the accident of birth—are furthered whenever we make bold progress toward a quality 0–5 education for all our children—especially the poorest born.

10

Seeing At-Risk Minority Males as Future Fathers and Workers

A disadvantaged toddler may be underserved in the United States today, but he can at least take comfort in knowing that politicians consider him "sympathetic" or "deserving" of support. Yet if that same child grows up in a single parent–headed household in a drug-ridden neighborhood, goes to inferior schools, falls so far behind that he is not reading by third grade, and in his teen years, starts to engage in destructive behavior, he is transformed into a negative stereotype and even vilified as the problematic young minority male that politicians prefer to ignore. Make no mistake: anyone who engages in violent and destructive behavior must be held accountable. Poor Americans would be the first to say that poverty does not give anyone an exemption from personal responsibility. Yet we must also ask what our collective responsibility is for doing so little during the years when the sympathetic poor preschooler becomes the unsympathetic minority male teen. And what is our responsibility to young men who have gone off track, joined a gang, or been to jail who now need to find the right path?

We cannot afford to give up on these young Hispanic and African American men. I once lobbied for a new initiative for work assistance to disadvantaged out-of-school youth and was told by a member of Congress that as sad as it was, we should focus our energies on the preschoolers because it was too late to reach youth who had already been through the criminal justice system. My mother, who cofounded The Family Learning Institute for children who were not reading by third grade, has even seen resistance to strategies aimed at minority kids in the later grades of *elemen-*

tary school. The young minority males from poor neighborhoods who are strong enough to reject gangs and drugs still face inferior schools, an unemployment rate as high as 36 percent, negative stereotypes perpetuated by the media, and discrimination in the labor market. In one study, testers provided with similar résumés applied in person for the same entry-level jobs, and only 14 percent of blacks reporting no criminal records received callbacks while 34 percent of whites did.[1] The local TV news is four times as likely to show a mug shot of a defendant if he is black than if he is white and twice as likely to show a black defendant being physically restrained.[2] As Marc Morial, president of the National Urban League, explains, media portrayal of young black males can lead to internalized stereotypes. "Too many of our young black males believe that manhood is defined by the ability to injure or damage another man rather than helping another man."[3]

WE CANNOT GIVE UP

Beyond the progressive and moral case, there is a pro-growth rationale for not giving up on at-risk minority males. Consider the following: in contrast to the rising labor force participation of low-income black women, especially single mothers, the participation of young low-skilled black men fell from 59.3 percent in 1989 to 52 percent in 1999.[4] At the same time, the decline of the manufacturing sector has eliminated many of the stable and good-paying jobs for low-skilled workers. The typical full-time wages earned by black men are more than 20 percent less than white men. Almost one out of four black men between eighteen and twenty-four live in poverty.[5] Most alarmingly, incarceration statistics suggest that one in three black males will spend time in prison during their lifetime. Ten percent of black men aged twenty-five to twenty-nine were in prison at the end of 2001.[6]

These are some of the most depressing statistics in American social and economic life. Still, we offer these young men pathetically little help. Politicians may not want to spend public capital or their own political capital on initiatives that reach young people who have chosen gangs or crime over school and jobs, but we pay high costs for writing off these young men: court and prison costs, forgone child support, and most important, the incalculable loss of untapped potential.

FUTURE FATHERS: A VITAL CONTRIBUTION TO MAKE

If we want single minority males to contribute to the workforce and our economic future, we need to stop considering them outside the family structure and realize that they are current and future fathers. Helping them secure jobs also ensures that they are able to support their children, whether they are living with their families or not.

Far too little has been done to create policies that link responsible fatherhood and economic opportunity.[7] Even the most positive working poor initiatives, like the expanded Earned Income Tax Credit and child care assistance, are aimed at poor women with children. Only 6 percent of poor nonresidential fathers received job training or job search assistance in 1999, compared to 20 percent of poor mothers.[8] The expansion of the EITC helped low-income single mothers make considerable progress in employment and earnings in the 1990s, yet young minority males continued to drop out of the labor force. The EITC for single workers introduced in 1993 is quite small—less than $400—and phases out before these workers have even made enough to rise above the poverty line. As antipoverty expert Bob Greenstein points out, this makes these single workers the only group in the United States that are taxed further into poverty. If we increased the EITC for single workers so that they received a 15.3 percent wage subsidy until they were above the poverty line, we would give hundreds of thousands of young men a greater incentive to seek a living wage in legitimate private-sector jobs.

Another crucial move toward rewarding, not punishing, those who work to support their children is to change our child support system. As it stands now, about two-thirds of nonresident fathers fail to pay child support.[9] As Jonathan Peterson of the *Los Angeles Times* has explained, "[Noncustodial fathers] are not just invisible in national policy. They are villains in popular culture, scorned as deadbeat dads."[10] While we should have little sympathy for the deadbeats who have financial resources but refuse to support their children, the fact is 75 percent of unwed fathers are involved and give some financial support during pregnancy. Interviews with fathers suggest that their lack of income is a major cause for declining involvement in later years.[11] There is an important distinction between "deadbeat" and "dead broke." Because child support lifts an estimated 500,000 children out of poverty each year, we need to ensure that our policies give poor dads every opportunity to do right by their families.[12]

One success of the 1996 welfare reform bill was that it created a much stronger enforcement mechanism for child support that tracks fathers through their work. However, under this system the combination of taxes and child support arrearages can mean that some working fathers have their paychecks reduced by more than 60 percent. Economist Harry Holzer and others have shown that this policy can actually discourage these men from work.[13] We could address this negative incentive by offering an EITC-type match on child support payments as Wendell Primus has suggested, or by forgiving arrearages for those who are making an effort to pay.[14] We should also give fathers every financial incentive to pay their obligations to their children by ensuring that some or all of each payment directly benefits his child—instead of reimbursing the state for welfare payments it would make to the child anyway.

A well-funded initiative for linking economic opportunity and responsible fatherhood has still not passed Congress despite a Clinton-Gore Fathers Work/Fathers Win proposal, and despite the call from many experts, including Bruce Reed and Jason DeParle, to make this the next phase of welfare reform. Yet promising models exist that could be expanded. For example, a Fatherhood Program in Georgia works with noncustodial parents who are unable to pay child support, offering them vocational training, job placement, and counseling as well as a chance to earn a GED. A program evaluation found that participants were employed faster and more often than nonparticipants, and that their children experienced statistically significant increases in health care coverage compared to children of nonparticipants.[15] A seven-city demonstration project started in 1994 called Parents Fair Share that combines job placement with parenting skills has shown some significant results, particularly for those fathers who were least employable and least involved with their children when joining the program.[16]

Beyond employment strategies, we need strong parenting programs because, while economic support is critical, it will never replace an absent father. "Beyond the statistics is the pain of real children," reads a statement from the Morehouse Conference on African American fathers. "Boys and girls, young men and young women, who bear, and often pass on to their own children, the pains of father hunger. There are the boys and young men who, without the protection and guidance of fathers, struggle each day to figure out what it means to be a man, improvising for themselves expedient, and too often violent and self-destructive, codes of manhood."[17] Because the challenges of engaging fathers in their kids' lives are multifaceted, successful programs often combine comprehensive services. In 1993, a reformed heroin addict named Joe Jones created the Men's Services Program in the slums of Baltimore to provide prenatal training to future fathers in an effort to prevent infant mortality and low-birth-weight babies. Jones soon provided a full range of services to help fathers become more active and engaged parents as well: peer support groups and counseling, parenting classes, and educational and job training assistance. Testifying before the Senate Finance Committee in 2001, Freddie Belton, a father of five and a recent graduate of Jones's program explained, "Before Men's Services I used drugs, was involved in crime, and wasn't on track to being the best father. But, with the help of Joe Jones and the program, I was able to beat the odds . . . if programs like Men's Services aren't around to help, a lot of kids will grow up without fathers and end up in the same situation. I know. I grew up without my father." [18]

FUTURE WORKERS: IT'S NOT TOO LATE

Despite the overwhelming numbers of young black males in the criminal justice system, we can turn millions of lives around if we are willing to make the investment. Without viable youth employment initiatives, the barriers to convincing young black men to reject gangs and drugs become even higher. In the HBO documentary *Back in the Hood: Gang War 2* a former gang leader, Leifel Jackson, tells how recruiting young men into gangs was made easier by cutbacks in funding for economic opportunities: "When money is took out of the communities for intervention and prevention programs, the kids are right back where I used to want them, on the corners doing nothing, then you're going to see a surge in killings because of the drugs." [19]

The two most successful models for putting more resources into positive economic options for disadvantaged minority males are so-called saturation strategies that build a mass of peer support within communities and the "new environment" model that gives young people a chance to learn and prosper in a fully supportive atmosphere.

Saturation—A Critical Mass of Peer Support

Saturation strategies recognize that young people trying to get on the right track alone can face enormous social pressure—even ostracism—for their choices. They need a "critical mass" of peer support through job training or educational opportunities. In 1994 Bob Rubin asked me to organize a small group of policy discussions on how to do more for young black males. Lawrence Katz, chief economist at the Labor Department, pointed out that training money was often too spread out to give youth enough peer support to reject gang membership for more positive job or educational opportunities. Our Youth Employment and Skills (YES) proposal suggested concentrating employment and training opportunities to serve entire neighborhoods.

The YES program almost passed in 1994, but the midterm change in Congress doomed the effort for several years. In 1998 we created Youth Opportunity Grants, a descendant of YES, as part of the Workforce Investment Act. Youth Opportunity Grants provide job training, education, and career counseling services to all youth ages fourteen to twenty-one in particular high-poverty areas, combining federal, state, and local resources with private-sector involvement. In 2001 we provided $275 million to serve sixty-three thousand disadvantaged youth. The community-based saturation model needs further experimentation and expansion, but in another terrible example of misguided priorities, the Bush administration eliminated the Youth Opportunity Grant program in 2004. A promising private-sector model that employs the saturation model is the Career Academy approach, which has been championed by former Citigroup CEO Sandy Weill. These academies provide career-focused internships, mentoring, and vocational training through intensive and supportive programs for 150 to 200 students within larger high schools. According to one evaluation, it boosted participants' average earnings more than $10,000 over the four years following expected high school graduation compared to nonparticipants.[20]

The New Environment Model

A second approach is to give young people a chance to gain skills, confidence, and independence in a fresh environment. A prime example is Job Corps, where young men and women leave their neighborhoods and live at residential Job Corps Centers across the country. Earnings among Job Corps graduates are about $1,150 higher than a control group, and the most recent study found that these gains were sustained more than two years after participants left the program. The program also results in a 15 percent increase in GED certification among non–high school graduates and a 22 percent increase in vocational degree receipts. Further, participants are less likely to be arrested for or convicted of a crime, or be the victims of crime.[21]

Other residential programs use intensive quasi-military practices. The National Guard's Youth ChalleNGe program targets at-risk high school dropouts between sixteen and eighteen and combines academics and community service with physical training. After they complete the five-month residential component, students are matched with a mentor for the following year. Twelve months after finishing the program 83 percent of its graduates are either working, in school, or in the military.[22]

Intense approaches like these are expensive. Job Corps costs about $14,000 per student per year. But a recent controlled study found that when one factors in the compounding benefit to society of increased earnings and education, as well as reduced crime, the program produces a net societal gain of $17,000 per participant—or a return of more than $2 on every $1 dollar spent. The study concluded that despite the upfront expense, "it will be difficult to find a less intensive alternative to Job Corps which has substantial positive effects."[23]

FUTURE CRIMINALS? WE CANNOT AFFORD TO GIVE UP

The most difficult population to reach is the one in our prison system. Six hundred thousand ex-offenders are released from prison each year. Economist Richard Freeman estimates the overall cost to society from crime at 4 percent of GDP a year, so programs that prevent both first-time and repeat offenses would have substantial benefits.[24]

The paradox is that job opportunities are dramatically reduced for anyone who has served jail time, but the best way to reduce recidivism is to ensure opportunities for post-release employment. No matter how tough it may seem to reach ex-offenders, and whether or not we see them as deserving, we need to recognize the importance of having them reenter society as productive working citizens. Chicago's Safer Foundation provides transitional support to released offenders, starting before release and continuing for a year after placement. Support includes literacy training, job readiness assistance, job placement assistance, and support to both employers and employees. In 1996, of eighty-four participants in the foundation's basic education course for sixteen- to twenty-one-year-olds, seventy-two completed the course, and of those who did, more than two-thirds were placed in education or jobs; after 180 days, only one had been convicted of a new crime.[25]

Gang intervention programs offer another promising means of addressing the factors that push young people to crime. Benny Hernandez, whom President Clinton invited to the signing of the Workforce Investment Act in 1998, was a gang member by age ten. Jailed by fifteen, he enrolled in prisoner education programs provided by the Texas Youth Commission and earned a GED. Upon his release from prison, he attended the University of Houston-Downtown and now plans on going to law school.[26] Intervention programs for gang members like Benny are already up and running in many communities. A well-regarded example is Silicon Valley's Mexican American Community Services Agency, which provides gang intervention programs such as Street Reach, that focuses on education, employment, counseling, and family services. The LA Bridges program has gone one step further, providing preventative programs such as education, job skills, and parenting classes alongside more controversial interventions in instances of gang-related violence. Crisis units diffuse tension, forge peace deals between warring gangs in southern Los Angeles, and build relationships with gang members that can reduce acts of killing and help facilitate the transition of young kids from gangs into education and job-training programs. An independent evaluation by Vital Research reports that it has reduced school suspensions, alcohol abuse, and arrests by more than two-thirds for participating kids, and association with gang peers by 48 percent.[27]

President Clinton noted the compelling public safety rationale for proactive support of ex-offenders as they return to their neighborhoods and families. In his last budget, we included proposals to establish "reentry partnerships" with community groups, "reentry courts" to help ex-offenders navigate their return to the community, and grants to support young offenders in particular. These proposals have languished under Bush, but in 2004 a bipartisan group in the House brought the issue forward by proposing a bill to offer comprehensive support of ex-offenders including housing, employment services, mental health, and counseling. Democratic representatives Stephanie Tubbs Jones and Danny Davis worked with Republicans Mark Souder and Rob Portman to introduce the Second Chance Act of 2004, for which President Bush voiced support in his 2004 State of the Union. Although political support from the Republican leadership has been disappointing, the bill's sponsors and at least President Bush's support show some bipartisan recognition that those leaving prison cannot be forgotten.

11

New Technologies: Tapping the Potential of People with Disabilities

In 1994, writer and Bank of America executive Joe Martin was diagnosed with amyotrophic lateral sclerosis, or Lou Gehrig's disease, after completing only the first chapter of his first book, *Fire in the Rock*. Eventually, the disease left him completely paralyzed. But with the help of a sophisticated new device called the Eyegaze, Martin learned to type using only the movement of his eyes, kept his job at the bank, finished his manuscript, and went on to write another book, *On Any Given Day*.[1] "My mother was able to make the whole world do whatever she wanted with a look," Martin explains. "As far as I know, this is the same system."[2]

Later, I tried the Eyegaze for myself at the Disability Network in Flint, Michigan, during a stop on President Clinton's "digital divide" tour. It was tricky at first. To write my name, I struggled to shift my gaze from the "G" to the "E" on the keyboard without hitting keys in between.

As President Clinton took his shot at maneuvering the Eyegaze, Nancy Cleveland of LC Technologies, which manufactures the device, explained that a single machine cost $15,000. Computer-assisted prosthetics now offer soldiers who have lost limbs new mobility but they cost up to $80,000.[3] Matthew Nagle, a twenty-five-year-old former high school football star, became completely paralyzed when he was stabbed in the neck in 2001. Now surgically implanted sensors can read his thoughts and allow him to move a robotic arm well enough to play a computer game or change the channel on his TV. This experimental technology costs about $50,000.[4]

These wondrous but costly inventions show how beyond the traditional divide between individuals with disabilities and the rest of society, we risk a growing disparity between people with disabilities who can and cannot afford such technologies.

The lack of any serious federal initiative to ensure that people with disabilities can access the high-tech discoveries that can help them become working, contributing members of society undermines the basic progressive notion of economic dignity. As former Congressman Tony Coelho, who has epilepsy, has said, for people with disabilities "work means much more than financial stability . . . It is a source of identity and social acceptance . . . Without work we are doomed to fail."[5] Failing to make these cutting-edge technologies widely available makes little economic sense when we desperately need to increase our labor force. Of the 19.9 million working-age people with disabilities in 2003, only 37.8 percent were employed, compared to 77.5 percent of those without disabilities. Not surprisingly, their poverty rate is more than twice the national average.[6]

Empowering these individuals will become more important as our workforce ages. According to Gregg Vanderheiden of the Trace Center at the University of Wisconsin, the share of people between the ages of fifty-five and sixty-four with functional limitations is more than five times that of the group between twenty-five and thirty-four.[7]

Ensuring that all significantly disabled Americans have access to rehabilitative technologies is a cost we as a nation can justify on both moral and economic grounds. Since these technologies facilitate employment, providing them fits a pro-growth progressive test: they are direct assistance that rewards work and gives Americans with serious disabilities the capacity to take personal responsibility for their financial independence. If we cannot agree on how to fully fund these initiatives, we should at least have an income-contingent, low-interest loan program that links repayment for assistive technologies to 5 percent to 10 percent of a disabled person's income a year. Even if this program had costs due to loan subsidies and even if some workers never have enough income to fully repay their loans, the tax revenues that would result from having these disabled Americans in the workforce could over time cover these expenses.[8]

BRIDGING THE INTERNET DIVIDE

The Internet has opened doors for many disabled people, but it is not straightforwardly or intrinsically accessible to people with visual, muscular, or mobile impairments. People with disabilities access the Internet at half the rate of those without disabilities and sixty percent report never having used a computer.[9] In a 2002 survey by the Pew Research Center, more than one in four disabled respondents said their disability impaired or made use of the Internet impossible.[10] If the technology sector, however, can be encouraged to incorporate accessibility goals into the earliest stages of their planning and development, accessible IT technologies could become the twenty-first-century equivalent of a wheelchair ramp, fundamental for equal access to work and education for people with disabilities. In 2000, Tom Kalil, Clinton's lead technology advisor, and I called top government scientists and technologists to the White House to search for ideas for broadening Internet accessibility for those with disabilities. One of the strongest conclusions was that if private firms made technologies like screen readers for the vision-impaired a clear goal, they could be integrated at the early stages of product development, when it would be less expensive. IBM has helped Sprint PCS improve its Web accessibility for the deaf and hard of hearing. IBM's former director of accessibility solutions, Cindy Drummond, explained: "We're finding . . . different motivators. Companies aren't required by law, but this is a great way to market and to appeal to the community."[11]

This is an area where the government can lead by example. In 1998, Congress approved an amendment to the Rehabilitation Act—known as Section 508—which requires all federal agencies to make their Web sites and information technology resources accessible to people with disabilities. Section 508 has encouraged a number of states to adopt similar standards, so much of the public effort to bridge the digital divide is being done with an eye on accessibility.

REWARDING WORK FOR ADULTS WITH DISABILITIES

Many of our support programs were designed a half-century ago, when people with disabilities were assumed to be fundamentally incapable of independence—and certainly not expected to work. Our policies continue to reflect such a "caretaker" view and as a result, impose substantial barriers and disincentives to work.

In the 1990s we made great strides addressing work disincentives in other areas, with policies like the Earned Income Tax Credit and efforts to increase the availability of child care for moderate-income families. But since the passage of the Americans with Disabilities Act (ADA) in 1990, our policies toward adults with disabilities have not caught up with this trend.

A key example is the substantial gainful activity threshold used to determine eligibility for the two major cash benefit programs for people with disabilities—Social Security's Disability Insurance (SSDI) and Supplemental Security Income (SSI). If you can earn even a meager income ($830 a month, or about $10,000 a year in 2005), these programs assume you must not be disabled and they therefore deny you benefits. Consequently, many people who are able to work have a disincentive to do so. Even more important, many people with disabilities face losing their Medicare and Medicaid coverage if they're employed because eligibility for these programs is tied to eligibility for SSDI and SSI respectively. In a bitter irony, Medicaid is one of the best and most comprehensive providers of the assistive technologies that would facilitate a disabled person's return to the workplace, but having a job can make the person ineligible for coverage!

In recent years, many politicians have been willing to admit that policies that, as economists David Stapleton and Richard Burkhauser explain, "will help you as long as you don't help yourself" [12] are absurdly counterproductive. One of the primary reforms came in 1998 with the Ticket to Work and Work Incentives Improvement Act, sponsored by Senators Kennedy, Jeffords, Moynihan, and Roth, and signed by President Clinton. This law makes it much easier for recipients of disability benefits to work in three major ways. First, it ensures they can continue receiving Medicare benefits for more than eight years while working. Second, it makes it much easier for recipients who lose their benefits because they start working to collect Social Security and SSI disability benefits if they become eligible again. Third, it created a Ticket to Work program that provides employment services to people with disabilities.

The act also expanded what is known as a Medicaid "buy-in" program (that was created in the 1997 balanced budget agreement), which allows individuals with disabilities who are working and have moderate incomes to buy discounted Medicaid coverage so that working does not deny them access to critically important assistive technologies. States were left to implement the buy-in program, yet so far nineteen states have not done so, and many offer less generous options than the rules allow.[13]

With states responding to fiscal strains by cutting back on Medicaid buy-in opportunities, additional federal support could help them retain, expand, or adopt buy-in programs. For millions of people with disabilities this would mean the difference between being able to choose *both* work and life-changing technologies or being forced to choose between the two.

Truly addressing this problem means more than just mitigating disincentives to work. It means actually rewarding those disabled people who choose to work. One possibility would be to model a new Disabled Worker Tax Credit (DWTC) on our nation's most successful rewarding work policy—the EITC.[14] Building on the EITC's benefit structure, a DWTC could offer lower-income disabled workers a more generous refundable credit, which would not only give this marginalized group a new incentive to enter the workforce, but also help compensate for additional costs like assistive technologies. For those who took out income-contingent loans to pay for work tools, this tax credit could also help them meet those costs.

12

Tomorrow's Innovators and Tomorrow's Innovation

As the dynamism economy fuels increasingly efficient global production, the U.S. economy will always want to specialize in whatever is at the cutting edge. The pressure to stay ahead of the curve has never been greater. As Benjamin Wallace-Wells, editor of *The Washington Monthly*, points out, "Fall five years behind on building car factories in the early twentieth century and you lost some profits; fall five years behind on hybrid cars and you may have lost an industry."[1] To avoid missing out on the riches of emerging industries, our workers and businesses have to relentlessly push the envelope of research and innovation.

My sister Anne, a professor of immunology at the University of Chicago, once took a napkin and drew for me rows of dots in a vertical pattern. In the last row she circled a single dot, and wrote "huge breakthrough." The first row she labeled "basic research": discoveries there might lead to an unpredictable dot in the next row. Combined with other unpredictable connections in later rows, the discovery might eventually lead a scientist to a cure for a major disease or the next information technology blockbuster. Her point was that no one knows how to connect all the dots in advance. While our system of patent protection offers private companies an incentive to do the research on the last row of dots—providing nineteen years of protection from competition on commercial research breakthroughs like Viagra or Lipitor—there is no way to give that same incentive for basic research done in the first row. Yet every great commercial breakthrough is achieved, in Sir Isaac Newton's famous phrase, "by standing upon the shoulders of giants." If the government does not invest in basic research, and the private sector sees it as too risky or damaging to their short-term bottom lines, we will have less innovation and discovery.

But, in fact, pure "curiosity-driven" research, pursued without any practical application in mind, has delivered some of our most important economic and social innovations. In 1831, when Michael Faraday was investigating the link between electricity and magnetism—which the ancient Greeks discovered when they rubbed amber against fur—he found that he could generate a sizable electric current by moving a magnet inside a coiled copper wire. Faraday's revolutionary discovery became the central component of an electric generator. It wasn't used commercially for another fifty years, but the lightbulb, the telephone, and the food processor wouldn't have been possible without it.

THE POLITICS OF UNDERINVESTMENT IN BASIC RESEARCH

The Politics of Instant Results

Just as private investors want to capture profits derived from the research they underwrite, politicians want to capture political credit for funding research that can be traced to major breakthroughs. Congress guides research by establishing priorities and rightly directing a portion of funding toward important goals like cures for breast cancer, AIDS, or diabetes. But this process creates a danger that Congress or even government agencies will make funding decisions based on immediate promise rather than long-term potential. In the field of immunology, for instance, it makes sense to focus federal research funding on responses to known threats such as anthrax and smallpox, but such funding should not come at the expense of basic immunology research that might ultimately help us respond to unforeseen bioterror threats in the future.

The negative repercussions of this demand for immediate results are being felt throughout the scientific community. Promising young scientists end up chasing funding for the "disease of the day," while governmental agencies too often shun riskier research to avoid the failure that is part-and-parcel of scientific innovation. Scientists joke that "you have to do the experiment before you can write the proposal." Private-sector research is a powerful driver of applied innovation, but only the government can fund pure research without financial concern for its immediate applicability.

And over the long term, it is the discoveries from this work that will drive technological innovation and productivity growth.[2]

The classic example of government research with broad, unforeseeable application is the Defense Advanced Research Projects Agency, or DARPA. Created in 1957 in the wake of *Sputnik,* for over four decades DARPA's steady commitment to fundamental "blue sky" research has led to a series of huge breakthroughs. In the 1960s, for example, AT&T told the agency that "packet-switched networks" would never work, but DARPA continued developing this technology, which eventually formed the basis of the Internet.[3] The agency has had a tremendous impact on the U.S. economy, funding research that has led to the personal computer, computer graphics, optical networks, and speech-recognition software. DARPA supported the founders of Google while they designed their groundbreaking algorithm.[4] Indeed, the agency is credited with helping start at least nineteen technologies that have grown into billion-dollar industries.[5]

In recent years, there has been a major shift in DARPA's research strategy toward short-term projects with specific "deliverables." In April 2005, John Markoff of the *New York Times* reported widespread criticism from the research community of DARPA's new "focus on short-term projects while cutting support for basic research," noting that "the shift away from basic research is alarming many computer scientists and electrical engineers, who warn there will be long-term consequences for the nation's economy."[6] Even a report by the president's own Information Technology Advisory Committee has called the changes a "crisis in prioritization."[7] Indeed, funding going to universities for computer science research was nearly cut in half from 2001 to 2004. Berkeley professor David Patterson warns that due to these DARPA cuts, "There will be great technologies that won't be there down the road when we need them."[8]

DARPA is not the only place where the recent Bush budget allocations are moving away from basic research. Other potential losers include research satellites that could forecast the types of solar storms that can affect our satellite infrastructure and electrical grid, as well as further research on high-energy physics. As the *Christian Science Monitor* has reported, "The United States unwittingly may be positioning itself for a long, steady decline in basic research—a key engine of economic growth—at a time when competitors from Europe to Asia are hot on America's heels."[9]

The Politics of Hide-and-Divide Science Budgeting

Much of the federal government's underinvestment in science starts with politicians' overriding desire to be "tough on spending" regardless of what the spending is for. Our mystifying budget process exacerbates this reflex by making it difficult to make a coherent set of decisions about science funding. Congress sets the NIH (National Institutes of Health) budget as part of the "Labor-HHS" spending bill, whose allocations often pit health research funding against compelling priorities like Head Start and community health initiatives. Funding for the National Science Foundation is in a separate spending bill and competes with housing programs, while NASA has to compete with veterans' benefits. To address these irrational budgetary distortions, Congress should have one unified science budget so that politicians can make a rational assessment of our nation's basic research needs.

The Physical Sciences Take a Backseat

During our years in the White House, a strong bipartisan effort doubled the NIH budget from $10.3 billion in 1992 to $20.4 billion in 2000. This was accomplished because disease is nonpartisan; we all have loved ones who have suffered from cancer or Alzheimer's. Personal tragedy often trumps politics, even in Washington. Some of the most touching moments I have seen have been when politicians of very different stripes have joined forces to raise funds for research against a condition that has affected their families.

At the same time, federal investment in basic research in engineering and physical sciences has been flat or down over the last three years,[10] because of both general budget pressure and the lack of a committed constituency. Over the last few decades, federal R&D funding has shifted away from technology—engineering, physics, math, and computer science—and toward life sciences. In 1981, 48 percent of the federal government's R&D spending went to technology, while 36 percent went to life sciences; in 2003, life sciences R&D rose to 54 percent and technology R&D declined to 32 percent.[11]

Not only is the decline in research in the physical sciences a setback for staying competitive in the dynamism economy, but ironically it could even impede biomedical science. Clinton NIH Director and Nobel Laureate Dr. Harold Varmus has pointed out that progress in biomedical research depends on advances in the physical sciences and engineering. Imaging technologies such as the MRI (magnetic resonance imaging) machine have their origins in basic physics research conducted in the 1930s and 1940s. We would not have sequenced the human genome without advances in computer algorithms, advanced microprocessors, and robotics. University presidents and researchers have to understand this bias against physical sciences and engage in a more sophisticated political strategy to highlight the long-term economic and health benefits of well-balanced support for research.

A NEW RESEARCH AGENDA

When we put the politics aside, it is clear that we need to create a new constituency for long-term basic research. We should identify those broad areas that fit what scientists call Pasteur's quadrant—where research can both address practical economic, health, or security challenges and expand fundamental understanding of the world around us.

Nanotechnology

An area where the United States is in danger of resting on its earlier lead is nanotechnology. Clinton administration technology wizard Tom Kalil, with the support of the Science Advisor's office and the Office of the Vice President, argued for a major National Nanotechnology Initiative (NNI) to increase funding, which Clinton launched in 2000 and which drew the enthusiastic support of former Republican Speaker Newt Gingrich. The initiative recognized that realizing the potential of nanotechnology—the science of manipulating the structure of atoms—requires long-term, risky research beyond the time lines of individual firms.[12] Based on early promising results, experts believe that nanotechnology will have applications in areas as diverse as computing, communications, health care, clean energy, space exploration, and national security. (Some speculate that its long-run impact could be as significant as research on antibiotics, the transistor, or the Internet.)

Even though we were one of the first nations out of the gate, we are far from winning the nanotech race. A White House report on the first five years of NNI warns that U.S. leadership is under "increasing competitive pressure from other nations."[13] According to the Task Force on the Future of American Innovation, a coalition of technology corporations, trade, academic, and scientific associations, "Asian countries are investing significantly in nanotechnology, and may have already surpassed the U.S. in promising areas of research." For instance, Chinese scientists claim to have developed a process for producing carbon nanotubes at sixty times the speed they are produced in the United States.[14]

Renewable and Clean Energy

The need for expanded research to develop transformative energy technologies has never been greater. Our reliance on fossil fuels is accelerating the rate of global climate change, and our dependence on oil has imposed substantial economic costs and leaves us dangerously dependent on unstable regimes like Saudi Arabia.[15] Despite the leadership of some companies, including General Electric which recently doubled investment in environmental technologies to $1.5 billion a year,[16] the U.S. private sector has reduced its commitment to environmental R&D each of the last four years—between 0.7 percent and 4.7 percent each year.[17] While this trend may reflect corporate America's lack of long-term perspective, there are two more basic reasons for such underinvestment in clean renewable energy. First, while our environmental, economic, and national security would be significantly enhanced if an American company developed technology that would help us achieve a more reliable and environmentally responsible energy future, for any single company, the chances of such a monumental breakthrough are low. Moreover, it is unlikely that such a company could capture, in profits, much of the value such an innovation would add to our environment and security. Second, the volatility in oil and natural gas markets adds significant risk to any investment in a new energy technology. While a particular alternative fuel or technology may seem cost competitive when oil is selling for $60 a barrel, it is hard to predict what oil will cost tomorrow, let alone next year. A drop in oil prices could destroy the market for new fuel research, perhaps before testing would even be complete. Given these realities, more and more policy makers argue that the U.S. government should engage in a new commitment on the order of the Apollo project to accelerate our transition away from fossil fuels.[18] But except for a brief period in 1999 and 2000, the real value of funding for renewable energy research has been consistently lower over the past twenty-five years than it was at the end of the 1970s.[19]

President Bush has committed new funding to hydrogen technology research, but it has come at the expense of other crucial research priorities. For instance, in his 2006 budget the president requested a 4 percent cut in the Department of Energy's (DOE) overall energy efficiency and renewable energy program funding. If the administration has its way, DOE solar R&D will be cut by 1.3 percent, geothermal by 8 percent, and hydropower by 90 percent.[20] Many of the initiatives the Clinton administration pushed in this area failed to take hold due to low oil prices and bitter partisanship. Clinton and Gore won a significant victory in getting more than $1 billion in funding in 1999 and 2000 for the Climate Change Technology Initiative, but even this only brought real funding to the level it had been at the end of the Carter administration. One of the most significant projects was a public-private Partnership for the Next Generation of Vehicles (PNGV) started in 1993, which invested more than eight hundred million dollars in public funds and nearly $1 billion in private funds to develop market-ready hybrid vehicles that averaged between 70 and 80 miles per gallon. The prototypes for three cars were developed and tested by 2000, but in 2002 Bush announced that he was scrapping the project and replacing it with a hydrogen-car initiative.[21]

The economic cost of not acting goes beyond the threat of oil shocks and climate change. Without strong investment we will likely forgo an opportunity to lead in an emerging environmental market—projected to be worth over $600 billion worldwide this year.[22] As much of the world moves to undertake serious emissions reductions under the Kyoto treaty, the potential for exporting low-emissions technology will increase dramatically in the next decade.[23] While we were once the world's leader in alternative energy technologies, today only two of the top twenty renewable energy companies are American.[24] Ten years ago, American companies controlled 50 percent of the market for solar cells, but today their market share has dropped to 10 percent;[25] Japan has gone from producing 60 percent as many solar cells as the United States in 1996 to producing twice as many today.[26] Japanese companies even dominate our domestic hybrid car market, the clean-energy area drawing most attention from Americans. In fact, Ford has had to depend on technology from Toyota to get its hybrid models to market.[27] Substantial government investment could catalyze breakthrough research and products in a number of exciting areas. Plug-in hybrid electric vehicles being developed by a group of activists and entrepreneurs transform existing hybrid cars like the Toyota Prius into plug-in hybrid vehicles that can go 30 miles or more before using any gas and average more than 100 miles per gallon. Government support for further research could help get this potentially transformative technology to the market.[28] Biofuels are another important area that holds great promise. Biofuel technology like cellulosic ethanol, often called "biomass," was labeled the "the new petroleum" by Senator Richard Lugar and former CIA Director Jim Woolsey.[29] As Brookings scholar David Sandalow says, this would support our farmers instead of Saudi Arabia. But projects like the DOE's Biomass/Biofuels Program and the U.S. Department of Agriculture's Natural Resource Conservation Services Biomass Research and Development Program are slated for significant cuts.[30]

Reducing the Time from Bug to Drug

Our government's primary response to the anthrax attacks of 2001 and the threat of bioterrorism has been to stockpile large quantities of medicines and vaccines. But biologists have warned the Defense Department of the new threat presented by genetically engineered pathogens. For instance, "stealth" viruses could infect people but remain dormant until activated by a particular trigger. We need to radically reduce the time required to develop countermeasures to man-made pathogens that we have never seen before. This does not mean simply finding a better vaccine, but improving our basic research capacity to identify new cures in a matter of weeks rather than years. In 2004 Congressman Jim Turner (D-TX) introduced a RAPID Cures Act which would make a much-needed step toward increasing government investment in such basic research.

THE SCIENCE AND TECHNOLOGY WORKFORCE: INCREASING THE POOL

The Bureau of Labor Statistics projects that between 2000 and 2010, eight of the nine fastest-growing occupations will require science or technology skills. Yet according to the National Assessment of Educational Progress, fewer than one-third of American students are proficient in math and science, and China and India are graduating five times as many engineers as we are.[31] At the same time, our scientific workforce is growing older—over half of Americans with science and engineering degrees are forty and older—and according to the National Science Foundation, a rising wave of retirements over the next two decades could threaten "the relative technological position of the U.S. economy."[32]

Much of this gap in our science and technology workforce could be closed if we address the dramatic underrepresentation of women and minorities in science, engineering, and math. Women represent 43 percent of our workforce, but make up only 23 percent of scientists and engineers. Blacks and Hispanics together represent about 30 percent of our workforce, but make up only 7 percent of scientists and engineers. In 2003, only sixteen African Americans and sixteen Hispanics received doctorates in mathematics—a combined total of only about 3 percent of the degrees in the field. Together, blacks and Hispanics received less than five percent of all doctorates awarded in physics, chemistry, and computer science as well.[33] Indeed, according to Dr. Shirley Ann Jackson, the president of Rensselaer Polytechnic Institute and first African American president of the American Association for the Advancement of Science, *the entire projected shortage of workers in fields like computer science, engineering, and physical science could be eliminated if women and minorities were represented in those fields in parity with their percentages in the total workforce.*

The key to achieving that goal is giving young women, minorities, and other underrepresented populations the exposure and confidence to pursue their interests in scientific fields. At age nine there is virtually no difference between girls and boys in terms of performance and interest in math and science. By eighth grade, however, twice as many boys as girls are interested in pursuing careers in these fields, and boys start outperforming girls in science by age thirteen and in math by age seventeen.[34] While the gender gaps in advanced science classes in high school are falling (although they remain wide in physics and computer science), this improvement is not being reflected in college majors or careers. Due to cultural factors, girls and young women are less confident about their math and science abilities, and less excited about scientific activities.[35]

Math and science after-school programs, clubs, and summer programs launched in partnership with business leaders, universities, or local science museums successfully build girls' and disadvantaged students' interests. Sally Ride, our nation's first female astronaut, has developed a nationwide network of clubs and camps that give girls hands-on opportunities to learn about science and have female scientists as mentors.

Another provocative idea is single-sex learning environments that are designed to eliminate, rather than perpetuate, the stereotyping that steers girls away from math and science. A recent comprehensive study in the

United Kingdom found that girls in girls-only schools were 30 percent to 40 percent more likely to take advanced science courses.[36] While any sex segregation in public schools should be monitored to make sure it doesn't reinforce harmful exclusion or stereotypes, the national imperative to close the gender gap in math and science achievement justifies increased experimentation. One of the leading examples of a successful all-girls math and science school is the Young Women's Leadership Charter School in Chicago. With a student body that is 81 percent African American or Hispanic and about 65 percent low-income, YWLCS has improved test scores across the board. In the school's first graduating class this year, 41 percent plan on majoring in science, math, or technology in college—compared to about 15 percent of female undergraduates nationwide.[37]

For these early intervention efforts to succeed in the long term, we need the support of colleges and universities. Professor Paul Romer argues that even if more students want to seek majors or advanced degrees in science and engineering, universities may not be able to accommodate them in the short term because institutional inertia makes it difficult to adjust the size of departments. As a result, it may be more difficult for all but the most competitive students to complete a degree. The solution may be government incentives for universities to expand their science and engineering departments and encourage greater enrollment. Romer recommends providing grants to undergraduate institutions that increase the share of their graduates with degrees in the natural sciences and engineering.[38]

Use Cutting-Edge Technology for Education

While many politicians lament the fact that American fifteen-year-olds score below the international averages on international math and science assessments, too few political leaders challenge the educational and technology community to make learning in these fields more engaging. Indeed, the only people intensely focused on using technology to keep our kids' attention on complex tasks are video game developers. Parents everywhere watch the same distracted children who struggle to do forty-five minutes of homework exhibit uncanny powers of concentration as they play *Halo 2* on their Xbox for hours. Imagine if video games made it half this much fun to identify chemical compounds?

Video game developers routinely spend $10 million developing a single game, but only a fraction of this amount is available to develop educational software designed to help teach math, science, or reading or improve kids' cognitive thinking. Education and technology experts believe that learning tools could be developed to teach math, geography, or science with the same science-fiction characters, search-and-destroy drama, and competition of the best video games *if* businesses were convinced that they could be lucrative markets. A collaboration between MIT and Microsoft, the Education Arcade project, is yielding marketable prototypes like *Hephaestus,* a multi-player online game where players compete for resources on a volcanic planet, but have to design their vehicles using real-world engineering principles.[39] So far only a few notable educational video games like *Where in the World is Carmen San Diego?* and *Math Blaster* have achieved moderate commercial success.

The government could jump-start the market with lucrative prizes and contracts for the creators of the best high-tech video games that teach subjects in engaging ways. If coalitions of school systems purchase the most popular video game teaching math it would provide the market demand for further development and investment.

Honoring Our Scientists

While many policy analysts emphasize the importance of encouraging American students to seek careers in science, young people who graduate with science PhDs face more years of study and less pay upon graduation than their peers who get professional degrees like MDs, JDs, and MBAs. While a promising law student jumps to clerking for a judge or finding a high-paying job after three years of law school, a science PhD spends five to six years achieving her doctorate, followed by another five or more years as a "postdoc"—with low salaries, few benefits, and often limited ability to pursue her own research.

These realities stymy all but the most dedicated students. As a recent article in *Science* noted, "scientists must now work until midlife before they can obtain a stable income and clear benefits."[40] This is a particular challenge for female—and increasingly, male—scientists for whom nearly a decade of eighty-hour weeks of laboratory research makes a scientific research career and starting a family extremely difficult.

Scientific agencies such as NSF and NIH should receive the resources to increase graduate student and postdoc salaries and health and pension benefits. Universities should do more to treat postdocs as young professionals doing substantive research, as opposed to quasi-grad students. They should also experiment with alternative tenure tracks and "stop the clock" policies for fathers or mothers who choose to take a year or two off for a young child, and provide more technical support for promising postdocs with significant family obligations. Such policies could help address the underrepresentation of female professors in science, but they would likely be appreciated by men as well. Finally, nothing honors those in basic science more than winning NIH and NSF grants. Ensuring that grants judged in the top 25 percent actually receive funding is vital to spurring those who choose basic research to stay in the profession.

PART FOUR

The Nation That Saves Together Grows Together

13

Spreading the Wealth Creation

The American Dream in large part tells a story of savings. Americans aspire not only to make ends meet from week to week but also to save and invest for the future. Personal savings is not only critical—alongside government savings or borrowing—to how much is invested in the economy, it is a vital ingredient in ensuring economic dignity and upward mobility. Savings are the means by which we move up and accumulate wealth, put a down payment on a home, maintain our economic dignity if we're laid off. It allows parents to invest in their children's education, and allows retirees to live out their days in comfort and security.

With savings, Americans enjoy the "magic of compound interest": even those who invest conservatively and get a return of 3 percent above inflation see their inflation-adjusted savings double every twenty-three years. And if you save enough to buy a home or put away a nest egg, you can borrow against your equity at lower rates, which allows you to increase your investments and watch your savings grow even further.

While Americans love to celebrate the success of families that build wealth and create a better life for themselves and their children, there has been, at least until recently, far too little focus on how wildly inefficient and inequitable our policies are for encouraging private savings. Defined benefit plans, which remain an important form of employer-provided pension by allowing workers to reap the benefits of higher market returns without assuming personal risk, remain an important way to save for retirement but have been in significant decline in recent decades. The 401(k) pension plan—now the most widely used employer-provided pension in the U.S.—

offers tens of millions of Americans opportunities to save, but we continue to have a Swiss cheese retirement savings system where more than half of all Americans are falling through the holes with no employer-provided pension of any kind in any given year. These holes do not simply reflect misguided private decision making or workers' lack of income. They are encouraged by a system that is completely counterproductive when it comes to increasing national savings and providing rational incentives to help more Americans create wealth. And neither party has effectively championed those workers who fall through the holes or the urgent imperative to turn our upside-down system right-side-up. Republicans often have the right rhetoric—praising, as President Bush does, the importance of ownership. Yet almost without exception their proposals exacerbate our system's inefficient and upside-down nature. Democrats have leveled strong critiques on the inequities of Bush's proposals but very rarely have made wealth creation and private savings a major plank of a progressive agenda. While progressives are certainly right to push for broader and more comprehensive social insurance in light of the increasing dislocation in the dynamism economy, pro-growth progressives should acknowledge that savings and wealth creation are also a critical component of an economic strategy for at least two reasons. First, even if our nation agrees on a new cost-sharing compact, many families may still need additional savings as a cushion against inevitable dislocation. Second, to the degree that our economy sees significant productivity gains or increases in asset values during periods when wages are stagnant, with increased savings and investment ordinary workers can share in a portion of those gains.

Rather than concentrating wealth in the hands of the few or focusing solely on spreading the wealth, we need to spread wealth creation opportunities to the tens of millions of hardworking American families who are currently struggling to save. To advance such a bold agenda, pro-growth progressives must make a frank and deservedly harsh critique of the upside-down nature of our current policies.

1. An Upside-Down System for Encouraging Savings

Imagine a hypothetical country—Fiscal Nation—with only one hundred families. The president convenes the families at the national meetinghouse to announce his policies to deal with the sorry state of personal savings. He identifies the fifty families that are living paycheck to paycheck with no savings and are the main source of the saving crisis and has them move to the right side of the room. He says that he has a new program to increase savings and bring more families into the process of wealth creation and ownership and that these families will get 5 percent of the new benefits. When some of the families start to complain, he explains that he needs to give the wealthiest 10 percent of families over half of the new benefits and that 5 percent is all he can afford for them.

Fiscal Nation's ridiculous savings strategy is disturbingly close to the allocation of savings incentives in the United States. Today, we spend about $150 billion in tax expenditures—exceptions to income tax—to encourage retirement savings. Of that amount, only about 10 percent goes to the bottom 60 percent of taxpayers and an astoundingly low 3 percent goes to the bottom 40 percent of taxpayers—the 57 million filers struggling the most to save. Those in the top 10 percent making over $100,000, and who are already saving the most, get 50 percent of our retirement savings dollars.[1] If the U.S. savings incentive system were turned into a logic question for the SAT, the principle describing it would be: "the harder it is for you to save, the less we help you; the easier it is for you to save, the more we help you."

The reason our system is so upside-down is that the only way we encourage savings is through tax deductions. We give everyone the opportunity to deduct some of his income before it is taxed and put it into savings accounts to grow tax-free until it is withdrawn. What too few people appreciate is that relying on tax deductibility turns our progressive tax system on its head. The higher your tax bracket, the bigger your deduction; the lower your tax bracket, the lower your deduction, and therefore the less incentive you have to save.

Consider what this system does for a high-powered management consultant who with her husband makes $500,000 and falls in the top 35 percent tax bracket. She is a triple-winner in our retirement security system. First, she has an employer-provided 401(k), with her employer matching funds for the first 6 percent of income she saves. Second, because she also has business income, she has access to a host of additional tax-deferred savings opportunities, including the chance to set aside up to $40,000 additional per year in a Self-Employment Plan (SEP) IRA and up to $11,000 a year in a 529 savings account for her children's college education. Third, because she is in the 35 percent bracket, for every $1,000 she deducts in either of these accounts, we let her keep $350 in cash that she would have had to pay in taxes. That $350 gets larger and larger through compound interest or investment earnings—and none of those earnings are taxed until the money is withdrawn.

Now consider the woman who cleans the CEO's office. She loses three times under our upside-down system. First, if she makes less than $30,000 a year there is a 75 percent chance that she will have no employer-provided pension and no matching contribution.[2] Second, the myriad opportunities for higher-income workers to contribute additional savings to IRAs and supplemental accounts are largely irrelevant for someone living paycheck to paycheck. Third, since she is only in the 10 percent bracket, even if she finds a way to squeeze $1 a month for savings, she gets only a 10 percent deduction—less than one-third of the incentives for the CEO. If she was one of the more than 50 million Americans who fall a bit lower in the income spectrum and owe no income tax this year, she would be given no financial incentive at all to participate in savings and wealth creation. Furthermore, if she does manage to accumulate modest savings, her family could be hurt if they are currently eligible for low-income programs that employ strict asset tests.

When one considers how difficult it is for lower-income people to save and how many are living paycheck to paycheck and up to their eyeballs in debt, this upside-down system is nothing short of scandalous.

Upside-Down Extends to Home Ownership

Community activists often point to the inequity between higher-income families, who can deduct the interest from their mortgages, and low-income renters—60 percent of whom spend more than half of their income on housing[3]—who get no deduction or support through the tax code. What is less recognized is that even among the two-thirds of Americans who own homes, our incentives to build home equity are upside-down. We spend over $100 billion a year allowing American families to deduct the interest that they pay on their mortgages (up to $1 million in mortgage debt) and the property taxes they pay on their homes. If you are fortunate enough to be in the 35 percent tax bracket you are a big winner again. First, you get to deduct 35 percent of your mortgage interest and property taxes—a rate three times higher than a moderate-income worker. Second, you are more likely to have a larger mortgage and property taxes to deduct against your income—meaning that you can deduct more income at a higher rate. But if you make $25,000 and are to scraping together a down payment on a modest house, here's what the government offers you: zero tax benefit for every dollar of mortgage interest you will pay and zero tax benefit to help offset your property taxes. Stunningly, the incentives for home ownership are even more upside-down than retirement savings. The bottom 40 percent get less than 1 percent of the benefit—less than $1 billion a year—while the top 10 percent get 54 percent of the tax expenditures.[4]

Upside-Down Fails on Growth

Our upside-down system is not only a travesty on equity grounds, it is a failure from a national savings and growth perspective. From a macroeconomic viewpoint, there are only two reasons to provide tax incentives for saving: increasing overall national savings, and overcoming what economists refer to as the myopia problem—people's tendency to save less than they need for retirement, because they either are not focused on the long term or are overly optimistic about what they will need to maintain their standard of living.

To see why our upside-down system fails to increase national savings, let's say that national savings is $200, because the government is saving $100 and the wealthiest people in the private sector are also saving $100. What if the government decides to spend $5 on tax deductions for savings that wealthy people put in tax-free retirement accounts? Clearly government savings would decline by $5 to $95. But what does research suggest would happen to overall national savings with such high-income tax incentives? Rather than actually accruing any new savings, high-income people are likely to take $5 of their existing savings and shift it into the new account to get the matching credit from the government.[5] What does this do to national savings? High-income people now have $105 in savings and the government has $95—there has been no overall improvement, just a windfall for the well off. Yet, studies point to an even more negative scenario. What if we assume high-income people might have been happy saving $100? The fact that the government essentially gives them $5 more might compel them to go out and spend an additional $5. What's the impact of this? The government is saving $95 and the well-off are saving $100. We've actually managed to harm national savings while giving the well-off a windfall.

What would happen if the government gave its $5 in savings incentives to moderate-income households that currently can't afford to save at all? If those families decide to put away $5 to get the matching $5 incentives, the policy would actually increase national savings. While government savings would go down to $95, the existing $100 being saved by well-off families, together with the $10 in the new accounts for hard-pressed families, would increase national saving to $205.

If government incentives do nothing to leverage new private savings then the tax dollars (as the first two scenarios showed) are at best a windfall for well-off people and at worst a drain on savings from our economy.

Moreover, the roughly $75 billion in tax revenue we spend on incentives for the top 10 percent cannot be justified as combating myopia. By definition, this group's higher income will afford them a more dignified retirement even if they undersave during their careers. The public policy goal of preventing undersaving should target middle- and lower-income workers, for whom a failure to save will leave them unable to maintain a decent standard of living in retirement.

Today, 37 percent of workers say they have not saved at all for retirement, and across income brackets 70 percent of workers report that they are more concerned with immediate financial goals such as paying bills or making home improvements than with saving for retirement.[6]

Their failure to save for retirement is a future liability on programs like Medicaid, food stamps, and Supplemental Social Security payments. Policies that encourage families with modest incomes to save more for retirement partially pay for themselves by reducing those families' future reliance on safety net programs.

In the ultimate embarrassing failure of our system, in 2004 total personal savings was lower than the amount the government spent encouraging people to save.[7]

2. Swiss Cheese

Our upside-down savings system has helped create a Swiss cheese retirement landscape, with tens of millions of Americans falling through gaping holes with no support to pull themselves out. For those who have one, an employer-provided 401(k) is an extremely effective savings mechanism for two reasons. First, it puts the human tendency toward inertia to good use. Once a worker elects to participate, a portion of his salary is automatically moved into his retirement savings account. Second, 88 percent of employers who offer 401(k) programs put in a matching contribution, so if an employee saves 5 percent of his income and his employer contributes the same amount, an employee automatically saves 10 percent of his salary.[8] Yet over 50 percent of working families do not have an employer-provided retirement savings account in any given year; 85 percent of workers in the lowest wage quintile have none, nor do 75 percent of Hispanic workers and 60 percent of black workers. These holes in our retirement savings system go far beyond the working poor and minority workers. Four out of every five small-business employees have no employer-provided pension.[9] According to a recent survey, fewer and fewer small businesses that do not have retirement plans say they are likely to implement one.[10] Only 14 percent of part-time workers participate in an employer-provided plan.[11]

Families can still save for retirement through an IRA, but the number that do is miserably low. In 1998, of all taxpayers twenty-one and over, only about 17 percent owned an IRA, and an astoundingly low 6 percent made a contribution that year. Unsurprisingly, workers with family income above $75,000 were more than twice as likely to contribute to an IRA than workers with incomes of $30,000.[12]

These deficiencies in our retirement system expose the premature declarations by some political pundits that we have already achieved a strong "investor class." Political strategists like to point out that the share of American stockowners jumped from 32 percent to 52 percent between 1989 and 2001, and the numbers of voters who own some stock has jumped to 70 percent[13]—with a strong expansion among prized suburban "swing" voters. While the growing number of stockholders may have real political implications, when one looks at the degree of wealth actually being accumulated by the typical family and the number of working families that still fall through the cracks, it is clear that a strong and widespread investor class remains an unfulfilled national aspiration.

In 2001, 43 percent of families had no retirement plan through either current or past employment.[14] Economist Edward Wolff estimated that in 1998, more than one in four families headed by a forty-seven- to sixty-four-year-old had no pension wealth outside Social Security—no IRA and no 401(k). Nineteen percent of families—and 43.1 percent of the black and Hispanic families in that age range—had so little wealth (including their nonretirement savings, homes, and projected Social Security benefits) that they could expect to fall into poverty in retirement.[15]

What is least understood about the rising investor class is that even among the half of Americans that own some form of stock, most families' holdings are relatively small. The typical middle-income American investor has only about $15,000 in stock. One-quarter of stockholding families have less than $5,000 in the market.[16] Among families closest to retirement—in the fifty-five- to fifty-nine-year-old range—half have less than $10,000 in an IRA or 401(k). The Congressional Budget Office (CBO) recently concluded that about half of all baby boomer households have inadequate retirement savings.[17] Pollster James Zogby found in the 2004 election cycle that the percentage of voters who identified themselves as part of the investor class actually fell to 30 percent, from 50 percent in 2000.[18]

3. Policy Responses from the Right and Left: Let Them Eat Icing Versus Missing in Action

The Bush administration has put forward a number of retirement security proposals, including expanding tax-deferred savings accounts and private accounts proposals for Social Security (which I will discuss in detail in later chapters). These proposals have been justified as part of an effort to create an "ownership society," as Bush explained in 2002, "where a life of work becomes a retirement of independence . . . government can help by expanding the rewards of saving and by strengthening protections for saving."[19]

The rhetoric of the ownership society has appeal because it paints a picture of every American having more opportunity to invest, save, and create wealth. Yet it is a clear case of false advertising—virtually every Bush administration retirement savings proposal would worsen the failings of our upside-down system and widen the gaping holes in the Swiss cheese.

Bush's Empty Retirement Savings Plan

To see how Bush's ownership policies ring hollow, let's go back to our Swiss cheese retirement system. Today only about half of American workers have an IRA or employer-sponsored 401(k) pension, and only about 5 percent of workers make the maximum allowable contributions each year. The other 95 percent either cannot afford to put away that much or are not saving at all.[20]

Yet when President Bush announced one of his first "ownership society" proposals in 2003—new Retirement Savings Accounts (RSAs) and Lifetime Savings Accounts (LSAs)—the accounts were designed so they provided new financial incentives to increase retirement savings for the 5 percent who were saving their maximum amount in IRAs or 401(k)s and no new incentive to the other 95 percent of Americans. President Bush essentially looked out at the 95 percent of U.S. citizens without cake and decided that the solution was to give the 5 percent of citizens with cake an extra helping of icing.

Currently, it is rare for a working couple to "max out" their IRA contribution by each putting in $4,000. Under President Bush's proposal, there would be nothing new for the 95 percent of families who fail to "max out," but the couple that does max out can not only increase their joint IRA limit to $10,000, but if they have two children, they can shelter another $20,000 through a new Lifetime Savings Account: an additional $5,000 for each of them plus $5,000 for each of their children. The result: the few well-off Americans who were up to their IRA limit can now go from $8,000 to three, four, or five times that much depending on the number of children they have. In addition, the RSAs and LSAs would remove the current restriction that forbid households making over $160,000 from reaping the tax benefits of a Roth IRA, a move that by definition helps only high-income households.[21]

New Incentives to Drop 401(k) Coverage

The Bush plan not only fails to provide new support for most workers, it also undermines employer-provided 401(k) plans. Because of current contribution limits on IRAs, a small business owner who wants to save more than $8,000 in a tax-deferred retirement account has to start a 401(k) plan and offer the benefit to his employees. With Bush's RSA and LSA, he could stash away as much as $30,000 in tax-free retirement savings before he had to provide plans to his employees. Al Martin, president of the Small Business Council of America, said that Bush's proposal "would gut the small business retirement plan system."[22]

A Blow to National Savings

Bush's RSA and LSA proposal is a perfect example of allowing the most well-off to shift their savings around to gain a tax windfall instead of increasing savings in the private sector. Economists at the Congressional Budget Office looked at the Bush plan and concluded that "Most taxpayers would simply save the same amount in one of the new accounts as they would have saved in one of their current tax-free accounts."[23] With little positive impact on private savings, the RSA/LSA proposal would become yet another drain on public savings, making our system even more inequitable and increasing the deficit for years to come.

Progressives Have Been Largely Missing in Action

Progressives have rightly spent considerable energy shining the public spotlight on how damaging Bush's policies could be. Yet, without a bold alternative, progressives risk being perceived as missing in action or naysayers regarding what should be a profound progressive cause to spread the wealth creation.

The inability to articulate a bold pro-wealth agenda does not mean progressives have not made any progress. In the 1990s, progressive savings advocates joined President Clinton to launch a number of pilot Individual Development Account (IDA) experiments that provided both technical assistance and generous matching contributions for savings to lower-income families. Yet, as Ray Boshara, a longtime IDA proponent, puts it "IDAs [are] a small but necessary down payment on [a] larger vision . . . it's time for the policy agenda to move well beyond IDAs." [24]

A couple of smaller savings ideas the Clinton administration was pushing were wrapped onto a "savers' credit" that was enacted as part of President Bush's 2001 tax cut package. While the credit offers a modest tax incentive for low-income savers, it is nonrefundable—which means that the more than 50 million American workers without tax liability cannot take advantage of the benefit. Remarkably, this small tax incentive for savings is one of the only tax cuts that the Bush administration is willing to allow to expire in 2006. In a recent positive step, in July of 2005, House Democratic leaders Nancy Pelosi, Charlie Rangel, and Rahm Emanuel put forward a solid package of progressive savings options under the banner of AmeriSave.

Yet, the only progressive proposal that approaches the necessary scale was President Clinton's 1999 Universal Savings Accounts. USA Accounts were an expansive initiative to spark individual ownership and wealth creation with starter funds for low-income workers and a generous schedule of matching tax credits for savings of lower- and middle-income workers. [25] In my four years as director of the National Economic Council, this was perhaps the new idea I was most proud of, though I cannot take full credit for its acronym. When we presented the proposal to President Clinton he asked me what we planned to call the new accounts. "Universal Savings Accounts," I said. Bob Shrum replied, "Fantastic, USA Accounts—great name." A split second of nonrecognition on my face made it clear to everyone in the room that I had never realized that Universal Savings Accounts had such a patriotic acronym. Bruce Reed joked that it was a good thing I had not called it the Universal Supplemental Savings Retirement Accounts, or I would have been pitching USSR Accounts to the president of the United States.

TOWARD A UNIVERSAL 401(K)

The right way to fill the gaping holes in our Swiss cheese savings system is to extend the features of our current system that work the best for all Americans. The more we learn about savings behavior, the more it is clear that encouraging savings among those who are either not saving or saving too little will require two things: providing greater matching financial incentives to encourage even hardpressed families to save and making it as easy and automatic as possible for these families to do so. Luckily, we have an effective model. Workers who participate in generous 401(k)s already reap the benefits of this system. What is needed is a Universal 401(k) system for all Americans.[26]

A Universal 401(k) can bring equity and efficiency to our system for encouraging savings by turning our current upside-down incentives right side up. Under the Universal 401(k), the government would offer a new retirement account with matching tax incentives to every working family. A Universal 401(k) would use refundable tax credits to match contributions made by those who need the most incentive to save—lower- and middle-income workers. For low-income families, the government could offer a generous $2-to-$1 matching tax credit on the first $2,000 that they accumulate in retirement savings. In other words, if a low-income family could save $667 a year, the government would contribute an additional $1,333 into their Universal 401(k). One hopes that the power of the 2-to-1 match and the prospect of accumulating $2,000 in annual savings would compel millions of families to get into the habit of saving at least $667 a year. We could also consider offering so-called starter funds—automatic tax credits deposited into a family's Universal 401(k) for a limited time period, to help give families an initial boost to save.

For middle-income families, the government could offer a somewhat less generous but still powerful $1-to-$1 match on savings, so that if a family contributed $1,000 to their Universal 401(k) they would get an additional $1,000 in matching funds. For more upper-middle-income families, the government could consider offering a 50 cent credit for every dollar of initial savings as well.

Some conservatives in Congress and the White House may argue that the government matches of a Universal 401(k) in the form of refundable tax credits are just a new entitlement. What they probably won't mention is that each and every one of them is currently offered a government-sponsored savings plan and a match out of taxpayer dollars, just as I was when I was at the White House. The federal Thrift Savings Plan (TSP) offers all federal employees a 401(k)-type account and a generous match. It is worth asking why members of Congress and White House staff can receive a matching credit from the taxpayer when they save, but the same arrangement for hardworking families represents an entitlement.

ADVANTAGES OF THE UNIVERSAL 401(K)

1. The Right Pension for the Dynamism Economy

A Universal 401(k) would address many of the most important features of our dynamism economy. Workers facing the prospect of increasing job change and potential dislocation would no longer have to struggle with multiple 401(k) accounts, IRAs, and other defined contribution accounts, but rather carry a single, completely portable Universal 401(k) with them for their entire adult life. Workers could roll over all accumulated retirement savings into their portable Universal 401(k) whenever they made a job change or left the workforce.[27]

This portability, alongside the Universal 401(k)'s constant financial incentive to save, could address what is a silent crisis in our current retirement savings system: the lack of accumulated retirement savings due to the tendency of younger and more moderate-income workers to "cash out" and take a lump sum from their 401(k) when they are changing jobs—even if they must incur a tax penalty. Alicia Munnell of Boston College estimates that a median-wage worker who consistently saves 6 percent of her salary with a 3 percent match would accumulate $300,000 by the time she retires, but because 55 percent of workers cash out their 401(k)s when they switch jobs, the real accumulation is only $42,000.[28]

If workers facing the choice to cash out are given an easy option to continue saving in a Universal 401(k) where generous matching incentives will continue independent of work status, it could compel far more of them to maintain their retirement savings. And to further combat cashing out, we could consider establishing *automatic rollovers* into a Universal 401(k) where workers provide their Universal 401(k) account information to employers on the first day of a new job and when they leave, any funds accumulated in an employer pension plan will be automatically rolled over to the Universal 401(k), unless the worker specifically directs the firm otherwise.

While the savings in a Universal 401(k) needs to be predominantly restricted for retirement, families struggling to build a nest egg in the dynamism economy also need to know that they will be able to access some of these funds in limited instances to cushion against economic emergencies and to engage in additional wealth creation activities. If withdrawal restrictions are set too loosely, it could lead families to draw down from their account too often to supplement their normal consumption. But we could make modest extensions to existing 401(k) withdrawal rules to give families more flexibility, including a new provision to allow workers who have been out of work for more than six months to withdraw up to 10 percent of an account's value without penalty, allowing families to cover medical expenses above 5 percent of their income out of their Universal 401(k), and making it easier to take temporary loans out against a Universal 401(k) to buy a home or invest in education. In addition, we should modify federal health and antipoverty programs to ensure that low- and moderate-income families who have accumulated modest assets in Universal 401(k) accounts are not disqualified from receiving social services.

2. A Plus for Working Mothers

The Universal 401(k) could become a powerful tool to spread wealth creation opportunities to parents who leave the workforce to care for a child. Working moms considering taking time off to spend with their kids lose more than their paycheck—they stop accumulating Social Security benefits and lose the ease of savings and generous matching incentives of an employer-provided plan. Even if they rejoin the part-time workforce down the road, they are unlikely to be offered pension options. In short, these parents forgo savings that can make the difference between an economically dignified or economically stressful retirement. The Universal 401(k) would be completely portable, and the incentives to save would not be contingent on employment, so a parent could maintain an account with a generous match even if she took time off to raise children.

3. Boosting Real National Savings

As discussed earlier, by encouraging those low- and moderate-income families currently saving the least to increase their savings, we would be increasing national savings instead of the Bush administration's plan to encourage better-off Americans to simply shift existing savings to take advantage of the windfall from the new tax incentive. The more the Universal 401(k) targets those not saving, the more each dollar of government funds would be leveraging new private savings. If the Universal 401(k) were financed in a deficit-neutral manner, and thus made no net change to public savings, it would ensure that the overall policy was making a substantial contribution to increasing overall national savings.

4. Spreading Automatic Savings Incentives

Research increasingly shows the impact of inertia in savings behavior. If people have to take a specific action—like writing a check and depositing it into an IRA—the less likely they are to save. But if savings happens automatically (unless they act to stop it or opt out of the program), then inertia becomes a powerful tool for savings. If Universal 401(k)s are constructed correctly they can harness this powerful tool.

The most effective way to make savings automatic is for employers to automatically deduct a specific amount from a worker's salary and deposit it in a retirement savings account.

But it turns out the human tendency toward inertia that makes auto-deductibility so important is just as big a factor in enrolling in the 401(k) in the first place. Ironically, our pension system creates obstacles to enrollment. Employees often have to wait six months to one year to enroll, which means that an employee who has become accustomed to a certain paycheck has to be prepared for his take-home pay to be reduced after six or twelve months as opposed to having savings deducted from day one. In addition, most companies require the employee to specifically opt in to become part of the pension plan instead of being automatically enrolled. An employee who is unaware of the benefits of a 401(k) plan, wary of forfeiting money from her paycheck, or simply forgets to fill out the paperwork will end up outside the powerful savings system that 401(k)s provide. The result is that in firms that offer 401(k) plans, one in four workers doesn't choose to participate.[29]

The difference between making an employee opt in to a pension plan and automatically enrolling him and requiring him to opt out if he is not interested may not seem like a big deal, but with the power of inertia, it has huge consequences.[30] Auto-enrollment programs, used by 7-Eleven, Hewlett-Packard, and other companies have been quite promising, with participation rates jumping above 85 percent within a short period of time.[31] Perhaps even more encouraging, a recent National Bureau of Economic Research paper found that among workers earning less than $20,000 a year, auto-enroll programs raised participation rates from 12.5 percent to a whopping 79.5 percent. The increases were most significant for low-income, black, Hispanic, and younger workers.[32] Unfortunately, only 8 percent of companies offer auto-enrollment—a small minority.[33] Peter Orszag estimates that if all firms switched to automatic enrollment, it would generate $20 billion a year in new private savings.[34]

Establishing a Universal 401(k) could expand auto-enrollment by assuaging the fears of companies who believe that auto-enrollment is paternalistic or aren't inclined to meddle in their workers' spending habits. Many of these employers may be more willing to employ automatic enrollment if failing to do so meant that their employees would miss generous matching tax incentives just because they forgot to check a box or didn't fully grasp the importance of saving. This same motivation might also inspire more employers to allow employees to enroll on the day they're hired instead of maintaining the conventional waiting period.

But while encouraging auto-enrollment is vital to helping increase retirement savings, it is on its own of little relevance to the half of American workers who currently lack an employer pension. Any effort to spread savings incentives must not only encourage increased enrollment in firms that already offer pensions, but help more employers offer employees this option in the first place.

Today, many employers—especially small businesses—want to offer a 401(k) plan but fear they cannot meet the nondiscrimination rules that require that a majority of lower-income employees participate in the plan, or they can't afford to give their workers a matching contribution. With the Universal 401(k) more companies may be willing to set up a system of automatic deductions for their workers because the matching incentives make it more likely that lower- and moderate-income workers will participate and therefore help management meet its nondiscrimination test.

5. Encouraging Savings of Partial Tax Refunds

Tax refunds, like the Earned Income Tax Credit and the Child Tax Credit, are an ideal place for many low- or middle-income families to start saving. The U.S. government distributes $228 billion in tax refunds each year. The average taxpayer receives a substantial annual refund; about $2,000, or 5 percent of typical family income. And because these refunds are, for the most part, delivered as a lump sum, individuals can save simply by checking a box on their tax return to direct the refund into a retirement account.

Under current law, however, taxpayers who want to do this have to deposit all of their refund into savings or nothing at all. As one might expect, hardpressed families may be reluctant to put all of their refund in a savings account when they are struggling to pay their bills.

One solution that was promoted by Treasury officials Mark Iwry and Jon Talisman during the end of the Clinton administration is to allow taxpayers to deposit part of their refund in a retirement account.[35] One study by Harvard Business School professors Peter Tufano and Daniel Schneider and University of Kansas professor Sondra Beverly found that in test programs, participants who were given the choice saved 47 percent of their refunds. H&R Block, the tax return preparation company, has found considerable demand among their lower-income clients to direct part of their tax refund into retirement savings, but under existing regulations, it is a two-step process of transferring a taxpayer's refund into an interim account and then transferring a portion into an IRA.[36] Peter Orszag has proposed that we could further contribute to automatic savings if a taxpayer could automatically deposit a percentage of his refund to his retirement savings unless he directed otherwise.

A Universal 401(k) could be designed to allow such refund splitting, and the generous matching financial incentives would encourage more workers to take advantage of it. A study conducted by the Retirement Security Project at Brookings and H&R Block showed that adding a 50 percent matching incentive raised participation rates in their refunds-splitting program and created a sixfold increase in average contributions compared to a control group.[37] Under the Universal 401(k) proposal the incentives would be even more powerful; a middle-income worker would see a box on her tax return that would allow her to direct half her refund into her Universal 401(k) and instantly double her money via the government's generous matching funds.

6. Applying the Right Focus—Targeting Today's Workforce

A Universal 401(k) puts the focus of progressive efforts where it should be—on the pension and personal saving crisis that affects today's working families. Every member of the workforce could see immediate benefits and start on the road to greater savings.

Recently there has been a spate of interesting ideas to focus progressive savings reform on giving children a savings account at birth. Scholars Bruce Ackerman from Yale Law School and Ray Boshara at New America Foundation have been particularly aggressive at pushing this idea of "baby bonds." In 2003 the British government created the Children's Trust Fund—an initiative to provide every baby born after September 1, 2003, with $400 to $800 in a new account. Such "baby bonds" are intriguing and far superior to any of President Bush's ownership proposals. Endowing newborns with their own savings accounts as an addition to a Universal 401(k) could be a way of spreading the culture of wealth creation and savings to the next generation. Yet, when prioritizing among scarce resources in a time of high deficits, progressives would make a serious mistake if they used the bulk of their political and financial capital for progressive savings on newborns. When half of all families and more than 80 percent of low-income families have no employee-sponsored retirement plan in any given year, our first goal should be to get them into the habit of saving and creating wealth.

While we do not know if accounts from birth will transform eighteen-year-olds into long-term savers or simply fund spring break trips, we know quite a lot about how to encourage savings among adults through automatic enrollment, deductions, and matching contributions. Furthermore, one of the most effective ways to encourage a culture of saving and investment among young people is to first instill the habit in their parents.

Advocates of more expansive baby bonds must address some tough questions. Do these proposals prevent parents from accessing these accounts—which are in their children's name—if they fall into poverty or need the funds to pay for their child's health or housing needs? Can they really keep costs from exploding by limiting these new baby bonds to infants born after legislation is passed? Is it really possible that the two-year-old and four-year-old siblings of all these newborns will not mind that they are left out in the cold? For many of us who worked on the 1988 Dukakis campaign the situation evokes the "notch baby" issue—which we affectionately put at the top of our "issues from hell" list. Because of a flaw in legislative technicalities, people born in 1916 received high Social Security benefits, but those born between 1917 and 1921—the notch babies—got noticeably less, inspiring them to launch a spirited if not angry political protest to raise their benefits. If the same happens with left-out siblings, the cost could expand exponentially and crowd out the resources needed for a Universal 401(k).

In sum, baby bonds are an intriguing idea worthy of experimentation. Legislative proposals similar to the ASPIRE act deserve support as long as the costs are kept modest.[38] Another idea with modest costs would be to give people an extra incentive—perhaps $100—if they deposited their entire child tax credit in an account for their child.

7. Encouraging Balanced, Diversified Wealth Creation

A Universal 401(k) would promote a stable base of diversified savings by requiring that matching contributions be invested in a range of broad-based index or investment options, which could be managed by qualified private-sector firms or through a version of the Thrift Savings Plan now used by federal workers. Additional contributions could be invested however the taxpayer chose.

In the past, when progressives promoted ownership and wealth creation, a major focus was worker ownership of businesses. In the 1970s, Senator Russell Long sponsored legislation that allowed employee stock ownership plans (ESOPs), in which employees gained the right to shares in the company over time. More recently, this concept has taken the form of stock options, and ordinary workers at companies such as Microsoft and Intel have become millionaires.

Where stock options and worker ownership come with diversified pension savings, they are a powerful tool for creating wealth and aligning workers' interests with those of the company as a whole. Some of the most successful Silicon Valley entrepreneurs such as John Doerr will attest to the power of stock options as a motivating tool for risk taking, hard work, and loyalty. Yet when worker ownership is encouraged for average-income workers without additional diversified savings, progressives need to be concerned about what amounts to a "double nondiversification risk." No financial officer would tell a friend or relative to put all of his economic savings in a single company. Yet, as we saw in the recent financial scandals, when a worker has too much equity in the company that he works for, and the company goes belly-up, he loses his savings *and* his job in one fell swoop. A Universal 401(k) ensures that workers are being encouraged to build a nest egg, not to put all their eggs in one basket.

PROGRESSIVE TAX REFORM FOR SAVINGS

Today in Washington, the debate over savings and wealth creation is increasingly viewed through the lens of tax reform. Shortly after his second inauguration, President Bush made clear that tax reform would be a top second-term priority and appointed a Presidential Tax Reform Commission with a stated goal of promoting savings and investment.

Certainly making our tax code simpler, fairer, more fiscally responsible, and easier for working Americans to save could help spread wealth creation and fuel shared economic growth. Yet as with his misnamed ownership society agenda, there is every indication that President Bush's tax reform aspirations will move our nation in the wrong direction on all these counts.

In Washington, Bush's successive rounds of tax cuts from 2001 to 2004 are cheerily bragged about in conservative circles as a well-planned incremental strategy to dramatically reduce or eliminate taxation on the wealth of the most well-off Americans. The strategy includes eliminating taxation of capital gains and dividends, eliminating taxes for the wealthiest estates, and removing limits on upper-income retirement accounts. What's striking about this reform effort is that rather than seeking to replace taxes on both work and investment with some form of consumption tax, this strategy is designed to relieve virtually all investment income of the wealthiest Americans from taxes while taxing the wages of the vast bulk of working Americans at far higher rates.

Traditionally, those who sought to eliminate taxes on savings and investment called for a consumption tax either in the form of a 25–50 percent national sales tax on final purchases, or a hefty value-added tax assessed on businesses at each level of production. The fatal flaw of these types of broad consumption taxes is that they turn our progressive tax system into a far more regressive and far less fair system. A 25 percent tax on a $4,000 washer and dryer—tacking $1,000 onto the purchase price—might represent a mere half of one percent of the income of someone making $200,000, yet it would place a five times higher burden on a typical earner making $40,000.

As problematic as such a broad-based consumption tax is, President Bush's strategy to tax work, but not investment income erodes our values of honoring work and shunning policies designed to foster a perpetual economic elite. Americans support policies that reward true entrepreneurial risk taking and the wealth that emanates from successfully navigating those risks. Our values have always honored and celebrated those whose rise comes through hard work and ambition. Our founders frowned on old European policies that favored the landed gentry over those who made their income through hard work. Progressive taxation, meanwhile, has mediated the balance between those who have already succeeded and those who are still trying to climb the ladder. While American culture often celebrates those whose efforts land them riches, we also expect those who have benefited so much from our nation's opportunities to pay a higher share of taxes. Fifty-seven percent of Americans support a tax system where higher-income people pay higher tax rates, and nearly 7 in 10 think that upper-income people pay too little in taxes.[39]

President Bush's effort is quietly but effectively moving America to a system where the burden of taxation is shifted away from the passive income of the most well-off to the wages of the most hardworking. Consider two hypothetical boyhood friends who meet on New Year's Eve at the age of forty-five to discuss their plans for the coming year. The first friend is a middle school science teacher in an urban school, making $50,000 a year, and has decided to tutor disadvantaged kids on the weekends to bring in another $10,000. The second friend has been a top investment banker and has accumulated $10 million in wealth that he can invest while he enjoys an early retirement. Both knew when choosing their career paths that our market system provides greater financial rewards to successful investment bankers than successful teachers. But they also understood that our progressive tax system asks those with the highest income to pay a higher share in taxes to help fund our society's military, health, and educational needs—including aid to the urban school where the friend who is a teacher worked.

Consider how Bush's ultimate vision of taxing work, but eliminating taxes on investment, affects the two friends in the coming year. The teacher will pay 7.65 percent of his income in payroll taxes on his additional $10,000 as well as 25 percent in marginal taxes—for a total of over 30 percent. Since our teacher friend is still trying to make ends meet, he has little discretionary income to save; as his income comes in, it will mostly be consumed by taxes and daily needs. The investment banker on the other hand believes he will make an 8 percent return through capital gains and dividend income, meaning he will earn $800,000 completely tax-free, enough income to finance his consumption and grow his principal every year, continuously expanding his wealth. When the investment banker dies, his children will be among the richest one-tenth of a percent of Americans to inherit an estate worth more than $10 million completely tax-free.

At a time when our dynamism economy is already moving toward winner-take-all outcomes, the Bush tax reform strategy dramatically reinforces gaps between big winners and the rest of us. The result is a more divided economy and society, hardly the vision of the American dream. It is a world where factory workers, nurses, police officers, and office managers who put in an extra hour of work see 30 percent of their income taxed, while those who see their dividends increase while they are napping will not pay a dime.

Warren Buffett—super investor and second richest man in the world—was one of the first to warn us of the impact of Bush's stealth tax reform approach. In 2003 he explained that with zero taxation on dividends, his board could simply choose to provide $1 billion in annual dividends to shareholders, and as he owns 31 percent of the company, he would get $310 million a year tax-free, driving his effective tax rate down to only 3 percent of his income! "And our receptionist?" Buffett asks. "She would be paying about 30 percent [in taxes], which means she would be contributing about 10 times the proportion of her income than I would to such government pursuits as fighting terrorism, waging wars and supporting the elderly. Let me repeat that point: her overall tax rate would be 10 times what my rate would be."[40] A recent analysis by the *New York Times* shows that this outcome is already starting to take shape: the richest 400 taxpayers, people who had incomes over $87 million dollars in 2000, paid roughly the same rate of taxes as those middle-class families who made between $50,000 and $75,000.[41]

Worse still, repealing the estate tax betrays the vision of America where economic success is fundamentally determined by hard work as opposed to the mere accident of birth. Rather than simply increasing the estate tax exemption, from $2 million per couple in 2001 to $4 million a couple or $7 million a couple, which would be the law in 2008 and 2009 respectively, President Bush has sought to permanently repeal the estate tax in its entirety. By aiming such a massive tax cut at the heirs of large estates, Bush is proposing perhaps the most regressive tax proposal in American history. Completely repealing estate taxes for couples with estates over $5 million could eventually provide more than $40 billion a year to only half of one percent of estates—including a staggering average of $17 million in tax cuts for the 750 estates worth over $20 million.[42]

Tax reform that allows the investment income from significant fortunes to be accumulated and passed down to heirs tax-free moves our nation closer to one where economic success will depend on whether your family has accumulated large assets, not on your own hard work, ambition, or entrepreneurial spirit.

In the coming tax reform debate, pro-growth progressives need to attack these policies not just as failed supply-side ideology but as an affront to America's core values. During the 2004 presidential campaign, Senator John Edwards used this theme as the basis for some of the campaign's most eloquent speeches. The question of the larger values behind the president's tax reform agenda, however, never broke through as a major theme in the campaign and remain unclear for many Americans. Going forward, this must be more than a single theme by a single candidate. Conservatives made policy and political gains in the 1970s and 1980s by arguing that some progressive policies run counter to the value of helping those who are taking responsibility for their own lives. Progressives must now show that the ideological zeal for supply-side tax cuts is moving federal policy far from the American tradition of valuing the hard work of the middle class.

In waging this debate, however, progressives must be careful not to fall into the trap of positioning themselves for work *as opposed to* wealth. Pro-growth progressives must have a message and policy framework that makes clear that we honor the work of lower- and middle-income America *and* want to use every means possible to promote wealth creation and upward mobility among the tens of millions of hard-working Americans who make up the backbone of this nation.

A Flat Tax Incentive

One progressive tax reform idea consistent with these values is what I have called a "Flat Tax Incentive" for savings. It would address the issue of our upside-down tax system and help spread wealth creation opportunities to millions of hardworking middle-income families, without adding new regressive burdens.[43] The idea is simple: instead of relying on tax deductibility, which gives those in the top tax bracket 35 cents for every dollar saved and those without income tax liability zero cents, we could introduce a flat 30-cent refundable tax credit for every dollar any worker saved, no matter what her profession, income, or socioeconomic class. The Flat Tax Incentive would simply say that that when a CEO and the person who cleans her office each put away an additional dollar, they both get the same tax incentive—hardly a proposal to soak the rich. After a brain storming session I held during the 2004 presidential campaign with Peter Orszag, Jason Furman, Robert Gordon, Jon Talisman, and Brian Deese, I pitched the idea of a flat tax credit to Senator Kerry, who liked it even though it was never accepted as a campaign proposal. While a 30 percent credit is substantially paid for by bringing down the incentive on those in the top 35 percent bracket, it would still require additional resources to pay for it. The tax reform plan put forward by Center for American Progress President John Podesta calls for a 25 percent credit that, while less generous for upper-middle-class savers, would be virtually deficit neutral.[44]

Replacing the deduction-based system with a flat tax credit represents a real progressive tax reform. It addresses a key failure in our current tax code and a critical shortcoming of current 401(k)s. Currently, only 5 percent of 401(k)-type plan participants and 1 percent of participants in households earning less than $40,000 contribute the allowable maximum. With a flat tax credit in addition to the Universal 401(k)'s matching incentives, lower- and middle-income workers would have an incentive to save beyond the $2,000 eligible for matching credits. For example, if you were a middle-class family making $50,000 a year and in the 15 percent tax bracket, you would not only get a $1-for-$1 match on your first $1,000, but an additional 30 percent credit on additional savings up to the existing IRA or 401(k) limit—twice the tax incentive you would get under our current system of deductibility. Of course, those in the highest 35 percent tax bracket would receive a somewhat less generous incentive than under the current deduction-based system—but there is little evidence to suggest this would in any way change their savings behavior.

If we really wanted to have a dramatic impact, we would also consider the idea of a flat or flatter tax incentive for housing so that our CEO and the person cleaning her office would both get a similar credit for mortgage interest and property tax payments.[45]

Increasing Savings Without Increasing the Deficit: A 5,000-to-1 Tax Cut

A new Flat Tax Incentive alongside a Universal 401(k) with generous matching credits and efforts to make savings easier and more automatic would build on the best aspects of our system and stake out a bold progressive vision to spread wealth creation in America. But, clearly, offering these generous matching contributions would not come without cost. Although one could argue that the cost to the deficit of these new incentives would be worth it because they would encourage a large increase in private savings, it would be more fiscally responsible to pay for even these pro-savings proposals without increasing the deficit.

The cost of financing a Universal 401(k) would depend greatly on how many people choose to participate. For example, if 50 million Americans leveraged $500 of refundable tax cuts a year, the cost would be $25 billion. And while the Flat Tax Incentive would be primarily paid for with savings from eliminating tax deductibility, it would require additional funds as well. Much of the cost could be covered, however, by allowing the estate tax exemption—currently at $3 million per couple—to rise to $5 million, but avoid the scheduled repeal for the richest estates in 2010. While a Universal 401(k) could provide new savings incentives for 50 million to 100 million taxpayers, retaining the estate tax for estates above $5 million per couple would only affect about ten thousand estates a year, while raising over $400 billion from 2011 to 2020.

This should not be a hard sell for a member of Congress at a town meeting. In the average state only those two hundred taxpayers with the absolute richest estates would pay somewhat higher taxes than under President Bush's proposal, while 1 million working families would receive a new tax cut to help them save and someday build their own estate. That means five thousand citizens get a tax cut for every one estate that sees somewhat higher taxes.[46]

14

Young Frankenstein Economics: Do Deficits Matter?

Washington's commitment to fiscal discipline reminds me of a scene from Mel Brooks's classic movie *Young Frankenstein*. Dr. Frankenstein, played by Gene Wilder, is preparing to confront the monster he has created. He tells his trusty assistants, played by Marty Feldman and Teri Garr, "No matter what you hear in there, no matter how cruelly I beg you, no matter how terribly I may scream, DO NOT OPEN THIS DOOR!" When he enters the room and the Frankenstein monster growls, Wilder pounds on the door. When he realizes that his assistants are following his instructions, he calls out, "Let me out. Let me out of here. Get me the hell out of here. What's the matter with you people? I was joking! Don't you know a joke when you hear one?"

Politicians on both right and left claim to be for fiscal discipline, but they want an escape hatch when more cherished priorities are at stake. Bloomberg News Washington Bureau Chief Al Hunt likes to tell how Congressman Jimmy Burke always said he was for balanced budgets, then proudly voted for every tax cut and spending increase that came his way.[1]

Most politicians have a strong tendency to recognize the economic benefits of fiscal discipline when they are arguing against someone else's priorities. In the Yugioh card games my stepson, Miles, and my godson, Derick, used to play, each card represents a creature with attack points that lose their power in specific situations. Conservatives similarly seem to find that fiscal discipline is a powerful rationale when they argue against an expensive Democratic spending proposal, but they don't think it's relevant to Republican proposals for lower taxes. Progressives certainly are more likely to exalt the virtues of deficit reduction, when proposals for upper-income tax cuts are on the line.

This does not mean all politicians are hypocrites when it comes to fiscal responsibility. Fiscal discipline should never become a policy idol. Deficit or debt reduction or even balanced budgets are not ends in themselves—they are means to achieving larger goals of growth, security, and shared prosperity. If we taxed all labor income at 75 percent to balance the budget or pay off the national debt, would we be better off? Certainly not. As supply-siders will happily tell you, taxes that high would decrease work incentives, encourage black markets, and undermine growth. Conversely, as progressives will gladly tell you, if we cut back on spending so much that we end up with a broken legal system, a 40 percent illiteracy rate, and a crumbling interstate highway system, we would have less growth and prosperity even with fiscal discipline.

The point is that fiscal discipline is inevitably an exercise in balance: finding the right mix between the economic benefits derived from fiscal discipline and those from lower taxes or higher public investment. Regardless of one's economic philosophy, making a good-faith effort to strike this balance is a crucial ingredient of shared economic growth.

FINDING THE BALANCE: TRUMPERS VS. BALANCERS

I can say from firsthand experience that when making a budget, it is hard to escape the basic mathematic equation that—at least in the short term—a dollar more for preschool education is a dollar less for deficit reduction. As the one person who worked closely with President Clinton on budgets from the campaign to his final day in office, I was often his sounding board for whether or not we were hitting the right balance. While members of the Clinton economic team differed on the margins, one of our shared values that kept us cohesive for eight years was our passionate agreement on striking a balance between fiscal discipline and strong progressive investments. This posture can put the pro-growth progressive at odds with "Supply-Side Trumpers" and "Progressive Trumpers" who believe their top priorities should completely trump any consideration of fiscal responsibility.

THE ATTACK OF THE SUPPLY-SIDE TRUMPERS

If I had written this book in my final years in the White House, I would have primarily addressed those who thought the Clinton economic team had gone too far in subordinating progressive investments to reduce the deficit and eventually saving surpluses.

Today those disagreements among progressives seem inconsequential compared to the all-out assault on fiscal responsibility we have seen from the Supply-Side Trumpers, who have placed tax cuts ahead of fiscal sanity at every turn. Indeed, the Bush administration has engineered a historic mutiny against the traditional conservative economic position that fiscal discipline is important to maintaining confidence and economic growth—presiding over what former Nixon Secretary of Commerce Peter G. Peterson has called "the biggest most reckless deterioration of America's finances in history."[2] Consider the following: when President Bush took office in 2001, Congressional Budget Office projections suggested surpluses of more than $5 trillion between 2006 and 2015.[3] Now, reasonable estimates by Goldman Sachs and others suggest that those surpluses will be replaced by deficits of nearly $5 trillion.[4] That's a $10 trillion deterioration in the ten-year budget outlook. To paraphrase the late Senator Everett Dirksen, $10 trillion here and $10 trillion there, and soon you are talking about real money.

The Bush administration's campaign to pass excessive tax cuts without offsetting savings was the single largest cause of this deterioration and the result of an active campaign to disregard fiscal discipline no matter what the circumstances. As recounted in Ron Suskind's book, *The Price of Loyalty,* when former Treasury Secretary Paul O'Neill raised serious concerns about "what rising deficits would mean for our economic soundness," he was cut off by Dick Cheney who pronounced, "Reagan proved deficits don't matter."[5] In his recent book, *Running on Empty,* Peter Peterson describes Bush's views on tax cuts and fiscal discipline as "not fact driven" but "faith driven" and notes that members of the administration as so sure "they are right" that they are "untroubled by their changing, competing, and even contradictory rationales."[6]

Breaking from Twenty Years of Balancing

It is hard to overestimate how radical the administration's shift on fiscal discipline has been. All of the major U.S. economic institutions—the Fed-

PRIOR REPUBLICAN CHAIRMEN OF THE COUNCIL OF ECONOMIC ADVISERS MAKE THE CASE FOR DEFICIT REDUCTION

- Reagan Council of Economic Advisers under Chairman Martin Feldstein: *"Measures to reduce the budget deficit would lower real interest rates and thus allow the investment sector to share more fully in the recovery that is now taking place primarily in the government and consumer sectors."* [7]

- Bush I Council of Economic Advisers under Chairman Michael Boskin: *"Economic theory and empirical evidence indicate that expectations of deficit reduction in future years, if the deficit reduction commitment is credible, can lower interest rates as financial market participants observe that the government will be lowering its future demand in the credit market . . . In other words, expectations of lower interest rates in the future will lower long-term interest rates today. Lower long-term interest rates will reduce the cost of capital, stimulating investment and economic growth relative to what would be predicted if expectations were ignored."* [8]

- Federal Reserve Chairman Alan Greenspan, former Chairman of Council of Economic Advisers under President Ford: *"[P]olicy makers should . . . recognize the important role that prudent fiscal policy can play in promoting national saving and maintaining conditions conducive to investment and continued strong growth of productivity. Beginning in the late 1980s, impressive progress was made in reining in federal expenditures and restoring a better balance between spending and revenues . . . Lower federal deficits and, for a time, the realization of surpluses contributed significantly to improved national saving and thereby put downward pressure on real interest rates. This, in turn, enhanced the incentives of businesses to invest in productive plant and equipment."* [9]

- N. Gregory Mankiw, former Chairman of the Council of Economic Advisers under President George W. Bush: *"When the government spends more than it receives in tax revenue, the resulting budget deficit lowers national saving. The supply of loanable funds decreases, and the equilibrium interest rate rises. Thus, when the government borrows to finance its budget deficit, it crowds out households and firms who otherwise would borrow to finance investment."* [10]

eral Reserve, the Office of Management and Budget, the Congressional Budget Office—through Democratic and Republican administrations have assumed in their economic models the basic economic relationship that higher deficits and lower savings raise interest rates and put a drag on growth. The two most prominent names in economic policy—the current Federal Reserve Chairman Alan Greenspan and his predecessor Paul Volcker—both make the case for deficit reduction. The Council of Economic Advisers under both President Reagan and the first President Bush clearly articulated the importance of fiscal discipline to savings and growth (see box on page 210) in their annual Economic Reports to the President.

Prior to the rise of the Bush Supply-Side Trumpers, the 1981 Reagan tax cut was the most famous example of supply-side ideology subordinating all other considerations. In his book, *The Triumph of Politics,* David Stockman, Reagan's first director of the Office of Management and Budget, denounced this period as a low point for honest fiscal policy, explaining how the Reagan team used a "magic asterisk" of unspecified and unrecognized future spending cuts in the budget to hide the likely impact of the tax cuts on the deficit.[11]

What is often overlooked, however, is that following the 1981 tax cut, Washington would go two decades before we saw another episode where fiscal responsibility was completely trumped by an administration's policy agenda.

President Reagan neither proposed nor signed another deficit-exploding tax cut after 1981. Instead, at the urging of Republican Senator Bob Dole he signed a major tax increase in 1982 to undo about 30 percent of the fiscal damage done by the 1981 bill. In 1983, following the recommendations of a bipartisan Social Security commission led by Alan Greenspan, he signed a Social Security bill that took tough fiscal measures including raising the payroll tax and the retirement age, and increasing the taxation of Social Security benefits.

As the run-up in defense spending continued to expand deficits, Congress passed the Gramm-Rudman-Hollings Act to reduce the deficit in 1985. And with the significant 1986 Tax Reform Act, all sides agreed to close personal and corporate tax loopholes as they reduced income tax rates so that the overall reform did not increase the deficit.

In 1990, facing mounting deficits, George Bush Sr. courageously worked with Democratic congressional leaders Tom Foley, Dick Gephardt, and Leon Panetta to raise taxes, cut spending, and institute tough new budget rules that required that any new tax cut or entitlement come with a plan for how to pay for it—the so-called pay-as-you-go budget rules. While the president took criticism from his own party for breaking his "read my lips" pledge, his real error was his unwillingness to stand proud and firm behind his decision. Bush's tacit acceptance that his decision was a mistake made him look weak and undermined the market's faith that he was serious about fiscal responsibility. The 1990 agreement was something Bush should have campaigned on in 1992, not run away from.

In 1993 Democrats took the lead on fiscal discipline as President Clinton proposed and later signed what turned out to be an economically crucial and effective deficit reduction bill. The bill passed with only Democratic votes because Republicans chose to test the new president by mounting an opposition without a counterproposal. By 1995 Clinton and the Republicans each put forward legislation to balance the budget. Although arguments over the differences between the proposals led to the well-known government shutdowns of 1995 and 1996, the one thing both Speaker Newt Gingrich and President Clinton firmly agreed on was that you had to balance the budget by paying for new initiatives. They had opposing visions of how to best achieve deficit reduction—Speaker Gingrich wanted to severely cut domestic programs enough to both cut taxes and balance the budget; President Clinton wanted to achieve balanced budgets on a slightly longer time line that protected the nation's safety net and expanded investments in children and rewarding work—yet both sides agreed that deficits mattered. During much of the 1990s, both sides also lived under pay-as-you-go budget principles. These principles were based on the common-sense notion that if you propose either a new entitlement or tax cut, you should have to come up with a way to pay for it so that the new initiative does not increase the deficit. This rule could be breached by a super-majority, 60 percent vote, but the rule served as a constant pressure to maintain fiscal discipline.

The bipartisan commitment to fiscal discipline was the baseline for our budget battles through the second half of the 1990s. Though the differences between our competing visions remained stark, good-faith negotiations allowed us to achieve consensus on the Bipartisan Balanced Budget Act of 1997, which significantly increased Medicare's solvency. Efforts were made to drain the emerging surpluses to support across-the-board tax cuts and transportation spending, but after President Clinton's 1998 State of the Union pledge to Save Social Security First, his commitment to pay down the national debt helped secure four consecutive years of surpluses.

Today, the political landscape has been turned upside down. With successive rounds of unaffordable tax cuts, followed by a prescription drug bill for Medicare that offers no offsetting savings and no provisions for the government to bargain with drug companies over rapidly rising costs, the Bush administration completely walked away from the discipline of "pay-as-you-go" budget principles and threw responsible bipartisan budgeting out the window. The conservative deficit hawk, so prevalent in the late 1990s, has become an endangered species. Nearly in lockstep, the Republican congressional leadership allowed the Bush tax cut agenda to trump all concerns over deficits and generational responsibility—with only a few principled Republican dissenters such as Senator John McCain.

One bellwether of the times has been the White House's attitude toward the Concord Coalition, a bipartisan organization committed to fiscal discipline and headed by such notable Republicans as former Senator Warren Rudman and Pete Peterson. The coalition has a reputation of being critical of anyone on either side of the aisle who strays from deficit reduction and increasing national savings. The Bush White House treated its members as pariahs for not going along with Supply-Side Trumpers. When Steve Friedman was chosen to replace Larry Lindsey as director of the National Economic Council—my old job—newspapers reported that having been former vice chairman of the Concord Coalition was a serious liability. He was forced to deny that his past connections implied anything about his support for President Bush's tax-cutting agenda.[12] Soon, I thought, Republicans would be brought before hearings and asked "Are you now or have you ever been a member of the Concord Coalition?"

ON THE DEATH AND DYING OF CONSERVATIVE FISCAL DISCIPLINE: THREE STAGES OF SUPPLY-SIDE TRUMPING

A dramatic transformation in the public debate doesn't occur overnight. The one that has occurred on deficits seems to have occurred gradually in three stages, which I will refer to as Defiance, Denial, and Deathbed Conversion, with apologies to Elisabeth Kübler-Ross.

Stage I: Defiance

The first component of the Bush administration's strategy to downplay the importance of fiscal responsibility was to question whether deficits have any effect on interest rates—an argument that seems to defy the basic logic of supply and demand. While all would agree that the supply of shoes and candy bars affects the price of those products, the Bush administration had to argue that the supply of capital available to homeowners and businesses would not affect the price—as measured through interest rates.

To understand the relationship between deficits and interest rates, we need to start at the beginning, with the idea of national savings. Let's go back to our hypothetical Fiscal Nation with one hundred families. If the one hundred families each had no savings, what would happen if Jill Entrepreneur wanted to buy new equipment to start a company? With no capital available to borrow, she would have to wait years for her family to save the money, and Fiscal Nation would be denied the productivity her company might have brought to the economy.

But if the hundred families worked hard and each put away $5,000 in Fiscal Bank, the nation would have a pool of $500,000 in national savings. Now when Jill Entrepreneur wants to buy the most up-to-date machines to start her business, she can borrow from the pool of $500,000 at a reasonable interest rate—let us say 5 percent—and can pay back the loans with the extra profit the new machines help bring in.

What happens if the government of Fiscal Nation does not bring in enough tax revenues to cover the cost of schools, roads, and other basic services, and runs a deficit of, say, $300,000? The government is forced to borrow $300,000 to finance its deficit, leaving only a $200,000 pool for the entrepreneurs to borrow from. Now when Jill Entrepreneur comes in the bank managers tell her that there is only $200,000 available, and because there is lots of demand for it, she will have to pay 8 percent interest. Jill decides that at this higher interest rate, she can borrow for only half as many new machines—meaning less potential for her company and Fiscal Nation's economy to grow.

Economists call this process "crowding out." When the government had to borrow $300,000, it crowded out the savings available for people like Jill Entrepreneur. Of course, if some of the $300,000 was going into important public investments—like education or research—such borrowing could be justified as promoting productivity, therefore outweighing the costs of crowding out some private investment.

In the United States, the level of government borrowing has played an important role in determining the size of our overall pool of net national savings—the overall amount of savings when you add together what is being borrowed or saved by the government, private individuals, and businesses. For example, if the private sector is saving 5 percent of GDP and the government is borrowing 3 percent, the total savings rate would be 2 percent. Savings done by U.S. businesses and individuals in the private sector—so-called private savings—has been in decline for the past two decades. With no truly successful strategy for increasing private savings, fiscal discipline has been the only surefire way to increase national savings. This means that the level of government borrowing plays a major role in determining how much capital is available for entrepreneurs and businesses, and how expensive it is for them to borrow. For example, the Clinton administration's commitment to deficit reduction and eventually saving surpluses was solely responsible for nearly doubling our pool of national savings. In 1992, private savings was 7.8 percent of GDP, but the government was crowding out this savings by borrowing 4.7 percent of GDP, leaving the overall pool of national savings at 3.1 percent. By 2000, private savings had fallen to only 3.5 percent of GDP, but instead of crowding out savings the government was actually "crowding in" additional savings by running a surplus of 2.4 percent of GDP. Government savings together with private savings produced an overall national savings rate of 5.9 percent in 2000, nearly twice the level of 1992. If private savings had remained constant over this eight-year period, the government's commitment to fiscal discipline would have more than tripled our overall pool of savings—to more than 10 percent of GDP. Likewise, the abandonment of fiscal discipline over the past four years is solely responsible for the dramatic decline in our pool of national savings to only 1.2 percent of GDP in 2004—its lowest level since 1934.

Temporary Suspension

To justify supply-side tax cuts over any concern about fiscal responsibility, the Bush administration had to deny that government borrowing ever leads to "crowding out." In early 2002, the Bush Council of Economic Advisers highlighted studies that showed no relationship between government borrowing and interest rates. In stark contrast to Republican economists under Reagan and the first President Bush, R. Glenn Hubbard, the head of the Council from 2001 to 2003, argued that, "We have very little empirical evidence to suggest much of a link between deficits and interest rates." [13]

Yet the studies the White House relied on shared a fundamental flaw. They all looked at the effects of *today's* deficits on today's interest rate, rather than how the *expectation* of deficits affected today's interest rates. A maxim of the "Rational Expectations" revolution led by conservative economists at the University of Chicago was that people respond to economic events when their expectations change, not when the actual event occurs. Think about what happens to a company's stock price when facing bankruptcy. On the day the company files its bankruptcy papers, there may be little impact on the stock price. By the Supply-Side Trumper logic, this is evidence that bankruptcy had no impact on the price. Yet you can bet that the day the market first learned that the company was facing severe financial distress and started *expecting* the company to go under, the stock price declined.

Likewise, when markets expect government borrowing to increase beyond projections, interest rates will go up, and when the government borrows less than previously expected (when there's a great supply of savings for private companies and home owners to borrow) interest rates will go down. When Brookings economists Peter Orszag and Bill Gale reviewed all available academic studies on the subject in 2002, they found that among the seventeen studies that accounted for changes in expectations about the deficit, sixteen found a connection between deficits and interest rates. [14]

Intended Consequences

The Trumper logic ignores perhaps the best evidence of how expectations of future deficits affect interest rates—real-life examples of changes in expectations about the direction of our fiscal future. In January 1993 many economists agreed with Bob Rubin's hypothesis that there was a significant "deficit premium" in the economy. Interest rates were higher than they should have been with such an uncertain economy because of negative expectations about the deficit—which was $290 billion in 1992 and projected to rise to $455 billion by the end of the decade even with a full economic recovery.

Rubin feared that even if the economy did start to rebound, the higher interest rates from the deficit premium would squash the expansion leading to a stop-and-start economy. With the economy showing negative growth in the first quarter of 1993 and unemployment near 10 percent in California and over 7 percent nationwide, this was a significant concern. [15]

Indeed, economic reporters, including Steve Mufson and John Berry in the *Washington Post*, had written about the possibility of a double-dip recession,[16] and in election week of November 1992, *Fortune* magazine offered a sober assessment of the economy: "Everywhere executives are grumbling in disappointment—they had expected things to be better by now. . . . The economy could be even weaker than the official figures show."[17]

Rubin figured that the markets would consider a Democratic president and a Democratic Congress a recipe for fiscal profligacy and would not expect much improvement on the deficit. But if Clinton could break the expectation of rising deficits, interest rates might drop right away—a view that was supported by CEA economists Chairman Laura Tyson, Alan Blinder, and Larry Summers, who laid out exactly this scenario for President-elect Clinton in our key transition meeting on January 6, 1993.

The first test of this theory came unexpectedly. Prior to his first *Meet the Press* appearance as Secretary of the Treasury, Lloyd Bentsen had met with George Stephanopoulos and me and gave us the strong impression that he was not going to be making any budget news ahead of the president. Whether by design or accident, Secretary Bentsen commented that we were so serious about fiscal discipline that we were willing to consider the most difficult of political moves—a modest energy tax. The market immediately took Bentsen's remarks as a sign of President Clinton's seriousness about deficit reduction. The next day, at one of our Roosevelt Room budget meetings, Bentsen came in with newspaper clippings saying that interest rates had dropped to a seven-year low based on his statement. Supply-Side Trumpers seem ideologically committed to arguing that President Clinton's fiscal policies did not change expectations about the deficit and lowered interest rates, but as the box on page 218 illustrates, the weight of the contemporaneous evidence is overwhelming that they did. Indeed, as chief economist at OMB Joe Minarik charted out, interest rates fell when prospects for the deficit reduction plan looked good, and rose when things looked shaky (see graph on page 220). Vice President Gore later referred to this period as a rare moment of intended consequences.

"Look Mom, Interest Rates Are Low Now"

The Bush Trumpers' response to this evidence is to advance the simplistic argument that because we experienced high deficits since 2001 while interest rates remained low, deficits can't possibly have an impact on interest rates.

INTENDED CONSEQUENCES: CONTEMPORANEOUS EVIDENCE
ON DEFICITS AND INTEREST RATES IN 1993

- *Financial Times,* January 26, 1993, on the heels of Treasury Secretary Lloyd Bentsen's *Meet the Press* appearance: *"The [bond] market opened markedly higher as investors and dealers got their first chance to react to Sunday's comments by Mr. Lloyd Bentsen, the new Treasury Secretary, which suggested the White House views cutting the deficit as a top priority."*

- *Washington Post,* January 29, 1993: *"The bond market continued to respond favorably to Clinton's promises to reduce the deficit and to Greenspan's latest comments. Since Election Day, interest rates on ten-year U.S. Treasury notes and thirty-year bonds have dropped by about half a percentage point."*

- *Los Angeles Times,* February 23, 1993, shortly after President Clinton released his economic plan: *"The yield on thirty-year Treasury bonds sank below 7.0 percent for the first time, closing at 6.93 percent, as investors continued to rush into bonds on the belief that interest rates overall are headed lower. Traders cited the move as a ringing endorsement of President Clinton's plan to cut federal spending while rejuvenating the economy."*

- *Wall Street Journal,* February 24, 1993: *"The spectacular bond market rally accelerated yesterday, with long-term Treasury bond yields plunging to another record low as investors rushed to embrace President Clinton's economic package."*

- *Cleveland Plain Dealer,* February 26, 1993: *"The bond market has staged a massive rally since President Clinton announced his plan to revive the economy last week, with yields on thirty-year Treasuries falling a third of a percentage point in just a week, leaving those already holding the bonds feeling significantly better off... Lower rates on Treasury securities, which fell below 7 percent Monday for the first time in sixteen years, will lead to lower rates on mortgages, corporate borrowing and other types of long-term debt, leading to a rush of refinancings."*

- *National Journal, February 27, 1993: "[I]n the bond market, the early take on President Clinton's economic plan is a big thumbs-up. Prices of thirty-year treasury bonds rose sharply and interest rates dropped in response the package. . . . The drop in interest rates is terrific news for the economy and for the Clinton administration: Cheaper credit should boost the recovery by stimulating demand for new houses and the big-ticket consumer goods, such as dishwashers and furniture, that follow housing purchases."*

- *Boston Globe, February 28, 1993: "During the week the market continued a rally that began after Clinton's State of the Union Message, further driving down long-term interest rates and making home mortgages the most affordable they have been in two decades."*

- *Los Angeles Times, April 3, 1993: "[B]ond buyers appeared sure that President Clinton's deficit reduction program would assure a steady decline in long-term interest rates. The result, said investment strategist Richard Eakle of Eakle Associates, was a bond market pumped up as if on steroids."*

- *USA Today, August 10, 1993, upon passage of the 1993 Deficit Reduction Act: "Fueling the bond rally: Traders cheered the passage of President Clinton's deficit-cutting plan, which they believe will keep long-term interest rates low."*

- *New York Times, August 24, 1993: "In pushing the nation to swallow the bitter medicine of deficit reduction, the Clinton administration promised that there would be a sweet reward: a sharp drop in interest rates that would give the economy a huge boost. Well, interest rates have fallen sharply."*

This argument ignores the demand side of the supply-demand equation. Let's go back to Fiscal Nation where the citizens accumulated $500,000 of total savings. The government still borrows $300,000, but the Nation is in such a depression that Jill Entrepreneur is now the only person who wants to borrow. If she borrows from the remaining $200,000 in savings and gets a low interest rate, it would be because no one else was in a position to borrow money, not because deficits do not matter. Indeed, had the

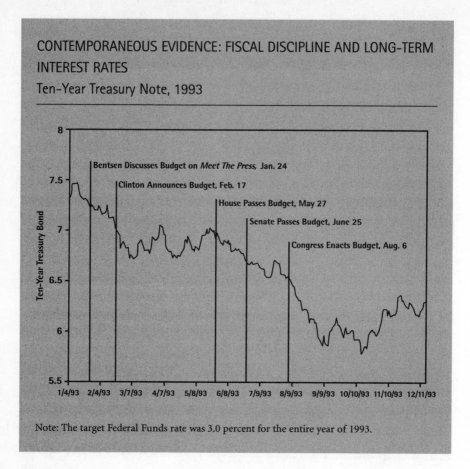

CONTEMPORANEOUS EVIDENCE: FISCAL DISCIPLINE AND LONG-TERM INTEREST RATES

Ten-Year Treasury Note, 1993

Note: The target Federal Funds rate was 3.0 percent for the entire year of 1993.

government run a balanced budget, and Jill Entrepreneur was the only citizen to borrow from $500,000 in savings, it's safe to assume she would have received an even lower interest rate.

This is exactly what happened in the recession and very slow recovery of 2001–2003. Long-term interest rates fell for two reasons: one, with such a weak economy, fewer businesses were demanding capital. Indeed, business investment declined 12 percent from the last quarter of 2000 to the first quarter of 2003. From 2001 to mid-2005, annualized business investment growth has averaged less than 1 percent. The second reason was that to jump-start the economy, the Federal Reserve lowered short-term interest rates from 6.5 percent to 1.0 percent during this period—an amazing 5.5 percentage points.

Evidence suggests that without the large increase in the long-term deficits, long-term interest rates might have even been lower, which would have helped our economy during the jobless recovery of 2002 and 2003. Consider that between December 2000—the month before President Bush took office—and December 2001, Greenspan cut the Federal Funds rate by 475 basis points. The relationship generally noted by bankers and economists is that when the Federal Funds rate—the short-term interest rate—falls, long-term interest rates tend to fall by about half as much. Yet long-term rates—the rates affected by deficit projections—barely changed, falling by only 15 basis points. Indeed, between 2001 and 2004, the spread between the Federal Funds rate and the ten-year bonds rate has been in the top 10 percent to 15 percent of its historical range.

The bottom line is that had the deficit not gone up so much, it is likely that long-term rates would have fallen even faster and further, meaning we would have had more economic stimulus in these weak years when we really needed it. In describing the effect of the 2001 tax cuts top Wall Street guru Abby Cohen noted, "Intermediate interest rates in the United States have not declined in recent months, even though the Federal Reserve has pushed short-term interest rates dramatically lower. And the reason is that many investors are concerned about the long-term implications of the change in fiscal policy." [18]

Those who want to contend that deficits do not matter also point to the curious period in 2005 when despite a rise in short-term rates, ten-year rates did not increase. Most economists have puzzled over what Greenspan has called a "conundrum." Some believe this is a temporary aberration due to the bond market undervaluing long-term fiscal risk. Others, like Merrill Lynch chief economist David Rosenberg and top investors like Pacific Investment Management company head Bill Gross, believe that current low rates are a reaction to prospects for weak economic growth and may even "assume a recession." [19] Interest rates may also be kept artificially low by substantial purchases of bonds by China, Japan, and other Asian countries seeking to keep their currency values artificially low. Others like Roger Altman point to the rare combination of a savings glut in developing nations that, due to global economic uncertainty, are willing to settle for low-yielding U.S. bonds. [20] Even if a temporary combination of perceived economic uncertainty and global imbalances are keeping interest rates lower than one would project, prudent fiscal policies should be based on sound economic principles and not the hope that aberrations or conundrums continue. While these circumstances are likely to be temporary, the policies that are increasing U.S. deficits are likely to be permanent changes that could damage our country's long-term fiscal health. Over time, as Alan

Greenspan has stated, "history suggests that an abandonment of fiscal discipline will eventually push up interest rates, crowd out capital spending, lower productivity growth, and force harder choices upon us in the future."[21] Or as President Bush's second Chairman of the Council of Economic Advisers, Greg Mankiw, wrote succinctly in his well-known economics textbook: "The most basic lesson about budget deficits follows directly from their effects on the supply and demand for loanable funds: when the government reduces national saving by running a budget deficit, the interest rate rises, and investment falls."[22]

Do Recessions and Wars Free Us from Having to Worry About Deficits?

When Democrats and some Republicans warned that long-term tax cuts would drive up the deficit for years to come, the Supply-Side Trumpers struck another defiant note. "We shouldn't worry about deficits during a time of recession," was a key mantra of the Bush team during 2001 and 2002—and a key justification for their successive rounds of tax cuts. This is one of those half-truths that should come with a warning label: the untruthful half could be harmful to your nation's long-term fiscal health.

Let's start with the truthful half. In times of economic weakness such as recessions, the government should be willing to borrow temporarily to increase spending or to give tax relief tightly designed to induce people to spend more. This is because in downturns what holds the economy back is a temporary lack of consumer and business demand, not limits on how much can be produced. The lack of demand threatens to push the economy into a downward cycle: people and businesses don't buy enough, so firms cut back on their own spending and lay off workers, who also cut back on spending—starting this negative cycle over again. In these circumstances, increased spending and reduced taxes can jump-start the economy and get consumers spending and businesses expanding and hiring (or at least not contracting and firing) to help restore a positive cycle of demand, expansion, and growth.

This was John Maynard Keynes's lesson to the world. It was also the infamous lesson the world learned from Herbert Hoover who tightened fiscal policy during a period of economic weakness, only to further push the economy on its way to recession and then the Great Depression.

So what does that mean in practical terms? It means that most of the time it makes sense for a nation to save more—to increase the pool of savings from which businesses and home owners can borrow and invest—but in times of economic weakness or war, the nation needs to make an exception to that rule.

But this strategy is by definition a temporary one. As Larry Summers used to say, "Breaking windows so you can hire window makers and window fixers may be a good way to get a little economic activity going, but it is not much of a long-term strategy." In other words, while it may be fine to have a temporary rise in the deficit during a war or recession, the key words are *temporary, war,* and *recession.* When long-term deficits are locked in, they will continue to harm the economy after the short-term problems have passed.

Imagine a family going through some hard times: the husband is ill and the wife loses her job. The wife tells her husband, "Go get us a loan. In times like these, it makes sense to borrow a bit to get by." He comes home from the bank and says, "I borrowed $20,000 to tide us over while I'm sick and you're not working. I also made arrangements for us to borrow an additional $100,000 every year for the next twenty years, so we can buy everything we have always wanted." The wife exclaims, "Why would you put us in debt for the next twenty years? We just needed a little help to get by right now!" The husband replies, "Well, you did say that in times like these it makes sense to borrow!"

This absurd hypothetical is stunningly close to the fiscal arguments the Bush administration has employed. The Bush team constantly uses the rationale of temporary economic downturn to argue for *permanent* tax cuts. For example, Treasury Secretary John Snow justified the administration's proposal to permanently cut dividend and capital gains taxes in 2003 by explaining, "A soggy economy is what we've got today. We're in a recovery, but it's not as strong and robust as it should be . . . the economy needs a boost and that's what the [president's tax cut package] is all about."[23]

Using the Keynesian logic of temporary deficits to jump-start the economy from the sluggishness it faced in 2001–2003, the administration pushed through tax cuts that if made permanent will increase the deficit by over $300 billion a year in 2011–2013, as well as in 2023, 2033, and 2043. Amazingly, the administration was also calling for making the estate tax repeal permanent, a move that would have had zero impact until 2011 when the tax cut was scheduled to expire, but would have increased the deficit by more than $745 billion in the decade from 2011 to 2020.[24] We sacrificed our fiscal health for decades to cure a temporary economic cold spell!

Bottom line: it's okay to let the deficit go up for a year or two to help stimulate an economy out of recession. It is a fiscal crime to use it as an excuse to put our nation in trillions of dollars of debt for decades to come.

Stage II: Denial

When the Bush team saw that defiance was failing to win converts, they moved on to their second stage: admit that *large* movement in the deficit might matter, but always present their tax cut and spending proposals as so modest and manageable that they could not lead to any negative impact.[25]

Hiding the Full Cost: The Dieter's M&M Fallacy

The first step in denial is what I call the Dieter's M&M Fallacy: a lot of a little never adds up to a lot. (Some people in my family refer to the Jewish Fallacy of Noshing.) I know this fallacy well. If Ronald Reagan was known for the jelly beans in the Oval Office, the Clinton White House was flush with bowls of M&Ms. They were a constant temptation, so one day I bought a regular vending machine pack of M&Ms, emptied out the contents and counted forty-four pieces. If the whole pack had 260 calories, I calculated that each M&M had 5.9 calories. I reasoned that as long as I limited my handfuls to ten M&Ms, I was having only 59 calories, hardly enough to effect my weight. The fallacy should be obvious: no matter how many handfuls I had in a day, I could always tell myself, "Well, I should have not had the previous fifteen handfuls, but this next one—being only 59 calories—can't possibly make a difference." Painful diets were the product of this delusional thinking.

Unfortunately, the Dieter's M&M Fallacy has pervaded the fiscal policy of the Bush administration. Imagine if President Bush had come into office proposing a budget-busting tax cut and acknowledged that it would cost $3.7 trillion by 2015—or $5.1 trillion including additional interest costs.[26] Or, imagine if he had acknowledged that this tax cut would give the top 1 percent of taxpayers the money needed to close the entire shortfall in Social Security for seventy-five years. It might have spurred a broad national debate about the country's priorities. In 1995, when Speaker of the House Newt Gingrich proposed an expensive and sweeping tax cut within a balanced budget, his transparency allowed the public to debate the tradeoffs between large tax cuts and tough measures like dramatically cutting Medicaid and eliminating the Department of Education. The apparent lesson the Bush administration has drawn from Gingrich's budget defeats has been to carefully and meticulously avoid having to face that open debate by presenting tax cut after tax cut in bite-size pieces, thereby obfuscating the cumulative costs these policies impose on America's future.

Consider the administration's 2001 tax cut. When it was signed into law, the administration claimed it would cost $1.35 trillion. But guess what that left out? It ignored the associated interest costs from the higher debt the tax cuts would leave. It explicitly ignored the fact that these full tax cuts would only be delivered to millions of families if we added hundreds of billions of additional dollars to the deficit to prevent the Alternative Minimum Tax from taking them back. And it assumed the tax cuts would expire at the end of 2010 and, like Cinderella at midnight, tax rates would suddenly revert back to their previous higher levels. And sure enough, soon after the 2001 tax cuts were enacted, the IMF found that taking all of its likely costs into account, the total was likely to reach *$2.5 trillion, nearly twice the reported price tag.*[27]

The Cinderella tax cuts—or "sunsets"—were the most disingenuous parts of this strategy. The basic idea was to hide the true costs of the tax cut by pretending that it would expire at midnight—even though once it was passed it would be virtually politically impossible not to extend it. Bush's Cinderella tax cuts were explicitly designed and passed with no intention— none, zippo—of ever being allowed to expire. Even before these tax cuts were passed, Republicans such as Representative Bill Thomas, chair of the tax writing Ways and Means Committee, was saying, "No one believes there will be any difficulty in extending them."[28] Senate Finance Committee Chairman Charles Grassley agreed: "Will a tax, once eliminated, be reestablished? I doubt it."[29] Indeed, this is precisely what has unfolded. Bit by bit, the Bush administration has passed tax cuts, made them look smaller by pretending they would sunset, and then immediately sought to make them permanent without suggesting how they would be paid for. In sum, President Bush has added more than $5.1 trillion to the deficit halfway through the next decade while continuing to maintain that all the tax cuts were modest and would have little impact on the deficit.

The Dieter's Refrigerator Walk

When confronted with the projected rise in deficits, how do Supply-Side Trumpers defend their policies? Believe it or not, they use the same supply-side arguments they used two decades ago to suggest that tax cuts will magically increase economic activity so much they will lower deficits. Remember when Arthur Laffer figured on the back of a napkin that if you cut taxes, revenues go up? This always reminded me of how my older brother Mike tried to hoodwink me when we were kids into believing that if you had to walk to the refrigerator, you would burn more calories going to get the ice cream than you would gain from eating it. Of course, my brother, who is a fit 155 pounds at age forty-eight, knew well—as do most people— that it is foolhardly to believe that you can lose weight by eating more desserts or lose deficits by passing popular, expensive tax cuts. While neither common sense nor evidence supports this assertion, it is made so frequently by supply-side advocates—including my frequent CNN debating partner and former presidential candidate Steve Forbes—that it is worth understanding how and why it fails.

When economists look at how a tax cut will affect the budget they look at either a "static" or a "dynamic" model. The static model assesses how much the tax cut costs, assuming nothing else changes. So if you give one million people a $500 tax cut, the costs would be $500 million and the static model would show a $500 million increase in the deficit.

The dynamic model says we should consider what effect the tax changes might have on how much people work. Supply-siders contend that if we look at this dynamic effect, tax cuts are such a strong encouragement for people to work harder that they might pay for themselves. They say that the added revenue from greater work effort and investment will create so much new income that there will be no loss to the Treasury even with lower tax rates. This may indeed be true in extreme cases—such as in some emerging economies or in the United States a half-century ago when John F. Kennedy wisely lowered the top tax rate from 91 percent. But there is simply no evidence that in most circumstances tax cuts ever come close to having such a large impact that they pay for themselves.

To see what a stretch the supply-side "eat more—lose weight" argument is, consider the following example. Let's say you make $100,000 in pretax income, work fifty hours a week, and pay a 25 percent income tax. That means the government is collecting $25,000 from you each year. What happens if your tax rate is lowered to 20 percent? Under the static model—assuming no change in your work effort—you will pay $5,000 less in taxes and the deficit will go up by the $5,000.

What would it take for such a tax cut to pay for itself? To generate an additional $5,000 in tax revenue at the lower 20 percent rate, you would have to earn $25,000 over your $100,000 in income. Assuming that you work by the hour, lowering your tax rate from 25 percent to 20 percent would have to inspire you to work 25 percent harder. How many people do you know who would work an extra five hundred hours a year—from 50 hours a week to 62.5 hours a week—simply because their tax rate drops from 25 percent to 20 percent?

Even if you are inspired by a tax cut to work more, tax experts Joel Slemrod and Jon Bakija point out that lowering tax rates could have exactly the opposite effect on your neighbors.[30] Many parents may decide that a tax cut allows them to pay their bills with less work and more time for their children. The empirical evidence supports common sense. Some people do work a bit harder when they are given tax cuts and bring in a little more revenue, but it's not nearly enough to keep the deficit from rising.

At the urging of the Bush administration, the independent Congressional Budget Office and the Republican-controlled Congressional Joint Committee on Taxation conducted "dynamic" analyses of the Bush tax cuts. Supply-Side Trumpers expected these studies to find that because of a magic work effect, the budgetary costs of the tax cuts would be reduced. But both CBO and JCT found, as most independent analysts have, that whatever benefits there were from the tax cuts were small and negated by the harm to the deficit. The CBO and another dynamic analysis by the OECD actually found that the administration's tax cuts could both raise deficits and hurt growth—a double whammy. And none of the evidence has supported their claims that the administration's cuts to the dividend and capital gains tax rates and the marginal income tax rates will significantly increase personal savings, and certainly not enough to counteract the damage they will do to national savings by running up the deficit.[31]

Popular supply-side mythology—which callers have repeated to me on countless radio shows—contends that the Reagan tax cut had such a positive effect on the work ethic, that it raised revenues. This is not even close to being true. This myth comes from the fact that overall revenues—income taxes and payroll taxes together—did go up in the 1980s. But this was entirely because Congress had raised Social Security payroll taxes in the 1977 Social Security Reform that kicked in during the early 1980s. In fact, individual income tax revenues, adjusted for inflation, fell in each of the three years after the 1981 tax cuts were passed even as the economy was recovering and were a major reason for the dramatic spike in the deficit. Individual tax payments per working-age person were lower in 1993 than they were when Reagan took office. On the other hand, after the 1993 deficit reduction act increased the top tax rates, the economy performed so well that individual tax payments grew from 1993 to 2001 at a very healthy average rate of 5.4 percent a year.[32] In the spring of 2005, Supply-Side Trumpers cooked up a new supply-side myth. They contended that projections that the 2005 deficit would likely drop to $333 billion—compared to 2004's record nominal $412 billion deficit—should be credited to the 2003 tax cuts.[33] It is a sad commentary on how far the fiscal debate has deteriorated that supply-siders are boasting about a deficit that is still almost $800 billion worse than the $430 billion surplus that was projected for 2005 when President Bush took office. Analysts, including former Bush economic advisor and current Congressional Budget Office Director Douglas Holtz-Eakin, say the improvement is due to temporary factors and should be taken with a grain of salt because there is "no question if you take yourself to 2008, 2009, or 2010" the deficit projections have not changed. Economists at Goldman Sachs agreed this was a temporary blip and projected that the ten-year deficit would still be $4.8 trillion.[34]

Super Backloading

The third strategy Supply-Side Trumpers use to deny the harm their policies are doing to the deficit is to hide the costs so far out in the future that it disappears from even a ten-year budget window—a practice that I call super backloading.

We used to joke in the White House that an easy way to balance the budget would be to make everybody an offer: you can get 50 percent off next year's tax bill if you pay it today. Of course, the problem is that advancing the revenue expected for next year into this year makes today's fiscal problems easier and tomorrow's harder. The current administration appears to take this joke seriously. Consider their proposal to change the way people save for retirement.

Currently, most retirement savings programs—other than the Roth IRA—allow a worker to take a tax deduction now as an incentive to save and then tax the worker when she withdraws her savings during retirement.[35] These programs generate a little less tax revenue now, but they allow us to count on more revenue in the future. The Bush administration's new proposals for Retirement Savings Accounts (RSAs) and Lifetime Savings Accounts (LSAs) reverse this model: higher-income savers would stow away after-tax income on the promise of tax-free withdrawals when they retire. Since these proposals cause high-income taxpayers to pay more taxes on their savings now, the LSAs and RSAs seem to cost virtually nothing in the first five to ten years. Yet, this is a short-term illusion. The low costs today come only by reducing the tax revenue we would now expect to collect twenty or thirty years down the road. Fiscally responsible deployment of such backloaded savings incentives requires offsetting long-term savings. Without such savings, as the Tax Policy Center points out, the revenue losses would "explode just as the baby boomers start to retire and the budget situation turns really bleak." These super-backloaded costs would eventually amount to $35 billion a year and equal one third what it would cost to make Social Security solvent for seventy-five years.[36] This is a case of reverse generational responsibility: we make our current fiscal situation look better than it is at the expense of robbing expected revenues from the next generation.

Stage III: Conversion

In the final episode of the Supply-Side Trumpers, they are born again as deficit hawks who conclude that the only way to address ballooning deficits is to cut back dramatically on progressive government programs. Like Star Wars, however, the last episode is actually part of the back-story. The final stage, a newfound focus on fiscal discipline to justify "starving the beast" by forcing cuts in progressive investments, was an aim of the plan from day one.

For the Supply-Side Trumper strategy to succeed, they must argue that deficits don't matter in the stages when they are pushing deficit-exploding tax cuts, and after the tax cuts are passed, turn the discussion back to the budget deficit. As leading supply-sider and tax-cut advocate Grover Norquist explains, the goal is "to shrink the size of government. Our goal is to cut it in half."[37]

In their recent budgets, the Bush team claims to have rediscovered the importance of tackling the deficit. But the discussion is carefully designed to make sure that the public treats the tax cuts and Bush's other priorities as as a fait accompli. As conservatives frame the discussion, the tax cuts are no longer debatable and the only way that we can get serious about cutting the deficit is to make radical cuts in key progressive programs. Every proposal—including gimmicks like a "global spending cap"—is aimed only at spending cuts, as if the dramatic fall in revenues has played no part in the escalation of the deficit. When the Bush budget team finally rediscovered pay-as-you-go budgeting in 2004, they sought to change the principle so only new entitlements—not tax cuts—had to be offset.

In a column for Bloomberg News, I compared President Bush's focus on cutting progressive programs after passing multitrillion-dollar tax cuts to a father of a financially stretched family who decides to lease three fully loaded Hummer H1s for the bargain price of $9,750 a month.[38] As the family's financial situation deteriorates, the father calls the family together for a belt-tightening discussion. He holds up a jar of organic chunky peanut butter and says, "Do you realize we are spending $4.49 on this? We could be saving $2.04 if we bought Skippy peanut butter for only $2.45."

His teenage son responds, "Like, Dad, man, why are you busting us about two bucks on peanut butter when you're spending, like, almost $10,000 a month on cars?" The father sternly responds, "Don't change the subject. We are talking about peanut butter."

Bush's 2006 budget reveals his strategy for converting to a fiscal belt tightener. His goal was clear: focus the fiscal debate on cutting programs for hardworking families and the poor—which are the financial equivalent of peanut butter—while ruling out any effort to add up, put on the table, or even acknowledge the budgetary equivalent of luxury Hummers—his tax cuts for the highest-income Americans.

Like the son in the family fable, most Americans understand the basic law that money is always fungible—a dollar on cars could also be a dollar spent on peanut butter. Yet Bush's entire budgetary case rests on the assumption that no one will notice or mention that his proposed spending cuts are dwarfed by the deficit-exploding tax reductions that he has signed for high-income Americans.

Consider some of the cuts that Bush claims are necessary to lower the deficit. First, he would cut $500 million for job training and dislocated workers in the midst of what is still the slowest jobs recovery since the 1930s. Second, he would virtually eliminate the $500 million Community Oriented Policing Services (COPS) program that put 100,000 officers on the streets when we are concerned about domestic terrorist threats. Third, he would impose $4.5 billion in net cuts to Medicaid for the poor and disabled when health care costs and the numbers of uninsured are rising. And fourth, he would scrap the $1 billion a year in funding for the GEAR UP and TRIO programs that reach out to economically disadvantaged children and encourage them to go to college even though our economy desperately needs a larger share of this population to get college degrees.

These cuts add up to only about $6.5 billion a year, yet in the same budget Bush calls for implementing two obscure tax provisions that increase personal exemptions and itemized deductions that the top 2 percent of Americans can use to reduce their tax payments to the tune of $115 billion over the next decade. That's enough to pay for the programs he wants to cut and still reduce the deficit by $50 billion. In addition, in the very same budget, they propose to make all the tax cuts for the top 1 percent permanent without any mention of how they will make up for the more than $400 billion in lost revenue this extension will cost over the next ten years.[39]

While spending has also grown significantly as large increases in defense and prescription drug spending were implemented without offsetting savings, the Bush administration continues to target its spending cuts on domestic investments that are least responsible for the explosion in the deficit. In an analysis I conducted with Brian Deese at the Center for American Progress, we found that when you exclude expenditure on defense, homeland security, and international affairs, the domestic discretionary spending the Bush budget aims to cut did not even grow as a percentage of our economy from 2001 to 2005.[40] So while the tax cuts have increased the deficit by as much as 2 percent of GDP—or $300 billion a year—the Bush economic team focused on an area of spending that had not even grown as a percentage of the economy.[41] The tax cuts—which the administration's own Mid-Session Budget Review in 2004 confirmed were the largest legislated cause of our fiscal deterioration—helped drive down revenues as a share of the economy in 2004 to their lowest levels since 1959, and income tax revenues to their lowest since 1951. This cannot be attributed solely to the poor economy, because revenues were lower than they were during the recessions of the 1970s and 1980s.

The recent conversion to fiscal discipline isn't about finding *real* ways to reduce the deficit: it is about exploding the deficit and then using it as a reason to limit government's role to help those most in need.

1 5

Lessons in Fiscal Discipline

While supply-siders may seize upon a temporary aberration in interest rates to justify further deficit-exploding tax cuts, current circumstances and recent history only confirm why the reasons for returning to fiscally responsible policies remain strong and numerous.

REASON ONE: FISCAL RECKLESSNESS INVITES UNNECESSARY RISK

One of the core principles of any strong nation or strong economy should be to maintain solid foundations—avoiding unnecessary risks and steering clear of situations where your basic economic security becomes overly dependent on the whims of the market or the actions of others. The unpredictability of the dynamism economy should compel policy makers to secure a sound foundation of confidence and savings through fiscal discipline. In an environment where global capital markets are increasingly fluid—and investors increasingly fickle—the perception of fiscal recklessness can trigger a sudden loss of confidence. If we are dependent on borrowing from foreigners, we are vulnerable if they decide we are too risky a bet and start lending their money elsewhere, which would produce a sharp drop in the dollar. To then encourage lenders, we would have to offer higher and higher interest rates, which could stymie the stock market, investment, and the economy at large. This is what economists refer to as a "hard landing."

This concern is far from academic. Over the past three years, an *un-*

precedented 100 percent of the approximately $1 trillion increase in our federal debt went to foreign interests. Today 40 percent of our debt is held outside the United States; 20 percent in Japan and China alone. Robert Shapiro, of the Progressive Policy Institute and former Undersecretary of Commerce, estimates that foreign debt holders are "skimming off 30 percent of our annual gains in national wealth."[1]

The degree to which these investors are nervous about the Bush administration's historically weak fiscal policies represents a substantial risk for our economy. *Fortune* magazine reported on December 13, 2004, that President Bush's reelection was a primary reason for the subsequent fall in the dollar as fear that supply-siders would continue to run up the deficit discouraged some from buying dollars or lending to the United States. "International displeasure with President Bush and U.S. fiscal policy has helped push the dollar down more than 3 percent against the euro to an all-time low."[2] Foreign purchases of U.S. securities fell to a twelve-month low at the end of 2004, which the *New York Times* called a "bad omen for America's continued ability to finance its deficits on the terms currently being offered."[3] In January 2005 a distressing headline in the *Financial Times* read "Central Banks Shun U.S. Assets." It was followed by a report that a majority of central bank reserve managers, on whom we counted to finance 83 percent of our current account deficit last year, were shifting their portfolios to the euro, "an action likely to undermine the dollar's value on currency markets."[4]

Some of the most serious, conservative economists in the business have started to raise red flags. While many feel that some orderly downward movement in the dollar may benefit the U.S. economy, the prevailing sentiment is that our long-term fiscal deterioration, coupled with this excessive dependence on foreign investors, has left us dangerously exposed. In a speech in May 2005, IMF Managing Director Rodrigo de Rato warned that if we fail to address these imbalances "we run the risk of investors drastically reducing the flow of capital into the United States," in which case "the dollar could depreciate rapidly, currency and capital markets could become disorderly, and interest rates could rise sharply, posing a serious threat to global economic stability."[5] In the current environment, says former Nixon Commerce Secretary Peter Peterson, "almost anything might push currency markets over the tipping point—an act of terror, a bad day on Wall Street, a disappointing employment report, or even a testy report by a central banker.[6] Former Federal Reserve Chairman Paul Volcker puts the chances of a currency crisis within the next five years at 75 percent.[7]

In December 2004 the *New York Times* profiled Masatsugu Asakawa, an official at the Japanese Finance Ministry. Asakawa manages the Japanese government's U.S. dollar holding, valued at $720 billion, the largest in the world. These days he is so nervous that he carries an electronic currency monitor with him everywhere. Lately, dollar movements have been giving Asakawa some sleepless nights. "This thing wakes me up; it is terrible," he said. "Fortunately, my wife is very understanding." While Asakawa has assured market watchers that Tokyo has no immediate plans to unload its dollar assets, the fact that the central banker in Japan sleeps next to a currency monitor should give us all a bad night's sleep.[8]

In late February 2005 the dollar fell to a six-month low after the South Korean Central Bank indicated that it planned to "diversify" its currency holdings away from the dollar.[9] While the South Koreans recanted their comments the next day, the dollar received another blow in early March when Japan's Prime Minister Junichiro Koizumi testified before the Japanese parliament that "diversification is necessary."[10] Policy makers in Russia, China, India, Taiwan, and Thailand have all expressed reservations about continued dollar purchases—leading the *Wall Street Journal* to call diversification by foreign central banks the "new bogeyman haunting the dollar and U.S. fixed-income markets."[11]

Could a hard landing—usually associated with developing nations— happen to the world's richest nation? In a 1995 paper, former Chairman of the Council of Economic Advisers N. Gregory Mankiw and Johns Hopkins professor Laurence Ball wrote, "Despite the vagueness of fears about hard landings, these fears may be the most important reason for seeking to reduce budget deficits . . . If policy makers are prudent, they will not take the chance of learning what hard landings in G7 countries are really like."[12]

REASON TWO: ENSURING AMERICA
CAN RESPOND TO THE UNFORESEEN

With America having just lived through several years of peace and prosperity, the need for fiscal discipline to "save for a rainy day" may have seemed somewhat abstract as President Bush entered office in January 2001. But the combination of a recession, September 11, and continuing terrorist threats should have made the need real and compelling.

The fiscal harm from the combined costs of recession, tax cuts, an expensive fiscal stimulus package, homeland security, and wars in Afghan-istan and Iraq were significantly mitigated because we entered this unfortu-nate period from a position of fiscal strength. When President Clinton left office, the independent Congressional Budget Office projected that the pre-vious four consecutive years of surpluses would continue and would reach $397 billion in 2004 alone, due in no small part to the fact that Clinton had convinced congressional leaders in both parties to save the surpluses to en-sure Social Security's solvency. Not five years later, the costs of war, reces-sion, terrorism, and large tax cuts wiped out the expected surpluses and left the United States with a $412 billion deficit in 2004—a nominal record and $800 billion worse than previous projections for that year. Imagine if we had entered this period with deficits projected at $400 billion; we would have faced dangerous deficits of over $1.2 trillion—or over 10 percent of our GNP!

It is ironic and disappointing that the Bush administration has con-sciously chosen to leave its successors far less prepared for the next rainy day, particularly in light of the increased turbulence on the foreign policy front. Neutral forecasters project deficits between $450 billion and $500 bil-lion over the next ten years, even assuming a steady economic recovery and no new military crises.[13] The Bush fiscal policies have left future administra-tions with no fiscal cushion to deal with the next unforeseen military or eco-nomic crisis. Americans would likely have responded positively to a call for mutual sacrifice to ensure that we could meet our national security obliga-tions without serious harm to our fiscal strength. Following September 11, over 70 percent of Americans said they were willing to forgo tax cuts to en-sure that we had the resources to win the war on terrorism.[14] When Senator John McCain voted against the dividend and capital gains tax cuts in 2003, he explicitly stated that he could not in good conscience support expensive tax cuts in light of "the obvious and serious threats facing us today."[15]

REASON THREE: PROVIDING FOR ECONOMIC JUMP-STARTS AND MAINTAINING CONFIDENCE IN THE DYNAMISM ECONOMY

Changing labor market realities are making it increasingly evident that reigniting the American jobs machine after the economy has stalled re-quires both effective fiscal stimulus and long-term fiscal policies that in-spire confidence in America's long-term investment climate.

Why? In past economic downturns, employers were more likely to lay off workers in response to slack demand and then refill those positions when demand picked up. In contrast, today's economy is increasingly characterized by permanent job change. In the most recent economic downturn, 79 percent of the job losses were due to significant changes in competitive conditions or product lines and were never coming back—even when the economy did.[16] This new reality of the dynamism economy makes aggressive, well-targeted short-term stimulus even more important to limit falls in demand that lead to excessive job destruction. It also creates a premium on maintaining sound long-term fiscal polices that inspire the confidence and the risk taking needed to create new companies, new expansion, and new permanent job hires.

Simply put, fiscal policy in the dynamism economy needs a two-punch combination: a strong, high-bang stimulus to jump-start the economy and a simultaneous commitment to long-term fiscal discipline. The Bush team got things precisely backward. From the onset of the recession in 2001 through 2003, the administration's tax cut proposals were explicitly designed to provide the least possible short-term stimulus to spark or maintain jobs, and they have hurt confidence by dramatically increasing the deficit decades into the future.

This backward approach was employed right from the start. Indeed, in the form that the Bush administration first proposed their 2001 tax cut—not a penny would have reached taxpayers' pockets during the year we were in recession. Only under Democratic pressure did the administration even agree to include a timid plan to advance $300 rebates due in 2002 to the fall of 2001. To make things worse, the administration designed this $300-per-taxpayer advance in a way that prevented it from going to the more than 50 million low-income taxpayers most likely to spend it and help fuel a recovery. This was both anti-growth and anti-progressive. The independent consulting firm Economy.com found that the effect of the 2001 tax cut had essentially zero stimulative impact during the recession. The aggressive monetary easing by the Federal Reserve was far more responsible for keeping the recession relatively short and shallow.[17]

In the aftermath of 9/11, as the economy was in the midst of continuing job loss, the administration had the opportunity to reach across party lines. However, the administration rejected Democratic calls for stimulus proposals such as fiscal relief to states to help them avoid raising taxes and fees or a temporary rebate for payroll taxes for firms that make new hires. Instead, the administration pushed not only for a capital gains tax cut, but also for the retroactive elimination of the corporate Alternative Minimum Tax (AMT)—a provision in the tax code designed to prevent large corporations from avoiding all taxation. The Congressional Budget Office found that Bush's tax proposals were the "least likely to generate significant stimulus" of any proposals under consideration. Worse still, the proposal to eliminate the corporate AMT was put forward on October 5, 2001—just weeks after 9/11 and during a period in which the Bush administration was fighting an extension of unemployment insurance. It would have cost $25 billion—and given more than $7 billion to just sixteen companies—with no guarantee of any positive effect for jobs. Ironically, it would have given Enron a $254 million tax cut. As the CBO explained, "its bang for the buck is small because it is primarily a reduction in taxes on the return from capital that is already in place, not an incentive for new investment."[18]

As our economy continued to lose jobs in 2003, the administration called for capital gains and dividend tax cuts with 62 percent of the benefits going to the top 1 percent of taxpayers.[19] As ten Nobel laureates and more than four hundred other economists explained in the *New York Times,* "Regardless of how one views the specifics of the Bush plan, there is wide agreement that its purpose is a permanent change in the tax structure and not the creation of jobs and growth in the near term."[20] Goldman Sachs Chief U.S. Economist, Bill Dudley, estimated that the dividend tax cut offered only 8 cents on the dollar in stimulus—ten times less than providing fiscal relief to states.[21]

These tax cuts also undermined confidence in the U.S. economy. Over the past two years, many investors and independent organizations have voiced concern that deficits will drive up interest rates and weaken future productivity. In June 2003 the Bank for International Settlements—an organization for central bankers—noted that the Bush tax cuts hurt global confidence in U.S. public finances. In 2004 and 2005, both the International Monetary Fund (IMF) and the Organization for Economic Cooperation and Development (OECD) have argued that U.S. budget deficits have fueled economic imbalances that pose a serious threat to international growth.[22]

One sign of lagging confidence is that foreign direct investment in the United States has continued to fall even in the most recent recovery. During the 1990s, it more than quadrupled from $19.8 billion in 1992 to $86 billion in 1996. By 2000 it had hit an all-time high of $314 billion. Predictably, it fell from its peak during the recession in 2001, but even after the recession, foreign direct investment continued to plummet for two years and by 2004 remained 32 percent below 2001 levels.

Apologists for Bush fiscal policy say that our eventual return to solid growth in 2004 is proof that the backward policies were a success. But from a jobs and income perspective, the recovery was historically weak. In June 2005, real weekly wages were actually lower than they were in November 2001—the month the recession ended.[23]

And what about job creation? During the 2004 presidential election, there was so much political jostling about Bush being the first president since Hoover to preside over a net job loss that many people did not digest the indisputable facts: this has been the weakest job recovery since the 1930s. It took until May 2005 for the private sector to add a single, net new job during the Bush presidency,[24] at which point our economy was more than 8 million private-sector jobs behind the pace of job creation we would expect in a typical recovery since the 1950s. In the first forty-four months of the recovery, employment grew only a little over 2 percent. In the last four comparable recoveries, employment grew at five times that rate—11 percent. To give some perspective, while job growth *averaged* 237,000 during the eight years President Clinton was in office, only seven times in the first fifty-two months of the Bush presidency was job growth even over 200,000.

It is certainly possible that part of the weak job growth we have seen in the initial phases of the past two recoveries may be due in part to changes in the increased frequency of permanent job loss in the dynamism economy. Yet this new reality shows why powerful short-term stimulus combined with a continuation of long-term fiscal discipline might have helped maintain a stronger job market after the recession of 2001.

The Democratic congressional leaders, Nancy Pelosi and Senator Tom Daschle, had it right when they called for tax cuts, such as onetime business investment incentives and state unemployment assistance that, because they were concentrated and temporary, would have had a greater economic bang in the short term when we needed it with no negative impact on long-term deficits or confidence.

REASON FOUR: ADDRESSING KNOWN CHALLENGES

With only a few years left until the first baby boomers start to retire, the United States financial situation resembles that of a family with thirteen-year-old triplets, all headed to expensive Ivy League schools. The parents could continue running monthly credit card balances, but a larger predictable debt hovers on the horizon. You wouldn't have to be a financial planner to know that the responsible thing would be to save more now, or at least begin to pay down the credit card debt.

Reducing the deficit and saving surpluses to prepare for the inevitable costs of the baby boomer retirement follows the same logic. Paying down debt now would put us in a better position to handle the coming expenses without facing enormous interest costs and excessive debt levels. Indeed, our fiscal challenges extend well beyond Social Security. Medicare faces the same demographic challenges, but the costs will be magnified by the accelerating cost of health care overall. Indeed, the costs of keeping the Medicare Hospital Insurance Program solvent over the next seventy-five years are more than twice the cost of fixing Social Security. And with each passing month, we seem to learn more about the spiraling costs of Bush's Medicare prescription drug bill. The latest estimates come with a shocking conclusion: the drug bill will cost $8.7 trillion—more than twice the cost of keeping Social Security solvent for seventy-five years.[25] We will face other challenges for seniors as well: the costs of long-term care, which are the fastest-growing portion of Medicaid, will continue to rise. The population over eighty-five could more than triple from 4 million to 18 million people in the next fifty years, putting increased cost pressures on Medicaid, which funds nursing home expenses for those who have spent down all of their other assets.[26]

These coming challenges were a primary reason that fiscal conservatives from both parties believed the United States should keep deficits as low as possible, if not run surpluses to pay down debt. While the Bush economic team was correct that as a percentage of our national income the current deficits are *not the worst* in the past few decades—that argument sets a very low bar for the decade in which the baby boom retirement will begin. As recently as 2001, some top policy makers worried that we might be paying off our national debt too quickly. By 2005 the Bush administration's abandonment of fiscal discipline had so changed the fiscal landscape that David Walker, head of the Government Accountability Office, made this stunning revelation: by 2040 all expected federal revenues will barely pay the interest on the federal debt.[27]

REASON FIVE: PRESIDENTIAL LEADERSHIP SETS THE COURSE FOR MUTUAL RESTRAINT OR OPEN FLOODGATES

Over the past two decades, we have seen repeatedly that when it comes to fiscal discipline, a president's evenhanded leadership can have very positive consequences. If my battle scars in the White House taught me anything, it was that fiscal responsibility was about making everyone unhappy in a way that seemed fair and justifiable. When a president holds himself to a high standard of fiscal responsibility, he has the moral high ground to ask the same restraint from others.

After announcing his Save Social Security First pledge in 1998, President Clinton was in a stronger position to resist Republican efforts to drain the surplus for across-the-board tax cuts because he was willing to oppose even Democratic proposals to use the surplus to increase spending on the Highway Transportation Bill.[28] Likewise, the elder President Bush's willingness to put his own "read my lips" pledge on the table in the 1990 deficit reduction agreement gave him more authority to ask for restraint from congressional Democrats.

When George W. Bush broke with the established Washington practice of "pay as you go" and put forward a $2 trillion tax-cut proposal in 2001 with barely a thought for how to pay for a penny of it, he virtually assured that no one else was going to apply fiscal discipline to their proposals. In the 1990s, the first question anyone asked a political figure with a new tax cut or spending program was, How are you going to pay for it? Under President Bush, that question disappeared.

In 2001 Senator Daschle brought Bob Rubin, Larry Summers, and me to a Democratic senators' lunch. When we suggested that any Democratic prescription drug plan should include some savings to offset the cost, several senators wanted to throw us out of the room. If President Bush gets to push $2 trillion in tax cuts with no offsets, they argued, why should we have to come up with painful choices to pay for our initiatives?

Much of the reason that President Bush's belated efforts in 2005 to cut the deficit were received with such skepticism is that they were widely seen as tactics to apply fiscal discipline to progressive priorities, not as a sincere commitment to true fiscal restraint. In 2004 when a handful of Republican senators joined Democrats to reinstitute "pay-as-you-go" budget rules that required that any new tax or spending program be paid for, the White House pushed its own version of PAYGO rules that applied only to new spending, taking tax cuts—whether corporate subsidies or popular tax cuts—off the table. Republicans have also circulated a "global" spending cap proposal, which would impose a cap on all government spending but do nothing to stem the increase in the cost of tax cuts going to high-income Americans in coming years.

REASON SIX: THE VIRTUOUS CYCLE OF THE 1990s

Perhaps no discussion is more simplistic and unhelpful than the chicken-and-egg debate over whether lower deficits create growth or growth creates lower deficits. The answer is both. The right lesson to be learned from the 1990s is that fiscal discipline creates confidence that helps maintain sustainable growth that in turn leads to more income, more revenue, and lower deficits—the so-called virtuous cycle.

The virtuous cycle of the 1990s was spurred by the initial deficit reduction in 1993, but the movement toward balanced budget goals in 1995, the 1997 Balanced Budget Agreement, and President Clinton's commitment to save surpluses all contributed to an investment-led recovery and sustained economic expansion. The commitment to fiscal discipline in 1993 was a critical tipping point. As economic growth generated increased revenues, the bipartisan commitment to continued fiscal discipline meant that the government was saving more and increasing the capital available to meet booming investment demand. Business investment grew by between 7.8 percent and 12.5 percent every year from 1993 through 2000, making it the best eight-year period of peacetime investment expansion in our nation's history. The increased availability of capital coming from reduced government borrowing helped keep the expansion from running into an inflationary wall and forcing the Federal Reserve to raise interest rates. In 1999 unemployment was at a thirty-year low; yet core inflation still fell to an annual rate of 2.1 percent—its lowest since 1965.[29]

When Republicans weighed in against the 1993 deficit reduction plan, they made Chicken Little look like Pangloss. Senator Phil Gramm (R-TX) called the plan a "one-way ticket to a recession," and Representative Newt

THE 1993 DEFICIT REDUCTION PLAN AND THE VIRTUOUS CYCLE

- Alan Greenspan: *The 1993 Deficit Reduction plan was "an unquestioned factor in contributing to the improvement in economic activity that occurred thereafter."* [30]

- Paul Volcker, Federal Reserve Board Chairman (1979–1987): *"The deficit has come down and I give the Clinton administration and President Clinton himself a lot of credit for that. [He] did something about it, fast. And I think we are seeing some benefits."* [31]

- Goldman Sachs: *"The swing in federal budget position from a deficit of $290 billion in 1992 to a surplus of $124 billion in 1999—roughly matching the improvement in the general government position—has lowered equilibrium bond yields by a full 200 basis points."* [32]

- *BusinessWeek: "Clinton's 1993 budget cuts, which reduced projected red ink by more than $400 billion over five years, sparked a major drop in interest rates that helped boost investment in all the equipment and systems that brought forth the New Age economy of technological innovation and rising productivity."* [33]

- Lehman Brothers: *"Lower deficits, lower long-term rates, and higher real growth was the overall promise. With the data now rolling in . . . it seems clear that President Clinton has delivered on all three counts."* [34]

Gingrich (R-GA) predicted that the bill would "kill jobs and lead to a recession." [35] But, with nearly 23 million jobs created along with a near-doubling of productivity growth, widespread income gains and record small business creation, the supply-siders' projections were a bit off the mark. While the 1990s saw an unusually positive confluence of events—including the rise in information technology, improved productivity after a painful restructuring of the corporate sector, and a Federal Reserve chairman who was not too quick to apply brakes as the economy picked up speed—the overwhelming consensus from such experts as Chairman Greenspan, Paul

Volcker, *Fortune, BusinessWeek,* Lehman Brothers, and Goldman Sachs was that fiscal discipline was a key ingredient in the 1990s expansion (see box above).

This virtuous cycle increased the United States' ability to play a leading role in global economic policy. In 1993 *New York Times* reporter Steven Greenhouse explained, "in recent years, America's economic partners [Germany, Japan, or other members of the Group of Seven], often scolded Washington for not putting its own economic house in order before telling others what to do." [36] By the 1997 Denver G-8 meeting, the only criticism we received at the meeting was that we should have showed more modesty when we talked about the U.S. fiscal and economic strength.

More important, the United States' ability to provide critical leadership in stabilizing financial crises in Mexico, Russia, and Asia was substantially enhanced by having its fiscal house in order. It is hard to imagine that we would be able to marshal comparable leverage and leadership today if we faced a global economic threat similar to the Asian financial crisis of the late 1990s.

The benefits to fiscal discipline require an ongoing commitment. When President Clinton took office, Bob Rubin feared that there was a deficit premium: meaning interest rates were significantly higher than they should be because investors did not expect that Washington would tackle the deficit. In 1997, when I took over from Laura Tyson as head of the National Economic Council, there seemed to be just the opposite: a "fiscal discipline" discount. Top economists at investment banks told me that interest rates were lower than they would normally expect given the strong state of the economy because there was now a built-in expectation that both political parties were committed to reaching a balanced budget. My fear was that if we failed to meet that expectation in 1997 it could lead to a spike in interest rates as there would be little expectation of major deficit reduction in the election year of 1998.

While not as significant for deficit reduction as the 1990 and 1993 deficit reduction agreements, the 1997 Bipartisan Balanced Budget Agreement was crucial in that it demonstrated a continuing bipartisan commitment to fiscal discipline. Both sides agreed to significant savings in Medicare to strengthen its long-term solvency, [37] while letting each side have its share of "wins." Republicans got a cut in the capital gains rate, while we won $75 billion in support for working families. We created the Children's Health Insurance Program (CHIP), enacted the Hope Scholarship tax credit, repealed many of the provisions President Clinton found most troubling in the 1996 welfare reform bill, and passed a $500 child tax credit while making sure that millions of low-income families would receive it.

Young Frankenstein and the Virtuous Cycle: Save Social Security First

Perhaps even more consequential than the 1997 Balanced Budget Agreement, were President Clinton's policies to prevent emerging surpluses from being drained away. In 1998, after twenty-eight years of deficits, the government was in the black. In January the Congressional Budget Office projected a virtual balance for 1998 and $660 billion in cumulative surpluses between 1999 and 2008.[38]

To get a quick start on dealing with these surpluses, I called early National Economic Council (NEC) meetings to look at three interrelated issues: the new surpluses, Social Security, and taxes. To guard against the risk that someone on the economic team would leave their schedule lying around and tip off reporters that we were dealing with such controversial issues so early on, we simply called them "special issues" meetings. It soon became clear to me that our NEC discussions were moving toward the idea of linking the surplus to Social Security. Paul Begala, who was then a counselor at the White House, was ecstatic at the development and even suggested we make a December announcement—a month before the State of the Union. It took two more meetings with President Clinton in early January, however, before we decided to create a true Young Frankenstein vault: no one should be allowed to draw down the emerging surpluses until we had enough to cover the long-term Social Security shortfall.[39] In the first State of the Union draft, Michael Waldman and I named this policy Save the Surplus for Social Security. On his first reading, Clinton scratched out our words and wrote a far more memorable phrase: "Save Social Security First."

It is hard to underestimate the importance of the policy. As Michael Waldman wrote in his book *POTUS Speaks*, when President Clinton delivered the line at the 1999 State of the Union, Gingrich and others felt compelled to applaud. Suddenly, the landscape changed.

Before the State of the Union, there had been growing bipartisan support to use the surplus to expand spending in the Transportation Reauthorization legislation scheduled for a vote early in the year. Republicans in both the House and the Senate were already pushing proposals to drain the surpluses for tax cuts.[40] In our NEC "special issues" meetings, we were fully aware of how lethal these proposals could be for the emerging surpluses. We knew that if Congress agreed to spend tens of billions of dollars from the surplus on transportation, Republicans would have a powerful political argument: if we can use surpluses for spending, why can't we return those surpluses to the people through a large tax cut. When we chose to hold to our Save Social Security First position and oppose spending surpluses on the transportation bill, President Clinton was in a stronger political position to also oppose and even veto Republican tax cuts that would have drained the surplus. By the end of the decade, the Republican leadership dropped its push for surplus-draining tax cuts and instead chose to compete with the president to develop the strongest "lock box" for protecting the surpluses and fastest plan to pay down the debt. In January 2000, in an attempt to preempt President Clinton's budget release, House Speaker Hastert instructed Budget Chairman John Kasich to "eliminate all federal debt held by the public" by 2015.[41]

On the eve of Alan Greenspan's reappointment to a fourth term as Federal Reserve Chairman in 2000, we gathered in the president's private dining room. President Clinton praised Greenspan for his wise monetary policy choices at a time when the economic rulebooks didn't apply. Greenspan returned the compliment by saying he couldn't have done it without Clinton's commitment to fiscal discipline. At first, Clinton thought he was referring to the 1993 deficit reduction act, but Greenspan told him he also meant the outcome of his Save Social Security First pledge. "You created a political competition between the parties on who was best on debt reduction. That was something I never thought I would see in my lifetime."

In Clinton's last four budgets (1998 to 2001), the government ran cumulative surpluses of $559 billion instead of the $1.7 trillion in deficits CBO had projected in 1993—beating expectations by $2.3 trillion. At the end of 2001 publicly held debt was $2.9 trillion lower than was projected in 1993.

While long-term interest rates increased during 1999 as the demand for capital surged, the virtuous cycle—the crowding in of hundreds of billions of savings—kept interest rates far lower than they would have been absent fiscal discipline and Save Social Security First. In April 2000 Goldman Sachs analyzed the impact of the fiscal turnaround on long-term ten-year interest rates. They found that the swing from a $290 billion deficit in 1992 to a $127 billion surplus in 1999 was responsible for a 200–basis point drop in interest rates.[42] Had Goldman compared the $127 billion surplus to the

$400 billion deficit that was projected when President Clinton came into office, the effect on interest rates would have been even greater. Even so, the 200–basis point swing was the equivalent of a $3,000 annual tax cut for every home owner with a $150,000 mortgage, and most important, allowed for economic expansion to continue to generate more investment rather than fuel inflation.

Excesses that led to a bubble in technology and Internet stocks helped end this record expansion, but this virtuous cycle improved the lives of tens of millions of American families by leading to real income increases for high-income, middle-class, and working poor Americans, more than forty consecutive months of unemployment below 5 percent, historic declines in poverty, and lasting productivity gains. These were hardly facts in support of a radical change in U.S. fiscal strategy.

16

Balancing Fiscal Discipline in the New Supply-Side Reality

While the Bush administration has been guilty of casting aside all fiscal restraint, it would be wrong to imply that there are no skeptics of fiscal discipline on the left. Congressional Democrats supported the Clinton administration's policies to lower deficits and save surpluses in the 1990s, but they were far from unanimous. Some progressives endorsed measures like Save Social Security First more out of a belief that it was a deft tactic to block regressive Republican tax cuts than out of an appreciation for the pro-growth progressive benefits of deficit reduction. Throughout the nineties, several very thoughtful progressive intellectuals—the "Three Bobs": Bob Reich, former Secretary of Labor, Bob Kuttner, co-editor of the *American Prospect,* and Bob Borosage, head of the Institute for America's Future[1]—launched tough critiques of the Clinton economic team, claiming we were sacrificing major progressive priorities at the altar of balanced budgets and surpluses. They argued that had we been less concerned about deficits, we would have done more to push progressive policies in education, health care, and infrastructure investment.

At a workshop sponsored by the Progressive Policy Institute and the *American Prospect* to find common ground among different progressive elements, Larry Mishel of the Economic Policy Institute and I agreed that some of our disagreements reflected our strategic differences about what a Democratic president could accomplish with a Republican Congress more than disagreement over core economic values. While the Clinton White

House certainly would have preferred to make greater investments in early childhood programs, global poverty reduction, and health care, we believed that had we failed to apply fiscal discipline to our own priorities, we would have gotten only marginally more progressive investments while making it more politically difficult to hold the line against the type of fiscally reckless tax cuts we have seen since 2001.

Yet, beneath differences over budget strategy and historical memory, it is important to analyze what unites and divides progressives on fiscal policy. Pro-growth progressives and progressive deficit skeptics agree on the crucial notion that public investment is every bit as critical to our nation's economic well-being as private investment. Fiscal discipline lowers interest rates and creates a favorable investment climate that sparks private-sector investment in new productive equipment and innovations. However, the public investment perspective rightly posits that $10 billion dedicated to basic research or successful early childhood programs may do more for long-term productivity than the private-sector benefit of paying down the deficit by the same amount. As Bob Reich correctly notes, "public investments in education, health care, transportation, and the environment are complements to private investments. Businesses can't be highly productive unless their employees are highly productive."[2]

But pro-growth progressives and progressive deficit skeptics disagree on how heavily fiscal discipline should be weighted in forming economic policy and how much worthy progressive investments should trump concerns over the size of the deficit. Like the Supply-Side Trumpers, these deficit skeptics elevate public investments by at times downplaying or even trivializing the importance of fiscal discipline. When Bob Kuttner criticized our Save Social Security First proposal, he accused us of "surplus worship," arguing that "growth has picked up smartly in the past few years, and savings rates have nothing to do with it."[3] Such arguments pave the way for the progressive trumper rationale that fiscal discipline can be abandoned as long as the cause is progressive investments as opposed to supply-side tax cuts.

Those of us who call for additional new investments in education, research, and rewarding work incentives must be willing to acknowledge the economic benefits of fiscal discipline and explain why such well-targeted public investments are, on balance, beneficial to shared growth. The proposals for new public investments in this book are vital for creating shared prosperity, but each has to be balanced against the need for offsetting savings and fiscal responsibility. During the 1992 presidential campaign, Clinton always said our economic challenge had to address two deficits: the fiscal one and a deficit in investments in people. For pro-growth progressives, finding the right balance is agonizing precisely because we recognize the importance of both.

The Clinton budget team often took heat for being too stingy for progressives and too expansive for pure deficit hawks. I received many unhappy calls from both Democratic fiscal discipline hawks like Senator Bob Kerrey and Texas Congressman Charles Stenholm as well as exasperated progressives like Jeff Faux, founder of the Economic Policy Institute. Faux called me once to say, "When you wanted to focus on deficit reduction in the 1992 campaign, I swallowed and went along. When you decided to go for a balanced budget in 1995, I swallowed harder. When you thought you wanted to save surpluses to pay down some of the debt, I could barely take it. But now you want to save the surplus to pay off all the debt—you have just gone too far!"

With Supply-Side Trumpers having so successfully exploded the deficit, pro-growth progressives may find that drawing the right balance between policies desperately needed to provide more economic dignity, fair starts, and upward mobility and efforts to reduce the deficit will be an even more difficult and critical challenge than it was in the 1990s. If pro-growth progressives are focused solely on repairing the fiscal damage done by Bush policies, they could become willing accomplices in the Supply-Side Trumper's "starve the beast" strategy. On the other hand, progressives must recognize that fiscal responsibility done right can promote not only growth and confidence but progressive values as well.

APPRECIATING THE PROGRESSIVE VIRTUES OF FISCAL DISCIPLINE

1. Fiscal Discipline Promotes Progressive Outcomes When It Promotes Sustained Economic Growth

In our first year in the White House, James Carville claimed that he no longer wanted to come back in another life as Willie Mays; he wanted to come back as a bond market, because the economic team seemed to go to such lengths to please it.

Carville's joke strikes a chord for many progressives who believe that even if fiscal discipline has economic benefits, they flow directly to the bond market and financial institutions and not to the pockets of poor and middle-class families.

Yet for progressives who focus mainly on how expansive fiscal policy can prime the pump, the 1990s showed a different scenario: the potential for fiscal discipline to foster the type of long, stable, low-inflation expansion and monetary flexibility that can lead to very progressive labor market outcomes for even the lowest-income workers. The sound fiscal discipline and the monetary flexibility it fostered helped sustain a record expansion that fueled the demand for more workers, leading to more than forty consecutive months of unemployment below 5 percent.[4] Employers were forced to reach beyond their normal pool of potential workers to recruit, train, and hire minority and economically disadvantaged workers who were traditionally shut out of the labor market.

In Kansas City, where unemployment dropped to 3.2 percent in 2000, H&R Block put a technology facility within easy access of a poor neighborhood and offered two hundred low-skilled applicants $8 or $9 an hour—plus bus fares—to work as call center operators.[5] With unemployment down to 2.2 percent in Iowa, Rock Communications, a small printing company in the Quad Cities, hired dozens of local prisoners at full-time wages—thirteen of whom stayed on after their release.[6]

Unemployment among African Americans fell from 14.0 percent to a record low 7.0 percent; among Hispanic Americans it also dropped to historic lows. The poverty rate followed, falling to 11.3 percent in 2000, its lowest level since 1974, from 15.1 percent in 1993. The poverty rate for blacks fell from 33.1 percent to 22.5 percent—its lowest level on record. For Hispanics, it fell from 30.6 percent in 1993 to 21.5 percent in 2000, and slightly further in 2001. After falling 14 percent between 1979 and 1993, the average family income for families in the lowest quintile grew 24 percent from 1993 to 2000.[7]

The expansion may have also made highly vulnerable workers more resistant to ups and downs in the economy. Larry Summers and MIT macroeconomist Olivier Blanchard describe an economic process in Europe in the 1980s that they call "hysteresis" in which some workers are out of work so long that they lose many of the productive skills and habits needed to reintegrate into the workforce. Long-term spells of joblessness can lead to permanently higher rates of unemployment.[8] Conversely, a long-lasting expansion that reaches deep into the labor market has the potential for "reverse hysteresis" as more and more people who were out of work acquire résumés, work references, and skills to weather economic downturns and find work more quickly in the future.

There are some signs that this has happened. Even as African Americans struggled through the job loss of 2001 and 2002, former Urban League economist William Spriggs noted: "People are coming out of a favorable labor market. They are still optimistic, and they are more skilled, which means they are more willing to continue to look for work."[9]

2. Restoring Trust in Government

Another major dispute among progressives is whether fiscal discipline helps or hurts "trust" in progressive government. Progressive Trumpers argue that the key to rallying support for progressive policies is to promote bold programs that will demonstrate the tangible benefits of progressive investment over supply-side economics. They fear that too much concern for fiscal discipline will lead to timidity and voters will choose conservatives because they have not been offered a true progressive alternative.

Progressive Balancers see fiscal discipline as the bar progressives need to clear to build public trust in government—a prerequisite for attracting support for expansive government initiatives. This was a critical component of Governor Clinton's and the DLC's vision of the Democratic Party in the late 1980s and early 1990s, and one that Clinton established as a working premise of his presidency. It also became a cornerstone of New Labour in Great Britain. Following a 2002 Progressive Governance Meeting in London, Bruce Reed, Sidney Blumenthal (who coordinated much of the "third way" dialogue between Clinton and Blair), and I broached this subject directly with Blair. He was adamant that fiscal discipline "was a threshold" that New Labour had to meet to earn the trust to engage in more expansive progressive policies.

The most widely cited study on trust in government was conducted by the University of Michigan and found that public confidence increased in 1994 for the first time in a decade and nearly doubled—from 21 percent to 40 percent—between 1994 and 1998.[10] Indeed, when OMB director Frank Raines and I trekked up to Capitol Hill in 1998 to get support for our Save Social Security First policies, Raines always started his presentation with these poll results to show how deeply fiscal responsibility resonated with the public.

3. Stockman Risk: Can Middle-Class Entitlements Squeeze the Poor?

While Democrats often fear that supply-side tax cuts are designed to "starve the beast" and kill policies directed to poor Americans, Larry Summers and I, as well as top OMB officials Jack Lew and Sylvia Mathews, often discussed a different "starve the beast" fear: that when generous programs for the middle class face unexpected cost increases, the politicians will respond to the resulting higher budget deficits by cutting programs for the poor. Our code for this was "Stockman Risk"—named after Reagan OMB Director David Stockman, who came to regret the deficit-exploding budgets he presided over.

Stockman Risk, as we defined it, is a difficult calculation for progressives. Programs that serve both those in poverty and the middle class—most famously Social Security—have stronger constituencies and are more politically resilient. But if large increases in middle-class entitlements lead to spiraling deficits, programs for the poor and the politically weak are usually first on the chopping block.

Bob Greenstein, the tireless head of the Center on Budget and Policy Priorities and one of the nation's top advocates for the poor, argues that higher deficits, no matter how they are caused, can eventually put anti-poverty programs at risk. Discussing the impact of the long-term deficits caused by the Bush tax cuts, Greenstein wrote, "With low-income children being one of the nation's weakest political constituencies, programs to assist them will likely suffer from the deep budget cuts that will become almost inevitable." [11]

4. Deficit Reduction Can Be Done in a Progressive Manner

Bringing down the deficit in a progressive manner requires a three-part focus. In looking for a balance between spending cuts and revenue increases, we should first ask who can best bear the burden of deficit reduction and who will benefit most from the stronger economy it would bring about. In the 1993 Deficit Reduction Act, President Clinton's plan asked those in the top 2 percent to face higher tax rates because wealthier Americans had both the greatest ability to bear the short-run costs of balancing the budget and the most to gain if our deficit reduction gamble worked. Clinton was right. Those in the top 1 percent who faced the biggest brunt of the 1993 Deficit Reduction Act ended up with annual income gains of

$188,000 *after taxes* in the four years after the tax increases, and a $423,000 increase by 2000.[12]

Yet when asking for sacrifice from the most well-off, pro-growth progressives cannot ignore the warning from conservative critics that at some point, increases on higher-income taxpayers appear punitive and can chill risk taking and discourage investment. Still, given the impressive growth in the 1990s, it is hard for conservatives to argue seriously that returning tax rates for the wealthiest Americans to their pre-Bush levels—a measure that would raise close to $1 trillion in additional savings over the next decade—would somehow cripple any hope for greater investment or economic expansion. In fact, the surge in income for the wealthiest in the 1990s powerfully demonstrated that if such tax rates are part of an effort to strengthen economic confidence, the economic benefits of deficit reduction can vastly overwhelm the burden of slightly higher taxes.

Second, progressives need to recognize that trying to both reduce the deficit and push a progressive investment agenda simultaneously requires even more painful fiscal choices. In the 1993 Deficit Reduction Act, for example, President Clinton added $100 billion in progressive investments and cut $500 billion from the deficit over five years. We needed $600 billion to finance both goals. It was no secret that some of the most politically challenging measures could have been avoided had we dropped some of our largest progressive initiatives. For example, at one point late in the budget fight, a small group of senators met with administration economic officials and quietly noted that we could drop the highly controversial 4.3-cent gas tax increase, which Democrats were being attacked for, if we eliminated our large expansion of the Earned Income Tax Credit. To their credit, Clinton and Gore would not consider the proposal.

Third, while fiscal discipline does not mean giving up on major progressive initiatives, it may mean pursuing some of them through staged expansions. Fiscal concerns made it harder for President Clinton to make the dramatic increases in Head Start funding in his initial budget that he spoke of during the 1992 campaign. However, by fighting for sound increases each year, he was able to more than double Head Start funding over eight years, from $2.8 billion in 1993 to $6.2 billion in 2001, even as deficits disappeared. When deciding whether to seek progressive goals through bold leaps or a series of measured steps, our strategies must be based on the political context.

When deciding whether to seek progressive goals through bold leaps or progressive steps, our strategy should be based on a pragmatic assessment of what is most viable. With a Republican Congress for six of Clinton's eight years, bold new authorizations were politically difficult. A single Republican committee chair could kill any new initiative through inertia, stalling, stubbornly refusing to allow votes in committee, or by blocking legislation we supported from moving to the floor. Step-by-step increases through the appropriations process—where the president had the power and platform to threaten vetoes of the spending bills Congress sent him every year—were a far more viable strategy. Yet by choosing to battle for increases every year in preexisting discretionary programs, we were able to add $1 billion to funding for after-school care and expand initiatives to put computers in classrooms, and close the digital divide, from $23 million to nearly $800 million a year.

By using these three strategies the Clinton White House was able to make substantial movement on progressive goals, even in the context of deficit reduction and budget surpluses. Federal spending on the EITC, child care, Medicaid, and the state Children's Health Insurance Program (CHIP) grew from $32.4 billion in 1992 to $66.7 billion in 1999.[13] Resources for programs and tax credits supporting preschool through post-secondary education increased from $26.7 billion in 1993 to $59.6 billion in 2001. The Earned Income Tax Credit went up under President Clinton from $8.7 billion in 1993 to $26.1 billion in 2001, a remarkable increase in a time of deficit reduction. Dislocated worker training was tripled; the Women, Infants and Children's program was fully funded.

The 1993 Deficit Reduction Act and the 1997 Balanced Budget Agreement not only avoided virtually any cuts in aid to the poor, they included a spate of new progressive measures, such as a direct student loan program; the first federal Empowerment Zones for poor rural and urban areas; $500 child tax credits for millions of working poor families; health care for 5 million poor children; a new Hope Scholarship program and Lifetime Learning tax credits; and the restoration of basic cash assistance to many elderly or disabled legal immigrants who had been removed from the public assistance rolls in previous legislation.

Still, some progressives argue that President Clinton's commitment to fiscal discipline prevented his administration from seeking bold, large-scale progressive initiatives. This assertion does not hold up under scrutiny. Universal health care was the boldest progressive initiative in generations. In 1999 Clinton tried to pass the USA Account proposal, one of the largest pro-savings initiatives ever for working poor and moderate-income Americans, which would have cost more than $350 billion over a decade. While implementing these broad initiatives proved impossible in the difficult political climate of the day, it is hardly accurate to say the administration failed to stand up for broad plans for progressive change.

GOING FORWARD

A commitment to fiscal discipline does not mean that progressives should give up on bold goals. Progressives could benefit by employing the following four strategies:

1. Articulate a Bold Commitment to Progressive Values

Even where political or fiscal constraints limit immediate movement toward progressive goals, it is vital that progressives not only articulate bold goals but link them to core progressive values. President Clinton gathered support for substantial Earned Income Tax Credit increases even in a difficult budgetary environment in 1993 because he connected that policy with the basic value that no working parent should raise his or her children in poverty. Progressives should not only call for a bold new universal preschool initiative, but clearly tie it to the value of fair starts; not only promote a new cost-sharing compact, but link it to the value of ensuring economic dignity; not only design bold new efforts to spread the wealth creation, but connect them to Americans' optimistic desire for upward mobility.

Making these connections is an area where I feel we underperformed in the last years of the Clinton administration. While we made significant progress for children, we did not do enough to frame it in the context of fair starts and explain that our efforts were only a down payment toward the ultimate goal of universal preschool and universal health care for all children. Part of this failure may be because it is the nature of any outgoing White House staff to stress how much your administration has done, rather than what is left undone. Yet, had we done more to highlight the gap between our current state of affairs and our progressive values, we could have helped provoke our national conscience to propel us more quickly toward these goals.

2. Continually Show the Long-Term Trade-offs Created by Short-Term Choices

If progressives were more successful in defining and making tangible bold policy aims, the trade-offs between public investment and wasteful spending or reckless tax cuts for the most affluent would be more apparent.

Bush's tax cuts for only those making over $300,000 cost our nation $89 billion in 2004[14]—perhaps ten times more than the cost of quality after-school care for every child or enough to save Social Security without a single penny of benefit cuts. Yet in the absence of compelling progressive initiatives, these trade-offs are not apparent. Working parents were not aware that a powerful plan for after-school care or health care was being sacrificed to fund tax cuts for those averaging more than $1 million in annual income.

Progressives have been successful when they demonstrate the clear trade-offs at stake. In 1995, President Clinton explained why a balanced budget plan that included large tax cuts would also have to make large cuts to Medicaid, Medicare, and education. During the Reagan presidency, the dynamic president of the Children's Defense Fund, Marian Wright Edelman, gave masterful presentations with statistics showing how far the money spent on each MX missile or B-1 bomber could go in serving women and children in low-income programs such as Medicaid.

No one is more aware of the power of progressives starkly presenting these trade-offs than the Bush White House. They purposely hid the long-term costs and trade-offs of their tax cuts because they knew all too well that if they had said from day one, "We want a permanent tax cut three times larger than what is needed to fix Social Security," the public would have not supported them. A well-connected Republican admitted to me in January 2005 that Republicans were unlikely to call for a vote on permanent extension of the tax cuts for high-income taxpayers while Social Security reform was on the table because they feared it would allow Democrats to highlight the trade-off between tax cuts for the richest Americans and potential benefit cuts to Social Security.

Had there been more support for President Clinton's initial proposal to dedicate a portion of surpluses to extend Social Security's solvency and more understanding that those funds could reduce benefit cuts, it would have been far more difficult for those very resources to have been diverted to tax cuts for the most well-off. The Supply-Side Trumpers' great marketing success was using sleight of hand and budget tactics to hide the trade-offs. Progressives' and fiscal conservatives' great failure was letting them get away with it.

Progressives should consider legislative mechanisms for drawing attention to these kinds of trade-offs. One approach is to propose capping tax cuts' benefits for the wealthiest to ten times the size of the benefit received by the typical middle-class family. This would make clear that progressives were not opposed to tax cuts—even for the most well off—but simply wanted to limit their costs to bring down the deficit or fund critical education, savings, or adjustment policies. Another avenue worth considering is the use of dedicated funding streams. At the state level, potentially controversial tax increases have been enacted when their revenues are explicitly linked to funding popular progressive goals such as increased education or health care expansions. Many states including Oklahoma, Colorado, and Illinois use tobacco taxes to fund health care initiatives. Communities such as Portland, Oregon, and Miami, Florida, have passed referenda to raise property taxes to fund early childhood education.[15]

3. Create a New Culture of Experimentation, Evaluation, and Investing in Success

FDR once counseled that when it comes to aiding the disadvantaged, "it is common sense to take a method and try it: if it fails, admit it frankly and try another. But above all, try something." Unfortunately, we haven't taken his advice. Part of the problem is that the culture in Washington tends to discourage experimentation and evaluation, and when it is put to use, a pernicious double standard is often applied to programs that impact the poor. Most people appreciate that a cure for cancer or a new weapons system is worth several experiments, evaluations, and adjustments. Yet when a program is designed to provide children fair starts, help disadvantaged adults, support school-to-work programs, or reduce global poverty, conservative critics tend to look at any critical evaluation, not as a learning tool, but as a reason to jettison the entire enterprise. When faulty and incomplete studies in the early 1990s suggested that some of the benefits of Head Start may fade out over time, there were calls to cut back or eliminate the program rather than to look at what investments later in a child's life might maintain its benefits.

Moving toward a culture of experimentation and evaluation requires four understandings: First, while rigorous evaluations are vital, they can at times be subjective, preliminary, or flawed. A culture where one bad evaluation can kill a project chills rigorous examination. Second, we must eliminate the double standard on programs for the poor. If we believe in fair starts, and if eliminating child poverty is a national imperative, an evaluation that shows a child poverty program is not effective should first be a call to revise and improve that project—not eliminate it. Third, where it is clear that a progressive program is fatally flawed, progressives should take the lead in calling for eliminating that failed program and instituting an effective one. Progressives may have a legitimate fear that any admission of error will be used to undermine the entire policy position. But if we are to foster greater confidence among taxpayers that their dollars are being well spent, pro-growth progressives must champion the elimination of wasteful and ineffective programs.

Fourth, we need to invest in success. We have too few processes for identifying and expanding successful programs, and too many successful programs do not get the support they deserve. The nonprofit Teach for America has been lauded as a model program. Bush mentioned the program by name in the 2002 State of the Union and suggested that more young people consider joining it. And yet because of a lack of funding, Teach for America has to turn down ten thousand applicants every year who want to serve their country by teaching in poor areas. Last year, Teach for America had acceptance rates as low as most Ivy League schools.[16] Programs such as Job Corps and Youth Build struggle for funding, despite consistently showing solid results. There is something wrong with this picture.

One effective approach we used in the Clinton administration was to set up programs where applicants competed for challenge grants—a process that spurs innovation, partnership, and stronger efforts, and could be applied on a much grander scale. President Bush has called for a Millennium Challenge Account to reward effective efforts to reduce global poverty. We could also have a Domestic Millennium Challenge Account that invests in and expands programs that successfully reduce poverty in the United States.

4. Focus on the Values Behind Progressive Balance on Fiscal Policy

Pro-growth progressives should not shy away from basing their arguments for fiscal discipline on the larger values of generational responsibility. Leaving our children better off—both nationally and within each family—is a powerful American value across the political spectrum. Politicians from both sides of the aisle are more likely to withstand the attacks on their tough deficit reduction votes if they stand firm on such values.

But the legislation most responsible for the explosion of the deficit in the last several years—tax cuts and the prescription drug bill for seniors— has had nothing to do with a thoughtful acknowledgment of how much we are borrowing from, instead of investing in, our children's future.

LESSON IN REALITY: A FINAL CAVEAT

Any White House wrestles with the trade-off between headline-grabbing, potentially history-making bold proposals and the pragmatic, modest gains that are more likely to succeed. If you shoot for the moon and fail—as we did on universal health care—you wonder how many more people you might have helped had you been more practical. When you focus on what is realistic and clearly achievable, however, you wonder whether you should have made a bold moral statement.

Our efforts on global poverty reduction illustrate this tension. Upon leaving the administration, many of us who worked on global development and AIDS were discouraged by the lack of support among the public and the Republican Congress for overseas development assistance. We had many budget meetings where President Clinton gnashed his teeth and decried Republican congressional opposition to virtually anything that involved using American taxpayer dollars in foreign countries. The president was beside himself when a major Republican congressional leader "bragged" that he had never had a passport.

In 1999 we had beat back the Republican Congress's effort to cut the foreign assistance budget by 15 percent and House Majority Whip Tom DeLay then promised he would politicize our successful effort during the 2000 campaign as a case of Democrats choosing "Ghana over Grandma."[17] It was the latest in what seemed like an annual ritual with the Republican Congress in the 1990s: they would call for dramatic cuts in our development budget, and we would have to fight to restore funding and then to make increases knowing that it would lead to accusations of big spending.[18] In 2000 we called for debt relief for poor nations, for increasing the international AIDS budget to $466 million (more than triple its level only two years before),[19] and for bumping up education and child labor efforts by about $100 million as well. While we knew that these funding increases were far from what was needed, we also knew that in a political environment where Republicans often followed the lead of the powerful chairman of the Senate Foreign Relations Committee Jesse Helms, who described development assistance as "pouring money down a rat hole," a request for more than $1 billion would cause a backlash.[20] Indeed, it took an inspired all-out push from the administration and multitudes of advocacy groups to pass the legislation.

After September 11, the world changed. In what would have been an unthinkable move only two years earlier, President Bush announced in 2003 a major increase in AIDS funding and billions of dollars for a new Millennium Challenge Account to reward poor countries that performed well. While both these programs have their flaws, that a Republican president was willing to support such substantial increases in development assistance was an important and commendable breakthrough—even if it was provoked by larger geopolitical concerns.[21]

These unexpected events caused many of us to second-guess whether we should have aimed even higher on overseas development assistance. Even if it had been a losing battle, shouldn't we have used our last year to sound the clarion call with a multibillion-dollar AIDS proposal? Even if we couldn't have passed a new large-scale AIDS initiative, by proposing one, we would have been the first administration to lay out the high moral marker. For years President Clinton wanted to be bolder on development assistance. Why hadn't we matched that desire with a Marshall Plan for AIDS and global poverty reduction?

At first blush, I regretted having missed an opportunity by being too practical. Yet further reflection forced me to question whether I realistically believed a bolder proposal would have helped more people's lives or did I regret having failed to put forward a proposal that would have seized the moral high ground? We would have had the distinction of being the first to propose a visionary, multibillion-dollar AIDS initiative, but would it really have resulted in more help to real people?

This is a far tougher calculation.

I remember all too well the political mood of the time and the partisan opposition to any legislation that would bring President Clinton or Vice President Gore any glory. Even modest international environmental efforts, including data dissemination that might have warned millions of the December 2004 tsunami, were virulently opposed simply because Vice President Gore supported them.

In 2000 the administration had to pull out every stop and still get lucky just to secure $1 billion in funding for AIDS, education, and debt relief to poor nations. Indeed, part of the reason for the success of our legislative strategy on debt relief for poor nations was our explicit decision to not overplay it as a part of the Clinton legacy. In a meeting in the Roosevelt Room, Tom Hart, one of the leaders of the debt relief coalition, profusely thanked Secretary Larry Summers, Treasury Undersecretary Tim Geithner, and me for our work but explained that the best thing we could do was to go radio silent for four weeks, because if the initiative was perceived to be a Clinton-led effort, they would not be able to get the Republicans we needed on board. A historic White House meeting on debt relief that brought together an amazing range of political perspectives—from Reverend Pat Robertson and conservative Congressman John Kasich to Cardinal Theodore McCarrick, Bono, and liberal Congresswoman Maxine Waters—took place only because Kasich and I met secretly and agreed that he would write a letter to President Clinton requesting the meeting so that they could say, "Kasich requested this meeting with President Clinton on debt relief."

A top debt relief advocate told me recently that he feared that if Clinton called for a major Marshall Plan on AIDS and debt relief, it would have branded it as a Clinton-Gore idea and doomed its passage during an election year. This would have been a major defeat, as debt relief freed up $2.5 billion a year in debt payments for health and education in the world's poorest countries and helped lay the foundation for the increased bipartisanship on global poverty that came into fuller force after September 11.[22]

17

Generational Responsibility: Savings and Social Security

Back in the 2000 presidential campaign, George Bush promoted plans to transfer—or "carve out"—a portion of payroll taxes that currently fund Social Security into private accounts that individuals could invest in equities and bonds. With President Bush's reelection the debate moved to the top of policy discussions in Washington. The stated goals of those pushing for carve-out accounts—higher savings, prefunding retirement security, greater individual choice, spreading wealth creation—seem to have much common ground with pro-growth progressives. Yet at almost every turn, their arguments for private accounts are a massive case of false advertising. For the pro-growth progressive, however, the challenge is to not only expose the false case being made but also offer a viable alternative that both secures the core promise of economic dignity provided by Social Security and gives Americans separate opportunities to build savings and wealth.

THE SQUIRREL COLONY

While Social Security is one of the best-loved social programs in U.S. history, the financing structure is among the least well understood. Many citizens believe that—like squirrels stashing acorns—when they pay money in Social Security payroll taxes, it is put in a stash to be drawn upon in their retirement.

But Social Security is more like a squirrel colony in which each generation of young worker squirrels pools a fixed share of the acorns they gather to help feed older squirrels during the long, cold winters. Every squirrel contributes the same percentage of their take, but they agree to give a slightly larger share of the total to the poorest elderly squirrels, disabled worker squirrels, and the young of squirrels who cannot work or are decreased. What gives the current acorn-gathering squirrels security is not that there are individual stashes of acorns somewhere for each of them, but that there is a generational compact; they know that when they are old, the next generation of worker squirrels will return the favor by sharing some of their acorn bounty. Since acorn contributions are mandatory and pooled, each generation of retiring squirrels knows it can count on a set amount of acorns in old age.

Now, imagine that one day leading squirrel demographers find some disturbing population trends in the colony: squirrels are living longer; having fewer squirrel babies; a large number of them are set to retire at about the same time. They determine that soon there will be far too few worker squirrels gathering acorns to provide the burgeoning number of squirrel retirees with the same number of acorns that previous generations received in their retirement.

With too few worker squirrels per squirrel retiree, the math is pretty simple. If nothing is done, there will either not be enough acorns for future squirrel retirees to get their promised share (leading to acorn cuts) or future worker squirrels will have to give a higher percentage of their acorns (a higher acorn tax) to the burgeoning retiree squirrel population, leaving fewer acorns to feed their own children. The squirrel colony could borrow to make up for coming shortfall, but that will saddle the next generation of squirrels with a mountain of acorn debt.

THE GENERATIONAL COMPACT: SOCIAL SECURITY

Suffice it to say, this squirrel colony bears a striking resemblance to our Social Security system. Like the worker squirrels, human workers and their employers set aside a fixed share of wages to support current retirees. The amount set aside is equal to 12.4 percent of the first $90,000 of wages paid to the workers, with 6.2 percent paid by the workers and 6.2 percent paid by the employer. The understanding is that they, too, will receive the benefits when they retire, paid for by the next generation of workers, who will set aside the same amount of their own earnings. Policy wonks refer to this as a "pay-as-you-go" system.

If this elegant, generational pay-as-you-go compact has worked so well so far, why can't it continue? Simply put: demographics. The millions of babies born after World War II will begin retiring in 2008. With life expectancy increasing, the period over which these baby boom retirees will draw Social Security benefits will lengthen, and as fertility rates decline, there will be fewer and fewer workers to support the burgeoning number of retirees. While 39.9 million retirees will collect Social Security in 2005, by 2025 there will be 64.5 million; and by 2045 there will be 79.7 million— nearly double the number in 2005. Over the same period, the number of workers will grow by only one-fifth. Since 1975, about 3.3 workers have paid into the Social Security system for each beneficiary. By 2025, that ratio will fall to only 2.3 workers for each beneficiary, and by 2045 to 2.0.[1]

The problem is clear: there will not be enough acorns to go around. According to projections by the Social Security Administration, the combination of payroll taxes and payments from the Social Security Trust Fund will be able to pay full scheduled benefits to retirees until 2041. After that, if no changes are made, the system will only be able to pay about 74 cents out of every dollar in scheduled benefits.

Currently, we still collect more payroll taxes than we need to pay benefits. Per the Social Security reforms signed by Ronald Reagan in 1983, the government uses extra payroll taxes to buy bonds, which are deposited in the Social Security Trust Fund to build interest and help extend the period that Social Security will still be able to pay full benefits. The fact that this trust fund does not contain a mountain of acorns does not mean, as President Bush has stated, that it is the equivalent of an empty cabinet in West Virginia. The bonds held by the Social Security Trust Fund are legal instruments—backed by the full faith and credit of the United States government—that ensure Social Security payroll taxes that are collected and the interest they accumulate will be paid to beneficiaries. Because these bonds will be held and redeemed by taxpayers to benefit future seniors, what will matter most for our overall economic well-being is whether we have increased our national savings enough to meet these obligations without harming our standard of living and our ability to invest in our future.

THE EMPTINESS OF FIXING SOCIAL SECURITY
WITHOUT INCREASING SAVINGS

If politicians were simply looking for a superficial fix to Social Security's future finances, they could pass legislation requiring the U.S. government in 2041 to borrow the funds necessary to pay out benefits at their current levels. Or we could borrow trillions of dollars now, so that individuals or the government could invest them on behalf of Social Security. Both borrowing strategies are fool's errands. The first is reverse generational responsibility: avoiding the need to save by legislating increased borrowing from the next generation. The other is like starting an IRA by running up a MasterCard. You are creating an asset in one account that may possibly grow in the future by creating a debt in another account that is certain to accumulate interest charges.

These two borrowing options highlight a crucial point about Social Security reform: the entire economic virtue of acting early to save its solvency is based on the assumption that this generation is committing to save more now to lighten the burden of the baby boom retirement on coming generations. This is why it has been a matter of consensus in Social Security circles for years that any solution must improve national savings and fiscal discipline today. Past entitlement reform efforts and the recommendations of the 2001 Social Security Commission agreed that the aim of reform was to prepare our economy and government finances for the baby boom retirement down the road. Without saving more, we are like parents who specify in their will that their children should run up their credit cards to settle their debts. More to the point, we are saddling the next generation with a lower pool of savings for investment and hundreds of billions of dollars of higher interest payments on the national debt.

Increasing national savings and investing in the things that will make us more productive—education, technology, and research—will build the skills of our people and create more savings for our businesses to invest in new technologies. Simply put: if you want two workers to produce the acorns previously produced by three workers, it will sure help if those two workers are smarter, more productive, and able to benefit from the latest technologies.

Without this commitment to savings and investing in our future, we risk either taking away Social Security's ability to provide economic dignity to our seniors or making the cost of future retirement security so high that we reduce the resources for the next generation to provide for and invest in their children. As Alan Greenspan has written, "increasing our national saving is critical. . . . The effective application of our capital to its most highly valued use is going to become, if anything, more important, as we strive to increase the resources available to provide for the retirement of the baby boomers without, in the future, significantly reducing the consumption of workers."[2]

The most traditional solutions for generating additional Social Security savings are the most painful: tax increases or benefit cuts. To the degree that some workers pay more payroll taxes or some beneficiaries get fewer benefits than current law calls for, the gap between scheduled benefits and expected revenues closes. Yet these are not the only ways to close the solvency gap. We could specify cuts in other areas of the budget and redirect the savings to Social Security. We could roll back some of the recent tax cuts for the most well-off and redirect those revenues to prevent harsh tax increases or benefit cuts. Just as the parents of triplets all headed to Ivy League schools would be better off if they reduced their luxury spending until they know they can afford the tuitions, our nation should pull back tax cuts for the most fortunate until we know we have the savings to meet our Social Security and Medicare challenges.

In the 1990s, a unique option emerged that was not available in the previous decades, nor is likely to be viable in the foreseeable future: dedicating projected budget surpluses for Social Security. To reduce the likelihood that surpluses would be completely drained by popular new tax cuts or spending, President Clinton called for using surpluses to pay down the national debt while dedicating the interest savings to increasing the solvency of Social Security. After the Clinton administration succeeded in linking surpluses and Social Security, nearly every reform plan floated in the late 1990s—from advocates as diverse as John Kasich, Newt Gingrich, Phil Gramm, Bill Archer and Clay Shaw, and Henry Aaron and Bob Reischauer—dedicated part of the projected surplus to Social Security solvency. Yet with Al Gore's loss in 2000, we never achieved a legislative agreement to lock away Social Security surpluses to ensure they were dedicated to increasing national savings and strengthening Social Security solvency. Without such legislation, projected surpluses remained available for non–Social Security spending and were committed to new tax cuts under the Bush administration. While *Saturday Night Live* had a good time making fun of Al Gore's description of a Social Security "lock box," as Gore has said recently, no one is laughing now.

Backward Steps on National Savings

Our hypothetical parents with triplets heading to college would lose a lot of sympathy if the moment they recognized their rapidly approaching financial burden, they took out five times more debt to buy a multiyear time-share on Martha's Vineyard.

Such financial recklessness produces two distressing realities. One, the parents now need to save five times as much just to get back to the level of debt they had when they first recognized the coming tuition payments. Two, while it might have been difficult but tolerable to borrow much of the triplets' tuition, now these loans will have to be added on to the larger mountain of debt they've incurred to fund their time-share—putting the entire family in a much more dangerous financial position.

This hypothetical describes exactly the reversal the Bush administration has made on the goal of increasing national savings to manage the demographic burden on Social Security. The two signature accomplishments of their first-term agenda, an all-out effort for permanent tax cuts and a prescription drug bill for Medicare, were passed without concern for how to pay for them and are draining the very savings needed for Social Security. The gap in Social Security over the next seventy-five years is about $4.0 trillion adjusted for inflation; if made permanent the comparable cost of Bush's tax cuts would be $12.3 trillion and the prescription drug bill would be $8.7 trillion.[3] Together these proposals will cost five times more than what is needed to make Social Security solvent for seventy-five years! Amazingly, the tax cuts going to only the top 1 percent of Americans—a group with an average income of $1.2 million—would alone keep Social Security completely solvent for seventy-five years without any additional borrowing, tax increases, or benefit cuts.[4]

When you consider the harm the Bush administration has already done to national savings, even a fiscally responsible Social Security plan that increased national savings would at best be a case of "five steps backward, one step forward" on savings. Yet from the president's Social Security rollout at the 2005 State of the Union, his economic team has defended plans that do not even pretend to take a baby step forward on national savings.

Diverting Funds to Individual Accounts: Not a Plus for Savings

From a distance, President Bush's proposals to carve out a portion of the Social Security payroll tax for individual accounts seem to meet the test of adding to national savings. That is because privatization proposals are often billed as the equivalent of the squirrel colony encouraging younger squirrels to stash away extra acorns to supplement their retirement savings when the squirrel worker shortage hits. Unfortunately, diverting—or carving out—a portion of one's payroll taxes to private accounts does nothing to increase savings. Let's say a fifty-five-year-old couple has been putting 12.4 percent of their income into their 401(k) retirement accounts. One day, their twenty-five-year-old son convinces them to take a quarter of that money and put it in his IRA because he believes he can get a higher return in growth stocks. How much more is the family saving? Clearly, no more at all. All they've done is shift funds they had already saved from a secure and stable account to a riskier one.

Carve-out individual accounts do exactly the same thing. By shifting to a system where 8.4 percent of taxable payroll goes to traditional Social Security and 4 percent goes to private accounts, we are still saving 12.4 percent of taxable payroll for Social Security, but now part of the savings is invested at a higher risk. Worse, these private accounts could actually lower overall national savings. If workers falsely believe that the payroll taxes diverted into their private accounts represent an increase in retirement savings, it could lead some to cut back their pension or personal savings.[5]

Borrowing for New Accounts Does Not Repair the Damage

If younger squirrels decide to move 33 percent of what they normally contribute to retiree squirrels to build their own stash, current squirrel retirees would obviously face a 33 percent shortfall. The same is true with Social Security privatization. If the 12.4 percent payroll tax is already committed to keeping Social Security 100 percent solvent until 2041, and younger workers are now allowed to take about 33 percent of it for their own accounts, it also creates a hole in what current and future retirees are promised. Indeed, the president's plan to divert 33 percent of payroll taxes from Social Security will drive the system into insolvency eleven years earlier than if nothing were done.[6]

The money that is needed to fill this hole is called the "transition cost" of moving Social Security from a completely pay-as-you-go system to one which is partially prefunded. Rather than finding spending cuts or new revenues to pay for these transition costs and increase national savings, the president's plan aims to borrow the money, thereby simply shifting existing savings from one pot to another and making no forward progress. In fact, Social Security expert Jason Furman found that filling the gap would require $4.9 trillion in borrowing over the first twenty years of the program ($3 trillion if adjusted for net present value) and would increase the national debt for over sixty years.[7]

The White House defense of this massive new borrowing is that it would have no negative effect on national savings, as the increase in government borrowing would be transferred to private savings in these new accounts. This defense highlights how dramatically we have lowered our national standards for what Social Security reform should accomplish. Only a few years ago experts from all sides of the political spectrum believed that *increasing* national savings was the core justification for an early Social Security solution. Now the White House's new gold standard is that after you take five giant steps backward on national savings, simply do no further harm.

Also troubling, the White House defense of massive new government borrowing assumes that a Social Security plan that dramatically increases the federal debt will not affect economic confidence. While projections when President Bush took office that the United States would become debt free may have been optimistic, the run-up in the projected national debt during his tenure has been stunning. In 2008, the national debt is projected to be $5 trillion higher than projected when President Bush took office, and we are now on course to double it by 2030. Under President Bush's privatization plan, government borrowing is projected to nearly triple over that time, growing to equal in size to the entire American economy.[8] This dramatic increase in debt would damage economic confidence for several reasons.

First, confidence in the world's major economies is often affected by how they are seen to address their traditional economic Achilles' heels. For Japan and China, the test is usually the degree to which they pursue bank reform and confront the problem of nonperforming loans. For Europe, the test is progress on labor market rigidities. For the United States, the test has long been how well we keep our fiscal house in order. True, we have had a volatile record on fiscal discipline and have shown little appetite for dealing with major entitlements like Medicare and Social Security unless a real crisis is only a few years away. But the government summoned the political will to make difficult fiscal choices on Social Security in 1977 and 1983, and Medicare in 1993 and 1997. While the surpluses the United States ran in the late 1990s provided a major boost in economic confidence and foreign direct investment, if new policies expanded, extended, and accelerated our national debt, the United States would be seen as a debtor nation.

White House economists counter with a curious argument. They argue that if markets currently think the United States will have to incur debt decades from now to fund our Social Security shortfall, then borrowing the money now will not harm economic confidence. In essence, they are saying that to the degree markets have a worst-case expectation—that we will deal with Social Security by massive borrowing in the future—there is no harm in locking in that worst-case expectation by borrowing now. But massive borrowing to deal with Social Security solvency is harmful because it signals that the United States may never be expected to reduce the national debt or make fiscally and politically tough choices when confronting major entitlement challenges.

Second, Social Security plans that call for enormous increases in the national debt but promise essentially to pay the money back down the road are unlikely to mitigate much of the damage to confidence such an explosion of government borrowing caused. Contrary to the carefully orchestrated impression put forward by the Bush administration and the Republican National Committee that the debt will rise only for a single decade, the president's private account proposal increases the national debt for over sixty years! Former Secretary of the Treasury Bob Rubin has rightly noted, however, that projected savings over a half century from now "will do nothing" to reduce the potential for negative impacts now on our financial stability.[9] While certainly "borrow now, save later" plans that call for some form of fiscal discipline down the road are preferable to plans that call for only borrowing, they hardly inspire confidence.

Moreover, while it makes sense for the painful elements of Social Security reform to be phased in, plans that do not increase savings and even increase the national debt in the short and medium term allow this generation to pass the burden of savings down the road. It is a bit like a college president who faces deteriorating buildings deciding that instead of soliciting additional funds from alumni to fix them, he will pass a resolution instructing his successor to cut professors' salaries and increase tuition to pay for them years from now.

Last, private account advocates who are nonchalant about running up the national debt rarely mention the billions of dollars in additional interest payments that taxpayers will bear for decades to come. Between 2011 and 2050, additional interest payments on new debt due to Bush's privatization plan would total $6.5 trillion—or $163 billion a year on average—in inflation-adjusted dollars. By the 2030s, we would be spending more money each year on interest payments than on the entire United States Army and four times the projected homeland security budget. Because the majority of this debt would likely be held by foreign creditors, it would increase our vulnerability to outside economic events, and ship our debt servicing outlays overseas—including nearly $1 trillion to China over forty years—rather than back into the U.S. economy.[10]

The irony is that for all President Bush's talk of a Social Security "crisis," the administration admits that private accounts will not increase Social Security's solvency. Indeed, during the rollout of the President's plan in February 2002, a top White House Social Security advisor was asked, "Would it be fair to describe . . . the personal accounts by themselves as having no effect whatsoever on the solvency issue?" He replied, "That's a fair inference."[11]

18

Break a Leg: Should We Save Social Security As We Know It?

Beyond issues of national savings, pro-growth progressives who want to champion economic dignity and upward mobility must clearly define Social Security's distinctive role in pursuing these goals. The United States retirement security system has often been described as a three-legged stool: one leg consists of personal savings and home equity; the second, pensions; and the third, Social Security, which has always been distinguished as the only guaranteed, risk-free leg. While failure to save, poor choices, bad luck, or a weak economy can undercut the first two legs, Social Security was designed to be the leg that ensures a modicum of economic dignity during retirement even if everything else goes wrong.

There are historical, economic, and human nature rationales for having one leg of the retirement stool provide benefits that are guaranteed and not subject to the state of the economy, the stock market, or even individual savings patterns. Most advanced societies have retirement systems that recognize the human tendency to be myopic about long-term savings and retirement needs, and the risk of unplanned events. In the United States, Social Security was a specific response to the Great Depression. According to the Social Security Administration, "in 1934 over half of the elderly lacked sufficient income to be self supporting."[1] Even in today's economy, the risk-free quality of Social Security is essential. Consider the fate of older workers who saw their jobs, pensions, savings, health benefits, and housing values all spiral down when their companies were hit by scandal or a dramatic stock collapse in 2001 and 2002. The only portion of their finances that avoided this downward spiral was Social Security. At age eighty, Henry Pierce was informed that his struggling former employer, Special Metals, was going to cut his $400 monthly pension and his health benefits by more than 65 percent. With large-scale layoffs in the area, Pierce has also seen the value of his house erode in recent years. He is bracing himself to live on Social Security alone: "That's what keeps me going," he explained. "If it weren't for that, I wouldn't have nothing."[2]

While pro-growth progressives should certainly support measures like a Universal 401(k) that increase investment and wealth creation by strengthening the first two legs of our retirement system, we should still ask why we would want to inject market risk and economic uncertainty into the only leg that is currently risk free. Indeed, those like myself who want to create incentives to encourage more investment through a universal pension should be the most adamant about ensuring that this increased risk taking is balanced by keeping Social Security a rock-solid guarantee.

ARE MANY HAPPY RETURNS A SURE THING?

The benefits of maintaining Social Security as the risk-free leg of retirement are ignored or downplayed by private account advocates who stress potential high returns as a near certainty. Vice President Dick Cheney claims not only that "young workers who elect personal accounts can expect to receive a far higher rate of return on their money than the current system could ever afford to pay them," but that such investments in "securities markets are the best, *safest* way to build substantial personal savings."[3] (Emphasis added.) Statements like these make higher returns seem like a sure thing—free money. Of course, there is no such thing. Investments in the stock market offer higher returns to compensate for the risk that investors could lose some or all of their money. If major companies could guarantee returns as solid as a U.S. government bond, they would not have to compensate their stockholders with higher returns. As Harvard economist Robert Barro points out, "the premium on stocks is compensation for risk." Simply put, Barro writes, "there is no free lunch of assured higher returns."[4] This is why the Congressional Budget Office calculates the "risk-adjusted" returns when it evaluates the prospect of investing Social Security dollars in the market. For the purpose of making long-term budget calculations, they believe market investments will—when one adjusts for the risk of both higher and lower returns—perform about the same as a risk-free government bond. The very design of President Bush's Social Security plan vividly demonstrates what the higher risk of equity investments could mean for individual workers and retirees.

Under the plan, for every dollar you shift into your private account, a dollar plus 3 percent after inflation—or 6 percent if you assume a 3 percent inflation rate—is deducted from your guaranteed Social Security benefit. In other words, President Bush is betting that the dollar you invest in your private account will return more than this 6 percent nominal rate so that you are better off. Indeed, the White House predicts that a future Social Security recipient who invests 50 percent of his account in stocks will get a 7.6 percent return (assuming a 3 percent inflation rate) and therefore do better than if he had remained in the traditional Social Security plan.

The president's plan is the functional equivalent of a financial advisor telling workers to borrow from their MasterCard at 6 percent to invest in an IRA in the hopes of getting a high enough return to allow them to pay back the credit card loan and still make a profit. Under the Bush plan, a worker who diverts money and makes only a 5 percent return will not be able to pay off this loan at 6 percent interest and will thus be worse off. No competent financial advisor would encourage a client to borrow from his credit card and risk losing money in the hope that he might make a 1 percent to 2 percent additional return in the stock market. Nonetheless, the very core of the Bush plan is to encourage even working poor Americans to make precisely this wager with their guaranteed Social Security benefits.

While the vice president and others may tell Americans that, based on historical patterns, moving from guaranteed benefits to investing in the market is the "safest" way to build retirement savings, they fail to mention a number of risks.

Red Sox Risk

Over the past 135 years, investments in the stock market have returned about 4 percent more than government bonds. This is a sound basis for most Americans to put a portion of their long-term pension investments in broadly diversified stock holdings. Yet, will this pattern continue to be such a sure thing that Social Security recipients should bet even the risk-free leg of their retirement stool on higher returns? History provides no assurance that the decade or year to come will follow the patterns of the century, decade, or year that just passed. Ask anyone who relied on historical precedent to bet that the Red Sox would not win the World Series in 2004 or that no team could come back from a 3–0 deficit to win a best-of-seven playoff series.

It is worth noting that the pattern of stocks outperforming government bonds in the United States was not repeated in the most advanced industrialized nations. From 1900 to 2003, average inflation-adjusted equity returns were 3.3 percent in France, 3.0 percent in Germany, and only 2.2 percent in Italy.[5] Even in the United States, the market has gone down or performed worse than government bonds for long periods. The S&P fell after 1968 and did not regain its value after accounting for inflation until 1983. Indeed, in 1979, *BusinessWeek* had a cover entitled "The Death of Equities." These periods are ancient history to many young adults, who, according to a 1999 study, expected the market to increase by a whopping 20 percent annually during their lives.[6]

More and more economic and Wall Street experts acknowledge Red Sox risk, arguing that the spread between risk-free bonds and the real return on equities may be narrower in the future than it has been. While the White House assumes a 6.5 percent real return from equities, the chief economists at JP Morgan, Moody's, Lehman Brothers, and Merrill Lynch all believe that the rate of return will be only 4.0 percent. David Rosenberg of Merrill Lynch believes that the White House estimate "stretches the imagination."[7] When you put this 4 percent estimate on the mixed bonds and stock portfolio that the White House recommends, the real return—even without adjusting for risk—is barely enough to pay back the 3 percent the White House plan subtracts from your Social Security benefit without being worse off. If partial privatization becomes law, the government will ask tens of millions of Americans to risk lower Social Security benefits for the hope of marginally higher returns.

The White House argues that this risk can be mitigated with a "life cycle approach" to investment, which would move participants away from higher-risk equities and into bonds as they got closer to retirement. Yet Yale professor Robert Shiller found that when you adjust future returns based on international averages, the typical Social Security recipient would do worse under the president's plan 71 percent of the time—even with the life cycle option—than under the traditional Social Security system.[8]

All long-term estimates are by definition speculative and varying. Some economists believe that future market returns are likely to be lower because stock price/earning ratios are now historically high. Others predict lower U.S. growth because the American labor force is shrinking or because of fierce competition from new equity markets in other parts of the globe. These variables and unknowns certainly do not rule out the possibility that the returns in the twenty-first century could be as strong or stronger than they were in the twentieth. But they should caution us not to assume that historical trends are a sure bet.

Timing Risk—The Twins Scenario

Even if the historic trend of the market outperforming government bonds continues in this century, a second substantial risk is that your benefits could be paltry if you retire during a market downturn. Imagine twin brothers born in 1907. They both worked in an auto plant; one retired in 1972 at sixty-five and the other retired in 1974 at sixty-seven. Because Social Security protects recipients from market risk, both would receive benefits according to the same formula. Now what if both men had individual retirement accounts and invested in the same market portfolio. Because the stock market declined precipitously from '72 to '74, the brother who retired at the end of 1974 would have received an annuity from his individual account 40 percent less than the one his twin received when he retired at the end of 1972.[9]

Twin brothers retiring before and after the tech bubble burst in 2000 would have had similarly disparate returns. If the twins were enrolled in a partial-privatization plan, the brother who retired in 1999 would receive a monthly benefit 36 percent higher than his brother who retired in 2002. Yet this only tells part of the story. Those who retire in down years, like Mr. Pierce, may also see their pension, housing values, and savings decline as well. But unlike Mr. Pierce, they won't have a guaranteed Social Security benefit.

Bail-Out Risk

One can only imagine the pressure for a deficit-exploding bailout if millions of retirees or near-retirees lost pensions and personal savings and faced greatly diminished Social Security benefits during an election year. Indeed, before Social Security initial benefits were automatically indexed to wages in 1972, Congress repeatedly gave exceptional increases to benefits during election years even without such a downturn. Such "bailout" risk could be substantial. Economist Christian Weller at the Center for American Progress estimates that the cost of ensuring that retirees do not suffer from market downturns would be between $600 billion and $900 billion over the next seventy-five years.[10]

Some privatization advocates have even put forward what has been described as a pre-bailout feature, with the prospect of higher returns but also a guaranteed level of benefits. Economists of all stripes agree that this type of "pre-bailout," or minimum guarantee from your individual account, encourages excessive risk taking through what they call "moral hazard": if the government protects you against your bad investment decisions, you would be far more inclined to make riskier choices than if you had to bear the full costs of your actions. If you give me $10,000 and tell me that no matter how I invest it I am guaranteed a 3 percent profit—I have a huge incentive to bet on long shots. Even if I lose my $10,000, the government would guarantee me a $10,300 bailout. These proposals would encourage recipients to make the riskiest investment possible, knowing they could keep all the gain in their private accounts if they hit it big, and that their fellow taxpayers would pick up the tab if they bet wrong.

Exploding Hidden Fee Risk

Suppose that in order to set up an individual account you had to pay a 25 percent tax on all of its earnings that would go directly to well-off Wall Street employees. That doesn't sound like a political winner, does it? Yet in a typical IRA, the bank or the brokerage firm charges the account holder an annual management fee that is often 1 percent of the account's balance.[11] That may not sound like a lot, but it means that over forty years, 20 percent to 30 percent of the account goes to the financial institution.[12] And the more frequently you trade the assets in your account, the higher the transactions costs. Austan Goolsbee, professor of economics at the University of Chicago Graduate School of Business, predicted that if individual accounts are managed like an average 401(k), Wall Street stands to pocket $940 billion in administrative fees, an amount that would be the "largest windfall gain in American financial history."[13]

The histories of private accounts in Chile and Great Britain are cause for concern. Hidden fees and transaction costs drained over 20 percent of the accounts' value in Chile, and in Britain fees spiraled so far out of control—over 40 percent in some cases—that the government was forced to restrict trading and investment options in the accounts.[14]

In response to concerns about high transaction costs, the Bush administration put forward a plan that limits investment choices and would be managed by a quasi-government entity modeled on the Thrift Savings Plan (TSP) currently offered to government employees. The TSP has kept administrative costs low and represents a sensible way to offer low-cost, reasonably diversified investment options.[15] Yet, while the TSP model is a sensible way to lower the high costs of pensions in the private sector, it is still not clear why one would want to add the risk that Social Security transaction costs would explode as the TSP was forced to dramatically ramp up to cover nearly 150 million workers. Even Bush's Presidential Management Agenda ranks Social Security as the government's most efficient program.[16] Economist Dean Baker at the Center for Economic Policy Research estimates that even if private accounts restricted investment choices and maintained lower transaction costs, the costs would be five times higher than current Social Security.[17]

UNDERVALUING SOCIAL SECURITY:
OR GREASING THE SLIPPERY SLOPE TO PRIVATIZATION

The architecture and rhetoric behind virtually all Social Security privatization proposals share one aspect: they are designed to encourage Americans both to undervalue the broad, guaranteed benefits of Social Security and to overvalue the benefits of the newly created private accounts.

Consider a worker who has $10,000 to ensure the security of himself and his family. He takes $5,000 and invests it in the stock market. With the other $5,000 he buys his family fire, auto, and life insurance. After one year the stock market goes up 5 percent, so his investment is worth $5,250. But he concludes he has taken a loss on his second $5,000 investment because he is still alive, his house hasn't burned down, and his family avoided a major car accident. As a result, he cancels all of his insurance because his stock investment appears to be bringing a higher return. Of course, this is absurd behavior: you cannot determine the value of insurance by looking at year-by-year returns.

When President Bush claims that Social Security has "a paltry rate of return compared to conservative stocks and bonds"[18] he is encouraging Americans to make precisely this foolish comparison. Consider a more accurate comparison: On the first day of a new job your employer offers two retirement savings options. Option One provides a 3 percent return above inflation and Option Two often provides a 5 percent return above inflation. The second might seem pretty attractive if that were all the information you were given. But what if the benefits administrator explained that, unlike Option Two, Option One is 100 percent guaranteed, will give you a higher retirement benefit as a percentage of your income if you fall into poverty, and provides you with monthly disability insurance and life insurance that would provide full benefits to your surviving spouse in retirement and your children until they were eighteen years old?

The second option is Social Security. The survivor's insurance (worth about $353,000 in the private sector) and disability insurance (worth about $403,000 in the private sector) provided by Social Security are the difference between financial devastation and economic dignity for millions of Americans.[19] About one-third of Social Security payments, to 17 million Americans, go to non-retirees in the form of these insurance benefits. Seven million are disabled workers and their families, 55 percent of whom would live in poverty without these benefits.[20] Thanks to Social Security, 68 million children go to bed at night with the assurance that if a breadwinning parent were to die, survivor's insurance would replace part of the lost income they need for their economic well-being. One of the people who sat in the first lady's box for the 1998 State of the Union was a young woman named Tyra Brown. After her mother died when she was fifteen, she moved in with her grandmother and struggled to make it through high school and to get to college. "It wasn't easy," she explained, "but Social Security really helped, and we could count on that income to be there every month. And I don't think we could have made it otherwise. When my mom was alive she paid into the Social Security system, and although she wasn't able to get her retirement benefits, her Social Security contributions did help provide for me when I needed support."[21]

At an event at the Center for American Progress, I met a retired economist who told me the heart-wrenching story of his sister Susan's experience with Social Security's survivor's and disability insurance. Three years ago, her husband, Joseph,[22] was laid off from his prosperous job at an energy company; soon after he was diagnosed with a terminal brain tumor and began collecting disability insurance. He died on his fifty-seventh birthday, leaving behind seven children, two in college and three younger than eighteen. The youngest, age ten, was born with Down Syndrome and will need to collect disability for his entire life. But Susan and the children had Social Security survivor's insurance, and she was able to keep her house and send her children to college. For families like Susan and Joseph's, the insurance component of Social Security is the wall that keeps compounded misfortune from washing them over the edge. If the Bush administration wanted to create a transparent and accurate picture of the risks and rewards of private accounts, private accounts would be worth precisely the incremental value they added above Social Security benefits.

What is striking and revealing is the degree to which the entire structure of the Bush partial privatization plan is contorted to make people undervalue Social Security's full slate of benefits and overvalue private accounts. The basic argument for private accounts is that while $1,000 in payroll taxes might be worth $1,060 after one year in Social Security (with a 3 percent rate above inflation, which we will assume to be 3 percent), if you could invest that $1,000 in the market you might make 7 percent or $1,070 and be $10 better off. Since the White House recognizes that you need to pay back Social Security for the $1,060 value of the payroll taxes that were diverted, the value of the private accounts in this context should be $10.

Yet the president structured his plan so that all $1,070 stays in the private account while the loan of $1,060 from Social Security payroll taxes would be repaid by reducing traditional benefits by $1,060. This design serves two functions: it makes a private account that has added only $10 look like it has gained more than one hundred times that much, and it makes today's guaranteed Social Security benefit appear $1,060 less generous.

Their effort to make Social Security's guaranteed benefits look paltry does not end here. The entire Bush effort to improve solvency is achieved through a second round of cuts to traditional Social Security benefits. The result of these double cuts is to make traditional Social Security benefits all but disappear for many middle-income beneficiaries. By 2055, a median earner will see their traditional benefit cut by two-thirds; and according to Jason Furman a worker currently making $59,000 will see her guaranteed benefit cut by seven-eighths.

The depth of the White House's commitment to this deceptive strategy was evident when a *Washington Post* story incorrectly assumed that the White House plan would require that private accounts pay back the diverted payroll taxes to Social Security (in the above hypothetical the account would pay back $1,060 and be left with a value of $10). The White House launched an all-out assault on the story, releasing a fact sheet calling the story "flat wrong" and "completely inaccurate."[23] Yet for a Social Security recipient, it would not make a penny of difference whether the offset came out of his private account or Social Security benefit, as a top White House staffer confirmed in a February briefing.[24] So why the hysterics?

What really upset the White House was not the *Post*'s technical error, but the fact that the story gave readers an accurate picture of the relatively meager and uncertain benefits of the Bush private account plan. Ensuring that a partial privatization plan inflates the true value of private accounts and demeans the true value of the Social Security guaranteed benefit is fundamental to those who would like to see private accounts as merely a first step in a slippery slope toward dismantling the Social Security compact as we know it.

What makes Social Security a crown jewel of progressive government is not only that it provides assurance of economic dignity for those who have taken personal responsibility, but it has been a compact between all working Americans—the middle class and healthy as well as the working poor and the disabled. Americans have embraced its progressivity: the idea that you pay more in the better off you are, and you get more back if misfortune strikes in the form of poverty, disability, or loss of a parent or spouse you rely on or if you just live longer than normal. Many Americans who never expect to be poor or disabled know that protection is there for anyone in their family who may need it. This progressive compact has had a powerful political dimension. Because Social Security is a progressive program that the middle class believes in, it has never been as politically vulnerable as programs that benefit only those who are poor or disabled.

Yet if private accounts in Social Security can be distorted to encourage the healthy and well-off to see Social Security, not as a universal compact, but as a bad deal, they will gradually use their political clout to pull out of it altogether. This process could transform what is today a progressive compact into a two-tiered system of private accounts for the fortunate and a politically weak welfare program for the elderly poor and those with disabilities.

LEAVING WEALTH TO HEIRS: A FALSE CASE FOR PRIVATIZATION

One prominent argument for partial privatization is that private accounts would let a worker who died before he collected Social Security leave what he accumulated to his surviving heirs. President Bush has stated: "It's your money, and when you pass on, you can leave it to whomever you want. That's not the way the system works today." [25] While allowing workers to accumulate savings that they can leave to their surviving family certainly spreads wealth creation, the argument that it must be done by partially privatizing Social Security is disingenuous for two reasons.

First, the call for inheritability is another way that private account advocates ignore or undervalue Social Security's guaranteed benefits. As just discussed, survivors' benefits in essence allow the millions of workers and retirees to leave to their children under eighteen and their spouses over sixty their benefits during the time their loved ones need them most.

Second, if we want to increase the degree to which Social Security allows workers who die before they reach retirement age—or before they enjoy a typically long retirement—to bequeath some of their benefits to their heirs, it can easily be done without private accounts or partial privatization. The only issue is cost. Whether you use traditional Social Security or private accounts, increasing a worker's ability to bequeath benefits requires huge amounts of new resources, from more borrowing, more taxes, or more benefit cuts.

To see why this entire issue is about cost, not privatization, remember that Social Security functions as an annuity. If someone lives a long time, it is more costly for the Social Security system. But if a person dies sooner than average, the savings to the Social Security system compensates for the costs of the people who live longer. This is no small issue—especially for older women. Unmarried women make up more than 60 percent of all households over eighty-five, and 28 percent of women sixty-five or older are poor or near poor. [26] One out of four elderly women living alone relies on Social Security as her only source of income. [27] For the growing number of women who outlive their husbands and live into their nineties, it is literally a lifesaver.

Now let's say that every Social Security recipient could bequeath the benefits they did not receive to their heirs. To do this, Social Security would lose the savings that allow it to provide benefits for those women and men who live longer than expected. The key to adding such a new and expensive feature is not partially privatizing Social Security, it is finding considerable new funds to allow bequeathments by those who die early without having to pay lower benefits to those who live longer than average. If inheritability is a desired policy goal, it requires more resources, not privatization.

NOT THE WAY TO HELP MINORITIES

Privatization advocates also use statistics on workers dying before or shortly after reaching retirement to argue that the current system has a negative bias against minorities—particularly black males. As President Bush said earlier this year, "African American males die sooner than other males do, which means the system is inherently unfair to a certain group of people." [28] Private account advocates use the alarming statistic that black males have an average life expectancy of sixty-eight years—nine years less than the national average—to suggest that they will collect Social Security for only three years. [29] This is a serious issue that deserves serious consideration, yet like inheritability, it in no way argues for private accounts.

First, this use of average life expectancies is grossly misleading. As economist and *New York Times* columnist Paul Krugman points out, the lower average life expectancies for African Americans in general, and males in particular, reflect higher death rates from causes such as crime and infant mortality that happen at early ages and have no impact on Social Security. [30] In fact, at the age of sixty-five, African American males can expect to collect Social Security for 14.6 years—only two years less than white males, and four times as long as you'd expect if you looked only at the average life expectancy. Oddly, the administration has been using this same argument about Hispanic Americans, even though they can expect to live about three years longer than whites and therefore benefit even more from the current structure of Social Security. [31] As a 2005 National Council of La Raza report stated, "because of longer relative life expectancies than their peers, Latinos gain on a lifetime basis when one compares the disability, survivor, and retirement benefits received with taxes paid by the average Latino worker." [32]

Second, when you examine actual life and work histories, Social Security is an advantageous deal for African American males. The system's highly progressive benefit structure means that low-income earners get a larger share of their wages replaced by Social Security. Since African Americans still make up a disproportionate number of low-income workers, the progressive structure means their guaranteed benefits are high relative to the taxes they pay. Over time, African American workers in the bottom 20 percent of wage earners receive on average nearly twice as much in benefits as they paid in taxes, while Hispanics at this income level receive 1.5 times as much as they paid in taxes. [33] Furthermore, African Americans are much more likely to receive survivor's and disability benefits. They make up only 13 percent of the population, but 18 percent of workers collecting disability benefits. Nearly a quarter of black children collect survivor's benefits.[34] A recent GAO report concluded that African Americans actually get more from Social Security relative to what they paid in than whites.[35] As with inheritability, however, if privatizers want to make benefits more generous to African American males, they could use additional resources to make our current benefit structure more generous to those who die earlier.

19

Toward a Progressive Consensus on Retirement Savings and Wealth Creation

I have often seen polls that seem to suggest that the public held contradictory views on retirement security and Social Security reform. When asked whether they would like an individual account that offered more personal choice to invest for higher returns, they responded positively. But they also said they wanted a rock-solid Social Security benefit that was protected from market risk.

The wrong lesson to draw from this poll is that Americans are confused or stupid, or that the only thing standing between saving Social Security as we know it and privatization is a great marketing campaign. The right lesson is that the majority of Americans support the underlying logic of the three-legged retirement stool. Most of us want to have both some rock-solid protection if everything goes wrong and the opportunity to invest and take some risks for the chance of greater economic wealth. Neither progressives nor conservatives have articulated a vision for retirement security that meets both of these aspirations. Conservatives offer little rationale for why private savings can only be increased by injecting risk into Social Security through private accounts. Progressives, on the other hand, make powerful critiques against privatization and arguments for the need to keep Social Security a risk-free, guaranteed benefit but rarely present bold progressive options that offer middle-income and working poor Americans significant new opportunities to save and create wealth through the other legs of the retirement system—pension coverage and personal savings.

The pro-growth progressive should seek to strengthen Social Security as we know it—guaranteed, solvent, and risk-free—while promoting American's wealth creation aspirations, and strengthening the employer-pension leg of our retirement stool with a new Universal 401(k).

1. Real Generational Responsibility and Savings

Pro-growth progressives should establish a threshold test for any Social Security reform proposal: it *must* increase savings and generational responsibility. Any reform plan needs to increase savings, at the very least, to repair some of the damage done by the Bush administration's tax cuts, and certainly must not further increase our public debt in the short or long term.

Plans that either increase borrowing or lock in the historic fiscal deterioration of the last few years seemed designed by the Mad Hatter, who said, "Up is down and down is up." Passing on more debt and risk to the next generation turns the entire justification for generational responsibility on its head. Many of the Republican plans depend on adding trillions of dollars to the debt to create private accounts.

Sadly, the most prominent Republican plans for Social Security reform in the fall of 2005 have completely abandoned any pretense of fiscal or generational responsibility. A report by the Center for Budget and Policy Priorities found that rather than attempting to increase national savings, the seven major Republican congressional plans would on average raise the national debt by a staggering 46.8 percent GDP by 2050, while several call for no difficult choices even to increase savings down the road. The goal of increasing national savings and generational responsibility, which had for decades been the core justification for addressing Social Security's long-term solvency sooner rather than later, has now been replaced with an obsession with partial privatization. Perhaps the most cynical of these proposals are the ones by Representative Jim McCrery and Senator Jim DeMint that both increase the debt and make no progress on strengthening Social Security's solvency. These plans seek to score political points by claiming falsely that they prevent "a raid" on the Social Security Trust Fund, yet their real purpose is to use this argument as a Trojan horse to borrow nearly a trillion dollars to lay the foundation for larger-scale Social Security privatization. Ironically, rather than protecting Social Security surpluses, Senator DeMint's proposal would divert $1 trillion of them into new private accounts and away from the bonds that ensure these surpluses are dedicated to paying future benefits and extending the program's solvency.[1] Pro-growth progressives should set a strong principle that the only way to truly restore Social Security solvency is to increase national savings now.

2. Universal 401(K) in Addition to Social Security

The linchpin for a progressive consensus on retirement savings could be a combination of a bold new Universal 401(k) outside of Social Security and a fair and progressive financing plan to keep Social Security solvent for the next seventy-five years.

A Universal 401(k) can provide the common ground that Democrats and Republicans need if they are going to work toward an agreement that is both pro-growth and progressive. In 1999, when President Clinton proposed USA Accounts, both parties were too suspicious of each other to recognize the benefits the plan offered. We should not miss this opportunity again.

When one sheds ideological preconceptions, each and every one of the stated goals of the privatizers could be more effectively achieved with a Universal 401(k). Take savings: unlike the President's plan to divert payroll taxes to create private accounts, which amounts to nothing more than shifting money from one pot to another without adding any new savings, the generous matching incentives in a Universal 401(k) would encourage more low- and moderate-income families to put away new savings and actually boost national private savings. What about ownership? President Bush's private account is essentially taxed 70 percent to 100 percent, because for every dollar you make in your private account, your Social Security benefit is cut by 70 percent to 100 percent of that gain. Americans would actually "own" 100 percent of their Universal 401(k) in addition to their guaranteed Social Security benefit. Indeed, while seniors would be wise to convert much of their Universal 401(k) accounts into sound annuities, there is no question that if a worker died early, the savings would go to her heirs without harming Social Security solvency at all.

Some progressives resist Universal 401(k)s because they fear that the cost of setting them up might drain resources that could have gone to Social Security solvency or other progressive causes. This concern is misguided and highlights the lack of emphasis that too many progressives put on promoting individual savings, investment, and spreading wealth creation. As the Universal 401(k) is completely separate and distinct from Social Security, it neither injects risk into Social Security nor seeks to unravel support for it by diverting payroll taxes. Rejecting a progressive savings account that is portable enough for the dynamism economy and that turns our upside-down savings incentives right-side-up out of fear that it will become too popular is like rejecting an after-school initiative out of fear that it will draw resources away from Head Start. Fighting to keep Social Security solvent and guaranteed may be the most important policy goal for progressives, but if we are to champion economic dignity and upward mobility, it cannot be our only goal for savings and retirement security.

Progressives have spent so much time rightly opposing what is wrong about private accounts within Social Security that they downplay what is right about increasing individual investment, ownership, and savings outside of Social Security. When I was in the White House I met with scholars at the libertarian CATO Institute and Jose Piñera, former Chilean Minister of Labor and Social Security, and the architect of Chile's partial privatization program. I was not impressed or persuaded—particularly because of Chile's alarmingly high administrative costs and only 50 percent participation rate. Yet, as Minister Piñera showed me one of the small "bank account pamphlets" used to record account transactions, I agreed completely with his general point that when workers own and control their investment accounts, it can have a powerful impact on savings behavior and a greater understanding of the magic of compound interest. I witnessed this transformation firsthand when all of us at the White House were offered a chance to participate in the federal version of a 401(k)—the Thrift Savings Plan, or TSP. The TSP offered a dollar-for-dollar match on the first 3 percent of your income that you contributed and a 50 percent match on the next 2 percent. In other words, if you contributed 5 percent of your income to savings, the government would add an additional 4 percent. Many young White House staffers who had never thought about saving a penny for their retirement not only started savings but actively followed the market and their investments. Everywhere I went one of them would ask me (under the false notion that an economic policy advisor was a competent personal financial advisor) what I thought they should contribute, and how they should divide up their contributions between the five diversified investment options.

There is something hypocritical and paternalistic about progressive policy makers who invest their own money and follow the market but believe that when helping ordinary workers the sole focus should be on strengthening the safety net. A lack of progressive passion for spreading investment and wealth creation opportunities for typical working families may give the impression that we are anti–stock market, anti–higher returns, and anti–risk taking. If we want voters to believe that we are focused on their economic aspirations, we will have to do better.

3. Mutual Sacrifice and Responsible Financing

While a Universal 401(k) would be a great mechanism to increase savings, it would not help make Social Security solvent. While the Social Security Trust Fund can pay full benefits until 2041 and is hardly, as President Bush has claimed, "in crisis," when it comes to long-term financing challenges for Social Security or Medicare, it is better to live by Ben Franklin's maxim about an ounce of prevention. If our nation can increase savings and direct them to Social Security, we can take more modest measures now instead of severe efforts decades down the road.

Most elected officials—with a few notable exceptions—go to great lengths to avoid presenting Social Security reform ideas that would entail pain or sacrifice because they do not want to give their opponents potent ammunition. Political consultants read candidates the equivalent of their Miranda rights: "Any candid statement calling for Social Security cuts or tax increases can and will be used against you in the court of public opinion and your next election." When I was a consultant to the television show *The West Wing,* I had President Jed Bartlet privately tell his communications director Toby Ziegler, "There is no way you can fix Social Security without raising someone's taxes or cutting someone's benefit. And this may be the largest forum in Washington where anyone has ever admitted that."

If any congressman is willing to take on the third rail, he has to meet what I call the Town Hall Test. He has to explain to a room of his constituents why the pain he voted for was necessary and unavoidable, and why he believes the burden will be equitably shared. By the summer of 2005, the White House and congressional Republicans had failed the Town Hall Test miserably, not only because voters were wary of private accounts, but also because the White House plan put the entire burden of increasing solvency on benefit cuts.[2] They have tried to sell this benefit-cut-only approach in two ways: first by trying to argue that it is not a benefit cut at all, and then by trying to argue that their benefit cuts will protect the middle class and the poor.

During the president's failed sixty-day tour to make the pitch for his misguided Social Security reform, he argued that benefits would not be cut because they would be adjusted for inflation as opposed to wage growth, as they are under current law. At first blush it may seem reasonable to have benefits grow with inflation rather than wages because it would assure that decades from now, retirees would maintain their buying power for typical consumer goods like toothpaste. However, maintaining the link between Social Security and wages is critical to ensuring that retirement does not mean a devastating fall in a worker's standard of living. For example, an inflation guarantee in 1940 would ensure only that a senior today could afford a 1940s retirement, not one that has kept up with the improvements in our standard of living, which now includes widespread car ownership, airconditioning, prescription drugs, computers, and television. By ensuring that benefits are linked to lifetime wages, Social Security now makes up 36 percent of pre-retirement income, which then serves as a building block for a dignified retirement that is hopefully supplemented by a pension and savings.[3] If benefits are linked to inflation, however, Social Security will eventually replace only 20 percent of a typical worker's wages—making devastating economic falls in retirement far more likely. Indeed, if the inflation rate had been applied to Social Security benefits since 1940 instead of the wage index, people retiring today at age sixty-five would receive 55 percent less in benefits, and there would be three times as many retirees— more than 30 percent—living in poverty.[4]

The White House sought to make this proposal more palatable by protecting the lowest 30 percent of workers who make about $20,000 today, under what they call "progressive price indexing." However, because the White House relies on a benefit-cut-only approach, the cuts for the other 70 percent of workers are quite deep. A twenty-year-old today, making what in today's terms would be about $58,000, would eventually see a 42 percent cut in benefits.[5] Far from calling for mutual sacrifice, this proposal would require a worker making $40,000 to accept a benefit cut more than half the size of someone making $4 million—one hundred times his salary.

Members of Congress in both parties should fear flying tomatoes if, after passing President Bush's successive tax cuts for well-off Americans, they restore Social Security's solvency only through significant benefit cuts. How could a member of Congress tell working families that they have no choice but to accept deep sacrifices to fix Social Security when the portion of recent tax cuts for the top 1 percent of taxpayers (whose average income is over $1.2 million) would have kept the program solvent for seventy-five years without a single penny of benefit cuts? Americans understand that each dollar of federal revenue can just as easily be spent on education or defense as on tax cuts or Social Security. They always suspect that the sacrifice being asked of them could be avoided by cutting wasteful spending or by raising someone else's taxes. Legendary Senate Finance Chairman Russell Long often recited his poem, "Don't tax him, don't tax me, tax that fellow behind the tree." A Social Security solution that asks ordinary workers for sacrifice must first meet the test that such sacrifice is necessary and fairly applied.

This is not to suggest, as some progressive lawmakers have, that we should make Social Security solvent just by repealing high-income tax cuts and make no other benefit or revenue changes. Nonetheless, if the White House and Congress call for mutual sacrifice with a straight face, a contribution from repealing part of recent high-income tax cuts must be a substantial part of the solution.

The 3 Percent Solution

A compromise that would allow a progressive congressman to pass the Town Hall Test and not put the entire burden of fixing Social Security on the highest income earners would be for Republicans and President Bush to repeal a portion of the tax cuts to the very highest earners to make up at least half the savings for Social Security's solvency. In exchange, the Democratic leadership would agree to work with the Republican leadership to find the rest of the savings through modest, progressive adjustments to the program's current revenue and benefit structure. Together with a Universal 401(k), these components would form the basis of an overall retirement security package that would reject privatization, while making Social Security's guaranteed benefits solvent for seventy-five years and vastly increasing savings, ownership, and wealth creation.

The best option for generating savings from the highest earners would be a 3 percent Social Security surcharge on all income over $200,000— whether from income, dividends, or capital gains—to be used to increase national savings and Social Security solvency.

This surcharge is preferable to other options, such as the proposal put forward by Senator Lindsey Graham (R-SC) to raise the amount of income subject to payroll taxes from the first $90,000 up to $200,000.[6] While it is rare and politically gutsy for a conservative Republican senator to put a progressive tax option on the table, a 3 percent surcharge on all income over $200,000 has two distinct advantages over his proposed extension of payroll taxes. First, the 3 percent solution is more progressive—

particularly for the self-employed. The surcharge would affect only about 2 percent of taxpayers, and it would be less than recent tax cuts this income group has already received. In comparison, raising the payroll tax cap by a dramatic amount could be a particular burden for the self-employed because they bear the full 12.4 percent of the payroll tax. It could levy an additional $7,000 in taxes for a self-employed small business owner making $150,000. Second, a surtax on all income—and not just wages—does not encourage high-income earners to employ tax strategies to disguise wage income as dividends or capital gains to avoid the higher payroll tax. Under the Graham plan, a small business owner making $150,000 in wages will pay an extra $7,000 in taxes, but a more sophisticated executive who earns $500,000 a year purely in dividends and capital gains will contribute nothing to Social Security solvency.

4. True Bipartisanship, or How to Hold Hands and Jump Together

If history is any guide, the best recipe for Social Security's solvency is a truly bipartisan process driven by the leaders of both parties. While politicians are eager to take credit for major legislative accomplishments, when it comes to tough choices on Social Security or Medicare, most want political cover. As Richard Darman, the OMB Director for President George H. W. Bush, explained, both parties have to agree to "hold hands and jump together."

This is not to say that neither party should ever step out on a limb alone. But when major deficit reduction or entitlement savings bills have been purely partisan, politicians often remember how it felt when the limb was sawed off. Republicans still blame their votes in 1985 to freeze the Cost of Living Adjustment in Social Security for their loss of the Senate in 1986. Democrats who passed Clinton's 1993 deficit reduction without a single Republican vote are still subjected to hostile political ads for counting more Social Security benefits as taxable income (even though the change affected only the 13 percent of recipients with the highest income, the additional revenues were used to protect Medicare from insolvency, and President Reagan signed a provision taxing the benefits of twice as many people in 1983).

Recent history suggests that three elements are needed for major legislation on entitlement savings that does not put political careers at risk: the support of major leaders in each party; a true willingness to compromise;

and forums where both parties can put options on the table without fear that they will be used against them.

In 1983 Ronald Reagan and House Speaker Tip O'Neill used the President's Social Security Commission to push through painful adjustments with true bipartisan cover. While most commissions do not lead to more than a report, Reagan and O'Neill deftly used the commission as a foil to conduct actual negotiations. Reagan appointed Alan Greenspan as his negotiator and O'Neill used Social Security legend Robert Ball, which according to Jack Lew, former OMB Director and Tip O'Neill staffer, allowed the two leaders to exchange offers in the context of the commission and to disassociate themselves from unpopular proposals that were leaked or went astray. The commission's recommendations served as the blueprint for the 1983 Social Security amendments, which, among other things, cut benefits by gradually raising the retirement age to sixty-seven by 2027 and raised revenues by accelerating increases in payroll tax rates and subjecting a portion of benefits for high-income beneficiaries to income tax.

The same is true of the 1997 Bipartisan Balanced Budget Act, which included politically difficult measures to protect Medicare solvency but garnered majority support from each party because it had the blessing of President Clinton and House Speaker Gingrich, as well as Senate Majority Leader Trent Lott and Minority Leader Tom Daschle.

In 1997 Clinton Chief of Staff Erskine Bowles skillfully got an agreement to let OMB director Frank Raines, legislative director John Hilley, and me, along with Democratic congressional budget chiefs Congressman John Spratt and Senator Frank Lautenberg, negotiate in confidence with Republican budget chiefs Pete Domenici and John Kasich. Because we were assured that what was said in the room stayed in the room, we could explore options knowing Clinton and the congressional leadership of both parties would support a final agreement.

After President Clinton's call to Save Social Security First in the 1998 State of the Union, I struggled to find a way for the NEC and the White House to promote a constructive dialogue during a midterm election year that would lay a foundation for bipartisan negotiations in 1999. After my first proposals were shot down within the White House, I got an agreement for President Clinton to ask the AARP (American Association of Retired Persons) and the deficit hawks at the Concord Coalition to host bipartisan forums around the country, in which either he or Vice President Gore, along with Republican and Democratic members of Congress would participate in an open discussion on Social Security reform. We were trying to neutralize the third rail by creating a no-fire zone on Social Security. The gesture of bipartisanship was greatly appreciated as key Republicans senators and congressmen attended both the meetings and a White House conference in December.

Yet the larger political environment was obviously highly divisive in late 1998 and 1999. Never was the atmosphere more bizarre than at the December 1998 White House Conference on saving Social Security. Several Republican congressmen who praised the president's bipartisanship and stressed that only his leadership could get things through voted for impeachment only weeks later.

Even in a better political environment, the power of inertia always lengthens the odds against solving long-term entitlement challenges. The controlling equation in Washington is often: high perceived political risk + high ideological division + high number of years till the crisis point = INERTIA. Indeed, there is no historical precedent for addressing a major entitlement challenge—whether to Social Security or Medicare—well in advance of a crisis. When George Will said a Social Security solution will come about three weeks before the checks would bounce, he was more historically accurate than flip.[7] In 1977 and 1983 when Congress took tough steps for Social Security, they had no choice. Estimates in 1977 showed that the Disability Insurance (DI) trust fund could be depleted by 1979 and the Old Age and Survivors Insurance (OASI) fund depleted by 1983; projections in early 1983 showed the OASI fund could dry up later that year. Similarly when President Clinton addressed Medicare in 1993, he faced an insolvency date of 1999.

President Bush has tried to force Washington into urgent action by describing the coming Social Security financial challenge as a "crisis." Yet it is hard to call a 2041 insolvency date a crisis. Without true bipartisan political cover, most members of Congress will think that the term-limited White House is rolling the dice, and if a partisan agreement backfires, it is the Congress that will be around to pay for it. To many in Congress, our push for Social Security reform in the late 1990s was about the desire of two retiring politicians—Bill Clinton and House Ways and Means Chairman Bill Archer—to capture a legacy before they left office. In 1999, when I called a congressional staffer to find out how a Social Security briefing I had conducted with Special Assistant to the President Jeff Liebman had gone, the staffer admitted that after we left, one congressman said, "I don't need to support the Bills' Legacy project, I'm not going anywhere."

President Bush has yet to show the spirit of compromise or the willingness to create a truly bipartisan forum needed to reach a politically acceptable and fiscally responsible Social Security agreement. While the 2001 Social Security Commission included some knowledgeable experts and registered Democrats, only those who opposed the Democratic leadership on the issue of partial privatization were asked to join the commission—hardly the formula for constructive bipartisan negotiations.

When it comes to fiscal policy, the administration has consistently relied on what I have called the "Rightward Sweep": start to the right and hope to get enough unified support in the House to ram through your ideal legislation; then fake just far enough left in the Senate to persuade a handful of Democrats to join, before cutting as far back to the right as possible in conference committee. While this may be a politically effective strategy for passing fiscally irresponsible tax cuts, it is a politically ineffective strategy for passing fiscally responsible Social Security reform. By insisting on private accounts, the Bush administration has failed to create a bipartisan environment likely to encourage Democrats to hold hands with Republicans and jump together. The result of this failure is that the only type of Social Security reform the Republican majority is likely to support on a party line vote is a free lunch, Alice-in-Wonderland plan that will pass trillions of dollars in additional debt to the very generations that responsible Social Security reform should benefit. Surely, Americans deserve better.

Acknowledgments

With this book, as with most things in my life, I have been blessed with more support and good fortune than any one person deserves.

John Podesta, president of the Center for American Progress, and Sarah Rosen Wartell allowed me to focus a significant chunk of the past eighteen months on the research and writing of this book. Al From and my longtime policy partner Bruce Reed at the Democratic Leadership Council provided me with early research support for which I am very thankful.

I am also very appreciative of those who offered excellent advice on large sections of the book or gave in-depth advice on a particular section, including Rekha Balu, David Ellwood, Liz Fine, Jason Furman, Robert Gordon, Bob Greenstein, Ed Gresser, Jonathan Gruber, Harry Holzer, Andy Imparato, Chris Jennings, Tom Kalil, Andrea Kane, Lawrence Katz, Karen Kornbluh, James Kvaal, Joan Lombardi, Sylvia Mathews, Ron Minsk, Peter Orszag, Meeghan Prunty, Robert Rubin, Bob Shireman, Anne Sperling, Karen Tramontano, Bill Treanor, and Michael Wessell. Michael Waldman deserves special thanks not only for his commentary but for coaching me through the entire process.

I had many conversations with a variety of people that helped me formulate various parts of this book as well as the decision to write a book, including Allison Abner, Alex Arriaga, Rob Atkinson, Dean Baker, Michael Barr, Paul Begala, Sandy Berger, Sarah Bianchi, Alan Blinder, Robert Boorstin, Erskine Bowles, Lael Brainard, Matt Browne, James Carville, Lou DeMatte, Patrick Dorton, Oeindrilla Dube, Rahm Emanuel, Kris Engskov, Lee Feinstein, Michael Ferguson, Tim Geithner, Gary Gensler, Claudia Goldin, Steve Goss, Ann Gust, Kevin Hassett, Steve Hess, Melody Hobson, Russell Horwitz, Mark Iwry, Shirley Ann Jackson, Jonathan Kaplan, Sally Katzen, Ron Klain, Lori Kletzer, Jeanne Lambrew, Thea Lee, Arthur Levitt, Jeff Liebman, Mack McLarty, Joanne McGrath, David Milliband, Larry Mishel, Janet Murgia, Jerry Noyce, Jon Orszag, Leon Panetta, Michael

O'Hanlon, Alice Rivlin, Dorothy Robyn, Ken Rogoff, Nancy Roman, David Rothkopf, Ceci Rouse, Lee Sachs, Sheryl Sandberg, Howard Schultz, Rob Shapiro, Gerry Shea, Gayle Smith, Larry Sperling, Mike Sperling, Lawrence Summers, Jon Talisman, Elizabeth Warren, Matt Winkler, Janet Yellin, and Heather Zichal.

Beyond representing me, Bob Barnett has been a valued and trusted advisor and counselor. I want to thank Ruth Fecych for her adroit editing and heroic patience. Patricia Romanowski gave the manuscript a fine copyedit, Edith Lewis carefully shepherded it through the production process, while Gypsy da Silva and Terra Chalberg provided helpful assistance. I particularly want to thank David Rosenthal for taking a chance on me and this book.

I benefited from dedicated assistance managing my office while writing this book from Jeremy Bayer, Bonnie Berry, Owen Davies, David Garrison, Richard Lum, Brian Walsh, and particularly Mark Schuman, who gave a dedicated and inspired effort in the final months of the book.

I owe a special thanks to Sam Elkin for his excellent research on the fiscal responsibility and Social Security chapters. I also received fine research assistance from Sara Aronchick, Radha Chaurushiya, Jacob Leibenluft, Gabriel Wildau, and most especially Josh Lynn who proved invaluable after joining me in the spring of 2005. And when I needed great relief pitching to pull me through from the first draft to galleys, Amias Gerety was a terrific closer—tireless and insightful.

Authors often note the one person they could not have written their book without. This book is no exception. Brian Deese was more than the world's greatest researcher: at every stage, he was my number-one sounding board, advisor, critic, colleague, and friend. With his combination of brilliance, work ethic, and unflappable disposition, he will be a leading policy light for decades to come.

I am forever grateful to President Clinton, not only for giving me the opportunity to serve, but for insisting on rigorous economic policy formulation through the National Economic Council and for his willingness to face tough political resistance to implement responsible policies. Both during and after the White House, Hillary Clinton has been an inspiration to me on issues from health care to the education of girls in the world's poorest nations. What I will always appreciate most about both President Clinton and Senator Clinton is that they never let you forget that behind even the most arcane budget item or policy issue are real people who simply want opportunity and a fair chance.

Al Gore was an integral and outstanding part of the White House economic team from day one. He was our leader on many issues from technology policy to climate change and was personally very supportive of me, for which I am very appreciative. I am indebted not only to my White House colleagues and economic team but also to the tremendous civil servants whose dedication and expertise too often go without proper thanks. My deepest appreciation goes to the more than one hundred policy experts I learned so much from at the NEC, who helped shape my ideas and analysis over several years. I owe a special debt of gratitude to my chief of staff, counselor, and life support, Melissa Green.

I want to particularly thank the following people for their advice and influence for nearly twenty years and often longer: Roger Altman, Paul Dimond, Dawn Johnsen, Robert Katzmann, Sylvia Mathews, Howard Shapiro, Josh Steiner, George Stephanopoulos, Larry Summers, Tom Kalil, and Laura Tyson.

I want to also note those who were particularly supportive when I first started in economic policy, including Chris Edley, Elgie Holstein, Steve Hess, Jackie Parker, the late Kirk O'Donnell, Dan Tarullo, Governor Mike Dukakis, whose presidential campaign I proudly served on, and of course, Governor Mario Cuomo, who taught me so much as my boss for nearly three years and whose passion for justice remains a never-ending inspiration to me.

I owe a special debt to two Bobs: Bob Reich for taking me in during the summer of 1984 when I was just a first-year law student, encouraging me to further develop my thinking on progressive economic policies, and for giving me years of wise counsel. I could not be blessed with a wiser or more supportive mentor than Bob Rubin. When you are in Bob Rubin's orbit, you have the privilege of working with someone who is not only a friend and colleague, but a master at building trust, collegiality, and decision-making processes based on rigor, humility, and responsibility.

In addition to being my heroes, my parents and siblings each influenced my policy beliefs and the contents of this book. My father's legal work inspired my chapter on workers with disabilities and much of my writings on equal opportunity; my mother's work as a pioneer on education reform has long inspired my views on education policy; my brother Mike contributed ideas that I used in my discussions on progressive taxation; my immunologist sister Anne gave me significant advice on the science portion of the book. And when I write on the potential of young urban youths and after-school programs, I am inspired by the Mosaic Youth Theatre of Detroit founded and run by my brother Rick. While they come from neighbor-hoods where 50 percent of their peers drop out of high school, over twelve years an amazing 95 percent of Mosaic kids have not only graduated, but gone on to college. I am also thankful for the support during this process of my brother- and sisters-in-law, Ethan, Peggy, and Valeria, my many Sper-ling, Bukstel, and Hyman relatives, and so many friends, among them Shirley Brandman, Darryl Wilburn, Bill Godfrey, Heidi Chapman, Tom Herwig, and Steven and Joanne Spencer.

At times it seemed that a day never went by in the White House when Erskine Bowles did not ask me: "Boy, when are you going to get married?" In August 2004, I married my best friend and soulmate, Allison Abner. There has never been a day that I have been working on this book where I have not felt sustained by her emotional support, wise counsel, and sense of justice. My new in-laws, Olivia Abner and Tony Abner, were always patient and supportive during the writing of this book.

For the last thirteen years I have been grounded and blessed by a godson Derick Chapman and a goddaughter Samantha Chapman who have been like my own children to me. I have also been fortunate to have in my life a multitude of spirited nieces and nephews from the Israelsohn, Spencer, Abner, and Sperling (both Detroit and Milwaukee) families. With my mar-riage, I received the additional blessing of a loving son Miles. At ten years old, he is already trying to challenge Derick at video games and is certainly challenging his mother and me with the most penetrating philosophical questions.

The other dedication in this book is to Chris Georges, a *Wall Street Jour-nal* reporter and one of my closest friends. He left us way, way too soon, but he remains an inspiration to his family and friends to never think you're a big shot, always stick up for the little guy, and never let even the toughest obstacles keep you from living life to the fullest.

Notes

Introduction

1. A number of conservative commentators resurrected this quote during the debate over the Bush tax cut, suggesting that JFK used the "rising tide" quote to justify his tax reduction and reform agenda. I have found no evidence of this. Instead, the only documented uses of the phrase in the Public Papers of the Kennedy Presidency are in reference to (a) the value to the whole country of public works projects in specific states (the Fryingpan-Arkansas project, the TVA, the Greers Ferry Dam, etc.) and (b) the value for all countries in pursuing freer trade.

Part One: The Pro-Growth Progressive

Chapter 1: Growing Together in the Dynamism Economy

1. Joseph Schumpeter, *Capitalism, Socialism and Democracy* (New York: Harper, 1942).
2. Nitin Nohria, Davis Dyer, and Frederick Dalzell, *Changing Fortunes: Remaking the Industrial Corporation* (Hoboken: John Wiley & Sons, 2002), 4; cited in John Micklethwait and Adrian Wooldridge, *The Company: A Short History of a Revolutionary Idea* (New York: Modern Library, 2003), 129–130.
3. Micklethwait and Wooldridge, 129.
4. Gary Rivlin, "Who's Afraid of China?," *New York Times,* December 19, 2004.
5. Douglas Hayward, "Streamlined Links with Business Partners," *Financial Times,* April 29, 2002. See also, David Rocks, "Dell's Second Web Revolution," *BusinessWeek Online,* September 18, 2000.
6. "The Giant in the Palm of Your Hand—Nokia's Turnaround," *Economist,* February 12, 2005; Alan Cowell, "After Cutting Its Phone Prices, Nokia Raises Its Outlook," *New York Times,* September 10, 2004; Terry Maxon, "Cell Phone Buyers May Wait for Next Big Thing, But What Else Can It Do?," *Dallas Morning News,* February 23, 2005; Steve Lohr, "As Cellphones Bulk Up, How Much is Too Much?," *New York Times,* May 4, 2005.
7. Martin Baily, "Macroeconomic Implications of the New Economy," Institute for International Economics, September 2001.
8. Scott Bradford and Robert Lawrence, *Has Globalization Gone Far Enough? The Costs of Fragmentation in OECD Markets* (Washington, DC: Institute for International Economics, February 2004), 32.
9. Bureau of Labor Statistics.

10. These issues are further discussed in Gene Sperling, "Raising the Tide and Lifting All Boats," *Progressive Politics*, July 2004.

11. Andy Grove, "Business Software Alliance: The Coming Software X Curve," PowerPoint presentation, October 9, 2003, http://www.globaltechsummit.net/press/AndyGrove.pdf.

12. "Into the Unknown," *Economist*, November 13, 2004.

13. Greg Schneider, "Touch and Pay, Here to Stay Self-Checkout Machines Offer Empowerment to Shoppers, Cost-Efficient Service to Retailers," *Washington Post*, October 12, 2002.

14. "Men and Machines," *Economist*, November 13, 2004.

15. Mei Fong, "A Chinese Puzzle: Surprising Shortage of Workers," *Wall Street Journal*, August 16, 2004.

16. "India's Riding the Manufacturing Wave," *Economic Times*, November 24, 2004; Diane Lindquist, "Governments Move Toward Outsourcing," *San Diego Union Tribune*, August 22, 2004. World Bank GNP per capita 2003, Atlas method Mexico $6,200; India $530.

17. Priya Srinivasan, "A World of Opportunities," *Business Today*, December 19, 2004.

18. In August 2000, amidst fear of rising heating oil prices, the Clinton administration agreed to a "swap" from the SPR—a temporary release that had to be replenished.

19. Organization for Economic Cooperation and Development (OECD), "Employment Protection: Costs and Benefits of Greater Job Security," Policy Brief, October 18, 2004.

20. Bureau of Labor Statistics, Business Employment Dynamics Survey.

21. Bureau of Labor Statistics, Business Employment Dynamics Survey. Note: Because of differences in methodology there is some discrepancy between these statistics and the BLS payroll survey data.

22. U.S. Census Bureau, Current Population Survey, Historical Income Tables.

23. U.S. Census Bureau, Current Population Survey, Historical Poverty Tables.

24. U.S. Census Bureau, Current Population Survey, Housing Vacancies and Homeownership.

25. Frederick Jackson Turner, "The Significance of the Frontier in American History," Paper presented to the American Historical Society, University of Wisconsin, 1893.

26. David W. Noble, *Historians Against History: The Frontier Thesis and the National Covenant in American Historical Writing Since 1830* (Minneapolis: University of Minnesota Press, 1965).

27. Business Roundtable, Washington, DC, May 23, 2004.

28. Pew Research Center for the People and the Press, "The 2005 Political Typology: Beyond Red vs. Blue," May 10, 2005.

29. Paul Samuelson, "Where Ricardo and Mill Rebut and Confirm Mainstream Economists Supporting Globalization," *Journal of Economic Perspectives*, Summer 2004.

30. Robert J. Shiller, *The New Financial Order* (Princeton: Princeton University Press, 2003), 108.

31. David DeKok, "Pennsylvania Lawmakers Move to End Job Outsourcing," *Patriot-News*, February 25, 2004.

32. Daniel Kadlec, "Where Did My Raise Go?," *Time*, May 26, 2003.

33. Shiller, 2003, 10.

34. Michael Schroeder and Timothy Aeppel, "Skilled Workers Mount Opposition to Free Trade, Swaying Politicians," *Wall Street Journal*, October 10, 2003.

35. William Gates Sr. and Chuck Collins, "Tax the Wealthy: Why America Needs the Estate Tax," *American Prospect*, June 17, 2003.

36. "Transcript: Bill Moyers Interview with Bill Gates Sr. and Chuck Collins," Public Broadcasting System (PBS), January 17, 2003.

37. Congressional Budget Office (CBO), "Effective Federal Tax Rates, 1997 to 2000," August 2003. Figure in 2000 dollars.

38. Bureau of Labor Statistics, Displaced Workers Survey, 2002.

39. Because of changes by the Bush administration, extended unemployment insurance has been even more restricted. It has kicked in only for those states that can meet complicated formulas showing that they are particularly hurting during such downturns. See Jessica Goldberg and Wendell Primus, "A Description of the Unemployment Provisions in the Economic Stimulus Package," Center on Budget and Policy Priorities, March 28, 2002.

40. Erica Groshen and Simon Potter, "Has Structural Change Contributed to a Jobless Recovery," *Current Issues in Finance and Economics,* vol. 9, no. 8, Federal Reserve Bank of New York, August 2003.

41. David Ellwood, "Grow Faster Together, or Grow Slowly Apart," Aspen Institute, 2002.

42. Kris Maher, "Skills Shortage Gives Training Programs New Life," *Wall Street Journal,* May 3, 2005.

43. Norman R. Augustine and Burton Richter, "Our Ph.D. Deficit," *Wall Street Journal,* May 4, 2005; Organization for Economic Cooperation and Development, "Science, Technology and Industry Outlook," 2004.

44. Peter G. Peterson, "A Prominent Executive Argues for More Statesmanship from Our CEOs," *Newsweek,* June 13, 2005.

45. Jerome Friedman, "Will Innovation Flourish in the Future?," *Industrial Physicist,* August 2002.

46. Friedman, 2002.

Chapter 2: Three Progressive Values

1. Rebecca Blank, "Can Equity and Efficiency Complement Each Other?," University of Michigan, January 2002.

2. Marian Wright Edelman, "25 Lessons for Life," in *The Measure of Our Success: Letter to My Children and Yours* (New York: Perennial, 1993).

3. Bureau of Labor Statistics, "Number of Workers Exhausting Unemployment Insurance Benefits Sets Record Level for a December," Center on Budget and Policy Priorities, January 30, 2002.

4. Barbara Ehrenreich, *Nickel and Dimed* (New York: Metropolitan Books, 2001), 25.

5. Katherine Newman, *Falling from Grace: Downward Mobility in an Age of Affluence* (Berkeley: University of California Press, 1999), 173.

6. NBC News Wall Street Journal Poll, May 31, 2003.

7. U.S. Census Bureau, Current Population Survey, Historical Income Tables.

8. Alexis de Tocqueville, *Democracy in America,* Book III, Chapter XIX, translated by Henry Reeve, Project Gutenberg, 2005.

9. Pew Research Center, "The 2004 Political Landscape," November 5, 2003.

10. Gosta Esping-Anderson, "Inequality of Incomes and Opportunities," Universitat Pompeu Fabra, unpublished manuscript, 2005.

11. Gary Solon, "A Model of Intergenerational Mobility Variation Over Time and Place," in Miles Corak, ed., *Generational Income Mobility in North America and Europe* (Cambridge: Cambridge University Press, 2004), 38–47.

12. Katharine Bradbury and Jane Katz, "Are Lifetime Incomes Growing More Unequal," *Current Issues in Economics,* Federal Reserve Bank of Boston, Quarter 4 2002.

13. "Meritocracy in America?" *Economist,* December 29, 2004.
14. Thomas Hertz, "Rags, Riches, and Race," American University, April 9, 2003.
15. John Adams, "Thoughts on Government: Applicable to the Present State of the American Colonies," in Charles Francis Adams, *The Works of John Adams, Second President of the United States with A Life of the Author* (Boston: Charles C. Little and James Brown, 1851), 199.
16. Massachusetts Constitution, chapter V, section II.
17. Thomas Jewett, "Jefferson, Education, and the Franchise," *Early America Review,* Winter 1996–1997.
18. Ariel Halpern, "Poverty Among Children Born Outside of Marriage: Preliminary Findings from the National Survey of America's Families," Assessing the New Federalism Discussion Paper, Urban Institute, December 1999.
19. Children's Defense Fund (CDF), "Defining Poverty and Why It Matters," August 2004.
20. Andrea J. Sedlak and Diane D. Broadhurst, "National Incidence Study of Child Abuse and Neglect," Administration for Children and Families, 1996.
21. Mark Nord, Margaret Andrews, and Steven Carlson, "Household Food Security in the United States, 2003," Food Assistance and Nutrition Research Report, no. 42, October 2004.
22. National Center for Education Statistics, "Condition of Education: Early Literacy Activities," 2003.
23. Children's Defense Fund, 2004.
24. Quoted in Philip Kurland and Ralph Lerner, eds., *The Founders' Constitution* (Chicago: University of Chicago Press, 1986), Web Edition, Chapter 4, Document 7, http://press-pubs.uchicago.edu/founders.
25. Franklin D. Roosevelt, "Message to Congress on Tax Revision," June 19, 1935.
26. Dan Ackman, "Top of the News: Death and Taxes," Forbes.com, February 14, 2001.

Part Two: A New Compact on Globalization

Chapter 3: Toward a New Consensus on Trade

1. Eric Schmitt, "An Unlikely Champion of New Trade Pact with China," *New York Times,* April 17, 2000.
2. U.S. Census Bureau, "Foreign Trade: Trade in Goods," 2004.
3. U.S. Trade Representative (USTR), "NAFTA at Ten: A Success Story," December 1, 2003.
4. "When Neighbors Embrace," *Economist,* July 3, 1997; "Tequila Slammer: The Peso Crisis, Ten Years On," *Economist,* December 29, 2004.
5. Sandra Polaski, "NAFTA's Promise and Reality," Carnegie Endowment for International Peace, 2003, p. 26.
6. Oxfam, "Dumping Without Borders," August 2003.
7. Robert B. Zoellick, "Speech to the National Foreign Trade Council," July 26, 2001.
8. Robert Scott, "Hidden Costs of NAFTA," Economic Policy Institute, April 2001.
9. Howard Lewis and J. David Richardson, *Why Global Commitment Really Matters!,* Washington, D.C.: Institute for International Economics, October 2001, 16.
10. Newman, 1999, 174.
11. Bureau of Labor Statistics, Displaced Workers' Survey, 2004.
12. Lori Kletzer, *Job Loss Due to Imports: Measuring the Costs* (Washington, D.C.: Institute for International Economics, September 2001), 55.

13. Philippe Legrain, *Open World: The Truth About Globalisation* (London: Abacus, 2002), 39.

14. John Hilsenrath and Rebecca Buckman, "Factory Employment Is Falling World-Wide," *Wall Street Journal,* October 20, 2003.

15. E-Loan's experiment has been profiled in numerous publications in the past year. John Lancaster, "Outsourcing Delivers Hope to India," *Washington Post,* May 8, 2004.

16. Reed Abelson, "States Are Battling Against Wal-Mart Over Health Care," *New York Times,* November 1, 2004.

17. Michael Skapinker, "Inside Track: Why Nike Has Broken into a Sweat," *Financial Times,* March 7, 2002.

18. U.S. International Trade Commission, "Chapter 95, Toys, Games and Sports Equipment; Parts and Accessories Thereof," Harmonized Tariff Schedule of the United States, 2005.

19. Edward Gresser, "Toughest on the Poor: Tariffs, Taxes and the Single Mom," Progressive Policy Institute, Policy Report, September 2002.

20. James Brooke, "An Orange Grove Illustrates Japan's Economic Woes," *New York Times,* January 27, 2002.

21. Progressive Policy Institute, "Developing Countries Often Treat One Another Badly," Trade Fact of the Week, September 10, 2003.

22. William J. Clinton, "Speech to the World Economic Forum," Davos, Switzerland, January 29, 2000.

23. Susan Aaronson, *Taking Trade to the Streets* (Ann Arbor: University of Michigan Press, 2001), 110.

24. Inter-American Conference on the Maintenance of Peace in Buenos Aires: http://www.ibiblio.org/pha/7-2-188/188-06.html.

25. Quoted in Alfred E. Eckes, *Opening America's Market: U.S. Foreign Trade Policy Since 1776* (Chapel Hill: University of North Carolina Press, 1995), 167.

26. Glenn Simpson, "Multinationals Take Steps to Avoid Boycotts over War," *Wall Street Journal,* April 4, 2003. In another instance, complaints that French-owned Sodexho was feeding the U.S. Marine Corps in Iraq were quickly hushed up when it became clear that scrapping the contract would direct the pain on the company's 110,000 employees across the United States. See Paul Blustein, "House Members Target Sodexho for French Ties," *Washington Post,* March 29, 2003.

27. Progressive Policy Institute, "The Muslim Middle East's Share of World Trade Has Dropped by 75 Percent Since 1980," Trade Fact of the Week, September 4, 2002.

28. John Pomfret, "Chinese Are Split over WTO Entry; Monopolies Fear Western Influence," *Washington Post,* March 12, 2000.

29. See Michael Laris, "U.S. Details Embassy Bombing for Chinese: Beijing Officials Remain 'Skeptical' at Washington's Explanation of Accidental Attack," *Washington Post,* June 17, 1999.

30. "U.S. Spy Plane Heads Home," CNN.com, July 3, 2001.

31. Evelyn Iritani, "U.S., China Aim to Separate Trade from Tensions," *Los Angeles Times,* April 6, 2001.

32. State Department, 2005.

33. Philip Pan, "Hu Tightens Party's Grip On Power," *Washington Post,* April 24, 2005.

34. AFL-CIO, "Section 301 Petition Before the Office of the United States Trade Representative," 29, 44–45.

35. United States Trade Representative, "2004 Report to Congress on China's WTO Compliance," December 11, 2004.

36. U.S. China Economic and Security Review Commission, "Annual Report 2004," June 10, 2004.

37. U.S. State Department, Bureau of Democracy, Human Rights, and Labor, "China: Country Reports on Human Rights Practices—2004," February 28, 2005.

38. Jim Yardley, "China Plans to Cut School Fees for Its Poorest Rural Students," *New York Times,* March 13, 2005.

39. Internet World Stats, "Internet Usage Stats and Telecommunications Market Report," www.internetworldstats.com.

40. Jim Yardley and David Barboza, "Help Wanted: China Finds Itself With a Labor Shortage," *New York Times,* April 3, 2005.

41. Mei Fong, "A Chinese Puzzle: Surprising Shortage of Workers Forces Factories to Add Perks," *Wall Street Journal,* August 16, 2004.

42. C. Fred Bergsten, "An Action Plan to Stop Market Manipulators Now," *Financial Times,* March 14, 2005.

43. "Mitch: A Path of Destruction," BBC News, November 5, 1998.

44. Food and Agriculture Organization (FAO), "Analysis of the Medium-Term Effects of Hurricane Mitch on Food Security in Central America," November 30, 2003.

45. "Americas Nations Plead for Aid After Mitch Disaster," BBC News, November 4, 1998.

46. Yoweri Museveni, "We Want Trade, Not Aid," *Wall Street Journal,* November 6, 2003.

47. Hilde Johnson, Center for Global Development Event, April 29, 2003.

48. Oxfam, "Rigged Rules and Double Standards," 2002.

49. Oxfam, 2002, 47.

50. In his advocacy work, top development economist Jeffrey Sachs has long stressed the importance of lowering trade barriers for global poverty reduction. See Jeffrey Sachs, *The End of Poverty* (New York: Penguin Press, 2005). ("Sustained economic growth requires that poor countries increase their exports to rich countries.")

51. For an excellent analysis of AGOA's benefits and challenges, see Helene Cooper, "Fruit of the Loom: Can African Nations Use Duty-Free Deal to Revamp Economy," *Wall Street Journal,* January 1, 2002; and William Cline, "Trading Up: Strengthening AGOA's Development Potential," Center for Global Development, June 2003.

52. Oxfam, 2002, 54.

53. Mark Malloch Brown, UNDP estimate, as quoted in Nicholas Kristof, "Farm Subsidies That Kill," *New York Times,* July 5, 2002.

54. Nicholas H. Stern, appearing on "All Things Considered," National Public Radio (NPR), November 22, 2002.

55. International Food Policy Research Institute, cited in Kevin Hassett and Robert Shapiro, "How Europe Sows Misery in Africa," *Washington Post,* June 22, 2003.

Chapter 4: A New Cost-Sharing Compact

1. John Rawls, *A Theory of Justice* (Cambridge, MA: Belknap Press, 1971).

2. Nick Turner, "Silicon Valley's No Place to Find a Job," *Investor's Business Daily,* November 23, 2004.

3. Thomas Friedman, *The Lexus and the Olive Tree* (New York: Farrar, Straus, Giroux, 1999), 448.

4. I have discussed many of these issues earlier in "A New Consensus on Free Trade," *Washington Post,* March 1, 2004; "Raising the Tide and Lifting All Boats," *Progressive Politics,* July 2004; and "How to Be a Free Trade Democrat," *Foreign Policy,* March–April 2004.

5. Alan Krueger, "Economic Scene; Rapid Productivity Growth Probably Did Not Cause Slow Post-Recession Job Growth." *New York Times,* November 13, 2003.

6. Strategic Early Warning Network (SEWN), www.steelvalley.org.

7. Matt Vidal, Josh Whitford, Joel Rogers, and Jonathan Zeitlin, "Challenges & Options for Wisconsin Component Manufacturing: Final AMP Report to the Wisconsin Manufacturing Extension Partnership," Center on Wisconsin Strategy, June 2003.

8. The eight separate departments and agencies involved in the adjustment process are: the Department of Agriculture, Department of Commerce, Department of Defense, Department of Education, Department of Labor, Department of Housing and Urban Development, Department of Treasury, and the Small Business Administration.

9. Marcus Stanley, Lawrence Katz, and Alan Krueger, "Developing Skills: What We Know About the Impacts of American Employment and Training Programs on Employment, Earnings, and Educational Outcomes," Harvard Economics Department Working Paper, October 1998.

10. North Carolina Rural Economic Development Center, Institute for Entrepreneurship, New Opportunities for Workers Program, http://www.ncruralcenter.org.

11. Center for American Progress, "A Progressive Response to High Oil and Gasoline Prices," May 6, 2005.

12. Elizabeth Warren, "Sick and Broke," *Washington Post,* February 9, 2005.

13. COBRA stands for the Consolidated Omnibus Reconciliation Act of 1986.

14. Kaiser Family Foundation, "Trends and Indicator in the Changing Health Care Marketplace," 2004.

15. Lynn Etheredge and Stan Dorn, "Health Insurance for Laid-off Workers: A Time for Action," Economic and Social Research Institute Current Policy Briefing Series, February 2003.

16. U.S. Department of Labor, Employment, and Training Administration, "Trade Adjustment Assistance (TAA) Estimated Number of Workers Covered by Certifications," November 5, 2004.

17. Lori Kletzer and Howard Rosen, "Easing The Adjustment Burden on U.S. Workers," in *The United States and the World Economy: Foreign Economic Policy for the Next Decade,* C. Fred Bergsten, ed. (Washington, DC: Institute for International Economics, 2005), 333.

18. William Schweke, "Promising Practices to Assist Dislocated Workers," North Carolina Rural Economic Development Center, September 2004.

19. Schweke, 2004.

20. Jennifer Ginsberg, "New Mortgage Insurance Offered in West Virginia," *Charleston Gazette,* October 8, 2004; Jennifer Harmon, "Mass. Housing Agency Working to Keep Borrowers Housed," *Origination News,* September 1, 2004; and Rebecca Lipschutz, "Massachusetts Housing Program Offers Buffer for Some Buyers," *The Sun,* July 16, 2004.

21. Harold Brubaker, "Longevity No Shield Against Layoffs," *Philadelphia Inquirer,* May 27, 2001.

22. Kevin Maler, "Older and Unemployed," *Saint Paul Pioneer Press,* January 27, 2002.

23. Lori Kletzer and Robert Litan, "A Prescription for Worker Anxiety," Brookings Institution Policy Brief no. 73, March 2001.

24. U.S. Department of Labor, Employment and Training Administration, "Training and Employment Guidance Letter No. 02–03," August 6, 2003.

25. Lori Kletzer, "Trade-Related Job Loss and Wage Insurance: a Synthetic Review," *Review of International Economics,* vol. 12, no. 5, 2004.

26. Diana Farrell, "Governing Globalization," *McKinsey Quarterly,* number 3, 2004.

27. U.S. Department of Labor, Employment and Training Administration, "Trade Adjustment Assistance (TAA) Estimated Number of Workers Covered by Certifications," November 5, 2004.

28. U.S. Department of Labor, "WIA Participants by Program," www.doleta.gov/performance/charts.

29. Government Accountability Office (GAO), "Trade Adjustment Assistance: Reforms Have Accelerated Training Enrollment, But Implementation Challenges Remain," September 22, 2004.

30. Bureau of Labor Statistics.

31. eBay First Quarter 2005 Financial Report.

32. Rob Atkinson, "Modernizing Unemployment Insurance for the New Economy and the New Social Policy," Progressive Policy Institute, February 19, 2002.

33. Establishment of new hotline could come alongside an expansion of the government's retraining Web site. More intensive services would be available at the One-Stop Centers based on state and local eligibility rules.

34. Stanley, Katz, and Krueger, 1998.

35. Howard Rosen, "Trade-Related Labour Market Adjustment Policies and Programs," New America Foundation, 2004.

36. Stanley, Katz, and Krueger, 1998.

37. Thomas Kane and Cecilia Rouse, "The Community College: Educating Students at the Margin Between College and Work," *Journal of Economic Perspectives,* vol. 13, no. 1, 1999, 63–84. See also, Duane Leigh and Andrew Gill, "Labor Market Returns to Community Colleges: Evidence for Returning Adults," *Journal of Human Resources,* no. 2, vol. 32, Spring 1997.

38. Stanley, Katz, and Krueger, 1998.

39. Jeffrey Mayer, "Do It Like Dell: Improve Your Processes for Maximum Results," *Solid Innovations Newsletters,* January 18, 2005.

40. William Holstein interview with Sidney Harman, "In Outsourcing, You Yield an Opportunity," *International Herald Tribune,* June 12, 2004.

41. Shvetank Shah, "India's Dwindling IT Labor Advantage," *Optimize Magazine,* September 2004. Stephanie Overby, "India Sees IT Wages Rise," *CIO Magazine,* February 1, 2004. Gaurav Bhagowati, "India 2005: Facing the Challenges of Labor Shortage and Rising Wages," Outsourcing Center, Everest Group, January 2005. See also Jim Yardley and David Barboza, "Help Wanted: China Finds Itself with a Labor Shortage," *New York Times,* April 3, 2005.

42. Jim Yardley and David Barboza, "Help Wanted: China Finds Itself with a Labor Shortage," *New York Times,* April 3, 2005; Mei Fong, "A Chinese Puzzle: Surprising Shortage of Workers," *Wall Street Journal,* August 16, 2004.

43. Doug Tsuruoka, "Rural U.S. Seeks Place on IT Map," *Investor's Business Daily,* January 11, 2005.

44. Deloitte and Touche, "Calling a Change in the Outsourcing Market," April 2005.

45. Broadband Business Forecast, "And Now in 16th Place: The U.S. Falls Farther Behind in Broadband," May 3, 2005.

46. Pew Internet and American Life, www.pewinternet.org.

47. Andy Grove, "Business Software Alliance, The Coming Software X Curve," PowerPoint presentation, October 9, 2003, http://www.globaltechsummit.net/press/AndyGrove.pdf.

48. Tsuruoka, 2005.

49. Tony Adams, "Towns Get High-Speed Internet; BellSouth Brings Digital Bounty to Rural Georgia," *Columbus Ledger-Enquirer,* June 12, 2003.

50. Michael Currie Schaffer, "Mayor's Plan to Go Wireless Makes Debut," *Philadelphia Inquirer,* April 8, 2005.

51. Ed Frauenheim, "Made in Lower-Cost America," CNet News.com, February 8, 2005.

52. "U.S. Health Insurance Premiums Rise 59%, Since 2001," *Bloomberg News,* September 9, 2004.

53. This result was the highest rating received by any issue in the twenty-two years that NFIB has taken the survey. National Federation of Independent Businesses, "Small Business Problems and Priorities," June 15, 2004.

54. Ceci Connolly, "U.S. Firms Losing Health Care Battle, GM Chairman Says," *Washington Post,* February 11, 2005.

55. Mike Madden, "Frist, Clinton Team Up on Medical Data Bill," *The Tennessean,* June 17, 2005.

56. The primary aspect of the tax code that creates this dynamic is a provision called "deferral," which allows U.S. companies to defer paying taxes on profit earned abroad until it is brought back to the United States. The result of deferral, interacting with a number of other international provisions in our tax code, is to significantly reduce the effective corporate tax rate on income earned abroad. In short: our tax code provides an affirmative incentive for firms to shift jobs and production overseas, rather than create jobs here in the United States.

57. David Brumbaugh, "Tax Exemption for Repatriated Foreign Earnings," *Congressional Research Service,* October 22, 2003.

58. David Audretsch and Roy Thurik, "Sources of Growth: The Entrepreneurial Versus the Managed Economy," CEPR Discussion Paper no. 1710, Centre for Economic Policy Research, 1997. Audretsch and Thurik find that those European economies that have had the most success fostering entrepreneurship, like the United Kingdom, have seen higher rates of growth and lower unemployment relative to countries like France and Germany, which have maintained more managed, less entrepreneurial economies.

59. Office of Advocacy, U.S. Small Business Administration, from data provided by the U.S. Bureau of Census.

60. National Association of Small Business Investment Companies, "The U.S. Small Business Investment Company Program: History and Current Highlights," www.nasbic.org.

61. Jesse Jackson, "The Great Challenge of This Generation: Leave No One Behind," Commencement Address, Kennedy School of Government, Harvard University, June 8, 1999.

62. Michael Porter, "The Competitive Advantage of the Inner City," *Harvard Business Review,* May–June 1995.

63. Michael Barr, "Access to Financial Services in the 21st Century: Five Opportunities for the Bush Administration and the 107th Congress," Brookings Institution, Center on Urban and Metropolitan Policy, June 2001.

64. Adena Ventures, www.adenaventures.com.

65. See www.advantagevalleyels.com and Thomas S. Lyons, "The Entrepreneurial League System®: Transforming Your Community's Economy Through Enterprise Development," prepared for the Appalachian Regional Commission, March 2002.

66. Sheila McNulty, "Short on Frills, Big on Morale," *Financial Times,* October 31, 2001.

67. Michelle Conlin, "Where Layoffs Are a Last Resort," *BusinessWeek,* October 8, 2001.

68. John Nolan, "Union Official Expects Close Ratification Vote on Goodyear Contract," *Associated Press,* August 22, 2003; "Goodyear Could Close Alabama Plant, Layoff 15 Percent," *Associated Press,* September 23, 2003; "Securing Jobs, Saving Goodyear," United Steelworkers of America, www.uswa.org.

Chapter 5: Raising Global Boats

1. Two of the most powerful of these articles are Keith Bradsher, "Bangladesh Survives to Export Again," *New York Times,* December 14, 2004; and Peter Fritsch, "As End of Quota System Nears, Bangladesh Fears for its Jobs," *Wall Street Journal,* November 20, 2003.
2. "Women to Bear Brunt If Bangladesh Textile Industry Collapses," Agence France Presse, December 19, 2004.
3. Keith Bradsher, "Fresh Hope for Third-World Textile Makers," *New York Times,* December 14, 2004.
4. Richard Freeman and Kimberly Elliott, "The Role Global Labor Standards Could Play in Addressing Basic Needs," in J. Heymann, ed., *Global Inequalities at Work: Work's Impact on the Health of Individuals, Families and Societies* (Oxford: Oxford University Press, 2003), 74.
5. International Labor Organization, "Bitter Harvest: Child Labor in Agriculture," 2002. It is important to note that this is a problem in the United States as well as in developing countries. Human Rights Watch reported that as many as 300,000 children are working on corporate farms in the United States and, particularly in the area of fresh produce, the ILO Section 182 and more general antichild labor provisions are not being adequately enforced. Human Rights Watch, "Child Labor in Agriculture," June 11, 2002.
6. International Center for Trade and Sustainable Development, "WTO Ministerial Prep Meeting Tackles New Round," *Weekly Trade News Digest,* March 13, 2001.
7. Rajrsasyi Rao, "India Losing Child-Labour Battle," BBC News, May 6, 2002. See also, Human Rights Watch, "Small Hands of Slavery: Bonded Child Labor in India," September 1996. International Child Labor Program, U.S. Department of Labor, "India," Country Reports, www.dol.gov.
8. Kimberly Elliott, "Labor Standards and the Free Trade Area of the Americas," Institute for International Economics, August 2003, p. 13.
9. UNICEF, *State of the World's Children,* 1997, p. 60.
10. BBC News Cambodia Country Profile, July 15, 2004. UNDP, "Human Development Reports: Cambodia," 2003.
11. Susan Postlewaite, "As Unions Grow, an Industry Booms," *Business Week,* October 22, 2001.
12. Richard Freeman and Kimberly Elliott, *Can Labor Standards Improve Under Globalization?,* Washington, DC: Institute for International Economics, 2003, p. 118.
13. David Moberg, "Trading Down," *Nation,* December 22, 2004.
14. Karen Tramontano, "Stitching Up Global Labor Rights," *Washington Post,* December 11, 2004.
15. Sandra Polaski, "Cambodia Blazes New Path to Economic Growth and Job Creation," Carnegie Endowment International Peace, July 2003.
16. "Bangladesh, Other Asian Countries Among Losers as Textile Quotas End," Agence France Presse, December 19, 2004.
17. Freeman and Elliott, 2003. Outline this research in detail in their chapter, "The Market for Labor Standards."
18. Peter Ford, "Redefining Social Responsibility," *Christian Science Monitor,* June 13, 2003.
19. Paul Fireman, "Steps We Must Take on Third World Labor," *Washington Post,* October 17, 1999.
20. Fair Labor Association, "Annual Public Report," 2004.
21. Jake Batsell, "Fair Chance at Starbucks: Small Coffee Farmers Learn From Giant," *Seattle Times,* June 10, 2003.
22. Kelly Damore, "Coffee Talk," Oxfam America, February 15, 2004.

23. Tosin Sulaiman, "Clean Diamond Act to Help U.S. Producers Stay Clear of 'Conflict Diamonds,'" *Knight Ridder,* May 7, 2003; Amnesty International, "Déjà Vu: Diamond Industry Still Failing to Deliver on Promises," October 2004; Richard Morgan, "Qualitative Success," *Mining Journal,* December 3, 2004.

24. Alison Maitland, "Bitter Taste of Success: Corporate Social Responsibility Part IV," *Financial Times,* March 11, 2002.

25. Dani Rodrik, "Why Do More Open Economies Have Bigger Governments?" *Journal of Political Economy,* vol. 6, no. 5, 1998.

26. Robert Menendez, "Menendez Announces New Era in U.S.–Latin America Policy," Press Release, November 5, 2003.

27. George Psacharopoulos and Harry Anthony Patrinos, "Returns to Investment in Education: A Further Update," World Bank Policy Research Working Paper 2881, 2002. George Psacharopoulos, "Returns to Investment in Education: A Global Update," *World Development,* vol. 22, no. 9, 2002, 1325–43.

28. For a broad overview of the academic studies showing the return to investment in girls' education see Barbara Herz, and Gene Sperling, "What Works in Girls' Education: Evidence and Policies from the Developing World," Council on Foreign Relations, 2004.

29. David Dollar and Roberta Gatti, "Gender Inequality, Income, and Growth: Are Good Times Good for Women?," World Bank Policy Research Report on Gender and Development, Working Paper Series No. 1, 1999.

30. T. Paul Schultz, "Returns to Women's Schooling," in Elizabeth King and M. Anne Hill, eds., *Women's Education in Developing Countries: Barriers, Benefits, and Policy* (Baltimore: Johns Hopkins University Press, 1993).

31. K. Subbarao and Laura Raney, "Social Gains from Female Education," *Economic Development and Cultural Change,* vol. 44, no. 1, 1995, 105–28. World Bank, *Engendering Development,* World Bank Policy Research Report, 2001.

32. World Bank official Don Bundy and his team coined this phrase in an influential report "Education and HIV/AIDS: A Window of Hope," World Bank Education Section, Human Development Department, 2002.

33. Damien De Walque, "How Does Educational Attainment Affect the Risk of Being Infected by HIV/AIDS? Evidence from a General Population Cohort in Rural Uganda," World Bank Development Research Group Working Paper, Washington, DC: World Bank, March 2004.

34. D. A. Shuey, et al., "Increased Sexual Abstinence Among In-School Adolescents as a Result of School Health Education in Soroti District, Uganda," *Health Education Research,* vol. 14, no. 3, 1999, 411–19.

35. Herz and Sperling, 2004, p. 46. In Kenya, enrollment jumped to 7.2 million students from 5.9 million students; in Uganda, enrollment jumped to 6.5 million from 3.4 million, and in Tanzania, enrollment doubled to 3 million.

36. Steven Morley and David Coady, *From Social Assistance to Social Development: Targeted Education Subsidies in Developing Countries,* Washington, DC: Center for Global Development/IFPRI, 2003.

37. Morley and Coady, 2003. T. Paul Schultz, "School Subsidies for the Poor: Evaluating the Mexican Progresa Poverty Program," *Journal of Development Economics,* vol. 74, no. 1, 2004.

38. Shahid Khandkher and Mark Pitt, "Subsidy to Promote Girls' Secondary Education: The Female Secondary Stipend Program in Bangladesh," World Bank, 2003.

39. U.S. Foreign Agriculture Service, *The Global Food for Education Pilot Program: A Review of Project Implementation and Impact,* 2003.

40. Hillary Clinton, "Speech at Council on Foreign Relations," Washington, DC, April 20, 2004.

41. For earlier discussions of these issues, see Gene Sperling, "Toward Universal Education," *Foreign Affairs,* September/October 2001 and "Educating the World," *New York Times,* November 22, 2001.

42. Emily Fredrix, "Hillary Clinton Says U.S. Should Take Lead to Promote Girls' Education," *Associated Press,* April 20, 2004. Nita Lowey, "Senator Clinton, Congresswoman Lowey Introduce The Education for All Act of 2004," Press Release, September 29, 2004.

43. See also Gene Sperling, "Ethiopia Provides Glimpse of Hope for Its Future," *Bloomberg News,* April 15, 2002.

44. I have discussed this issue earlier in "Education Could Be America's Best Defense," *Financial Times,* June 22, 2004.

45. Author interview with George Saitoti, April 28, 2004.

Part Three: A Workforce for the Dynamism Economy

Chapter 6: A Pro-Growth Model for Rewarding Work

1. Sarah Jay, "The Neediest Cases: Woman Works Toward a Career and Reunites with Her Daughter." *New York Times,* December 25, 1995.

2. Indeed, we often said that we should change its name to the "Rewarding Work Tax Credit." In 1997, during Tony Blair's campaign for Prime Minister, his top domestic policy advisor David Miliband came to Washington to talk about policy ideas with people like Bruce Reed, Sidney Blumenthal, and myself. We made the point that we wished the EITC had a simpler name. He clearly got the point, for the British version of the EITC is known as the Working Tax Credit.

3. White House Press Release, "Good News for Low-Income Families: Expansions in the Earned Income Tax Credit and the Minimum Wage," December 4, 1998. Office of Management and Budget, Budget of the United States, 2006, Historical Tables.

4. In the first two weeks of the administration when we were engaged in our first budget meetings, I asked Bob Greenstein at the Center for Budget and Policy Priorities to estimate what increase in the EITC was needed to meet President Clinton's antipoverty pledge. These were the numbers I used in these budget discussions with President Clinton.

5. Alan Greenspan, *Hearing Before House Financial Services Committee,* July 18, 2001.

6. *Record of Discussion of FLSA of 1938,* Department of Labor, p. 873, quoted in Jonathan Grossman, "Fair Labor Standards Act of 1938: Maximum Struggle for a Minimum Wage," Department of Labor, www.dol.gov.

7. David Card and Alan Krueger, "Minimum Wages and Employment: A Case Study of the Fast-Food Industry in New Jersey and Pennsylvania," *American Economic Review,* vol. 84, no. 4, 1994.

8. Eileen Applebaum et al., "The Minimum Wage and Working Women," Rutgers University, June 18, 2004.

9. Nada Eissa and Jeffrey Liebman, "Labor Supply Response to the Earned Income Tax Credit," *Quarterly Journal of Economics,* vol. 111, no. 2, 1996, 605–37.

10. Bruce Meyer and Dan Rosenbaum, "Welfare, the Earned Income Tax Credit, and the Labor Supply of Single Mothers," NBER Working Paper 7363, National Bureau of Economic Research, September 1999. Another study, by V. Joseph Hotz, Charles H. Mullin,

and John Karl Scholz, has looked at families on or formerly on welfare in California alone, so their results are not affected by policy changes in different states enacted in the mid-1990s, such as experiments with welfare reform. They show that EITC increases in 1994 that expanded the credit substantially more for families with more than one child led employment rates for those families to rise by 6 to 8 percentage points more than for families with only one child. "The Earned Income Tax Credit and the Labor Market Participation of Families on Welfare," University of California–Los Angeles, March 2005.

11. Economic Policy Institute, "Snapshot: State Minimum Wages on the Move," December 1, 2004.

12. Lee Hockstader, "Santa Fe Wrangles over 'Broad' Living Wage Bill," *Washington Post,* February 26, 2003.

13. Nancy Cleeland, "Living Wage Laws Reducing Poverty, Study Shows," *Los Angeles Times,* March 14, 2002.

14. Neil Irwin, "Living Wage Impact Seen as Minimal," *Washington Post,* March 5, 2002.

15. For more information see, State EITC Online Resource Center, www.stateEITC.org.

16. Rachel Gordon, "S.F. Bonus for Families Earning IRS Tax Credit," *San Francisco Chronicle,* February 3, 2005.

17. Karen Schulman, "The High Cost of Child Care Puts Quality Care Out of Reach for Many Families," Children's Defense Fund, 2000.

18. Isabel Sawhill and Adam Thomas, "A Hand Up for the Bottom Third: Toward a New Agenda for Low-Income Working Families," Brookings Institution, 2001. Currently there is a child care tax credit that offers about $1,000 for child care services for each child up to two children. The benefit offers only 20 percent of the average child care costs, but the credit is nonrefundable, which means that it is of no help to working families who are too poor to pay taxes.

19. Steven Raphael and Michael Stoll, "Can Boosting Minority Car Ownership Narrow Interracial Employment Gaps?," Berkeley Program on Housing and Urban Policy, Working Paper 00–002, 2000.

20. Volpe Center, "National Transportation Technology Plans," Chapter 13, May 2000. See also, Center for Urban and Metropolitan Policy, "Moving Beyond Sprawl: The Challenge for Metropolitan Atlanta," Brookings Institution, March 2000.

21. Harry Holzer, John Quigley, and Stephen Raphael, "Public Transit and the Spatial Distribution of Minority Employment: Evidence from a Natural Experiment," *Journal of Policy Analysis and Management,* Summer 2003.

22. The basic problem was that because the EITC was refundable but the Child Tax Credit was not, it made a big difference in what order families were allowed to apply them. This was the issue of "stacking." A single mother with two kids who owed $1,000 in taxes, and was eligible for a $1,500 EITC paid no taxes and got a $500 refund. If she then applied for the nonrefundable Child Tax Credit, because she had no remaining tax liability, she would not get a penny of the $1,000 she was eligible for under the $500 per child tax credit. If she were allowed to take her Child Tax Credit first, she could put the $1,000 toward the taxes she owed, and, since the EITC is refundable, she could also get the full $1,500 refund.

23. Rob Wells, "Tax Bill Would Deny Key Benefit to Working Poor," *Associated Press,* July 3, 1997.

24. Daniel Mercado speaking at "News Conference on Administration's Proposal for Tax Credits for Working Families," July 10, 1997.

25. Ted Barrett and Steve Turnham, "DeLay Pushes New Tax Relief," CNN.com, June 3, 2003.

26. "The Non-Taxpaying Class," editorial, *Wall Street Journal,* November 20, 2002. "Lucky Duckies Again," editorial, *Wall Street Journal,* January 20, 2003. "Even Luckier Duckies," editorial, *Wall Street Journal,* June 3, 2003.

Chapter 7: The Work-Family Balancing Act

1. Karen Kornbluh, "The Parent Trap," *The Atlantic Monthly,* February 1, 2003.
2. Dan Pink interviewed workers who have chosen this route and suggested that this is a growing trend that is likely to permanently change the labor market. Dan Pink, *Free Agent Nation* (New York: Warner Books, 2002).
3. Laura Giannotta, "Letter to the Editor," *The Record (Trenton),* December 31, 1989.
4. Bureau of Labor Statistics. Clearly, these dramatic increases have been driven by myriad factors, many of which are unconnected to the work-family policies that I address in this chapter. As MIT economist Claudia Goldin explains, "Various features of the economic development process greatly altered the economic role of women. Changes in female labor force participation were effected mainly by advances in education, the growth of sectors such as clerical work and sales, and the shorter workday. The secular decline in fertility and its cyclical aspects that affected cohorts differentially, as well as a host of well-known advances in household production, also altered female employment." Nonetheless, as women's education and roles in society become increasingly equalized with men, policies affecting work-family choices are likely to be of increased importance in affecting decisions to enter the labor market. Claudia Goldin, *Understanding the Gender Gap* (Oxford: Oxford University Press, 1990), xiii.
5. Richard Freeman, "The U.S. Economic Model at Y2K: Lodestar for Advanced Capitalism?," NBER Working Paper 7757, National Bureau of Economic Research, June 2000.
6. National data for Japan, 2002, reported in *Japan Economic Newswire,* March 28, 2003.
7. Laura Tyson, "New Clues to the Pay and Leadership Gap," *Business Week,* October 27, 2003.
8. Anne Marie Chaker and Hilary Stout, "Mothers Who Take Time Off Must Play Career Catch-Up," CareerJournal.com, May 18, 2004.
9. Karen Kornbluh, "The Mommy Tax," *Washington Post,* January 5, 2001.
10. Lisa Belkin, "The Opt-Out Revolution," *New York Times,* October 26, 2003.
11. Quoted in Walecia Konrad, "Welcome to the Woman-Friendly Company," *Business Week,* August 6, 1990.
12. Dale Fuchs, "Spain Labors to Bring Home Baby—and the Bacon," *Christian Science Monitor,* June 26, 2003.
13. Anne Hélene Gauthier and Jan Hatzius, "Family Benefits and Fertility: An Econometric Analysis," *Population Studies,* vol. 51, 1997. Kevin Milligan has found even stronger results from examining a natural experiment in Canada. After the implementation of a generous government payment of up to $6,400, Milligan found that fertility rates increased by an average of 12 percent and by 25 percent in families eligible for the maximum subsidy. Kevin Milligan, "Subsidizing the Stork: New Evidence on Tax Incentives and Fertility," NBER Working Paper 8845, National Bureau of Economic Research, March 2002.
14. Thomas DiPrete et al., "Do Cross-National Differences in the Costs of Children Generate Cross-National Differences in Fertility Rates?," German Institute for Economic Research, Discussion Paper 355, July 2003.

15. Kajsa Sundstrom, "Can Governments Influence Birthrates," *OECD Observer*, Organization for Economic Cooperation and Development, December, 2001.

16. Jonathan Head, "Japan Sounds Alarm on Birthrate," BBC News, December 3, 2004.

17. "Kinder, Gentler," *Economist*, December 6, 2003.

18. Karen Kornbluh, "A Real Mother's Day Gift," Center for American Progress, May 7, 2004.

19. Women's Institute for a Secure Retirement, "Women & Pensions: Overview," Heinz Foundation, www.wiser.heinz.org.

20. Alicia Ault Barnett, "Perks for Part-Timers," *Business and Health*, September 1996.

21. David Cantor et al., "Balancing the Needs of Families and Employers: The Family and Medical Leave Surveys 2000 Update," Department of Labor, January 2001.

22. Cantor et al., 2001.

23. Debra L. Ness and Jodi Grant, "The American Work Place: Out of Sync with the American Family," Center for American Progress, May 7, 2004.

24. Several groups have been effective advocates for an extension of family leave, including the National Women's Law Center, led by Marcia Greenberger; the National Partnership for Women and Families, led by Debra Ness; and the Institute for Women's Policy Research, led by Heidi Hartmann.

25. Christopher Ruhm, "Parental Leave and Child Health," NBER Working Paper 6554, National Bureau of Economic Research, May 1998.

26. "Mother's Day: More Than Candy and Flowers, Working Parents Need Paid Time Off," Child Policy International Issue Brief, Columbia University, Spring 2002. International Labor Organization, "More Than 120 Nations Provide Paid Maternity Leave," Press Release, February 16, 1998.

27. See Christopher Ruhm, "The Economic Consequences of Parental Leave Mandates: Lessons from Europe," *Quarterly Journal of Economics*, 1998. Also see, Christopher Ruhm and Jackqueline Teague, "Parental Leave Policies in Europe and North America," NBER Working Paper 5065, National Bureau of Economic Research, March 1995.

28. Jon Gruber, "Incidence of Mandated Maternity Benefits," *American Economic Review*, June 1994. He finds that the cost of the benefit ranged from 1 percent to 5 percent of wages depending on demographic group. And he finds that the wage gap between potential mothers (women twenty to forty) and non-potential mothers (men twenty to forty and both sexes above forty) rose by about the cost of the leave.

29. Labor Project for Paid Family Leave, www.paidfamilyleave.org.

30. Arin Dube and Ethan Kaplan, "Paid Family Leave in California: An Analysis of Costs and Benefits," June 19, 2002.

31. California Economic Development Department, Paid Family Leave Program, May 27, 2005.

32. Joan Lombardi, *Time to Care* (Philadelphia: Temple University Press, 2002), 95.

33. Departments of Justice and Education, "Working for Children and Families: Safe and Smart Afterschool Programs," May 2000.

34. Janet Gornick, Marcia Meyers, and Katherine Ross, "Public Policies and the Employment of Mothers," Luxembourg Income Study Working Paper No. 140, Center for Policy Research, Syracuse University, 1996.

35. Policy Studies Associates, "Evaluation Results of the TASC Afterschool Program," February 2001.

36. Denise Huang et al., "A Decade of Results: The Impact of LA's Best Afterschool Enrichment Program on Subsequent Student Achievement and Performance," UCLA Graduate School of Education and Information Studies, June 2000.

37. Janet Gornick, Marcia Meyers, and Katherine Ross, "Public Policies and the Employment of Mothers," Luxembourg Income Study Working Paper No. 140, Center for Policy Research, Syracuse University, 1996; Thomas DiPrete et al., "Do Cross-National Differences in the Costs of Children Generate Cross-National Differences in Fertility Rates?," German Institute for Economic Research, Discussion Paper 355, July 2003.

38. Department of Education Web site, www.ed.gov.

39. Partnership for Family Involvement in Education, U.S. Department of Education, *Family Involvement in Education: A Snapshot of Out-of-School Time,* 1998.

40. Rich Lowry, "Bring Back the Stay-at-Home Mom," August 8, 2003, Townhall.com; Rich Lowry, "Democratic Shift on Welfare Reform," *The Advocate,* April 7, 2004.

41. Isabel Sawhill and Ron Haskins, "Work and Marriage: The Way to End Poverty and Welfare," Brookings Institution Policy Brief 28, 2003. See also Isabel Sawhill and Adam Thomas, "A Hand Up for the Bottom Third: Toward a New Agenda for Low-Income Working Families," Brookings Institution, 2001.

42. Gosta Esping-Anderson, "Inequality of Incomes and Opportunities," Universitat Pompeu Fabra, Unpublished Manuscript, 2005.

43. Smart Start, North Carolina, "Facts & Figures," www.ncsmartstart.org.

44. Helen Blank, Karen Schulman, Danielle Ewen, "Key Facts: Essential Information About Child Care, Early Education, and School-Age Care," Children's Defense Fund, November 1999.

45. Helen Blank, "Testimony Before the House Committee on Education and the Workforce," February 27, 2002.

46. Stephanie Mencimer, "Children Left Behind," *American Prospect,* December 30, 2002.

47. Christine Meyer, Swati Mukerjee, and Ann Sestero, "Work-Family Benefits: Which Ones Maximize Profits," *Journal of Managerial Issues,* Spring 2001.

48. Mackenzie Carpenter, "A Few Ounces of Prevention: Nationally Companies Recognize Need to Help with Family Care," *Pittsburgh Post-Gazette,* June 5, 1996.

49. Michelle Neely Martinez, "Work-Life Programs Reap Business Benefits," *HR Magazine,* June 1997.

50. Emery Dalesio, "Quiet Southern Software Giant Is Ready to Shout," *Los Angeles Times,* May 9, 2001; Geoffrey Wheelwright, "Profile: SAS Institute," *Financial Times,* December 15, 1999.

Chapter 8: Increasing the Labor Pool: A New Role for Colleges

1. David Ellwood, "Grow Faster Together or Grow Slowly Apart," Aspen Institute, 2002.

2. American Electronics Association, "Losing the Competitive Advantage? The Challenge for Science and Technology in the United States," February 2005.

3. Craig Barrett, "Fixing America's Educational System," *Chief Executive,* December 1, 2004.

4. Council on Competitiveness, "Benchmarking Competitiveness," www.compete.org.

5. Ina Mullis et al., "Mathematics and Science Achievement in the Final Year of Secondary School: IEA's Third International Mathematics and Science Study," International Association for the Evaluation of Educational Achievement, February 1998.

6. Benjamin Wallace Wells, "Off Track," *Washington Monthly,* March 2005.

7. Clare Ansberry, "A New Blue-Collar World," *Wall Street Journal,* June 30, 2003.

8. Anthony Carnevale and Donna Desrocher, "Help Wanted Credentials Required: Community Colleges in the Knowledge Economy," Educational Testing Service, 2001.

9. Laura Rendon, "Reconceptualizing Access in Postsecondary Education and Its Ramifications for Data Systems," National Postsecondary Education Cooperative, 1998.

10. There have been mild disputes over the years as to the exact promise Lang made and the statistics of success, but nothing that has undermined the basic lesson of this story. *60 Minutes,* CBS News, May 23, 2004 and February 23, 1986.

11. William Bowen and Derek Bok, *Shape of the River: Long-Term Consequences of Considering Race in College and University Admissions* (Princeton: Princeton University Press, 1998).

12. In fiscal year 2001, Congress appropriated $295 million. Through fiscal year 2001, the program has given 243 partnership grants and 30 state grants. Funded at $306 million in 2003, there are currently 289 grants to partnerships between schools, colleges, and other organizations, and another 35 related grants to states.

13. After GEAR UP passed, Steve Zwerling, then at the Ford Foundation, set up a permanent organization, the National Council for Community and Education Partnerships (NCCEP), to lobby and promote programs like GEAR UP and Project GRAD.

14. U.S. Department of Education, "National Evaluation of GEAR UP: A Summary of the First Two Years," Office of the Under Secretary, Policy and Program Studies Service, 2003.

15. David Leonhardt, "As Wealthy Fill Top Colleges, Concerns Grow Over Fairness," *New York Times,* April 22, 2004; Anthony Carnevale and Stephen J. Rose, "Socioeconomic Status, Race/Ethnicity and Selective College Admissions," Century Foundation, March 2003.

16. Department of Education, "High Hopes for College for America's Youth," Department of Education Fact Sheet, February 4, 1998.

17. Students who signed the pledge in middle school were more than four times as likely to enroll in a public four-year college upon graduating high school than their counterparts outside the program. And compared to other students at Indiana's public universities who did not receive any assistance, freshmen enrolled in the program were twice as likely to stay in college through their first year of school. Lumina Foundation, "Meeting the Access Challenge," August 2002.

18. Michael Winerip, "A Promise of Education and Its Lasting Legacy," *New York Times,* April 23, 2003.

19. U.S. Census Bureau, Current Population Survey, School Enrollment, Historical Tables.

20. Kevin Carey, "A Matter of Degrees," Education Trust, May 2004.

21. General Accounting Office (GAO), "College Completion: Additional Efforts Could Help Education with Its Completion Goals," May 2003.

22. Laura Horn, Rachael Berger, and C. Dennis Carroll, "College Persistence on the Rise," National Center for Education Statistics, November 2004; Organization for Economic Cooperation and Development, "Education at a Glance," 2003.

23. Bill Gates, "Speech to the National Education Summit on High Schools," February 26, 2005.

24. American Institutes for Research and SRI International, "The National School District and Network Grants Program Year 2 Evaluation Report," April 2004.

25. Khandi Bourne-Bowie, "Retention Depends on New Models of Student Development," *Black Issues in Higher Education,* March 30, 2000.

26. Patricia Gándara and Julie Maxwell-Jolly, *Priming the Pump: Strategies for Increasing the Achievement of Underrepresented Minority Undergraduates* (New York: The College Board, 1999). Similar programs, including the University of California, San Diego's Oasis Summer Bridge Program and the University of South Carolina's "University 101,"

have shown equally strong improvements. GAO, "Completion," 2003; "Georgia Tech Ranked as Top Producer of African American Engineering Graduates," *Atlanta Inquirer,* August 28, 2004; Phaedra Brotherton, "Minority Bachelor's Degrees on the Rise," *Black Issues in Higher Education,* June 7, 2001.

27. Florida State University, "Living and Learning in the Halls," www.housing.fsu.edu.
28. Cecilia Rouse and Thomas J. Kane, "The Community College: Educating Students at the Margin Between College and Work," *Journal of Economic Perspectives,* vol. 13, no. 1, Winter 1999.
29. See, for example, Susan Gooden and Lisa Matus-Goldman, "Opening Doors: Students' Perspectives on Juggling Work, Family and College," MDRC, July 2002.

Chapter 9: Take Universal Preschool Seriously, Please

1. Ron Haskins and Cecilia Rouse, "Closing Achievement Gaps," The Future of Children, Policy Brief, spring 2005.
2. Betty Hart and Todd Risley, *Meaningful Differences in the Everyday Experiences of Young American Children* (Baltimore: Brookes Publishing, 1995), 176.
3. Average math scores are 21 percent lower for black children and 19 percent lower for Hispanic children than their white counterparts. Valerie Lee and David Burkam, "Inequality at the Starting Gate," Economic Policy Institute, 2002.
4. Elizabeth Gershoff, "Living at the Edge: Low Income and the Development of America's Kindergartners," National Center for Children in Poverty, November 2003.
5. Isabel Sawhill (ed.), *One Percent for the Kids: New Policies, Brighter Futures for America's Children* (Washington, DC: Brookings Institution, 2003). James Heckman argues that "The rate of return to a dollar of investment made while a person is young is higher than the rate of return to the same dollar made at a later age. Early investments are harvested over a longer horizon than those made later in the life cycle." James Heckman and Dimitriy Masterov, "The Productivity Argument for Investing in Young Children," Working Paper No. 5, Invest in Kids Working Group, October 2004.
6. Lawrence Schweinhart, "The High/Scope Perry Pre-school Study Through Age 40," High/Scope Educational Research Foundation, 2004.
7. Leonard Masse and W. Steven Barnett, "A Benefit-Cost Analysis of the Abecedarian Early Childhood Intervention," National Institute for Early Education Research, 2002.
8. Rob Grunewald and Art Rolnick, "A Proposal for Achieving High Returns on Early Childhood Development," Federal Reserve Bank of Minneapolis, December 22, 2004.
9. Business Roundtable and Corporate Voices for Working Families, "Early Childhood Education: A Call to Action from the Business Community," May 2003.
10. Robert Dugger, "American Kids, Workforce Quality and Fiscal Sustainability: A Multi-Year Plan for the Invest in Kids Working Group—Year 2," Invest in Kids Working Group Working Paper No. 4, Committee for Economic Development, January 2005. See also, Research and Policy Committee, "Preschool for All: Investing in a Productive and Just Society," Committee for Economic Development, February 2002.
11. Fight Crime: Invest in Kids, "Quality Pre-Kindergarten: Key to Crime Prevention and School Success," www.fightcrime.org.
12. Jeff Modisett, "Shifting the Emphasis from Prison to Education: How Indiana Saved over 40 Million," *Black Issues in Higher Education,* March 25, 2004.
13. Education Commission for the States, "Brain Research and Education: Neuroscience Research Has Impact for Education Policy," March 1998.

14. Head Start Bureau, "Head Start Program Fact Sheet," Department of Health and Human Services, February 24, 2005.
15. Jill Barshay, "Special Interests Strike Gold in Richly Targeted Tax Bill," *Congressional Quarterly Weekly,* October 16, 2004.
16. Committee on Education and the Workforce, Minority Staff, "FY 2006 Bush Budget: Breaks Promises, Underfunds K-12 Funding, and Forces Students to Pay More for College," February 7, 2005.
17. Gosta Esping-Anderson, "Inequality of Incomes and Opportunities," Universitat Pompeu Fabra, Unpublished Manuscript, 2005.
18. "Earlier Nurture for Young Minds," *Los Angeles Times,* October 16, 1996.
19. Ingrid Wickelgren, "Nurture Helps Mold Able Minds; Environmental Influences on Intelligence Levels," *Science,* March 19, 1999.
20. Danya Glaser, "Child Abuse and Neglect and the Brain: A Review," *Journal of Child Psychiatry,* vol. 41, no. 1, 2000.
21. Nicholas Zill et al., "Head Start FACES 2000 Survey," Administration for Children and Families, May 2003.
22. W. Steven Barnett, "The Battle over Head Start: What the Research Shows," National Institute for Early Education Research, September 13, 2002.
23. Tamara Henry, "Getting a Head Start: But Do the Program's Benefits Last?" *USA Today,* April 13, 1993.
24. Heather Weiss, "From the Director's Desk," *Evaluation Exchange,* vol. 9, no. 1, Spring 2003.
25. Administration for Children and Families, "Head Start Program Fact Sheet," 2004.
26. For more on the policy options and importance of early childhood education and quality child care, see Joan Lombardi, *Time to Care* (Philadelphia: Temple University Press, 2002).
27. North Carolina Smart Start, "Results," www.smartstart-nc.org/overview/results.htm.
28. FPG-UNC Smart Start Evaluation Team, "A Six-County Study of the Effects of Smart Start Child Care on Kindergarten Entry Skills," FPG Child Development Institute, University of North Carolina, September 1999.

Chapter 10: Seeing At-Risk Minority Males as Future Fathers and Workers

1. Devah Pager, "The Mark of a Criminal Record," Center for Demography and Ecology, University of Wisconsin-Madison, August 2002.
2. Robert Entman and Andrew Rojecki, "The Entman-Rojecki Index of Race and the Media," excerpted from *The Black Image in the White Mind* (Chicago: University of Chicago Press, 2001).
3. Marc Morial, "Keynote Address to the National Urban League Annual Conference," July 27, 2003.
4. Harry Holzer and Paul Offner, "Left Behind in the Labor Market: Recent Employment Trends Among Young Black Men," Brookings Institution, April 2002.
5. U.S. Census Bureau.
6. Thomas Bonczar, "Prevalence of Imprisonment in the U.S. Population, 1974–2001," Department of Justice, August 2003; Bureau of Justice Statistics, 2001.
7. See Peter Edelman, "The True Purpose of Welfare Reform," *New York Times,* May 29, 2002. ("Responsible fatherhood could be encouraged if the federal government pro-

moted ways to help young, less educated African-American men, who were left out during the economic expansion of the past decade, find work.")

8. Elaine Sorensen, "Helping Poor Nonresident Dads Do More," Urban Institute, May 2002.

9. Elaine Sorenson and Chava Zibman, "Poor Dads Who Don't Pay Child Support: Deadbeats or Disadvantaged?" Urban Institute, April 2001. I-Fen Lin and Sarah McLanahan, "Norms About Unwed Fathers Rights and Obligations," *Children and Youth Services Review,* vol. 23, 2001, 485–512.

10. Jonathan Peterson, "Debate over Welfare Reform Broadens to Include Fathers," *Los Angeles Times,* June 16, 2002.

11. Waldo Johnson, "Paternal Involvement Among Unwed Fathers," *Children and Youth Services Review,* vol. 23, 2001.

12. Elaine Sorensen and Chava Zibman, "Child Support Offers Some Protection from Poverty," Urban Institute, March 15, 2000.

13. Harry Holzer, Paul Offner, and Elaine Sorensen, "Declining Employment Among Young Black Less-Educated Men: The Role of Incarceration and Child Support," Urban Institute, April 2004.

14. Wendell Primus and Charita Castro, "A State Strategy for Increasing Child Support Payments from Low-Income Fathers and Improving the Well-being of Their Children Through Economic Incentives," Center on Budget and Policy Priorities, April 14, 2002.

15. Georgia Fatherhood Program, Georgia Department of Technical and Adult Education. Another court-supervised program in Florida, which helps poor dads who owe child support maintain their jobs, produced a four-to-one return on investment in terms of the benefits accrued to children. Florida Commission on Responsible Fatherhood, www.floridafathers.org.

16. Cynthia Miller and Virginia Knox, "The Challenge of Helping Low-Income Fathers Support Their Children: Final Lessons from Parents' Fair Share," MDRC, November 2001. (Although there were some significant achievements in the program, this evaluation acknowledges that the program "generally fell short of its initial goals.")

17. "Turning the Corner on Father Absence in Black America." Statement from the Morehouse Conference on African American Fathers, June 16, 1999.

18. Freddie Belton, "Testimony Before the Senate Finance Committee," October 11, 2001.

19. Interviewed on *The Tavis Smiley Show,* National Public Radio (NPR), August 3, 2004.

20. James Kemple, "Career Academies: Impacts on Labor Market Outcomes and Educational Attainment," MDRC, March 2004.

21. Sheena McConnell, "National Job Corps Study: The Value of the Output and Services Produced by Students While Enrolled in Job Corps," Department of Labor and Mathematica Policy Research, 1999.

22. National Guard Youth ChalleNGe Program, www.NGYCP.org. These results are impressive, even after taking into account the intensive screening process. Another program, the Junior ROTC Career Academy (JROTCCA) does not have a residential component but attempts to create a separate environment by using a school-within-a-school model, where participants attend classes as a coherent unit and are assigned a special set of teachers. JROTCCA adds ROTC-related extracurricular activities such as drill team exercises with an emphasis on discipline. An evaluation by the RAND Corporation found that students in JROTCCA programs have higher GPAs, lower absenteeism, and higher graduation rates than would have been expected without the program. Marc Elliott et al., "Evidence of Positive Student Outcomes in JROTC Career Academies," *National Defense Research Institute,* 2001.

23. Office of the Chief Economist, *What's Working (and What's Not): A Summary of Re-*

search on the Economic Impacts of Employment and Training Programs, Washington, DC: U.S. Department of Labor, 1995.

24. Richard Freeman, "Why Do So Many Young Men Commit Crimes and What Might We Do About It?" *Journal of Economic Perspectives,* vol. 10, no. 1, Winter 1996.

25. Department of Justice (DOJ), "Chicago's Safer Foundation: A Road Back for Ex-Offenders," June 1998. Another example is the Center for Employment Opportunities in New York, which puts participants through a "boot camp"–like day labor program within a week after release. After two to three months of day labor, as well as job readiness training, life skills training, and support for things like finding housing, the program helps participants find permanent jobs. According to a DOJ evaluation, 70 percent find full-time employment within two to three months. Peter Finn, "Successful Job Placement for Ex-Offenders: The Center for Employment Opportunities," Department of Justice, March 1998.

26. Lisa Chmiola, "Former Gang Member Turns His Life Around; Teen Meets President in White House," *Houston Chronicle,* August 10, 1998.

27. LA Bridges Program, "Fact Sheet," www.streetgangs.com.

Chapter 11: New Technologies:
Tapping the Potential of People with Disabilities

1. Roy Hoffman, "The Summer of '56," *New York Times,* December 9, 2001.

2. Ed Williams, "Joe Martin's Journey: The Making of a Novelist; Scholar, Bank Exec, Guy in a Wheelchair—It All Contributed to Who He Is," *Charlotte Observer,* November 18, 2001.

3. Vincent P. Bzdek, "A Lost Leg, But Hope for Wings; The Pilot's Prosthesis Is a Marvel, But Will It Let Him Fly?," *Washington Post,* January 11, 2004.

4. Richard Martin, "Mind Control," *Wired,* March 13, 2005. Kristin Philipkoski, "Patients Put on Thinking Caps," *Wired,* January 14, 2005.

5. Tony Coelho, "Our Right to Work, Our Demand to Be Heard: People with Disabilities, the 2004 Election, and Beyond," Speech at New York Law School, October 24, 2003.

6. U.S. Census Bureau, American Community Survey, 2003.

7. Gregg Vanderheiden, "Fundamental Principles and Priority Setting for Universal Usability," Trace Center, University of Wisconsin, www.trace.wisc.edu.

8. An income-contingent loan system for assistive technologies could build upon recent government programs to provide low-interest micro-loans to individuals purchasing assistive technologies, supported through President Clinton's Assistive Technology Act of 1998 and President Bush's New Freedom Initiative. The existing micro-loan programs make it possible for many individuals to afford much-needed items without resorting to public assistance, but they are insufficient for people with disabilities who do not earn enough to pay their loan back. Income-contingent loans would expand the support significantly.

9. "Falling Through the Net: Towards Digital Inclusion," Department of Commerce, October 2000.

10. Amanda Lenhart et al., *The Ever-Shifting Internet Population: A New Look at Internet Access and the Digital Divide,* The Pew Internet and American Life Project, April 16, 2003.

11. Suzanne Robitaille, "The ADA's Next Step: Cyberspace," *BusinessWeek,* July 28, 2003.

12. Richard Burkhauser and David Stapleton, "Employing Those Not Expected to Work: The Stunning Change in the Employment of Single Mothers and People with Disabilities in the 1990s," Cornell University, May 2003.

13. Scott Cinsavich and Gabriela Rado, "Medicaid Buy-In: Concept and Implementation," Institute for Community Inclusion Policy Brief, vol. 4, no. 2, April 2002. Centers for Medicare and Medicaid Services, "The New Freedom Initiative: The President's FY2006 Budget and CMS Accomplishments," June 6, 2005.
14. In 1999, Clinton proposed an annual tax credit to offset up to $1,000 in work-related expenses for disabled workers. In early versions of the Ticket to Work Act of 1999, we had included a more generous variant of this proposal, which would have given a 50 percent tax credit for up to $10,000 in work expenses.

Chapter 12: Tomorrow's Innovators and Tomorrow's Innovation

1. Benjamin Wallace-Wells, "Off Track," *Washington Monthly,* March 2005.
2. Thomas Kalil, "R&D on the Edge," *San Jose Mercury News,* March 10, 2001.
3. Janet Abbate, "Government, Business, and the Making of The Internet," *Business History Review,* vol. 75, no. 1, Spring 2001. DARPA's successful research strategy is based on an innovative management style that recruits many of its program managers from leading research universities who can serve in a temporary rotation. This rotation brings a steady stream of new ideas to the institution and helps identify some of the most promising research directions. In addition, DARPA has no "entitled constituencies." All of its research is performed externally, and DARPA can select whatever mix of performers (university, industry, national labs) make the most sense for the task at hand.
4. Thomas Kalil, "Google: Lessons for America's Innovation Policy," Center for American Progress, May 14, 2004.
5. National Research Council, Computer Science and Telecommunications Board, *Evolving the High-Performance Computing and Communications Initiative to Support the Nation's Information Infrastructure* (Washington, DC: National Academy Press, 1995).
6. John Markoff, "Pentagon Redirects Its Research Dollars," *New York Times,* April 2, 2005.
7. President's Information Technology Advisory Committee, "Cyber Security: A Crisis in Prioritization," March 25, 2005.
8. As quoted in Markoff, 2005.
9. Peter N. Spotts, "Pulling the plug on science?," *Christian Science Monitor,* April 14, 2005.
10. The Task Force on the Future of American Innovation, "The Knowledge Economy: Is the United States Losing Its Competitive Edge?," February 16, 2005.
11. American Electronics Association, "Losing the Competitive Advantage? The Challenge for Science and Technology in the United States," February 2005.
12. For an excellent discussion of the importance of government investment in nanotechnology, see Thomas Kalil, "Cutting-Edge Small Technology Deserves Big U.S. Investment," *Seattle Times,* June 28, 2001.
13. President's Council of Advisers on Science and Technology, "The National Nanotechnology Initiative at Five Years," May 17, 2005.
14. Task Force on the Future of American Innovation, 2005.
15. Robert Hormats, "Testimony Before the House Government Reform Subcommittee on Energy and Resources," April 6, 2005.
16. Jeffrey Immelt and Jonathan Lash, "The Courage to Develop Clean Energy," *Washington Post,* May 21, 2005.
17. Shamarukh Mohiuddin, "How America Lost Its Clean Technology Edge," Progressive Policy Institute Backgrounder, December 1, 2004.
18. The Apollo Alliance, a nonprofit coalition led by Senator Maria Cantwell, President of the United Steelworkers Leo Gerard, Representative Jesse Jackson Jr., and Founder of

the Sierra Club Carl Pope, uses this metaphor as its mission statement. www.apollo
alliance.org.

19. Fred Sissine, "Renewable Energy: Tax Credit, Budget, and Electricity Restructuring Issues," *Congressional Research Service,* March 9, 2001.

20. Ken Bossong, "White House Budget Slashes Clean Energy: A Look at the Administration's Budget Request for Sustainable Energy Programs in FY2006," Renewable Energy
Access, February 28, 2005.

21. Nedra Pickler, "Automakers Won't Reach Clinton Goal," Associated Press, August
13, 2001. Paul Coninx, "Will Hydrogen Bomb as a Fuel?," *Toronto Star,* October 12,
2002.

22. Mohiuddin, 2004.

23. Jacqueline F. Gold, "Bush, Oil, Batter Clean Energy Stocks," CNNMoney.com, November 5, 2004.

24. Department of Commerce, "Industry Facts," Office of Environmental Technologies Industries, 2004.

25. Katharine Mieszkowski, "How George Bush Lost the Sun," Salon.com, October 25,
2004.

26. David Morris, "Solar Comes to (Part of) the Earth," Institute for Local Self-Reliance,
December 18, 2003.

27. Paul Roberts, "Power Shortage: The U.S. Is Falling Far Behind Its Rivals in Developing
Alternative Energy Sources," *Los Angeles Times,* May 23, 2004.

28. John Carey, "Giving Hybrids a Real Jolt," *BusinessWeek,* April 11, 2005.

29. Richard G. Lugar and R. James Woolsey, "The New Petroleum," *Foreign Affairs,* Janu-
ary/February 1999.

30. Bossong, 2005. The president's 2006 budget also proposes cutting the Department of
Energy Biomass/Biofuels program 18 percent, the Department of Agriculture (USDA)
Natural Resources Conservation Service's Biomass Research and Development Pro-
gram would be cut by $2 million to $12 million, and the USDA's Commodity Credit
Corporation Bioenergy Program is also slated for a $40 million cut from $100 million
in FY05 to $60 million in FY06, down from $150 million in FY04.

31. National Assessment of Educational Progress, Department of Education, 2003; American Electronics Association, "Losing the Competitive Advantage? The Challenge for
Science and Technology in the United States," February 2005.

32. National Science Board, "Science and Engineering Indicators," May 2004.

33. National Science Board, "Science and Engineering Indicators," May 2004; see also "A
Record Number of Doctoral Degrees Awarded to African Americans," *Journal of Blacks
in Higher Education,* Spring 2005.

34. Sophia Catsambis, "The Path to Math: Gender and Racial-Ethnic Differences in Mathematics Participation from Middle to High School," *Sociology of Education,* 1994.

35. U.S. Department of Education, "Women in Mathematics and Science," July 1997. Bea-
triz Chu Clewell and Patricia B. Campbell, "Taking Stock: Where We've Been, Where We
Are, Where We're Going," *Journal of Women and Minorities in Science and Engineering,*
vol. 8, no. 3, 2002.

36. T. Spielhofer et al., "The Impact of School Size and Single-Sex Education on Performance," National Foundation for Educational Research, July 2002.

37. Rosalind Rossi, "Bright Future for All-Girls School's First Graduates," *Chicago Sun-
Times,* June 6, 2004.

38. Paul Romer, "Should the Government Subsidize Supply or Demand for Scientists and
Engineers," NBER Working Paper 7723, National Bureau of Economic Research, June
2000.

39. Kurt Squire and Henry Jenkins, "Games-to-Teach Project," PowerPoint Presentation, Massachusetts Institute of Technology, Fall 2002.
40. Erica Goldman and Eliot Marshall, "NIH Grantees: Where Have All the Young Ones Gone?," *Science,* October 4, 2002.

Part Four: The Nation that Saves Together Grows Together

Chapter 13: Spreading the Wealth Creation

1. Office of Management and Budget, Budget of the United States Fiscal Year 2005 Analytical Perspectives; Leonard E. Burman, William G. Gale, Matthew Hall, and Peter R. Orszag, "Distributional Effects of Defined Contribution Plans and Individual Retirement Accounts," Brookings Institution Discussion Paper No. 16, August 2004.
2. Craig Copeland, "Employment-Based Retirement Plan Participation: Geographic Differences and Trends," EBRI Issue Brief, No. 274, October, 2004.
3. William Apgar, "Rethinking Rental Housing: Expanding the Ability of Rental Housing to Serve as a Pathway to Economic and Social Opportunity," Joint Center for Housing Studies Working Paper 04–11, Harvard University, December 2004.
4. Committee for Economic Development, "Hidden in Plain Sight: A Look at the $335 Billion Federal Asset Development Budget," January 2004.
5. A number of academic studies confirm that giving new retirement savings incentives to upper-income earners results in a reshuffling of assets as these earners simply *shift* existing savings to get a better deal, while savings contributed to tax-preferred accounts by lower-income workers are most likely to represent new savings. Eric Engen and William Gale, "The Effects of 401(k) Plans on Household Wealth: Differences Across Earnings Groups," NBER Working Paper 8032, National Bureau of Economic Research, December 2000. See also Jane G. Gravelle, "Individual Retirement Accounts (IRAs): Issues, Proposed Expansion, and Retirement Savings Accounts (RSAs)," September 15, 2000; and Andrew Samwick, "Is Pension Reform Conducive to Higher Saving?," *Review of Economics and Statistics,* vol. 82, no. 2, 2000.
6. Employee Benefits Research Institute, "Retirement Confidence Survey," April 2005; "What Us Worry: Americans Fail to Plan Retirement," Dow Jones Newswires, May 25, 2005.
7. Elizabeth Bell, Adam Carasso, and C. Eugene Steuerle, "Retirement Savings Incentives and Personal Savings," Urban Institute, December 20, 2004.
8. Deloitte and Touche, "2004 Annual 401(k) Benchmarking Survey," April 4, 2004.
9. Annual pension coverage from the Joint Bureau of Labor Statistics/Census Current Population Survey, analyzed by the Economic Policy Institute, includes private wage and salary workers who worked at least twenty-six weeks and at least twenty hours a week.
10. Employee Benefit Research Institute, "The 2003 Small Employer Retirement Survey (SERS) Summary of Findings," June 3, 2003.
11. Economic Policy Institute, "Retirement Security Facts at a Glance," February 2003.
12. Craig Copeland, "IRA Assets and Characteristics of IRA Owners," *EBRI Notes,* Employee Benefit Research Institute (EBRI), vol. 23, no. 12, December 2002.
13. Survey of Consumer Finances, Federal Reserve Board, 2001; National Election Day Exit Poll Results, Voter News Service, 2000.
14. Ana M. Aizcorbe et al., "Recent Changes in U.S. Family Finances: Evidence from the 1998 and 2001 Survey of Consumer Finances," *Federal Reserve Bulletin,* vol. 89, January 2003, p. 14.

15. Edward N. Wolff, "Retirement Insecurity: The Income Shortfalls Awaiting the Soon-to-Retire," Economic Policy Institute, 2002.

16. Ruy Texeira, "The Myth of the Investor Class," *American Prospect,* May 5, 2003.

17. William Gale, Mark Iwry, Peter Orszag, "Retirement Saving and Long-Term Care Needs: An Overview," Retirement Security Project, Brookings Institution, September 2004.

18. Jonathan Riskind, "401(k) Reports Might Make Some Investors Bearish on Bush," *Columbus Dispatch,* October 24, 2004.

19. George W. Bush, "Remarks to Department of Labor Retirement Security Summit," February 28, 2002.

20. Only about 4 percent of workers max out on their IRAs, and only about 6 percent of workers' 401(k)s are constrained by the contribution limit. For the IRA figure, see Craig Copeland, "IRA Assets and Characteristics of IRA owners," *EBRI Notes,* Employee Benefit Research Institute (EBRI), vol. 23, no. 12, December 2002. For the 401(k) figure, see Congressional Budget Office (CBO), "Utilization of Tax Incentives for Retirement Saving," August 2003.

21. Since the people who max out their contributions to these accounts tend to be higher-income, the distribution of people who benefit is highly skewed. Over a twenty-five-year period, the top 10 percent of households would get slightly more than half of the benefits from the creation of LSAs, while the bottom 60 percent would only get 11 percent. By 2028, the bottom 60 percent would be receiving only 4 percent of the benefits, versus 66 percent—a full two thirds—for the top 10 percent. The effect of RSAs would be highly skewed as well. For example, more than 90 percent of the tax benefit from removing the Roth IRA income limit would go to households with over $200,000 in income and almost 40 percent of the benefits would go to the 0.4 percent of households with income over $500,000. Leonard Burman, William G. Gale, and Peter R. Orszag, "Key Thoughts on RSAs and LSAs," Urban Institute-Brookings Institution Tax Policy Center, February 4, 2004.

22. Al Martin, "Remarks to the Small Business Council of America," February 5, 2003.

23. Congressional Budget Office (CBO), "The Potential Economic Effects of Selected Tax Proposals in the President's 2006 Budget," March 2005.

24. Ray Boshara, Correspondence, *American Prospect,* June 2003.

25. For more on the USA Account proposal see "Press Briefing by Director of the National Economic Council Gene Sperling, and Deputy Secretary of Treasury Larry Summers," Press Release, Office of the Press Secretary, April 14, 1999. The USA Account proposal offered a new tax-deferred retirement savings account with progressive government matches and starter funds for low- and moderate-income savers. The USA Account proposal offered starter funds of $300 for all workers who earn less than $40,000 a year, phasing out for workers who earn up to $80,000. In addition to the starter funds, the proposal offered a 1-to-1 match on additional savings up to $1,000 including the government contribution for workers who earn less than $40,000, phasing down to a 50 percent credit for workers who earn between $80,000 and $100,000.

26. I have discussed the Universal 401(k) proposal in earlier pieces, see "New Ways of Saving," *New York Times,* November 18, 2002; "Building a Real Investor Class," *Blueprint Magazine,* June 30, 2003; "No Pain, No Savings," *New York Times,* January 5, 2005; and "A Progressive Framework for Social Security Reform," Center for American Progress, January 10, 2005.

27. The benefits of complete portability are explored in detail in Paul Weinstein, "Universal Pensions," Progressive Policy Institute, February 22, 2002.

28. Discussed in Lee Walczak and Richard Dunham, "I Want My Safety Net," *BusinessWeek,*

May 16, 2005. See also, Alicia Munnell and Annika Sunden, *Coming Up Short: The Challenge of 401(k) Plans* (Washington, D.C.: Brookings Institution Press, 2004).

29. William Gale, Mark Iwry, and Peter Orszag, "The Automatic 401(k)," Brookings Retirement Security Project, March 2005.

30. Adoption of auto-enrollment options has primarily occurred in large firms. Only about 1 percent of 401(k) plans with fewer than fifty participants had adopted automatic enrollment by 2003, compared with 24 percent of plans with over five thousand participants. Patrick Purcell, "Automatic Enrollment in Section 401(k) Plans," *Congressional Research Service,* October 14, 2004.

31. Andrew Balls, "The Path of Least Resistance in 401(k) Plans," NBER Web site, National Bureau of Economic Research, April 21, 2005.

32. Bridgitte Madrian and Dennis Shea, "The Power of Suggestion: Inertia in 401(k) Participation and Savings Behavior," NBER Working Paper 7682, National Bureau of Economic Research, May 2000.

33. William G. Gale, J. Mark Iwry, and Peter R. Orszag, "The Automatic 401(k): A Simple Way to Strengthen Retirement Savings," Retirement Security Project, Brookings Institution, March 2005.

34. Jonathon Weisman, "Automatic Signup in 401(k)s Backed: Provision Eyed for Social Security Bill," *Washington Post,* May 22, 2005.

35. Introducing an option on people's tax forms that allowed them to easily split their refunds would cost virtually nothing to implement, especially since participants in trial efforts expressed a willingness to pay a small fee of $5 or so to recoup the cost of directing their refund into two different accounts.

36. Peter Tufano, Daniel Schneider, and Sondra Beverly, "Splitting Tax Refunds and Building Savings: An Empirical Test," Havard Business School, February 2005.

37. Esther Duflo, William Gale, Jeffrey Liebman, Peter Orszag, and Emmanuel Saez, "Saving Incentives for Low- and Middle-Income Families: Evidence from a Field Experiment with H&R Block," Retirement Security Project, May 2005.

38. The America Saving for Personal Investment, Retirement and Education (ASPIRE) Act is a bipartisan bill that follows the outlines of the British proposal. See New America Foundation, "The ASPIRE Act (Kids Accounts)," July 22, 2004. Leader, "Saving from Birth," *Guardian,* April 11, 2003.

39. Associated Press-Ipsos Poll, April 4–6, 2005; Gallup Poll, April 4–7, 2005.

40. Warren Buffett, "Dividend Voodoo," *Washington Post,* May 20, 2003.

41. David Cay Johnston, "Richest Are Leaving Even the Rich Far Behind," *New York Times,* June 5, 2005.

42. Author's calculations based on Tax Policy Center, "Distributional Tables: Current Law Distribution of Estate Tax 2009," April 13, 2004, and Joint Committee on Taxation, "Estimated Revenue Effects of H.R.8," April 13, 2005; and Joel Friedman and Ruth Carlitz, "Estate Tax Reform Could Raise Much Needed Revenue," Center on Budget and Policy Priorities, March 16, 2005.

43. For my earlier discussion of the Flat Tax Incentive see "A Progressive Framework for Social Security Reform," Center for American Progress, January 10, 2005; and "U.S. Needs 'Flat Tax Incentive' to Spark Savings," Bloomberg News, April 19, 2005.

44. Center for American Progress, "A Fair and Simple Tax System for Our Future: A Progressive Approach to Tax Reform," January 31, 2005.

45. While not calling for a Flat Tax Incentive, Representative Harold Ford has also proposed replacing our system of tax deductibility on savings and mortgage payments with a system of refundable tax credits. Harold Ford, "For Children, a Stake in the Future," *Washington Post,* January 25, 2004.

46. If additional savings beyond the retention of a $5 million estate tax exemption were needed to cover the full costs of a generous Universal 401(k) plan, the government could transfer savings by closing egregious international corporate loopholes, including provisions in our tax code like the so-called deferral provision that provide an incentive for companies to locate production overseas.

Chapter 14: Young Frankenstein Economics: Do Deficits Matter?

1. See, for example, Albert R. Hunt, "The Fiscal Free Lunch Is Back," *Wall Street Journal*, May 16, 2002.
2. Peter Peterson, *Running on Empty* (New York: Farrar, Straus, and Giroux, 2004) xxv.
3. In January 2001 in "Budget And Economic Outlook: Fiscal Years 2002–2011," the Congressional Budget Office (CBO) projected surpluses of $5.610 trillion between 2002 and 2011. Author's calculation using a conservative assumption that the growth in surpluses would slow to only the rate of nominal GDP growth after 2011.
4. Goldman Sachs, U.S. Economic Research, "The Long-Term Deficit Outlook: What's a Few Trillion Among Friends," March 3, 2005.
5. Ron Suskind, *Price of Loyalty* (New York: Simon & Schuster, 2004), 291.
6. Peterson, 2004, xxiii–xxiv.
7. Council of Economic Advisers, "Economic Report of the President," February 1984.
8. Council of Economic Advisers, "Economic Report of the President," February 1991.
9. Alan Greenspan, "Federal Reserve Board's Semiannual Monetary Policy Report to the Congress," Before the Senate Committee on Banking, Housing, and Urban Affairs, July 16, 2002.
10. N. Gregory Mankiw, *The Principles of Economics* (New York: Harcourt, 1998), 555.
11. David Stockman, *Triumph of Politics* (New York: Harper and Row, 1986).
12. See for example: Marilyn Gleewax, "Bush's Economic Appointments Bring Up New Questions; Tax Cuts or Not?," *Atlanta Journal-Constitution*, December 17, 2002.
13. Quoted in Richard Stevenson, "On Tax Cuts and Deficits, a Battle of Believers," *New York Times*, February 10, 2002.
14. William Gale and Peter Orszag, "The Economic Effects of Long-term Fiscal Discipline," *Urban-Brookings Tax Policy Center Discussion Paper*, December 17, 2002.
15. Bureau of Labor Statistics, January 1993.
16. For example, the National Institute Economic Review reported that "the slowdown in world demand coincided with the transition from a robust U.S. recovery to fears of a 'double-dip' recession." R. Anderton, G. M. Caporale, and J. W. Veld, "The World Economy; Forecasts for 1993," *National Institute Economic Review*, November 1992. See also Steven Mufson and John Berry, "Economy Stuck in Park Looms over Campaign; Americans Get Grim News on Jobs, Incomes and Debt," *Washington Post*, September 10, 1992; and Mark Memmott, "Economy Slips into Another Dip," *USA Today*, July 23, 1992.
17. Joseph Spiers, "It's Looking Grim Again, But We'll Avoid a New Recession," *Fortune*, November 2, 1992.
18. Appearance on *Face the Nation*, CBS News, January 6, 2002.
19. David Rosenberg, "Yield to the Curve," Merrill Lynch, June 13, 2005; William Gross, "The Strange Tale of a Bare-Bottomed King," PIMCO, May/June 2005; Gregg Greenberg, "PIMCO's Bill Gross is Still Fond of Treasuries," TheStreet.com, June 21, 2005.
20. Roger Altman, "The 'Conundrum' Explained," *Wall Street Journal*, June 21, 2005. See

also Nouriel Roubini and Brad Setser, "Will the Bretton Woods 2 Regime Unravel Soon: The Risk of a Hard Landing in 2005–2006," New York University, February 2005.

21. Alan Greenspan, "Testimony to House Budget Committee," September 12, 2002.

22. Mankiw, 1998, 557.

23. Interviewed on *This Week with George Stephanopoulos,* ABC News, May 11, 2003.

24. Joel Friedman and Ruth Carlitz, "Estate Tax Reform Could Raise Much-Needed Revenue: Some Reform Options with Low Tax Rates Raise Very Little Revenue," Center on Budget and Policy Priorities, March 16, 2005.

25. For example, regarding the administration's tax cut proposal, Treasury Secretary John Snow has said that "the deficits that result are really modest and clearly manageable." Quoted in Carolyn Lochhead, "GOP and Democrats at Each Other's Throats Over Tax Bill," *San Francisco Chronicle,* February 28, 2003. Similarly, CEA chairman R. Glenn Hubbard said that "In the long term the only piece of this plan that is new is the dividend piece. And the cost of that ten years from now is $50 billion a year in an economy that by then would be $13 trillion." Quoted in Joseph Guinto, "Hubbard Touts Bush's Plan as Tonic for Ailing Economy," *Investor's Business Daily,* January 27, 2003. See also, R. Glenn Hubbard, "Economic Outlook and Economic Policy," September 19, 2002. (Hubbard argues that there is "essentially no empirical evidence that moderate changes in budget surpluses are related to long-term interest rates.")

26. The total cost of the tax cuts, including extending them and associated interest costs from 2001 through 2015, is $5.1 trillion dollars. The direct cost of these tax cuts from 2001 to 2015 is $3.7 trillion. Joel Friedman, Ruth Carlitz, and David Kamin, "Extending the Tax Cuts Will Cost $2.1 Trillion Through 2015," Center on Budget and Policy Priorities, February 9, 2005.

27. International Monetary Fund, "United States: 2001 Article IV Consultation," August 14, 2001.

28. Janet Hook, "Dividend Tax Down, But Not Out, in House's $550-Billion Plan," *Los Angeles Times,* May 2, 2003.

29. Julie Hirschfeld Davis, "Congress OKs $330 billion in Tax Relief," *Baltimore Sun,* May 24, 2003.

30. Joel Slemrod and Jon Bakija, *Taxing Ourselves: A Citizen's Guide to the Great Debate Over Tax Reform,* Cambridge: MIT Press, 1996.

31. Joint Committee on Taxation, "Macroeconomic Analysis of H.R. 2, The 'Jobs and Growth Reconciliation Tax Act of 2003,' " Congressional Record, May 8, 2003; Congressional Budget Office (CBO), "An Analysis of the President's Budgetary Proposals for Fiscal Year 2004," March 2003; and Organization for Economic Cooperation and Development, "Economic Surveys: United States," April 2004.

32. Author's calculations based on the methodology of Richard Kogan, "Will the Tax Cuts Ultimately Pay for Themselves?," Center on Budget and Policy Priorities, March 3, 2003.

33. Editorial, "Revenues Rising," *Wall Street Journal,* May 23, 2005.

34. In January 2001, the Congressional Budget Office (CBO) projected revenues of $2.6 trillion dollars in 2005 and budget surpluses of $433 billion. In January 2005, CBO projected revenues of $2.1 trillion and a 2005 deficit of $368 billion. Recent analyses of the incoming tax revenues project that revenues may come in about 15 percent above 2004 levels, an estimated $2.2 trillion. Congressional Budget Office (CBO), "Budget and Economic Outlook," January 2001, January 2005; Congressional Budget Office (CBO), "Monthly Budget Review," June 2005; Goldman Sachs, U.S. Economic Research, "Deficit Reduction: Don't Pass Up this Investment!," June 10, 2005. Jonathon Weisman, "Economic Growth, Tax Receipts Combine to Reduce the Deficit," *Washington Post,* July 2, 2005.

35. The one existing program that allows savers to put after-tax savings into their account that they later withdraw tax-free is the Roth-IRA. This Roth-IRA model is not conceptually flawed: only the pretense that it is a free lunch that does not impose long-term fiscal costs.

36. Leonard E. Burman, William G. Gale, and Peter R. Orszag, "Key Thoughts on RSAs and LSAs," Tax Policy Center, February 4, 2004.

37. Peter Gosselin, "Dimensions of Bush's Budget Come into Focus," *Los Angeles Times*, March 16, 2003.

38. See Gene Sperling, "Bush Budget Means Cutting Only Peanut Butter," Bloomberg News, February 14, 2005.

39. The Center on Budget and Policy Priorities estimates that the direct costs of extending the tax cuts will be $1.8 trillion through 2015. The Urban-Brookings Tax Policy Center estimates that the top 1 percent of earners get 24.6 percent of the benefits of the tax cuts. Joel Friedman, Ruth Carlitz, and David Kamin, "Extending the Tax Cuts Will Cost $2.1 Trillion Through 2015," Center on Budget and Policy Priorities, February 9, 2005; Urban-Brookings Tax Policy Center, "EGTRRA, JGTRRA, and WFTRA, Distribution of Federal Tax Change by Cash Income Percentile, 2005," April 6, 2005.

40. Gene Sperling and Brian Deese, "It's Not Spending, Stupid," Center for American Progress, January 2004.

41. James Horney and Richard Kogan, "Assessing the Administration's Five-Year Appropriation 'Caps,'" Center on Budget and Policy Priorities, March 1, 2005.

Chapter 15: Lessons in Fiscal Discipline

1. Robert Shapiro, "Tax Reform or Bust," *Blueprint Magazine*, May 31, 2005.

2. Nelson Schwartz, "The Dollar in the Dumps," *Fortune*, December 13, 2004.

3. Editorial, "Interest Rates and Deficits," *New York Times*, December 18, 2004. Net foreign purchases of U.S. securities fell sharply in October 2004 to $48.1 billion from $67.5 billion in September. "Foreigners Bought $48.1 billion of U.S. Assets in October," Bloomberg News, December 15, 2004.

4. Chris Giles, "Central Banks Shun U.S. Assets," *Financial Times*, January 24, 2005.

5. Janet Guttsman, "IMF: Imbalances Threaten World Economy," Reuters, June 20, 2005. In this speech De Rato specifically called for the U.S. to pursue "even bolder deficit reduction."

6. Peterson, 2004, 93.

7. As quoted in Peterson, 2004, 93.

8. James Brooke and Keith Bradsher, "Dollar's Fall Tests Nerves of Asia's Central Bankers," *New York Times*, December 4, 2004.

9. "Dollar Drops Most in Six Months; Bank of Korea May Diversify," Bloomberg News, February 22, 2005.

10. David Pilling and Song Jung-a, "Moves to Calm Markets as Koizumi Comments Send Dollar Falling," *Financial Times*, March 11, 2005.

11. Michael R. Sesit and Craig Karmin, "How One Word Haunts Dollar—Investors Tremble as Foreign Central Banks Speak of 'Diversification,'" *Wall Street Journal*, March 17, 2005. Phillip Day and Hae Won Choi, "Asian Central Banks Consider Alternatives to Big Dollar Holdings," *Wall Street Journal*, February 5, 2004.

12. Laurence Ball and N. Gregory Mankiw, "What Do Budget Deficits Do?" NBER Working Paper 5263, National Bureau of Economic Research, 1995.

13. Concord Coalition, "Current Policy Trends Lead to Large Sustained Deficits: Fiscal

Years 2005–2015," February 2005; Goldman Sachs, U.S. Economic Research, "Deficit Reduction: Don't Pass Up this Investment!," June 10, 2005.

14. Morton M. Kondracke, "Can GOP Beat 'Midterm Curse' This November?," *Roll Call,* February 28, 2002.

15. John McCain, Senate Floor Statement, March 18, 2003.

16. Erica Groshen and Simon Potter, "Has Structural Change Contributed to a Jobless Recovery," *Current Issues in Finance and Economics,* vol. 9, no. 8, Federal Reserve Bank of New York, August 2003.

17. In a chart that estimates the contributions of monetary and fiscal policy to real GDP growth, Mark Zandi, chief economist of Economy.com, estimates that the impact of tax cuts on GDP growth in 2001 was "0.0." See Mark Zandi, "Assessing President Bush's Fiscal Policies," Economy.com, July 2004, p. 4, table 3. Indeed, even when looking past the recession Zandi notes that tax cuts have had very little impact on the economy. "Nearly all the economic growth experienced since the President took office is due to the aggressive monetary easing and greater federal government largesse." Ibid, p. 3.

18. Congressional Budget Office (CBO), "Economic Stimulus: Evaluating Proposed Changes in Tax Policy," January 2002.

19. Tax Policy Center, "Distribution of Tax Change from Reduction in Rates for Long-Term Capital Gains and Qualifying Dividends, 2005," January 14, 2005.

20. Paid advertisement, *New York Times,* February 11, 2003.

21. Bill Dudley, "Fiscal Policy—In Search of Balance, Creativity, and Grit," Goldman Sachs, May 2, 2003.

22. Bank for International Settlements, "73rd Annual Report: April 1, 2002–March 31, 2003," June 30, 2003; Organisation for Economic Co-operation and Development, *OECD Economic Outlook,* No. 77, June 2005; International Monetary Fund, "2005 Article IV Consultation with the United States of America, Concluding Statement of the IMF Mission," May 25, 2005. See also "IMF, OECD See Economic Risks in Bush's Budget," *Wall Street Journal,* April 15, 2004; Martin Crutsinger, "IMF: U.S. Deficits Threaten World Finance," Associated Press, April 15, 2004.

23. Bureau of Labor Statistics.

24. Gene Sperling, "The Road to Zero: Still Not There Yet, Private Sector Job Growth Under President Bush," Center for American Progress, June 3, 2005.

25. "Annual Report of the Boards of Trustees of the Federal Hospital Insurance and Federal Supplementary Medical Insurance Trust Funds," Center for Medicare Services, March 23, 2005. See also Aaron Bernstein, "Social Security," *BusinessWeek Online,* January 14, 2005; and Editorial, "The Bigger Problem," *Washington Post,* December 27, 2004.

26. Congressional Budget Office (CBO), "Projections of Expenditures for Long-term Care Services for the Elderly," March 1999.

27. General Accountability Office (GAO), "Highlights of GAO Forum: The Long-Term Fiscal Challenge," February 2005.

28. See for example, Clay Chandler and Eric Pianin, "Clinton's Social Security Pledge Holds Off Surplus Spenders," *Washington Post,* February 9, 1998; and James Dao, "Balanced Budget Faces a Big Test: Transit Spending," *New York Times,* March 2, 1998.

29. Bureau of Labor Statistics.

30. Alan Greenspan, "Testimony Before the House Committee on Banking and Financial Services," February 20, 1996.

31. Quoted in *Audacity,* Fall 1994.

32. Goldman Sachs, "Undistorted by the Budget Surplus," GSWIRE, April 14, 2000.

33. Mike McNamee, "How Growth Could End the Budget Wars," *BusinessWeek,* May 19, 1997.

34. Lehman Brothers, January 10, 1994.
35. Phil Gramm, *Congressional Record,* August 5, 1993; Newt Gingrich quoted in "The Clinton Budget, Georgia Delegation," *Atlanta Journal-Constitution,* August 6, 1993.
36. Steven Greenhouse, "Bentsen Sits Tall at Group of 7 Talks," *New York Times,* March 1, 1993.
37. When President Clinton took office, Medicare was projected to face insolvency in 1999. Medicare savings within the 1993 Deficit Reduction Act extended solvency through 2002. By the end of 2000, stronger economic growth, reductions in waste and fraud, and savings included in the 1997 Balanced Budget Agreement extended the Medicare insolvency date to 2025.
38. Congressional Budget Office (CBO), "Budget and Economic Outlook," January 1998.
39. In 1999, faced with bigger projected surpluses, President Clinton called in the State of the Union for committing 60 percent of the surplus to Social Security—enough to keep it solvent for fifty-five years. He called for dividing the rest among Medicare and his new Universal Savings Accounts proposal.
40. Donald Lanbro, "House Vote on Tax Cut Pledged, Republicans See it as Central Issue," *Washington Times,* December 27, 1997. The Tax Payer Dividend Act, introduced by Rep. John Boehner and Sen. Spencer Abraham, would have set aside surplus revenue in a fund committed to finance tax cuts. See John Berlau, "Budget is Balanced, Now What to Do?," *Insight on the News,* November 17, 1997.
41. Dennis Hastert, "Speaker Hastert Calls for Paying Off the Debt by 2015," Press Release, January 19, 2000.
42. Goldman Sachs, "Undistorted by the Budget Surplus," GSWIRE, April 14, 2000.

Chapter 16: Balancing Fiscal Discipline in the New Supply-Side Reality

1. Several other prominent progressives named "Bob" support more balanced fiscal discipline, including former CBO Director Bob Reischauer, Bob Greenstein, the head of CBPP, and of course, Bob Rubin.
2. Robert Reich, "Massachusetts at a Crossroads: The High Road or the Low?" Remarks at the Old State House, Boston, Massachusetts, March 28, 2002.
3. Robert Kuttner, "Surplus Worship," *American Prospect,* May–June 1999.
4. Bureau of Labor Statistics. The forty-three consecutive months ran from July 1997 through January 2001.
5. Louis Uchitelle, "Companies Try Dipping Deeper into Labor Pool," *New York Times,* March 26, 2000.
6. Ann Harrington, "Anybody Here Want a Job?" *Fortune,* May 15, 2000.
7. Census Bureau, Current Population Survey, Historical Poverty Tables, Historical Income Tables.
8. Olivier Blanchard and Lawrence Summers, "Hysteresis in Unemployment," NBER Working Paper 2035, National Bureau of Economic Research, November 1989.
9. Quoted in Louis Uchitelle, "Blacks Lose Better Jobs Faster as Middle-Class Work Drops," *New York Times,* July 12, 2003.
10. Virginia Sapiro and Steven J. Rosenstone, "National Election Studies, 1998: Post-Election Study [dataset]," Center for Political Studies, University of Michigan, 1999.
11. Robert Greenstein, "House Child Credit Legislation Not Fiscally Responsible: Bill More Likely to Harm Children Than to Help Them," Center on Budget and Policy Priorities, June 23, 2003.
12. Congressional Budget Office (CBO), "Effective Federal Tax Rates, 1997 to 2000," August 2003. Figure in 2000 dollars.

13. David Ellwood and Rebecca Blank, "The Clinton Legacy for America's Poor," *American Economic Policy in the 1990s,* Jeffrey A. Frankel and Peter R. Orszag, eds. (Cambridge: MIT Press, 2002). The authors describe this as programs aimed at the poor other than AFDC/TANF, food stamps, and housing.

14. Congressional Budget Office (CBO), "Effective Federal Tax Rates under Current Law 2001 to 2014," August 13, 2004. Joint Economic Committee, Minority Staff, "New CBO Analysis Confirms That the Bush Tax Cuts Are Skewed Toward the Rich," August 2004. The income threshold for the top 1 percent was $356,709 in 2004. Urban Institute–Brookings Institution Tax Policy Center, "Income Breaks for Distribution Tables, 2001–2015," May 25, 2004. The cost of comprehensive after-school care is estimated between $5 billion and $10 billion a year. See below chapter 17, note 4, on the relationship between tax cuts for the top 1 percent and the Social Security shortfall.

15. Alliance for Early Childhood Finance, "Learning Community on Early Care and Education Finance Reform," January 25, 2004. Other states are also using dedicated sin taxes: Pennsylvania passed a controversial plan to raise $1 billion with video slot machines in order to relieve property taxes and fund education. In California, Proposition 10 dedicated tobacco taxes to fund early childhood development.

16. Despite Laura Bush's public support for the program and President Bush's own praise, Teach for America's funding has been cut. In 2003, only a year after winning a $2 million challenge grant, it received no funding from the AmeriCorps service budget. Joe Klein, "Who Killed Teach for America?," *Time,* August 17, 2003.

17. Tim Weiner, "Giving In on Foreign Aid Bill, GOP Finds an Election Issue," *New York Times,* November 5, 1999.

18. In 1995, Clinton was forced to threaten a veto when congressional Republicans approved a foreign aid bill that the Associated Press noted would have cut aid spending to its lowest levels in fifty years. David Briscoe, "As U.S. Trims Aid, Nations Brace for Impact," Associated Press, October 8, 1995. In the first two years of their congressional control, the Republican majority in Congress refused President Clinton's budget requests to meet the United States contribution to the World Bank International Development Association, the largest donor of international aid to Africa. This caused the United States to fall $800 million behind on its contributions to IDA, failing to meet even the promises made by the first President Bush. Jim Boyd, "For World's Poor, IDA Must Mend Fences with the United States," *Star Tribune* (Minneapolis, MN), February 3, 1997. Throughout much of the 1990s, the Republican Congress sought to limit the development assistance budget, often led by Senator Jesse Helms who described such aid as "pouring money down a rat hole." See Ben Barber, "U.S. Loses Leadership in Foreign Aid; Japan, France, Germany Are More Generous," *The Washington Times,* June 2, 1997. (America "faces a broad, sustained attack on foreign aid by conservatives at home. Senator Jesse Helms, the North Carolina Republican who chairs the Foreign Relations Committee, led the charge with his slogan that foreign aid is 'poured down a rat hole.' The conservative Heritage Foundation said aid is a form of welfare for countries that discourages competitiveness and innovation.")

19. Also during this time, the United States and UN Ambassador Richard Holbrooke were the first to present the burgeoning AIDS crisis to the UN Security Council as a security threat. Nancy Soderberg, *The Superpower Myth* (Hoboken: John Wiley & Sons, 2005), 349.

20. See Ben Barber, "U.S. Loses Leadership in Foreign Aid; Japan, France, Germany Are More Generous," *Washington Times,* June 2, 1997.

21. Lael Brainard, "With Help From the Famous, Foreign Aid Resurges," *Los Angeles Times,*

June 26, 2002. Gene Sperling, "Bush 'Goes to China' to Boost Aid for Poor Lands," Bloomberg News, March 26, 2002.

22. UNESCO, "HIPC Debt Relief in African Countries: Scope for Financing Education," November 2002; "Debt Relief and Beyond Report" transmitted by G7 Finance Ministers to the Heads of State and Government, Genoa, July 20–22, 2001.

Chapter 17: Generational Responsibility: Savings and Social Security

1. Social Security Administration (SSA), "2005 Annual Report of the Trustees of the Federal Old-Age and Survivors Insurance and Disability Trust Funds," March 23, 2005.

2. Alan Greenspan, "Statement Before Senate Budget Committee," January 28, 1999.

3. These estimates are of the costs over 75 years expressed in net present value terms. Richard Kogan and Robert Greenstein, "President Portrays Social Security Shortfall as Enormous. But His Tax Cuts and Drug Benefit Will Cost at Least Five Times as Much," Center on Budget and Policy Priorities, February 11, 2005.

4. The Congressional Budget Office (CBO) estimated in June 2004 that the seventy-five-year Social Security shortfall is 0.4 percent of GDP, while the Social Security Administration (SSA) estimates the shortfall at 0.7 percent of GDP. The total cost of the tax cuts just for the top 1 percent of income earners will amount over seventy-five years to 0.6 percent of GDP—more than enough to cover the shortfall according the CBO estimates, and enough to cover 86 percent of the shortfall as estimated by the SSA.

5. Douglas W. Elmendorf and Jeffrey B. Liebman, "Social Security Reform and National Saving in an Era of Budget Surpluses," *Brookings Papers on Economic Activity,* 2000; and Andrew Samwick, "Is Pension Reform Conducive to Higher Saving?," *Review of Economics and Statistics,* vol. 82, no. 2, 2000.

6. Jason Furman and Robert Greenstein, "What the New Trustees' Report Shows About Social Security," Center on Budget and Policy Priorities, March 24, 2005, extrapolating data from Stephen Goss, Chief Actuary, Social Security Administration, "Preliminary Estimated Effects of a Proposal to Phase In Personal Accounts," February 3, 2005.

7. Jason Furman, "The Impact of the President's Proposal on Social Security Solvency and the Budget," Center on Budget and Policy Priorities, July 22, 2005.

8. Jason Furman, William G. Gale, and Peter R. Orszag, "Should the Budget Be Changed to Exclude the Cost of Individual Accounts?," Center on Budget and Policy Priorities, December 13, 2004.

9. Robert Rubin, "Attention: Deficit Disorder," *New York Times,* May 13, 2005.

10. Gene Sperling and Christian E. Weller, "One of the Largest New Government Spending Programs in History: National Interest Payments Due to President Bush's Social Security Proposal," Center for American Progress, July 2005.

11. "White House Social Security Briefing," *Washington Post,* February 2, 2005. When the Congressional Budget Office (CBO) analyzed the most prominent of the plans put forward by the President's Social Security Commission—often referred to as "Model 2"—they found that while it did increase solvency, all of the increases in solvency came solely from benefits cuts that could have been done without any individual accounts or increases in the national debt. Indeed, the CBO found that the individual accounts alone actually made the fiscal situation worse. CBO, "Long-term Analysis of Plan 2 of the President's Commission to Strengthen Social Security," July 21, 2004.

Chapter 18: Break a Leg: Should We Save Social Security As We Know It?

1. Social Security Administration (SSA), "A Brief History of Social Security," http://www.ssa.gov/history/briefhistory3.html.

2. Robert C. Withers, "Benefits, Ballot Package Confuse Some Retirees," *Herald-Dispatch* (Huntington, WV), September 7, 2003.

3. Press Release, "Vice President Discusses Social Security Reform," Catholic University of America, January 13, 2005.

4. Robert Barro, "Why Private Accounts are a Bad Idea," *BusinessWeek,* April 4, 2005.

5. Elroy Dimson, Paul Marsh, and Mike Staunton, "Global Investment Returns Yearbook," 2004, 29.

6. A survey jointly conducted by Paine Webber and Gallup found that by the end of 1999, "investors under forty expected a return of 22 percent" annually—multiples above historic averages. See James Poterba, "The Rise of the 'Equity Culture': U.S. Stock Ownership Patterns 1989–1998," Massachusetts Institute of Technology, January 2001.

7. Mark Whitehouse, "Abreast of the Market: Stocks May Dash Social Security Privatizers' Expectations," *Wall Street Journal,* February 28, 2005.

8. Robert Shiller, "Life-Cycle Personal Accounts for Social Security: An Evaluation," Yale University, April 2005.

9. Dow at the end of September 1974 was 60 percent what it had been at the end of December 1972. Using monthly averages, S&P 500 in December 1974 was 57 percent what it had been in December 1972.

10. Christian Weller, "Social Security Privatization: Retirement Savings Gamble," Center for American Progress, February 2005.

11. A 1998 Labor Department study found the average costs for actively managed large equity funds to be 1.47 percent. Department of Labor, Pension and Welfare Benefits Administration, "Study of 401(k) Plan Fees and Expenses," April 13, 1998.

12. Congressional Budget Office (CBO), "Administrative Costs of Private Accounts in Social Security," March 2004.

13. Austan Goolsbee, "The Fees of Private Accounts and the Impact of Social Security Privatization on Financial Managers," University of Chicago, G.S.B., September 2004.

14. Peter Diamond, "The Future of Social Security for This Generation and the Next: Proposals Regarding Personal Accounts," Testimony Before the Subcommittee on Social Security of the House Committee on Ways and Means, June 18, 1998. Norma Cohen, a British reporter for *The Financial Times,* points out that after nearly twenty years of privatization, workers are rushing out of private pensions and back into the state system—half a million workers in 2004 alone. Even Britain's equivalent of the Chamber of Commerce now advocates for a return to a state pension system and supports increasing taxes to do so. Norma Cohen, "A Bloody Mess," *American Prospect,* February 2005. Adair Turner, chairman of Britain's Pension Commission, recently led an effort to detail the numerous continuing challenges facing the British retirement system; see Pension Commission (UK), "Pensions: Challenges and Choice," 2004.

15. Transaction costs in the TSP are kept quite low—only 0.1 percent—about 1/15 of the normal 401(k).

16. Presidential Management Agenda, "Executive Branch Management Scorecard," December 31, 2004.

17. Dean Baker and David Rosnick have estimated the administrative cost of Social Security at 0.6 percent of money paid out on a yearly basis. Dean Baker and David Rosnick, "Basic Facts on Social Security and Proposed Benefit Cuts/Privatization," Center for Economic and Policy Research, November 16, 2004.

18. George Bush, "President Participates in Social Security Conversation in Indiana," University of Notre Dame, March 4, 2005.
19. Greg Anrig, "Ten Myths About Social Security," Century Foundation, January 26, 2005.
20. Consortium for Citizens with Disabilities, "Social Security Facts: How Does Social Security Help People With Disabilities & Their Families?," March 14, 2005.
21. Quoted in White House Press Release, "Remarks at Roundtable Discussion on Women and Retirement Security," October 27, 1998.
22. The family that approached me and gave me the precise details of their situation requested that their names be altered out of respect for their privacy.
23. White House Press Release, "Fact Sheet: Setting the Record Straight," February 3, 2005.
24. "White House Social Security Briefing," *Washington Post,* February 2, 2005. (Basically, the net effect on an individual's benefits would be zero if his personal account earned 3 percent real rate of return.)
25. George Bush, "President Participates in Social Security Conversation in Indiana," University of Notre Dame, March 4, 2005.
26. Alicia Munnell, "Why are So Many Older Women Poor," Center for Retirement Research, Boston College, April 2004. See also Heidi Hartmann, "The Impact of Social Security Reform on Women," Institute for Women's Policy Research, 1998.
27. Social Security Administration (SSA), "Income of the Population 55 or Older, 2002," March 2005.
28. George W. Bush, "Conversation on Social Security Reform," Andrew W. Mellon Auditorium, Washington, DC, January 11, 2005.
29. National Center for Health Statistics, "Chartbook on Trends in the Health of Americans," 2004.
30. Paul Krugman, "Little Black Lies," *New York Times,* January 28, 2005.
31. Government Accountability Office (GAO), "Social Security and Minorities: Earnings, Disability Incidence, and Mortality Are Key Factors That Influence Taxes Paid and Benefits Received," April 2003.
32. National Council of La Raza, "The Social Security Program and Reform: A Latino Perspective," 2005.
33. GAO, "Social Security and Minorities," 2003.
34. National Committee to Preserve Social Security and Medicare, "Why Social Security Is Important to African Americans," February 2005.
35. GAO, "Social Security and Minorities," 2003. See also Kilolo Kijakazi, "GAO Report Shows Social Security Is Favorable to People of Color But Some Changes in It Could Harm Minority Communities," Center on Budget and Policy Priorities, May 12, 2003.

Chapter 19: Toward a Progressive Consensus on Retirement Savings and Wealth Creation

1. James Horney and Richard Kogan, "Private Accounts Would Substantially Increase Federal Debt and Interest Payments," Center on Budget and Policy Priorities, August 2, 2005.
2. Jason Furman, "The Impact of the President's Proposal on Social Security Solvency and the Budget," Center on Budget and Policy Priorities, July 22, 2005, Table 1.
3. Today, this average "wage replacement" for a worker who retires at sixty-five is 42 percent. As the retirement age increases to sixty-seven, the average wage-replacement for a sixty-five-year-old will decline to 36 percent.
4. Patrick Purcell, "Estimated Effect of Price-Indexing Social Security Benefits on the

Number of Americans 65 and Older in Poverty," *Congressional Research Service,* January 28, 2005.

5. Jason Furman, "An Analysis of Using 'Progressive Price Indexing' to Set Social Security Benefits," Center for Budget and Policy Priorities, March 21, 2005.

6. Jeff Bliss, "Graham, Kolbe Mull Tax Increases for Social Security," Bloomberg News, December 3, 2004.

7. George Will appearing on *This Week with George Stephanopoulos,* ABC News, November 3, 2002.

Index

About the Author

Gene Sperling is a Senior Fellow at the Center for American Progress. He was President Clinton's National Economic Advisor and Director of the National Economic Council from 1997 to 2001 and Deputy National Economic Advisor from 1993 to 1997. Mr. Sperling recently served as a top economic advisor to the Kerry-Edwards presidential campaign. He is a columnist and commentator for Bloomberg News, has been a contributing writer and consultant to the television show *The West Wing*, serves as director of the Center for Universal Education at the Council of Foreign Relations, is chair of the U.S. Global Campaign for Education, is a contributing editor for the DLC's *Blueprint* magazine, and is on the Board of Directors of the Philadelphia Stock Exchange. He has appeared on *Meet the Press, Face the Nation, This Week, Good Morning America, Nightline,* and is a frequent contributor on CNN and NPR. His articles have appeared in *The Atlantic, Foreign Affairs, The New York Times, The Washington Post, Inc* magazine, *Financial Times, Foreign Policy,* and elsewhere. He was raised in Ann Arbor, Michigan, attended the University of Minnesota, Wharton Business School, and the Yale Law School. He currently resides with his family in Washington, D.C.